The DOT Medical Examination

A Guide to Commercial Drivers' Medical Certification

Fourth Edition

Natalie P. Hartenbaum, MD, MPH

D1598988

PRESS

OEM Press
Beverly Farms, MA

The recommendations contained in this book are based on reports sponsored by the Federal Motor Carrier Safety Administration or other driver licensing agencies unless otherwise noted. They should be used only as guidelines and are not regulation unless specifically indicated as such. Sound medical knowledge and an understanding of the underlying disease process and progression must guide the final medical certification decision.

Library of Congress Cataloging-in-Publication Data

The DOT medical examination : a guide to commercial drivers' medical certification / [edited by] Natalie P. Hartenbaum.—4th ed.
    p. ; cm.
  Includes bibliographical references and index.
  ISBN-13: 978-1-883595-48-7 (alk. paper)
  ISBN-10: 0-205-54297-2 (alk. paper)
  1. Automobile drivers—Medical examinations. 2. Truck drivers—Medical examinations. I. Hartenbaum, Natalie P. II. United States. Dept. of Transportation.
    [DNLM: 1 Automobile Driving—standards—United States. 2. Licensure—standards—United States. 3. Commerce—standards—United States. 4. Physical Examination—United States. WA 275 D725 2008]
  TL152.35.D68 2008
  629.28'330973—dc22

                                                              2007032764

OEM Press® is a registered trademark of OEM Health Information

Questions or comments regarding this book should be directed to:

OEM Health Information, Inc.
8 West Street
Beverly Farms, MA 01915-2226
978-921-7300
978-921-0304 (fax)
info@oempress.com
5 4 3 2 1

CONTENTS

Contributing Authors   v

Foreword   vii
ROBERT SWOTINSKY, MD, MPH

Preface   ix

I. The Examination Process   1

1. Commercial Driver Medical Qualification: Past,
   Present, and Future   3
   NATALIE P. HARTENBAUM, MD, MPH

2. Commercial Driver Medical Certification—The
   Examination   12
   NATALIE P. HARTENBAUM, MD, MPH

3. Regulations, Advisory Criteria, Interpretations, and
   Frequently Asked Questions   23
   NATALIE P. HARTENBAUM, MD, MPH

II. Specific Medical Conditions   95

4. Cardiovascular Disorders   99
   NATALIE P. HARTENBAUM, MD, MPH

5. Pulmonary Disorders   132
   NATALIE P. HARTENBAUM, MD, MPH

6. Musculoskeletal Disorders   150
   ERIC WOOD, MD, MPH

7. Neurologic Disorders   167
   KURT T. HEGMANN, MD, MPH

8. Endocrine Disorders   199
   KURT T. HEGMANN, MD, MPH

9.   Psychiatric Disorders   234
     Kurt T. Hegmann, MD, MPH

10. Renal Disease   250
     Natalie P. Hartenbaum, MD, MPH

11. Substance Abuse and Medication Use   256
     Natalie P. Hartenbaum, MD, MPH

**III. Commercial Drivers' Health: Risks
     and Hazards   287**
     Natalie P. Hartenbaum, MD, MPH

Index   305

CONTRIBUTING AUTHORS

Natalie P. Hartenbaum, MD, MPH
Chief Medical Officer
OccuMedix
Maple Glen, Pennsylvania

Kurt T. Hegmann, MD, MPH
Research Associate Professor
Rocky Mountain Center for Occupational & Environmental Health
Department of Family and Preventive Medicine
University of Utah
Salt Lake City, Utah

Eric Wood, MD, MPH
Associate Residency Program Director
Rocky Mountain Center for Occupational and Environmental Health
University of Utah
Salt Lake City, Utah

FOREWORD

It is similar to quoting scripture: "According to Hartenbaum . . . ." My colleagues at Fallon Clinic often quote *The DOT Medical Examination*, the bible of DOT physicals. They each have their own copy. When new editions come out, they upgrade. When they encounter a complex DOT exam, they check the book. The original source material for this book is retrievable from various publications and Internet sites—but who has time to search for the information while the patient is in the exam room? Dr. Hartenbaum and her colleagues have distilled the relevant information on DOT physicals into this practical, organized handbook. No wonder it remains one of the best selling occupational health references!

More than eight million truck and bus drivers are subject to DOT physicals. Millions of others undergo DOT-like physical exams under state laws or company policies. According to the Federal Motor Carrier Safety Administration (FMCSA), more than 50,000 qualified medical examiners are required to meet the need for DOT physicals. The number of health care providers now performing these exams is likely much higher. Some do a few each year. Some do a few each day. Currently, any health care professional who is licensed to perform examinations can perform DOT physicals. Many experts and policy makers think the medical qualification process needs to be more tightly controlled and monitored. The qualifications and training of those who perform the exams are a key concern. FMCSA is in the midst of reviewing and revising its DOT physical guidelines, some of which are almost 20 years old. FMCSA also is considering establishing qualification and training requirements for medical examiners. This rapidly changing world of the DOT process makes this current edition of Dr. Hartenbaum's text an especially important resource.

The DOT Medical Examination, now in its fourth edition, has helped fill the gap. This book has raised awareness about the complexity and importance of these examinations. These exams are not all quickies; it takes a well-trained, experienced, and thoughtful examiner to recognize and appropriately address the complex ones. This book gives the answers where they exist, and the framework for making individualized assessments where necessary. Like the Bible, *The DOT Medical Examination* does not have every answer; implementation is left to the practitioner. Basing medical determinations on authoritative knowledge gleaned from this text is reassuring especially if one's determination later is challenged.

Dr. Hartenbaum and her colleagues also have developed several other educational opportunities for medical examiners. These include a continuing education program based on this book and offered by the American College of Occupational and Environmental Medicine (ACOEM); a quarterly newsletter (*CDME Review*) published by ACOEM; and commercial driver medical examiner courses sponsored by ACOEM. The physicians who wrote this book are leaders and experts on DOT physicals. They are also in the trenches, performing DOT physicals and supervising others who perform them. *The DOT Medical Examination* is a must-have reference for any health care professional who performs DOT physicals or wants to learn more about them.

Robert Swotinsky, MD, MPH
Chair, Occupational Medicine
Fallon Clinic
Worcester, Massachusetts

PREFACE

It is hard to believe that it's been over a decade since the first edition of this guide was published. Our hope for the first edition was that it would serve not only as a resource to occupational health professionals but also as a convenient reference for others involved in the commercial driver medical process. The extent to which this manual has been utilized has been beyond our imagination.

Much of the use of this book stems from the increasing attention that has been focused on the role that medical conditions may play in motor vehicle accidents. Several accident investigations by the National Transportation Safety Board (NTSB) have concluded that medical issues were a contributing cause. Although much of the information has been available for years, it was not easily accessible nor were many examiners aware of its existence or location. Hopefully, *The DOT Medical Examination: A Guide to Commercial Drivers' Medical Certification* bridged that gap.

Since the third edition, there have been many changes in the medical certification process with many more to come. The ones that will likely have the greatest impact are the creation of the Federal Motor Carrier Safety Administration's (FMCSA) Medical Review Board (MRB) and the convening of Medical Expert Panels (MEP) which are reviewing the medical standards and guidelines. The MRB and MEPs already have made significant recommendations to change the medication criteria and cardiovascular guidance.

Another major change is in the planned creation of a national registry of certified medical examiners, limiting the performance of the commercial driver medical examinations (CDME) to those who meet specific criteria. This is a far cry from when many of us started performing these examinations, having little to no guidance and no available training.

The original intent of this guide was to provide the examiner with the regulations and "official" guidance in one easy-to-access place. Over the previous two editions and continued in this fourth edition, we expanded the inclusion of guidance from the medical literature and other relevant studies. Comparisons with guidelines and regulations from countries also are included where available.

Welcome to Dr. Eric Wood who is joining the team for this edition. I continue to be grateful to Dr. Kurt Hegmann who tolerates my pestering to meet deadlines and frequent modifying of formats. I want to acknowledge and thank Dr. Sam Caughron and Dr. Tuenis Zondag who contributed to the first three editions. The support and encouragement by Curtis Vouwie of OEM Press continues to be invaluable.

And of course, I especially want to thank my husband Dave, who continues to encourage and support my continually evolving projects. Many of you have heard me refer to the Alissa and Sara test, the ultimate criteria to evaluate whether an individual is safe to drive a bus or other commercial motor vehicle. When I started in occupational medicine and with the training programs for commercial driver medical examiners, Alissa was an infant and Sara only a dream. As the CDME process has progressed since the first edition, so have they; both are now confident young woman.

We all hope this fourth edition meets your expectations and needs.

NATALIE P. HARTENBAUM, MD, MPH

I

The Examination Process

1

Commercial Driver Medical Qualification: Past, Present, and Future

NATALIE P. HARTENBAUM, MD, MPH

Health care professionals who examine commercial drivers to determine medical fitness often comment that the regulations are old and out of step with current knowledge. While this may be true, the current standard is a significant improvement over the initial criteria from June 7, 1939, requiring the following minimum qualifications: "Good physical and mental health; good eyesight; adequate hearing; no addiction to narcotic drugs; and no excessive use of alcoholic beverages or liquors" [1].

The Motor Carrier Safety Act of 1935 granted the Interstate Commerce Commission (ICC) the authority to require medical certification for operators of commercial motor vehicles (CMVs) but not physical examinations. A physical examination and Certificate of Physical Evaluation were not required until January 1, 1954.

The U.S. Department of Transportation (DOT) was created by an act of Congress in 1970. Responsibility for commercial driver qualification was transferred to the DOT the same year. Tighter medical qualification standards were announced 30 years to the day after issuance of the initial criteria, on June 7, 1969 [2].

Physical requirements at that time were similar to those of the current standard. In the original notice, insulin use in the 12 months preceding the examination was disqualifying, as was a blood pressure above 160/90 mm Hg. The audiometric criterion in the Notice of Proposed Rulemaking was an average loss not greater than 25 to 30 dB in the better ear. Examinations were proposed to be required annually. However, in the Final Rule, issued on April 22, 1970 [3], the frequency of the examination was changed to biennial. The blood pressure criterion also was changed to its current form, disqualifying only those whose elevated blood pressure was "likely to interfere with the driver's ability to safely operate a commercial motor vehicle." The Final

Rule also stated that only current use of insulin would be considered cause for disqualification. The use of hearing aids to meet the audiometric standard became permissible in 1971. At the same time, the maximal permissible hearing loss was increased to an average loss not greater than 40 dB in the better ear. Since 1971, although medical advisory criteria and other guidance have been updated, the physical qualification standards themselves have remained essentially unchanged.

Motor carrier safety had been under the authority of the FHWA until October 1999, when responsibility was transferred to the Federal Motor Carrier Safety Administration (FMCSA) which reports directly to the secretary of the DOT [4].

Over the years, there have been several changes to the medical examination process. When controlled substance testing was initially implemented, testing was part of the periodic medical fitness examination. Once a company was conducting random tests at a 50 percent annual rate, periodic controlled substance testing could be discontinued. In July 1997, reference to subpart H, drug testing, was formally eliminated, and any reference to drug testing as part of the physical examination was removed [5]. Now that random testing is fully in effect, the only situation where the drug test and the examination might be done at the same office visit is in a preplacement situation. Even in this circumstance, the medical evaluation and the drug test should be considered as two separate and unrelated processes.

A 1992 amendment to the Federal Motor Carrier Safety Regulations (FMCSRs) allowed licensed health care professionals other than physicians to perform the examinations [6]. Some physician assistants, advanced practice nurses under physician supervision, and doctors of chiropractic are now able to evaluate commercial drivers for qualification. These providers can perform commercial driver medical examinations only if the state in which they are licensed permits them to perform such examinations. The hope was that by expanding the examiner pool there would be greater flexibility in arranging the required examination and possibly lower cost.

As a result of the Americans with Disabilities Act, the Congress directed the Federal Highway Administration (FHWA) to perform a thorough review of the physical qualifications. Announcements that studies were proposed to consider the feasibility of relaxing the vision [7] and diabetes [8] standards were published in the *Federal Register* in 1992 and 1993, respectively. The diabetes waiver program would permit some drivers with at least a 3-year record of safe commercial vehicle driving to drive a CMV in interstate commerce. Several other conditions were set, including blood sugar monitoring and the reporting of any accident, whether or not it normally would have been reportable. Some commercial drivers with at least a 3-year safe driving record and at least 20/40 vision corrected or uncorrected in the better eye were eligible for the vision waiver program.

A suit filed by the Advocates for Highway and Auto Safety requested a review of the issuance of waivers to individuals who otherwise did not meet the federal standard. In 1994, the U.S. Court of Appeals for the D.C. Circuit found that the "agency's determination that the waiver program(s) will not adversely affect the safe operation of CMVs is devoid of empirical support" [9]. New applications for these waiver programs are not currently being accepted, but those drivers currently holding waivers were grandfathered to continue to operate in interstate commerce provided they continue to meet requirements [10, 11]. A hearing waiver program to review the hearing standard was proposed in 1993 but was never begun [12].

A 1996 Eighth Circuit Court decision, in *Rauenhorst v. United States Department of Transportation*, required the agency to consider granting a waiver to a driver who met the criteria for a waiver prior to the program being closed [13]. Interim procedures for waivers, exemptions, and pilot programs were announced in 1998 [14] and these were adopted as a Final Rule in 2004 [15]. Waivers and exemptions are temporary relief from one or more of the FMCSRs. Waivers are valid for up to 3 months, whereas exemptions may be valid for up to 2 years and are renewable. For both, the applicant must indicate how the same or a greater level of safety could be achieved if the relief were granted. An exemption decision requires an opportunity for public comment, through publication in the *Federal Register*, whereas waivers do not. Since that time, several hundred exemptions to the vision standard have been granted.

Since 2000, there have been many modifications in the medical certifications of insulin-taking diabetic drivers. A 2000 report to Congress [16] on the feasibility of qualifying individuals with insulin-treated diabetes reviewed the issue and offered suggestions on how to permit some drivers on insulin to operate commercial vehicles in interstate commerce. A July 31, 2001, *Federal Register* [17] notice requested as to whether some insulin-treated diabetics should be granted exemptions. An exemption program was announced in September 2003 [18] and the first four exemptions were granted in September 2005 [19]. There were very specific criteria for eligibility, including at least 3 years of safe operation of a CMV while on insulin.

The Safe, Efficient, Flexible and Efficient Transportation Equity Act: A Legacy for Users (SAFETEA-LU) [20] required the FMCSA to eliminate the 3-year commercial driving requirement for insulin-treated diabetics and these changes were announced in November 2005

[21]. In March 2006 [22], comments were sought on whether the prohibition on insulin-treated diabetics should be further modified, possibly eliminating the need for an exemption and allowing the medical examiner and/or the treating provider to determine whether the driver should be medically qualified.

To date, only vision and diabetes exemptions have been granted but the FMCSA Frequently Asked Questions [23] indicates that: "A CMV driver may apply for an exemption from any of the standards. Exemptions are granted only in those instances where the driver can show that safety would not be diminished by granting the exemption." Notice of applications from four drivers from the prohibition for drivers with epilepsy or other condition likely to cause the loss of consciousness [24] has been published in the *Federal Register* but there had been no further announcements at the time this chapter was prepared.

Drivers who have been unable to meet the first or second medical standard because of a loss or impairment of an extremity had been eligible for a limb waiver. In May 2000 [25], terminology for this variance from the standards was changed to refer to a Skill Performance Evaluation (SPE) certificate rather than a waiver. This is now signed by the Division Administrator of the FMCSA. A road test is also required prior to issuance of the SPE.

Consistent with the definitions used in the Transportation Equity Act for the Twenty-First Century (TEA-21), the FMCSA amended the definition of a commercial vehicle under 390.5, which is used for determining which vehicles are subject to the FMCSRs, including the medical standards [26]. The definition also now includes vehicles designed or used to carry more than eight passengers (including the driver) for direct compensation greater than 75 air miles. In the same announcement, the FHWA delayed requiring operators of smaller vehicles to meet the medical criteria but in 2003, published a Final Rule requiring these operators of smaller vehicles to also meet medical criteria [27]. These drivers are not required to undergo controlled substance or alcohol testing.

A 2001 Advanced Notice of Proposed Rulemaking [28], requested comments on requiring school bus drivers involved in interstate transport of students (excluding home to school and return) to comply with the FMCSRs, including a medical examination. In 2004, this rulemaking was withdrawn [29].

A significant change in the medical certification process was the development and implementation of a new form. The proposed new form was published in the *Federal Register* in 1998 [30], and the Final Rule was published on October 5, 2000 [31]. In 2003, an updated version of the form which included the new hypertension guidelines and other changes in the advisory criteria was published [32]. This form includes one page each for medical history, testing, and recording of the physical examination. Instructions to examiners, the role of the commercial driver, and inclusion of the advisory criteria bring the entire document to eight pages. The advisory criteria reference the conference/expert panel reports and provide phone numbers for additional questions on issues such as Coumadin use. The examiner also is advised that additional information, either from the treating provider or a specialist, may be necessary. The option to certify a driver for less than 24 months if a medical condition is present that does not disqualify, but would require more frequent monitoring, is clearly stated. The examiner is directed to sign the certificate only if the driver would be able to perform both driving and nondriving duties.

Drivers are instructed to complete the history segment and then sign a statement indicating that the history they provided is accurate. The medical history questions are more relevant, and there is a place to list any medication the driver is taking. In addition, questions on venereal disease and the place for recording serology are no longer included. Examiners are instructed to review medication, and a question on sleep disorders had been added. The testing and physical examination pages include many of the standards adjacent to where the examiner would enter findings, e.g., vision or blood pressure. Pulse after exercise is no longer required.

With the document including not just the history and physical examination but also some guidance material, it was anticipated that examiners would have and utilize the necessary information. In their 1998 report on a New Orleans bus accident [33], the National Transportation Safety Board (NTSB) identified the failure of the medical certification program to detect the driver's medical problems and remove him from service as one of the probable causes of the accident. They indicated that the new form was a substantial improvement in serving as a resource for the medical examiner.

Neither the form nor the certificate included must be used exactly as published. Forms and certificates used must be "substantially in accordance" with the published versions. The examination reporting form can be reformatted or completed electronically. The certificate (commonly referred to as the card) can be resized to fit into a wallet and is not required to be any specific paper stock weight.

SAFETEA-LU contained many additional requirements for the CMV operator medical program in addition to changes in the insulin exemption eligibility. One key requirement was for the establishment of a Medical Review Board (MRB). The role of the MRB is to provide scientific advice to FMCSA on ongoing medical issues, including identification of appropriate physical qualifications of commercial motor vehicle drivers, medical standards, and guidelines. They will also be involved in the development of the educational curriculum for training medical examiners who certify drivers meet the physical qualification standards and functional tests for drivers with certain disabilities [34]. MRB members serve for 2 years but can be reappointed depending on need. The MRB will hear reports from the various Medical Expert Panels convened to review the existing regulations and guidance. So far, the MRB has heard reports from the Diabetes, Licit Use of Schedule II Medications and the Cardiovascular Expert Panel. Additional recommendations from the MRB have been made on Schedule II Medications and Cardiovascular Disease prior to finalizing this chapter and are discussed in the specific chapters.

A Chief Medical Officer is also required by SAFETEA-LU who will work with the MRB. That position has not been fully defined nor appointed.

A final requirement of SAFETEA-LU is for the establishment of a National Registry of Certified Medical Examiners (NRCME) [35]. While Congress is requiring training and certification, they do allow for self-certification, although at the present time, that is not the direction the FMCSA is headed. Once fully implemented, those examiners who have completed the required curriculum and any required testing would be placed on the NRCME. Only an examiner on the NRCME would be able to perform commercial driver medical certification examinations. A Role Delineation Study has been completed which was used to create a task list of components of the commercial driver medical examination. A survey of medical examiners has also been distributed [36,37]. These will be used to develop the core curriculum for medical examiner training as well as the medical examiner certification test. The FMCSA reminds examiners that at the current time there is no requirement to be listed on a registry and that neither training nor certification are required. They also have not endorsed any medical examiner training, education or certification programs

There have been plans to merge the Commercial Driver's License and the medical qualification documentation since the early 1990s. Feasibility studies and a Pilot Program were conducted. A negotiated rule-making committee was formed in 1996 [38] and charged with identifying a method for merging the commercial driver's license process with the medical qualification process. At that time one of the identified needs was to improve the quality of the medical examinations. "Doctor shopping" and the lack of understanding by many examiners of the regulations and supporting material were identified as significant problems. Several proposals were discussed to enhance consistency among health care providers performing commercial driver medical examinations. The proposals ranged from requiring examiners to sign a statement indicating that they understand the regulations and agree to follow them to an extensive certification course. The final meeting of the committee occurred in November 1997.

This had not moved forward until late 2006 when a Notice of Proposed Rulemaking was published that would require interstate commercial driver's license (CDL) holders subject to the medical requirements of the Federal Motor Carrier Safety Regulations (FMCSRs) to provide proof of a current medical examiner's certificate to their State Driver Licensing Agency (SDLA) [39]. As this information would be available, CDL drivers would no longer be required to carry the medical examiner's certificate. Final Rule on this is still pending.

The MRB is meeting regularly and making recommendations, some of which may require rulemaking and others that may not. There is also likely to be many changes in the qualifications of commercial driver medical examiners, required training and certification. As examiners, it is important that we stay abreast of new developments and studies. Watch for *Federal Register* announcements that affect the medical qualification process. The American College of Occupational and Environmental Medicine (ACOEM) publishes a quarterly newsletter that reviews recent or pending modifications in the examination process.

References

1. Zywokarte S. Team Leader, Driver Medical Standards, FHWA. Personal communication, October 1996.
2. Qualification of drivers. *Fed Reg* 1969;34(June 7):9080–9085.
3. Qualification of drivers of commercial motor vehicles. *Fed Reg* 1970; 35(April 22):6458–6467.
4. Organization and delegation of powers and duties: Redelegation to the director, Office of Motor Carrier Safety. *Fed Reg* 1999;64(Oct. 29):56270–56271.
5. Commercial driver's license program and controlled substances and alcohol use and testing: Conforming and technical amendments. *Fed Reg* 1997;62(July 11):37150–37153.
6. Qualification of drivers: Medical examination. *Fed Reg* 1992;57(July 28):33276.
7. Qualification of drivers: Waiver applications—vision. *Fed Reg* 1992; 57(March 25):10295–10297.
8. Qualification of drivers: Waivers—diabetes. *Fed Reg* 1993;58(July 29): 40690–40697.

9. Qualification of drivers: Vision deficiencies—waivers. *Fed Reg* 1994; 59(Nov. 17):39386–39390.

10. Qualification of drivers: Vision and diabetes—limited exemptions. *Fed Reg* 1996;61(Jan. 8):606–611.

11. Qualification of drivers: Vision and diabetes—limited exemptions. *Fed Reg* 1996;61(March 26):13338–13347.

12. Qualification of drivers: Hearing deficiencies—waivers. *Fed Reg* 1993; 58(Dec. 15):65638–65643.

13. Qualification of drivers: Waiver application—vision. *Fed Reg* 1998;63(Jan. 8):1524–1537.

14. Federal Motor Carrier Safety Regulations: Interim Final Rule, Request for Comments. Waivers, exemptions, and pilot programs—rules and procedures. *Fed Reg* 1998;63(Dec. 8):67600–67612.

15. Federal Motor Carrier Safety Administration. Department of Transportation. Final Rule; Waivers, Exemptions, and Pilot Programs. *Fed Reg* 2004; 69(Aug. 20):51589-51598.

16. A Report to Congress on the Feasibility of a Program to Qualify Individuals with Insulin Treated Diabetes Mellitus to Operate Commercial Motor Vehicles in Interstate Commerce as Directed by the Transportation Equity Act for the 21st Century. July 2000.

17. Notice of intent to issue exemptions and request for comments; Qualification of Drivers; Exemption applications; Diabetes. *Fed Reg* 2001;66(July 31):39548–39553.

18. Department of Transportation, Federal Motor Carrier Safety Administration. Qualification of Drivers: Exemption Applications: Diabetes. Notice of Final Dispositions. *Fed Reg* 2003;68(Sept. 3):52441–52.

19. Department of Transportation, Federal Motor Carrier Safety Administration. Qualification of Drivers: Exemption Applications: Diabetes. *Fed Reg* 2005;70(Sept. 2):52465–67.

20. Safe, Efficient, Flexible and Efficient Transportation Equity Act: A Legacy for Users 2005. www.fhwa.dot.gov/safetealu/legis.htm.

21. Federal Motor Carrier Safety Administration, DOT. Notice of revised final disposition. Qualification of Drivers; Eligibility Criteria and Applications; Diabetes Exemption. *Fed Reg* 2005;70(Nov. 8):67777–67781.

22. Federal Motor Carrier Safety Administration, DOT. Advance notice of proposed rulemaking request for comments. Qualifications of Drivers; Diabetes Standard. *Fed Reg* 2006;71(March 17):13801–13805.

23. Federal Motor Carrier Safety Administration FAQs. Accessed May 18, 2007. www.fmcsa.dot.gov/rules-regulations/topics/medical/faq.asp.

24. Federal Motor Carrier Safety Administration, US Department of Transportation. Qualification of Drivers; Exemption Requests; Epilepsy and Seizure Disorders, Notice of applications for exemptions, request for comments. *Fed Reg* 2006;71(Oct. 13):60606–60607.

25. Federal Motor Carrier Safety Regulations; Technical amendments; Final rule; Technical amendment. *Fed Reg* 2000;65(May 1):25285–25290.

26. Federal Motor Carrier Safety Regulations: Definitions of commercial

motor vehicle—interim final rule; Federal Motor Carrier Safety Regulations: Requirements for operators of small passenger-carrying commercial motor vehicles—proposed rule. *Fed Reg* 1999;64(Sept. 3):48510–48517.

27. Federal Motor Carrier Safety Regulations, DOT: Safety Requirements for Operators of Small Passenger-Carrying Commercial Motor Vehicles Used in Interstate Commerce—Final Rule. *Fed Reg* 2003;68(Aug. 12):47860–47875.

28. Interstate school bus safety; Advanced notice of proposed rulemaking; Request for comments. *Fed Reg* 2001;66(Oct. 22):53373–53376.

29. Federal Motor Carrier Safety Administration, DOT. Interstate School Bus Safety; Withdrawal. *Fed Reg* 2004;60(March 24):13803–13805.

30. Physical qualification of drivers: Medical examination—certificate. *Fed Reg* 1998;63(Aug. 5):41769–41781.

31. Federal Motor Carrier Safety Administration, DOT. Physical qualification of drivers; Medical examination; Final rule. *Fed Reg* 2000;65(Oct. 5):59363–59380.

32. Federal Motor Carrier Safety Administration, DOT. Motor Carrier Safety Regulations, Miscellaneous Technical Amendments. *Fed Reg* 2003;68(Sept. 30):56196–56208.

33. National Transportation Safety Board. Highway Accident Report: Motorcoach Run-Off-the-Road. New Orleans, Louisiana, May 9, 1999: HAR-01-01, 08/28/2001 NTIS Report No. PB2001–916201.

34. Medical Review Board, FMCSA Website. www.mrb.fmcsa.dot.gov/index.htm. Accessed May 18, 2007.

35. National Registry of Certified Medical Examiners Website. http://nrcme.fmcsa.dot.gov/. Accessed May 18, 2007.

36. Notice of Intent to Survey Medical Examiners Who Certify the Physical Qualifications of Commercial Motor Vehicle Drivers. *Fed Reg* 2006;71(July 13):39697–39698.

37. Notice of Intent to Survey Medical Examiners Who Certify the Physical Qualifications of Commercial Motor Vehicle Drivers. *Fed Reg* 2005;70(Sept. 29):56964–56965.

38. Commercial driver physical qualifications as a part of the commercial driver's license process. *Fed Reg* 1996;61(April 29):18713–18717.

39. Medical Certification Requirements as Part of the CDL. Notice of proposed rulemaking (NPRM); request for comments. Federal Motor Carrier Safety Administration (FMCSA), DOT. *Fed Reg* 2006;71(Nov. 16):66723–66748.

2

Commercial Driver Medical Certification—The Examination

Natalie P. Hartenbaum, MD, MPH

An area of confusion for many examiners and carriers is which drivers are required to meet the Federal Motor Carrier Safety Regulation's (FMCSRs) medical criteria. Although almost all drivers who require drug and alcohol testing also require the medical certification, many will require the examination but not drug testing. For the purpose of the medical examination, a CMV is defined by 49 CFR 390.5 as follows:

> Commercial motor vehicle (CMV) means any self-propelled or towed vehicle used on public highways in interstate commerce to transport passengers or property when:
>
> (a) The vehicle has a gross weight rating or gross combination of 10,001 pounds or more; or
> (b) The vehicle is designed or used to transport more than 8 passengers (including the driver) for compensation; or
> (c) Is designed or used to transport more than 15 passengers, including the driver, and is not used to transport passengers for compensation; or
> (d) Is used in the transporting of materials found by the Secretary of Transportation to be hazardous under 49 CFR U.S.C. 5103 and transporting in a quantity requiring placarding under regulations prescribed by the Secretary under 49 CFR, subtitle B, chapter I, subchapter C.

Most states have adopted the medical criteria for their intrastate commercial drivers but some will grandfather or grant exemptions for some drivers who do not meet the standards. Whether the driver him- or herself crosses state lines is not the determining factor for intra- or interstate commerce, it is the property being transported that matters.

An FAQ uses the example of a FedEx or UPS driver who only operates within a single state but the property he is transporting is part of interstate commerce. Drivers who operate only in interstate commerce may not be required to meet the federal medical standards and the examiner should be aware of specific requirements for drivers involved in intrastate commerce in their state.

Since the North American Free Trade Agreement (NAFTA), drivers from Mexico or Canada may be operating commercial motor vehicles within the United States. There is a reciprocity agreement with both Canada and Mexico that permits drivers who meet medical criteria in their home countries to operate in the United States with some limitations. Canadian or Mexican drivers who are insulin-using diabetics, who have epilepsy, or who are hearing or vision impaired are not qualified to drive CMVs in the United States. Canadian drivers who do not meet the medical fitness provisions of the Canadian National Safety Code for Motor Carriers or Mexican drivers who do not meet the medical fitness provision of the *Licencia Federal de Conductor* but have been issued a waiver are not qualified to drive CMVs in the United States.

The medical examination to determine medical fitness for commercial drivers has very specific criteria. Drivers cannot be medically certified for longer than 2 years and there are many circumstances where the duration should be less, including drivers with hypertension or those with any medical condition, which may not remain stable for 2 years. Drivers operating with either a diabetes or vision exemption also must be examined at least annually. Many carriers are unaware that even if a driver has a current medical certification, they are required to be examined if their "ability to perform his/her normal duties has been impaired by a physical or mental injury or disease" [49 CFR 391.45c]. The initial determination to whether a new examination is required is the responsibility of the carrier. While the medical examiner is responsible for determining whether the driver meets the medical criteria, the employer is responsible to ensure the driver is medically fit and may require any driver returning from injury or illness to undergo a medical examination [1]. For a new driver, the carrier may accept a driver's current medical certificate or may require the driver to complete an examination by an examiner chosen by the carrier. Many carriers take this approach to meet their responsibility of ensuring the medical examiner is informed of the "minimal medical requirements and characteristics of the work to be performed" [2].

The examination currently can be performed by "a person who is licensed, certified, and/or registered, in accordance with applicable State laws and regulations, to perform physical examinations. The term includes, but is not limited to, doctors of medicine, doctors of osteopathy, physician assistants, advanced practice nurses, and doctors of chiropractic." There is currently no training or certification requirement but the Federal Motor Carrier Safety Administration (FMCSA) has likely already published an announcement proposing the format of the National Registry of Certified Medical Examiners (NRCME).

Currently examiners are expected to:

> 49 CFR 391.43 "(c)(1) Be knowledgeable of the specific physical and mental demands associated with operating a commercial motor vehicle and the requirements of this subpart, including the medical advisory criteria prepared by the FMCSA as guidelines to aid the medical examiner in making the qualification determination; and
>
> (c)(2) Be proficient in the use of and use the medical protocols necessary to adequately perform the medical examination required by this section.

The content of the medical examination reporting form (often referred to as the long form) used to document the examination, and the certificate (referred to as the medical card) the driver is required to carry and the carrier required to maintain, is contained in the Code of Federal Regulations (CFR) and therefore considered codified. While the specific information on the form and the certificate must be included, the exact format from the CFR is not required. The medical certificate does not have to be the exact size published in the *Federal Register* and there is no requirement for the weight of paper used. In addition to the requirement that the information on any medical examination form be essentially consistent with what is found in the CFR, the size of any documentation must allow it to be legible.

The medical examination reporting form was significantly updated [3] in 2000 and minor modifications were made in 2003 [4] (see Figure 3.1 on pages 34–42). Unlike the previous two-page (often two sides of one sheet) form, the current complete form is nine pages in length. Page 1 is the medical history. Examiners should carefully review this history, because there are several key items on which the driver may not fully understand the issue. For example, the driver may indicate no to the questions whether he has seizures, diabetes, or high blood pressure, as the driver may believe because he is currently under treatment and the condition is well controlled that he no longer "has" the condition. The driver would indicate on the form that he is taking medication for that condition, alerting the examiner of the clinical diagnosis. The examiner must also review any medication listed because that may also reveal medical conditions not indicated directly in the medical history. Examiners are directed to discuss with the driver the potential hazards of medications, both prescription and over the counter, and document that discussion on page 1 of the Medical Examination Report.

The driver is required to sign that the "above information is complete and true" and that they acknowledge that "inaccurate, false or missing information may invalidate the examination" on the first page. The FMCSA in the FAQs [5] indicates that they rely on the medical examiner's clinical judgment to decide whether additional information should be obtained from the driver's treating physician. In addition to invalidating the examination, a civil penalty could also be levied against the driver under 49 U.S.C. 521(b)(2)(b), either for making a false statement of for concealing a disqualifying condition.

The second page of the form is where the examiner records any testing: vision, hearing, blood pressure, urine dip. This page includes both medical criteria and recommendations. There is one discrepancy in section 5, blood pressure/pulse. In one place it indicates the driver be qualified if the blood pressure is ≤140/90 and in the table, it includes the blood pressure of 140/90 as eligible for only a 1-year certification. If the driver's blood pressure is *exactly* 140/90, he is on no medications for hypertension, and there is no other medical reason to limit duration of medical certification, that driver can be medically qualified for 2 years. The Cardiovascular Medical Expert Panel has made recommendations to modify the hypertension guidelines. Among the recommendations that the Medical Review Board accepted (word from FMCSA is pending), is the examiner should base the determination of stage on blood pressure at the time of the examination and that could decide on length of certification despite treatment. The target blood pressure should be <140/90.

Page 3 is for recording the physical examination. Although only height and weight is required to be recorded, examiners should calculate a Body Mass Index (BMI) (calculated using standard measurement as weight (lb)/[height (in.)] 2×703) because this is a useful tool for evaluating the risk for obstructive sleep apnea. The examiner should indicate "yes" for any abnormalities and then document in detail in the comment section. This page is where the examiner indicates whether the driver is qualified and the duration of certification. Requirements for any waiver, exemptions, or limitations (exempt intracity zone or use of corrective lenses or hearing aids) should also be recorded on this page.

The next five pages include the driver's role, 391.41—Physical Qualification for Drivers and instructions to examiners, including the advisory criteria. The advisory criteria are recommendations provided by the FMCSA to aid the examiner in determining whether the driver meets the medical standards. Although the examiner is not required to follow them, they are codified (have been published in the *Code of Federal Regulations*) and the examiner should give careful consideration and document thoroughly if they decide not to follow these advisory criteria. Included with the advisory criteria are instructions for the examiner to see conference reports or panel guidelines on specific medical topics [6–9]. Recommendations in these documents are not regulations but as they are referenced in the codified advisory criteria, the examiner is obligated to be aware of and consider them. They are available at the FMCSA website at *www.fmcsa.dot.gov/facts-research/research-technology/publications/medreports.htm.*

The examiner is instructed to sign the medical certificate only if the driver is fit to drive and also able to perform nondriving responsibilities as required. These are listed in the driver role section and include for example, coupling and uncoupling trailers, loading and unloading trailers, placing and removing tarpaulins, tying down equipment or materials, pushing or pulling hoses from a tanker, inspecting the vehicle, or transporting passengers or hazardous material. When an examiner signs the medical certificate, he is signing that the driver is able to perform duties of a commercial motor vehicle operator, not just duties for the specific employer [5]. The only restrictions an examiner may place on the driver is to require corrective lenses, a hearing aid, a waiver or exemption, or a skill performance evaluation certificate. Drivers also can be restricted to operate only within an exempt intracity zone. Some states will permit a driver who does not meet federal medical standards to operate interstate only. These states generally have a specific certificate for these drivers.

In many cases where the driver has existing medical conditions, additional medical information or a specialist evaluation may be required. Prior to requesting any additional information or examination, the party responsible for any additional costs, whether the employer or the employee, should be identified.

There are four absolute situations for which the driver cannot be qualified at the time of the examination. For vision and diabetes, the driver may be eligible for an exemption but the examiner should not sign the medical certificate until the driver has been granted the exemption. These four criteria are:

1. Vision must be at least 20/40 in each eye, with or without correction; peripheral vision must be ≥70 degrees in the horizontal plane; and the driver must be able to identify colors of traffic signals (red, green, and amber).

2. There must not be an average hearing loss greater than 40 dB at 500, 1,000, and 2,000 Hz in the better ear. This is calculated by adding the values at 500, 1,000, and 2,000 Hz in one ear and dividing by three. A hearing aid can be used to meet the criteria.
3. The driver cannot have a clinical diagnosis of diabetes mellitus requiring insulin for control.
4. An established medical history or clinical diagnosis of epilepsy is disqualifying.

Although the use of methadone is not codified as an absolute disqualification, it is explained in the advisory criteria, interpretations, and the FAQs, that a commercial driver should not be qualified if on methadone.

The old examination form included the instructions to examiners but the current one does not. These instructions are included in 49 CFR 391.43 and are duplicated here.

49 CFR 391.43—Instructions for Performing and Recording Physical Examinations

The medical examiner must be familiar with 49 CFR 391.41, Physical qualifications for drivers, and should review these instructions before performing the physical examination. Answer each question "yes" or "no" and record numerical readings where indicated on the physical examination form.

The medical examiner must be aware of the rigorous physical, mental, and emotional demands placed on the driver of a commercial motor vehicle. In the interest of public safety, the medical examiner is required to certify that the driver does not have any physical, mental, or organic condition that might affect the driver's ability to operate a commercial motor vehicle safely.

General information. The purpose of this history and physical examination is to detect the presence of physical, mental, or organic conditions of such a character and extent as to affect the driver's ability to operate a commercial motor vehicle safely. The examination should be conducted carefully and should at least include all of the information requested in the following form. History of certain conditions may be cause for rejection. Indicate the need for further testing and/or require evaluation by a specialist. Conditions may be recorded which do not, because of their character or degree, indicate that certification of physical fitness should be denied. However, these conditions should be discussed with the driver and he/she should be advised to take the necessary steps to insure correction, particularly of those conditions which, if neglected, might affect the driver's ability to drive safely.

General appearance and development. Note marked overweight. Note any postural defect, perceptible limp, tremor, or other conditions that might be caused by alcoholism, thyroid intoxication or other illnesses.

Head-eyes. When other than the Snellen chart is used, the results of such test must be expressed in values comparable to the standard Snellen test. If the driver wears corrective lenses for driving, these should be worn while driver's visual acuity is being tested. If contact lenses are worn, there should be sufficient evidence of good tolerance of and adaptation to their use. Indicate the driver's need to wear corrective lenses to meet the vision standard on the Medical Examiner's Certificate by checking the box, "Qualified only when wearing corrective lenses." In recording distance vision use 20 feet as normal. Report all vision as a fraction with 20 as the numerator and the smallest type read at 20 feet as the denominator. Monocular drivers are not qualified to operate commercial motor vehicles in interstate commerce.

Ears. Note evidence of any ear disease, symptoms of aural vertigo, or Meniere's Syndrome. When recording hearing, record distance from patient at which a forced whispered voice can first be heard. For the whispered voice test, the individual should be stationed at least 5 feet from the examiner with the ear being tested turned toward the examiner. The other ear is covered. Using the breath which remains after a normal expiration, the examiner whispers words or random numbers such as 66, 18, 23, etc. The examiner should not use only sibilants (s-sounding test materials). The opposite ear should be tested in the same manner. If the individual fails the whispered voice test, the audiometric test should be administered. For the audiometric test, record decibel loss at 500 Hz, 1,000 Hz, and 2,000 Hz. Average the decibel loss at 500 Hz, 1,000 Hz and 2,000 Hz and record as described on the form. If the individual fails the audiometric test and the whispered voice test has not been administered, the whispered voice test should be performed to determine if the standard applicable to that test can be met.

Throat. Note any irremediable deformities likely to interfere with breathing or swallowing.

Heart. Note murmurs and arrhythmias, and any history of an enlarged heart, congestive heart failure, or cardiovascular disease that is accompanied by syncope, dyspnea, or collapse. Indicate onset date, diagnosis, medication, and any current limitation. An electrocardiogram is required when findings so indicate.

Blood pressure (BP). If a driver has hypertension and/or is being medicated for hypertension, he or she should be recertified more frequently. An individual diagnosed with Stage 1 hypertension (BP is 140/90–159/99) may be certified for one year. At recertification, an individual with a BP equal to or less than 140/90 may be certified for one year; however, if his or her BP is greater than 140/90 but less than 160/100, a one-time certificate for 3 months can be issued. An individual diagnosed with Stage 2 (BP is 160/100–179/109) should be treated and a one-time certificate for 3-month certification can be issued. Once the driver has reduced his or her BP to equal to or less than 140/90, he or she may be recertified annually thereafter. An individual diagnosed with Stage 3 hypertension (BP equal to or greater than 180/110) should not be certified until his or her BP is reduced to 140/90 or less, and may be recertified every 6 months.

Lungs. Note abnormal chest wall expansion, respiratory rate, breath sounds including wheezes or alveolar rales, impaired respiratory function, dyspnea, or cyanosis. Abnormal finds on physical exam may require further testing such as pulmonary tests and/or x-ray of chest.

Abdomen and viscera. Note enlarged liver, enlarged spleen, abnormal masses, bruits, hernia, and significant abdominal wall muscle weakness and tenderness. If the diagnosis suggests that the condition might interfere with the control and safe operation of a commercial motor vehicle, further testing and evaluation is required.

Genital-urinary and rectal examination. A urinalysis is required. Protein, blood or sugar in the urine may be an indication for further testing to rule out any underlying medical problems. Note hernias. A condition causing discomfort should be evaluated to determine the extent to which the condition might interfere with the control and safe operation of a commercial motor vehicle.

Neurological. Note impaired equilibrium, coordination, or speech pattern; paresthesia; asymmetric deep tendon reflexes; sensory or positional abnormalities; abnormal patellar and Babinski's reflexes; ataxia. Abnormal neurological responses may be an indication for further testing to rule out an underlying medical condition. Any neurological condition should be evaluated for the nature and severity of the condition, the degree of limitation present, the likelihood of progressive limitation, and the potential for sudden incapacitation. In instances where the medical examiner has determined that more frequent monitoring of a condition is appropriate, a certificate for a shorter period should be issued.

Spine, musculoskeletal. Previous surgery, deformities, limitation of motion, and tenderness should be noted. Findings may indicate additional testing and evaluation should be conducted.

Extremities. Carefully examine upper and lower extremities and note any loss or impairment of leg, foot, toe, arm, hand, or finger. Note any deformities, atrophy, paralysis, partial paralysis, clubbing, edema, or hypotonia. If a hand or finger deformity exists, determine whether prehension and power grasp are sufficient to enable the driver to maintain steering wheel grip and to control other vehicle equipment during routine and emergency driving operations. If a foot or leg deformity exists, determine whether sufficient mobility and strength exist to enable the driver to operate pedals properly. In the case of any loss or impairment to an extremity which may interfere with the driver's ability to operate a commercial motor vehicle safely, the medical examiner should state on the medical certificate "medically unqualified unless accompanied by a Skill Performance Evaluation Certificate." The driver must then apply to the Field Service Center of the FMCSA, for the State in which the driver has legal residence, for a Skill Performance Evaluation Certificate under §391.49.

Laboratory and other testing. Other test(s) may be indicated based upon the medical history or findings of the physical examination.

Diabetes. If insulin is necessary to control a diabetic driver's condition, the driver is not qualified to operate a commercial motor vehicle in interstate commerce. If mild diabetes is present and it is controlled by use of an oral hypoglycemic drug and/or diet and exercise, it should not be considered disqualifying. However, the driver must remain under adequate medical supervision.

Upon completion of the examination, the medical examiner must date and sign the form, provide his/her full name, office address and telephone number. The completed medical examination form shall be retained on file at the office of the medical examiner.

Although a rulemaking is in progress that may eliminate the need for some drivers to carry a medical certificate or for the carrier to maintain an actual copy of the certificate, currently the carrier must maintain a copy of the medical certificate in the driver qualification file. The carrier is NOT required to have a copy of the medical examination reporting form (long form) although they are not prohibited from obtaining this. A HIPAA compliant release is required for release of the medical examination reporting form to the employer but one is not required to provide the medical certificate. If the employer does obtain a copy of the medical examination, it must be used and maintained consistent with any state or federal laws regarding personal health information.

The examiner who completes the examination must sign the medical certificate. If the driver loses the certificate or it is damaged, they may obtain a copy from either the examiner (who is required to maintain a copy) or the motor carrier. If the original Medical Examiner is not available, a different examiner in that office may sign the replacement certificate, although some examiners may require the driver to undergo a new physical examination [5].

References

1. Interpretation 49 CFR 391.45. www.fmcsa.dot.gov/rules-regulations/administration/fmcsr/fmcsrruletext.asp?rule_toc=760&section=391.45&section_toc=1783&guidence=Y. Accessed May 20, 2007.
2. Interpretation 49 CFR 391.41. www.fmcsa.dot.gov/rules-regulations/administration/fmcsr/fmcsrruletext.asp?rule_toc=760&section=391.41&section_toc=1781&guidance=Y. Accessed May 20, 2007.
3. Federal Motor Carrier Safety Administration, DOT. Physical qualification of drivers; Medical examination; Final rule. *Fed Reg* 2000;65(Oct. 5):59363–59380.
4. Federal Motor Carrier Safety Administration, DOT. Motor Carrier Safety Regulations, Miscellaneous Technical Amendments. *Fed Reg* 2003;68(Sept. 30):56196–56208.
5. Federal Motor Carrier Safety Administration Medical Frequently Asked Questions.www.fmcsa.dot.gov/rulesregulations/topics/medical/faq.asp. Accessed January 5, 2007.
6. Blumenthal R, Braunstein J, Connolly H, Epstein A, Gersh BJ, Wittels EH. Cardiovascular Advisory Panel Guidelines for the Medical Examination of Commercial Motor Vehicle Drivers. FMCSA-MCP-02-002. Washington: U.S. Department of Transportation, Federal Motor Carrier Safety Administration, October 2002.
7. U.S. Department of Transportation, Federal Highway Administration. Conference on Neurological Disorders and the Commercial Driver. Publication No. FHWA-MC-88-042. Washington: U.S. DOT, Federal Highway Administration, Office of Motor Carriers, 1988.
8. U.S. Department of Transportation, Federal Highway Administration. Conference on Psychiatric Disorders and the Commercial Driver. Publication

No. FHWA-MC-91-006. Washington: U.S. DOT, Federal Highway Administration, Office of Motor Carriers, 1990.

9. U.S. Department of Transportation, Federal Highway Administration. Conference on Pulmonary/Respiratory Disorders and the Commercial Driver. Publication No. FHWA-MC-91-004. Washington: U.S. DOT, Federal Highway Administration, Office of Motor Carriers, 1991.

3

Regulations, Advisory Criteria, Interpretations, and Frequently Asked Questions

Natalie P. Hartenbaum, MD, MPH

For many years, examiners thought that the only information they would need to perform a commercial driver medical examination was provided on the form. Whereas the old form, which had been in use until 2001, contained only the medical standards and instructions to examiners, the form which has been in use since then also includes the advisory criteria as well as the roles and responsibilities of the commercial motor vehicle operator. Although this new form can be considered to be self-contained, there are still many other parts of the Federal Motor Carrier Safety Regulations (FMCSRs) that the examiner must be aware of prior to signing the medical certificate. There are several other regulations, including those on Skill Performance Evaluation Certificates and Exemptions with which the examiner should be familiar. The conference reports or advisory panel guidelines now are referenced in the advisory criteria. Although they are not medical standards, these advisory criteria are considered codified because they are included in the *Code of Federal Regulations*. The FMCSA now includes Frequently Asked Questions (FAQs) on their website that addresses many of the common issues faced by commercial driver medical examiners.

This chapter includes most of the regulations relevant to the commercial driver medical certification program. There are also interpretations posted for many of the standards. These were initially published in the *Federal Register* on April 4, 1997, but are now available through the FMCSA website. FAQs posted as of May 21, 2007, are also included. Examiners should periodically monitor the FMCSA Web page for updates to the Regulatory Guidance or FAQs Updates as well as all the Regulations, Regulatory Guidance, Rulemaking Announcements, and Medical Conference Reports / Advisory Panel Reports and FAQs can be accessed through the Federal Motor Carrier Safety Administration's Internet site (*www.fmcsa.dot.gov*).

The entire medical examination form is included in this chapter. Portions of the final five pages of the form, including driver roles, instructions to examiners, and advisory criteria, have been reproduced for easier reading.

Most states have adopted the FMCSA medical criteria to some extent for their intrastate drivers. Some may permit exemptions, waivers, or have grandfather programs for those drivers operating in intrastate commerce prior to the state's adoption of the medical criteria. Examiners should be familiar with the intrastate medical criteria for their and surrounding states. The determination of whether the driver is operating in intrastate (within a single state) or interstate (between states) is dependent not on the driver but on the property being transported.

Note that the weight used to define a commercial vehicle in the FMCSRs (which includes the medical requirements) in 49 CFR 390.5 differs from that found in 49 CFR 382 (Controlled Substances and Alcohol Use and Testing) and 383 (Commercial Driver's License). In the sections on controlled substance testing and commercial driver's license, a commercial motor vehicle is defined as a motor vehicle or combination of motor vehicles used in commerce to transport passengers or property if the motor vehicle

1. Has a gross combination weight rating of 11,794 kg or more (26,001 lb or more) inclusive of a towed unit with a gross vehicle weight rating of more than 4,536 kg (10,000 lb); or
2. Has a gross vehicle weight rating of 11,794 kg or more (26,001 lb or more); or
3. Is designed to transport 16 or more passengers, including the driver; or
4. Is of any size and is used in the transportation of materials found to be hazardous for the purposes of the Hazardous Materials Transportation Act and that require the motor vehicle to be placarded under the Hazardous Materials Regulations (49 CFR part 172, subpart F).

To determine which drivers fall under the FMCSRs regarding medical examination, in addition to operators of vehicles that transport hazardous material requiring placarding, the following weights and passenger capacities are used:

1. Has a gross vehicle weight rating or gross combination weight rating, or gross vehicle weight or gross combination weight, of 4,536 kg (10,001 pounds) or more, whichever is greater; or

2. Is designed or used to transport more than 8 passengers (including the driver) for compensation; or
3. Is designed or used to transport more than 15 passengers, including the driver, and is not used to transport passengers for compensation; or
4. Is used in transporting material found by the Secretary of Transportation to be hazardous under 49 U.S.C. 5103 and transported in a quantity requiring placarding under regulations prescribed by the Secretary under 49 CFR, subtitle B, chapter I, subchapter C.

Selected Sections from
TITLE 49—TRANSPORTATION—

CHAPTER III—FEDERAL MOTOR CARRIER SAFETY ADMINISTRATION, DEPARTMENT OF TRANSPORTATION *current as of May 21, 2007*

§390.5 **Definitions—only those pertaining to examination are included—The complete section 390.5 can be found on the FMCSA web page.**

Commercial motor vehicle means any self-propelled or towed motor vehicle used on a highway in interstate commerce to transport passengers or property when the vehicle

(1) Has a gross vehicle weight rating or gross combination weight rating, or gross vehicle weight or gross combination weight, of 4,537 kg (10,001 lb) or more, whichever is greater; or

(2) Is designed or used to transport more than 8 passengers (including the driver) for compensation; or

(3) Is designed or used to transport more than 15 passengers, including the driver, and is not used to transport passengers for compensation; or

(4) Is used in transporting material found by the Secretary of Transportation to be hazardous under 49 U.S.C. 5103 and transported in a quantity requiring placarding under regulations prescribed by the Secretary under 49 CFR, subtitle B, chapter I, subchapter C.

Direct compensation means payment made to the motor carrier by the passengers or a person acting on behalf of the passengers for the transportation services provided, and not included in a total package charge or other assessment for highway transportation services.

Exempt intracity zone means the geographic area of a municipality or the commercial zone of that municipality described in Appendix F to Subchapter B of this Chapter. The term "exempt intracity zone" does not include any municipality or commercial zone in the State of Hawaii. For purposes of §391.62, a driver may be considered to operate a commercial motor vehicle wholly within an exempt intracity zone notwithstanding any common control, management, or arrangement for a continuous carriage or shipment to or from a point without such zone.

Interstate commerce means trade, traffic, or transportation in the United States—

(1) Between a place in a State and a place outside of such State (including a place outside of the United States);
(2) Between two places in a State through another State or a place outside of the United States; or
(3) Between two places in a State as part of trade, traffic, or transportation originating or terminating outside the State or the United States.

Intrastate commerce means any trade, traffic, or transportation in any State which is not described in the term "interstate commerce."

Medical examiner means a person who is licensed, certified, and/or registered, in accordance with applicable State laws and regulations, to perform physical examinations. The term includes, but is not limited to, doctors of medicine, doctors of osteopathy, physician assistants, advanced practice nurses, and doctors of chiropractic.

PART 391—QUALIFICATIONS OF DRIVERS—
Subpart E — Physical Qualifications and Examinations

§391.41   Physical qualifications for drivers.

(a) A person shall not drive a commercial motor vehicle unless he/she is physically qualified to do so and, except as provided in §391.67, has on his/her person the original, or a photographic copy, of a medical examiner's certificate that he/she is physically qualified to drive a commercial motor vehicle.

The United States and Canada entered into a Reciprocity Agreement, effective March 30, 1999, recognizing that a Canadian commercial driver's license is proof of medical fitness to drive. Therefore, Canadian commercial motor vehicle (CMV) drivers are no longer required to have in their possession a medical examiner's certificate if the driver has been issued, and possesses, a valid commercial driver's license issued by a Canadian Province or Territory. However, Canadian drivers who are insulin-using diabetics, who have epilepsy, or who are hearing impaired as defined in §391.41(b)(11) are not qualified to drive CMVs in the United States. Furthermore, Canadian drivers who do not meet the medical fitness provisions of the Canadian National Safety Code for Motor Carriers but who have been issued a waiver by one of the Canadian Provinces or Territories are not qualified to drive CMVs in the United States.

(b) A person is physically qualified to drive a commercial motor vehicle if that person—

(b)(1) Has no loss of a foot, a leg, a hand, or an arm, or has been granted a skill performance evaluation certificate pursuant to §391.49;

(b)(2) Has no impairment of:

(b)(2)(i) A hand or finger which interferes with prehension or power grasping; or

(b)(2)(ii) An arm, foot, or leg which interferes with the ability to perform normal tasks associated with operating a commercial motor vehicle; or any other significant limb defect or limitation which interferes with the ability to perform normal tasks associated with operating a commercial motor vehicle; or has been granted a skill performance evaluation certificate pursuant to §391.49.

(b)(3) Has no established medical history or clinical diagnosis of diabetes mellitus currently requiring insulin for control;

(b)(4) Has no current clinical diagnosis of myocardial infarction, angina pectoris, coronary insufficiency, thrombosis, or any other cardiovascular disease of a variety known to be accompanied by syncope, dyspnea, collapse, or congestive cardiac failure;

(b)(5) Has no established medical history or clinical diagnosis of a respiratory dysfunction likely to interfere with his/her ability to control and drive a commercial motor vehicle safely;

(b)(6) Has no current clinical diagnosis of high blood pressure likely to interfere with his/her ability to operate a commercial motor vehicle safely;

(b)(7) Has no established medical history or clinical diagnosis of rheumatic, arthritic, orthopedic, muscular, neuromuscular, or vascular disease which interferes with his/her ability to control and operate a commercial motor vehicle safely;

(b)(8) Has no established medical history or clinical diagnosis of epilepsy or any other condition which is likely to cause loss of consciousness or any loss of ability to control a commercial motor vehicle;

(b)(9) Has no mental, nervous, organic, or functional disease or psychiatric disorder likely to interfere with his/her ability to drive a commercial motor vehicle safely;

(b)(10) Has distant visual acuity of at least 20/40 (Snellen) in each eye without corrective lenses or visual acuity separately corrected to 20/40 (Snellen) or better with corrective lenses, distant binocular acuity of at least 20/40 (Snellen) in both eyes with or without corrective lenses, field of vision of at least 70° in the horizontal meridian in each eye, and the ability to recognize the colors of traffic signals and devices showing standard red, green, and amber;

(b)(11) First perceives a forced whispered voice in the better ear at not less than 5 feet with or without the use of a hearing aid or, if tested by use of an audiometric device, does not have an average hearing loss in the better ear greater than 40 decibels at 500 Hz, 1,000 Hz, and 2,000 Hz with or without a hearing aid when the audiometric device is calibrated to American National Standard (formerly ASA Standard) Z24.5-1951;

(b)(12)(i) Does not use a controlled substance identified in 21 CFR 1308.11 Schedule I, an amphetamine, a narcotic, or any other habit-forming drug.

(b)(12)(ii) *Exception.* A driver may use such a substance or drug, if the substance or drug is prescribed by a licensed medical practitioner who:

(b)(12)(ii)(A) Is familiar with the driver's medical history and assigned duties; and

(b)(12)(ii)(B) Has advised the driver that the prescribed substance or drug will not adversely affect the driver's ability to safely operate a commercial motor vehicle; and

(b)(13) Has no current clinical diagnosis of alcoholism.

§391.43   Medical examination; certificate of physical examination.

(a) Except as provided in paragraph (b) of this section, the medical examination shall be performed by a licensed medical examiner as defined in §390.5 of this subchapter.

(b) A licensed optometrist may perform so much of the medical examination as pertains to visual acuity, field of vision, and the ability to recognize colors as specified in paragraph (10) of §391.41(b).

(c) Medical examiners shall:

(c)(1) Be knowledgeable of the specific physical and mental demands associated with operating a commercial motor vehicle and the requirements of this subpart, including the medical advisory criteria prepared by the FMCSA as guidelines to aid the medical examiner in making the qualification determination; and

(c)(2) Be proficient in the use of and use the medical protocols necessary to adequately perform the medical examination required by this section.

(d) Any driver authorized to operate a commercial motor vehicle within an exempt intracity zone pursuant to §391.62 of this part shall furnish the examining medical examiner with a copy of the medical findings that led to the issuance of the first certificate of medical examination which allowed the driver to operate a commercial motor vehicle wholly within an exempt intracity zone.

(e) Any driver operating under a limited exemption authorized by §391.64 shall furnish the medical examiner with a copy of the annual medical findings of the endocrinologist, ophthalmologist or optometrist, as required under that section. If the medical examiner finds the driver qualified under the limited exemption in §391.64, such fact shall be noted on the Medical Examiner's Certificate.

(f) The medical examination shall be performed, and its results shall be recorded, substantially in accordance with the following instructions and examination form. Existing forms may be used until current printed supplies are depleted or until September 30, 2004, whichever occurs first.

Instructions for Performing and Recording Physical Examinations

The medical examiner must be familiar with 49 CFR 391.41, Physical qualifications for drivers, and should review these instructions before performing the physical examination. Answer each question "yes" or "no" and record numerical readings where indicated on the physical examination form.

The medical examiner must be aware of the rigorous physical, mental, and emotional demands placed on the driver of a commercial motor vehicle. In the interest of public safety, the medical examiner is required to certify that the driver does not have any physical, mental, or organic condition that might affect the driver's ability to operate a commercial motor vehicle safely.

General information.   The purpose of this history and physical examination is to detect the presence of physical, mental, or organic conditions of such a character and extent as to affect the driver's ability to operate a commercial motor vehicle safely. The examination should be conducted carefully and should at least include all of the information requested in the following form. History of certain conditions may be cause for rejection. Indicate the need for further testing and/or require evaluation by a specialist. Conditions may be recorded which do not, because of their character or degree, indicate that certification of physical fitness should be denied. However, these conditions should be discussed with the driver and he/she should be advised to take the necessary steps to insure correction, particularly of those conditions which, if neglected, might affect the driver's ability to drive safely.

General appearance and development. Note marked overweight. Note any postural defect, perceptible limp, tremor, or other conditions that might be caused by alcoholism, thyroid intoxication or other illnesses.

Head-eyes. When other than the Snellen chart is used, the results of such test must be expressed in values comparable to the standard Snellen test. If the driver wears corrective lenses for driving, these should be worn while driver's visual acuity is being tested. If contact lenses are worn, there should be sufficient evidence of good tolerance of and adaptation to their use. Indicate the driver's need to wear corrective lenses to meet the vision standard on the Medical Examiner's Certificate by checking the box, "Qualified only when wearing corrective lenses." In recording distance vision use 20 feet as normal. Report all vision as a fraction with 20 as the numerator and the smallest type read at 20 feet as the denominator. Monocular drivers are not qualified to operate commercial motor vehicles in interstate commerce.

Ears. Note evidence of any ear disease, symptoms of aural vertigo, or Meniere's Syndrome. When recording hearing, record distance from patient at which a forced whispered voice can first be heard. For the whispered voice test, the individual should be stationed at least 5 feet from the examiner with the ear being tested turned toward the examiner. The other ear is covered. Using the breath which remains after a normal expiration, the examiner whispers words or random numbers such as 66, 18, 23, etc. The examiner should not use only sibilants (s-sounding test materials). The opposite ear should be tested in the same manner. If the individual fails the whispered voice test, the audiometric test should be administered. For the audiometric test, record decibel loss at 500 Hz, 1,000 Hz, and 2,000 Hz. Average the decibel loss at 500 Hz, 1,000 Hz, and 2,000 Hz and record as described on the form. If the individual fails the audiometric test and the whispered voice test has not been administered, the whispered voice test should be performed to determine if the standard applicable to that test can be met.

Throat. Note any irremediable deformities likely to interfere with breathing or swallowing.

Heart. Note murmurs and arrhythmias, and any history of an enlarged heart, congestive heart failure, or cardiovascular disease that is accompanied by syncope, dyspnea, or collapse. Indicate onset date, diagnosis, medication, and any current limitation. An electrocardiogram is required when findings so indicate.

Blood pressure (BP). If a driver has hypertension and/or is being medicated for hypertension, he or she should be recertified more frequently. An individual diagnosed with Stage 1 hypertension (BP is 140/90–159/99) may be certified for one year. At recertification, an individual with a BP equal to or less than 140/90 may be certified for one year; however, if his or her BP is greater than 140/90 but less than 160/100, a one-time certificate for 3 months can be issued. An individual diagnosed with Stage 2 (BP is 160/100–179/109) should be treated and a one-time certificate for 3-month certification can be issued. Once the driver has reduced his or her BP to equal to or less than 140/90, he or she may be recertified annually thereafter. An individual diagnosed with Stage 3 hypertension (BP equal to or greater than 180/110) should not be certified until his or her BP is reduced to 140/90 or less, and may be recertified every 6 months.

Lungs. Note abnormal chest wall expansion, respiratory rate, breath sounds including wheezes or alveolar rales, impaired respiratory function, dyspnea, or cyanosis. Abnormal finds on physical exam may require further testing such as pulmonary tests and/or x-ray of chest.

Abdomen and viscera. Note enlarged liver, enlarged spleen, abnormal masses, bruits, hernia, and significant abdominal wall muscle weakness and tenderness. If the diagnosis suggests that the condition might interfere with the control and safe operation of a commercial motor vehicle, further testing and evaluation is required.

Genital-urinary and rectal examination. A urinalysis is required. Protein, blood or sugar in the urine may be an indication for further testing to rule out any underlying medical problems. Note hernias. A condition causing discomfort should be evaluated to determine the extent to which the condition might interfere with the control and safe operation of a commercial motor vehicle.

Neurological. Note impaired equilibrium, coordination, or speech pattern; paresthesia; asymmetric deep tendon reflexes; sensory or positional abnormalities; abnormal patellar and Babinski's reflexes; ataxia. Abnormal neurological responses may be an indication for further testing to rule out an underlying medical condition. Any neurological condition should be evaluated for the nature and severity of the condition, the degree of limitation present, the likelihood of progressive limitation, and the potential for sudden incapacitation. In instances where the medical examiner has determined that more frequent monitoring of a condition is appropriate, a certificate for a shorter period should be issued.

Spine, musculoskeletal. Previous surgery, deformities, limitation of motion, and tenderness should be noted. Findings may indicate additional testing and evaluation should be conducted.

Extremities. Carefully examine upper and lower extremities and note any loss or impairment of leg, foot, toe, arm, hand, or finger. Note any deformities, atrophy, paralysis, partial paralysis, clubbing, edema, or hypotonia. If a hand or finger deformity exists, determine whether prehension and power grasp are sufficient to enable the driver to maintain steering wheel grip and to control other vehicle equipment during routine and emergency driving operations. If a foot or leg deformity exists, determine whether sufficient mobility and strength exist to enable the driver to operate pedals properly. In the case of any loss or impairment to an extremity which may interfere with the driver's ability to operate a commercial motor vehicle safely, the medical examiner should state on the medical certificate "medically unqualified unless accompanied by a Skill Performance Evaluation Certificate." The driver must then apply to the Field Service Center of the FMCSA, for the State in which the driver has legal residence, for a Skill Performance Evaluation Certificate under §391.49.

Laboratory and other testing. Other test(s) may be indicated based upon the medical history or findings of the physical examination.

Diabetes. If insulin is necessary to control a diabetic driver's condition, the driver is not qualified to operate a commercial motor vehicle in interstate commerce. If mild diabetes is present and it is controlled by use of an oral hypoglycemic drug and/or diet and exercise, it should not be considered disqualifying. However, the driver must remain under adequate medical supervision.

Upon completion of the examination, the medical examiner must date and sign the form, provide his/her full name, office address, and telephone number. The completed medical examination form shall be retained on file at the office of the medical examiner.

(g) If the medical examiner finds that the person he/she examined is physically qualified to drive a commercial motor vehicle in accordance with §391.41(b), the medical examiner shall complete a certificate in the form prescribed in paragraph (h) of this section and furnish one copy to the person who was examined and one copy to the motor carrier that employs him/her.

(h) The medical examiner's certificate shall be substantially in accordance with the following form. Existing forms may be used until current printed supplies are depleted or until November 6, 2001, whichever occurs first.

Medical Examination Report for Commercial Driver Fitness Determination

The complete Medical Examination form and certificate can be found on pages 34–42.

The Driver's Role

Responsibilities, work schedules, physical and emotional demands, and lifestyles among commercial drivers vary by the type of driving that they do. Some of the main types of drivers include the following: turn around or short relay (drivers return to their home base each evening); long relay (drivers drive 9–11 hours and then have at least a 10-hour off-duty period); straight through haul (cross country drivers); and team drivers (drivers share the driving by alternating their 5-hour driving periods and 5-hour rest periods).

The following factors may be involved in a driver's performance of duties: abrupt schedule changes and rotating work schedules, which may result in irregular sleep patterns and a driver beginning a trip in a fatigued condition; long hours; extended time away from family and friends, which may result in lack of social support; tight pickup and delivery schedules, with irregularity in work, rest, and eating patterns; adverse road, weather and traffic conditions, which may cause delays and lead to hurriedly loading or unloading cargo in order to compensate for the lost time; and environmental conditions such as excessive vibration, noise, and extremes in temperature. Transporting passengers or hazardous materials may add to the demands on the commercial driver.

There may be duties in addition to the driving task for which a driver is responsible and needs to be fit. Some of these responsibilities are: coupling and uncoupling trailer(s) from the tractor, loading and unloading trailer(s) (sometimes a driver may lift a heavy load or unload as much as 50,000 lbs. of freight after sitting for a long period of time without any stretching period); inspecting the operating condition of tractor and trailer(s) before, during, and after delivery of cargo; lifting, installing, and removing heavy tire chains; and, lifting heavy tarpaulins to cover open top trailers. The above tasks demand agility, the ability to bend and stoop, the ability to maintain a crouching position to inspect the underside of the vehicle, frequent entering

Medical Examination Report
FOR COMMERCIAL DRIVER FITNESS DETERMINATION

649-F (6045)

1. DRIVER'S INFORMATION — Driver completes this section

Driver's Name (Last, First, Middle)	Social Security No.	Birthdate M / D / Y	Age	Sex □ M □ F	New Certification □ □ Recertification □ □ Follow-up	Date of Exam

Address	City, State, Zip Code	Work Tel: ( ) Home Tel: ( )	Driver License No.	License Class □ A □ C □ B □ D □ Other	State of Issue

2. HEALTH HISTORY — Driver completes this section, but medical examiner is encouraged to discuss with driver.

Yes No

- □ □ Any illness or injury in the last 5 years?
- □ □ Head/Brain injuries, disorders or illnesses
- □ □ Seizures, epilepsy
  - □ medication _____
- □ □ Eye disorders or impaired vision (except corrective lenses)
- □ □ Ear disorders, loss of hearing or balance
- □ □ Heart disease or heart attack, other cardiovascular condition
  - □ medication _____
- □ □ Heart surgery (valve replacement/bypass, angioplasty, pacemaker)
- □ □ High blood pressure _____ medication
- □ □ Muscular disease
- □ □ Shortness of breath

Yes No

- □ □ Lung disease, emphysema, asthma, chronic bronchitis
- □ □ Kidney disease, dialysis
- □ □ Liver disease
- □ □ Digestive problems
- □ □ Diabetes or elevated blood sugar controlled by:
  - □ diet
  - □ pills
  - □ insulin
- □ □ Nervous or psychiatric disorders, e.g., severe depression
  - _____ medication
- □ □ Loss of, or altered consciousness

Yes No

- □ □ Fainting, dizziness
- □ □ Sleep disorders, pauses in breathing while asleep, daytime sleepiness, loud snoring
- □ □ Stroke or paralysis
- □ □ Missing or impaired hand, arm, foot, leg, finger, toe
- □ □ Spinal injury or disease
- □ □ Chronic low back pain
- □ □ Regular, frequent alcohol use
- □ □ Narcotic or habit forming drug use

For any YES answer, indicate onset date, diagnosis, treating physician's name and address, and any current limitation. List all medications (including over-the-counter medications) used regularly or recently.

_____
_____
_____

I certify that the above information is complete and true. I understand that inaccurate, false or missing information may invalidate the examination and my Medical Examiner's Certificate.   Driver's Signature _____   Date _____

Medical Examiner's Comments on Health History (The medical examiner must review and discuss with the driver any "yes" answers and potential hazards of medications, including over-the-counter medications, while driving. This discussion must be documented below.)

_____
_____
_____

TESTING (Medical Examiner completes Section 3 through 7)
Name: Last, _____ First, _____ Middle, _____

3. VISION

Standard: At least 20/40 acuity (Snellen) in each eye with or without correction. At least 70 degrees peripheral in horizontal meridian measured in each eye. The use of corrective lenses should be noted on the Medical Examiner's Certificate.

INSTRUCTIONS: When other than the Snellen chart is used, give test results in Snellen-comparable values. In recording distance vision, use 20 feet as normal. Report visual acuity as a ratio with 20 as numerator and the smallest type read at 20 feet as denominator. If the applicant wears corrective lenses, these should be worn while visual acuity is being tested. If the driver habitually wears contact lenses, or intends to do so while driving, sufficient evidence of good tolerance and adaptation to their use must be obvious. *Monocular drivers are not qualified.*

Numerical readings must be provided.

ACUITY	UNCORRECTED	CORRECTED	HORIZONTAL FIELD OF VISION
Right Eye	20/	20/	Right Eye	o
Left Eye	20/	20/	Left Eye	o
Both Eyes	20/	20/	

Applicant can recognize and distinguish among traffic control signals and devices showing standard red, green, and amber colors ? ☐ Yes ☐ No

Applicant meets visual acuity requirement only when wearing:
☐ Corrective Lenses

Monocular Vision: ☐ Yes ☐ No

Complete next line only if vision testing is done by an opthalmologist or optometrist

Date of Examination _____ Name of Ophthalmologist or Optometrist (print) _____ Tel. No. _____ License No./ State of Issue _____ Signature _____

4. HEARING

Standard: a) Must first perceive forced whispered voice ≥ 5 ft., with or without hearing aid, or b) average hearing loss in better ear ≤ 40 dB

☐ Check if hearing aid used for tests. ☐ Check if hearing aid required to meet standard.

INSTRUCTIONS: To convert audiometric test results from ISO to ANSI, -14 dB from ISO for 500Hz, -10dB for 1,000 Hz, -8.5 dB for 2000 Hz. To average, add the readings for 3 frequencies tested and divide by 3.

Numerical readings must be recorded.

a) Record distance from individual at which forced whispered voice can first be heard.

	Right ear \ Feet	Left ear \ Feet

b) If audiometer is used, record hearing loss in decibels. (acc. to ANSI Z24.5-1951)

	Right Ear				Left Ear			
	500 Hz	1000 Hz	2000 Hz		500 Hz	1000 Hz	2000 Hz
			Average:				Average:

5. BLOOD PRESSURE/ PULSE RATE

Numerical readings must be recorded. Medical Examiner should take at least two readings to confirm BP.

Blood Pressure	Systolic	Diastolic	Reading	Category	Expiration Date	Recertification
			140-159/90-99	Stage 1	1 year	1 year if ≤140/90. One-time certificate for 3 months if 141-159/91-99.
			160-179/100-109	Stage 2	One-time certificate for 3 months.	1 year from date of exam if ≤140/90
			>180/110	Stage 3	6 months from date of exam if <140/90	6 months if ≤ 140/90

Driver qualified if ≤140/90.

Pulse Rate: ☐ Regular ☐ Irregular

Record Pulse Rate: _____

6. LABORATORY AND OTHER TEST FINDINGS

Numerical readings must be recorded.

URINE SPECIMEN	SP. GR.	PROTEIN	BLOOD	SUGAR

Urinalysis is required. Protein, blood or sugar in the urine may be an indication for further testing to rule out any underlying medical problem.

Other Testing (Describe and record) _____

7. PHYSICAL EXAMINATION

Height: _____ (in.) Weight: _____ (lbs.) Name: _____ Last, _____ First, _____ Middle,

The presence of a certain condition may not necessarily disqualifying a driver, particularly if the condition is controlled adequately, is not likely to worsen or is readily amenable to treatment. Even if a condition does not disqualify a driver, the medical examiner may consider deferring the driver temporarily. Also, the driver should be advised to take the necessary steps to correct the condition as soon as possible particularly if the condition, if neglected, could result in more serious illness that might affect driving.

Check YES if there are any abnormalities. Check NO if the body system is normal. Discuss any YES answers in detail in the space below, and indicate whether it would affect the driver's ability to operate a commercial motor vehicle safely. Enter applicable item number before each comment. If organic disease is present, note that it has been compensated for. See Instructions to the Medical Examiner for guidance.

BODY SYSTEM	CHECK FOR:	YES*	NO	BODY SYSTEM	CHECK FOR:	YES*	NO
1. General Appearance	Marked overweight, tremor, signs of alcoholism, problem drinking, or drug abuse.			7. Abdomen and Viscera	Enlarged liver, enlarged spleen, masses, bruits, hernia, significant abdominal wall muscle weakness.		
2. Eyes	Pupillary equality, reaction to light, accommodation, ocular motility, ocular muscle imbalance, extraocular movement, nystagmus, exophthalmos. Ask about retinopathy, cataracts, aphakia, glaucoma, macular degeneration and refer to a specialist if appropriate.			8. Vascular System	Abnormal pulse and amplitude, cartoid or arterial bruits, varicose veins.		
				9. Genito-urinary System	Hernias.		
3. Ears	Scarring of tympanic membrane, occlusion of external canal, perforated eardrums.			10. Extremities- Limb impaired. Driver may be subject to SPE certificate if otherwise qualified.	Loss or impairment of leg, foot, toe, arm, hand, finger, Perceptible limp, deformities, atrophy, weakness, paralysis, clubbing, edema, hypotonia. Insufficient grasp and prehension in upper limb to maintain steering wheel grip. Insufficient mobility and strength in lower limb to operate pedals properly.		
4. Mouth and Throat	Irremediable deformities likely to interfere with breathing or swallowing.						
5. Heart	Murmurs, extra sounds, enlarged heart, pacemaker, implantable defibrillator.			11. Spine, other musculoskeletal	Previous surgery, deformities, limitation of motion, tenderness.		
6. Lungs and chest, not including breast examination	Abnormal chest wall expansion, abnormal respiratory rate, abnormal breath sounds including wheezes or alveolar rales, impaired respiratory function, cyanosis. Abnormal findings on physical exam may require further testing such as pulmonary tests and/ or xray of chest.			12. Neurological	Impaired equilibrium, coordination or speech pattern; asymmetric deep tendon reflexes, sensory or positional abnormalities, abnormal patellar and Babinki's reflexes, ataxia.		

*COMMENTS: _____

_____

_____

Note certification status here. See Instructions to the Medical Examiner for guidance.

☐ Meets standards in 49 CFR 391.41; qualifies for 2 year certificate
☐ Does not meet standards
☐ Meets standards, but periodic monitoring required due to _____
☐ Driver qualified only for: ☐ 3 months ☐ 6 months ☐ 1 year ☐ Other _____

☐ Wearing corrective lense
☐ Wearing hearing aid
☐ Accompanied by a _____ waiver/ exemption. Driver must present exemption at time of certification.
☐ Skill Performance Evaluation (SPE) Certificate
☐ Driving within an exempt intracity zone (See 49 CFR 391.62)
☐ Qualified by operation of 49 CFR 391.64

Medical Examiner's signature _____
Medical Examiner's name _____
Address _____
Telephone Number _____

Temporarily disqualified due to (condition or medication): _____

Return to medical examiner's office for follow up on _____

If meets standards, complete a Medical Examiner's Certificate as stated in 49 CFR 391.43(h). (Driver must carry certificate when operating a commercial vehicle.)

36

49 CFR 391.41 Physical Qualifications for Drivers

THE DRIVER'S ROLE

Responsibilities, work schedules, physical and emotional demands, and lifestyles among commercial drivers vary by the type of driving that they do. Some of the main types of drivers include the following: turn around or short relay (drivers return to their home base each evening); long relay (drivers drive 9-11 hours and then have at least a 10-hour off-duty period), straight through haul (cross country drivers) and team drivers (drivers share the driving by alternating their 5-hour driving periods and 5-hour rest periods.)

The following factors may be involved in a driver's performance of duties: abrupt schedule changes and rotating work schedules, which may result in irregular sleep patterns and a driver beginning a trip in a fatigued condition; long hours; extended time away from family and friends, which may result in lack of social support; tight pickup and delivery schedules, with irregularity in work, rest, and eating patterns; adverse road, weather and traffic conditions, which may cause delays and lead to temperature. Transporting passengers or hazardous materials may add to the demands on the commercial driver.

There may be duties in addition to the driving task for which a driver is responsible and needs to be fit. Some of these responsibilities are: coupling and uncoupling trailer(s) from the tractor, loading and unloading trailer(s) (sometimes a driver may lift a heavy load or unload as much as 50,000 lbs. of freight after sitting for a long period of time without any stretching period); inspecting the operating condition of tractor and/or trailer(s) before, during and after delivery of cargo; lifting, installing, and removing heavy tire chains; and, lifting heavy tarpaulins to cover open top trailers. The above tasks demand agility, the ability to bend and stoop, the ability to maintain a crouching position to inspect the underside of the vehicle, frequent entering and exiting of the cab, and the ability to climb ladders on the tractor and/or trailer(s).

In addition, a driver must have the perceptual skills to monitor a sometimes complex driving situation, the judgment skills to make quick decisions, when necessary, and the manipulative skills to control an oversize steering wheel, shift gears using a manual transmission, and maneuver a vehicle in crowded areas.

§391.45 PHYSICAL QUALIFICATIONS FOR DRIVERS

(a) A person shall not drive a commercial motor vehicle unless he is physically qualified to do so and, except as provided in §391.67, has on his person the original, or a photographic copy, of a medical examiner's certificate that he is physically qualified to drive a commercial motor vehicle.

(b) A person is physically qualified to drive a motor vehicle if that person:

(1) Has no loss of a foot, a leg, a hand, or an arm, or has been granted a Skill Performance Evaluation (SPE) Certificate (formerly Limb Waiver Program) pursuant to §391.49.

(2) Has no impairment of: (i) A hand or finger which interferes with prehension or power grasping; or (ii) An arm, foot, or leg which interferes with the ability to perform normal tasks associated with operating a commercial motor vehicle, or any other significant limb defect or limitation which interferes with the ability to perform normal tasks associated with operating a commercial motor vehicle; or has been granted a SPE Certificate pursuant to §391.49;

(3) Has no established medical history or clinical diagnosis of diabetes mellitus currently requiring insulin for control;

(4) Has no current clinical diagnosis of myocardial infarction, angina pectoris, coronary insufficiency, thrombosis, or any other cardiovascular disease of a variety known to be accompanied by syncope, dyspnea, collapse, or congestive cardiac failure.

(5) Has no established medical history or clinical diagnosis of a respiratory dysfunction likely to interfere with his ability to control and drive a commercial motor vehicle safely.

(6) Has no current clinical diagnosis of high blood pressure likely to interfere with his ability to operate a commercial motor vehicle safely.

(7) Has no established medical history or clinical diagnosis of rheumatic, arthritic, orthopedic, muscular, neuromuscular, or vascular disease which interferes with his ability to control and operate a commercial motor vehicle safely.

(8) Has no established medical history or clinical diagnosis of epilepsy or any other condition which is likely to cause loss of consciousness or any loss of ability to control a commercial motor vehicle;

(9) Has no mental, nervous, organic, or functional disease or psychiatric disorder likely to interfere with his ability to drive a commercial motor vehicle safely;

(10) Has distant visual acuity of at least 20/40 (Snellen) in each eye without corrective lenses or visual acuity separately corrected to 20/40 (Snellen) or better with corrective lenses, distant binocular acuity of at least 20/40 (Snellen) in both eyes with or without corrective lenses, field of vision of at least 70 degrees in the horizontal meridian in each eye, and the ability to recognize the colors of traffic signals and devices showing standard red, green and amber;

(11) First perceives a forced whispered voice in the better ear not less than 5 feet with or without the use of a hearing aid, or, if tested by use of an audiometric device, does not have an average hearing loss in the better ear greater than 40 decibels at 500 Hz, 1,000 Hz and 2,000 Hz with or without a hearing device when the audiometric device is calibrated to the American National Standard (formerly ASA Standard) Z24.5-1951;

(12) (i) Does not use a controlled substance identified in 21 CFR 1308.11 Schedule I, an amphetamine, a narcotic, or any other habit-forming drug. (ii) Exception: A driver may use such a substance or drug, if the substance or drug is prescribed by a licensed medical practitioner who: (A) Is familiar with the driver's medical history and assigned duties; and (B) Has advised the driver that the prescribed substance or drug will not adversely affect the driver's ability to safely operate a commercial motor vehicle; and

(13) Has no current clinical diagnosis of alcoholism.

37

General Information

The purpose of this examination is to determine a driver's physical qualification to operate a commercial motor vehicle (CMV) in interstate commerce according to the requirements in 49 CFR 391.41-49. Therefore, the medical examiner must be knowledgeable of these requirements and guidelines developed by the FMCSA to assist the medical examiner in making the qualification determination. The medical examiner should be familiar with the driver's responsibilities and work environment and is referred to the section on the form, **The Driver's Role.**

In addition to reviewing the Health History section with the driver and conducting the physical examination, the medical examiner should discuss common prescriptions and over-the-counter medications relative to the side effects and hazards of these medications. History of certain conditions may be cause for rejection, particularly if required by regulation, or may indicate the need for additional laboratory tests or more stringent examination perhaps by a medical specialist. These decisions are usually made by the medical examiner in light of the driver's job responsibilities, work schedule and potential for the conditions to render the driver unsafe.

Medical conditions should be recorded even if they are not cause for denial, and they should be discussed with the driver to encourage appropriate remedial care. This advice is especially needed when a condition, if neglected, could develop into a serious illness that could affect driving.

If the medical examiner determines that the driver is fit to drive and is also able to perform non-driving responsibilities as may be required with his/her license. The certificate must be dated. **Under current regulations, the certificate is valid for two years, unless the driver has a medical condition that does not prohibit driving but does require more frequent monitoring.** In such situations, the medical certificate should be issued for a shorter length of time. The physical examination should be done carefully and at least as complete as is indicated by the attached form. Contact the FMCSA at (202) 366-1790 for further information (a vision exemption, qualifying drivers under 49 CFR 391.64, etc.).

Interpretation of Medical Standards

Since the issuance of the regulations for physical qualifications of commercial drivers, the Federal Motor Carrier Safety Administration (FMCSA) has published recommendations called Advisory Criteria to help medical examiners in determining whether a driver meets the physical qualifications for commercial driving. These recommendations have been condensed to provide information to medical examiners that (1) is directly relevant to the physical examination and (2) is not already included in the medical examination form. The specific regulation is highlighted and it's reference by section is highlighted.

Federal Motor Carrier Safety Regulations
-Advisory Criteria-

Loss of Limb:
§391.41(b)(1)
A person is physically qualified to drive a commercial motor vehicle if that person:
Has no loss of a foot, leg, hand or an arm, or has been granted a Skill Performance Evaluation (SPE) Certificate pursuant to Section 391.49.

Limb Impairment:
§391.41(b)(2)
A person is physically qualified to drive a commercial motor vehicle if that person:
Has no impairment of: (i) A hand or finger which interferes with prehension or power grasping; or (ii) An arm, foot, or leg which interferes with the ability to perform normal tasks associated with operating a commercial motor vehicle; or (iii) Any other significant limb defect or limitation which interferes with the ability to perform normal tasks associated with operating a commercial motor vehicle; or (iv) Has been granted a Skill Performance Evaluation (SPE) Certificate pursuant to Section 391.49.

A person who suffers loss of a foot, leg, hand or arm or whose limb impairment in any way interferes with the safe performance of normal tasks associated with operating a commercial motor vehicle is subject to the Skill Performance Evaluation Certification Program pursuant to section 391.49, assuming the person is otherwise qualified.

With the advancement of technology, medical aids and equipment modifications have been developed to compensate for certain disabilities. The SPE Certification Program (formerly the Limb Waiver Program) was designed to allow persons with the loss of a foot or limb or with limb impairments to qualify under the Federal Motor Carrier Safety Regulations (FMCSRs) by use of prosthetic devices or equipment modifications which enable them to safely operate a commercial motor vehicle. Since there are no medical standards equivalent to the original body or limb, certain risks are still present, and thus restrictions may be included on individual SPE certificates when a State Director for the FMCSA determines they are necessary to be consistent with safety and public interest.

If the driver is found otherwise medically qualified (391.41(b)(3) through (13)), the medical examiner must check on the medical certificate that the driver is qualified only if accompanied by a SPE Certificate. The driver and the employing motor carrier are subject to appropriate penalties if the driver operates a motor vehicle in interstate or foreign commerce without a current SPE certificate for his/her physical disability.

Diabetes
§391.41(b)(3)
A person is physically qualified to drive a commercial motor vehicle if that person:
Has no established medical history or clinical diagnosis of diabetes mellitus currently requiring insulin for control.

Diabetes mellitus is a disease which, on occasion, can result in a loss of consciousness or disorientation in time and space. Individuals who require insulin for control have conditions which can get out of control by the use of too much or too little insulin, or food intake not consistent with the insulin dosage. Incapacitation may occur from symptoms of hyperglycemic or hypoglycemic reactions (drowsiness, semiconsciousness, diabetic coma or insulin shock).

The administration of insulin is, within itself, a complicated process requiring insulin, syringe, needle, alcohol sponge and a sterile technique. Factors related to long-haul commercial motor vehicle operations, such as fatigue, lack of sleep, poor diet, emotional conditions, stress, and concomitant illness, compound the dangers, the FMCSA has consistently held that a diabetic who uses insulin for control does not meet the minimum physical requirements of the FMCSRs.

Hypoglycemic drugs, taken orally, are sometimes prescribed for diabetic individuals to help stimulate natural body production of insulin. If the condition can be controlled by the use of oral medication and diet, then an individual may be qualified under the present rule. CMV drivers who do not meet the Federal diabetes standard may call (202) 366-1790 for an application for a diabetes exemption.
(See Conference Report on Diabetes Disorders and Commercial Drivers and Insulin–Using Commercial Motor Vehicle Drivers at:
http://www.fmcsa.dot.gov/rulesregs/medreports.htm)

Cardiovascular Condition
§391.41(b)(4)
A person is physically qualified to drive a commercial motor vehicle if that person:
Has no current clinical diagnosis of myocardial infarction, angina pectoris, coronary insufficiency, thrombosis or any other cardiovascular disease of a variety known to be accompanied by syncope, dyspnea, collapse or congestive cardiac failure.

The term "has no current clinical diagnosis of is specifically designed to encompass: "a clinical diagnosis of" (1) a current cardiovascular condition, or (2) a cardiovascular condition which has not fully stabilized regardless of the time limit. The term "known to be accompanied by" is designed to include a clinical diagnosis of a cardiovascular disease (1) which is accompanied by symptoms of syncope, dyspnea, collapse or congestive cardiac failure; and/or (2) which is likely to cause syncope, dyspnea, collapse or congestive cardiac failure.

It is the intent of the FMCSRs to render unqualified, a driver who has a current cardiovascular disease which is accompanied by and/or likely to cause symptoms of syncope, dyspnea, collapse, or congestive cardiac failure. However, the subjective decision of whether the nature and severity of an individual's condition will likely cause symptoms of cardiovascular insufficiency is on an individual basis and qualification rests with the medical examiner and the motor carrier. In those cases where there is an occurrence of cardiovascular insufficiency (myocardial infarction, thrombosis, etc.), it is suggested before a driver is certified that he or she have a normal resting and stress electrocardiogram (ECG), no residual complications and no physical limitations, and is taking no medication likely to interfere with safe driving.

Coronary artery bypass surgery and pacemaker implantation are remedial procedures and thus, not unqualifying. Implanted automatic cardiac defibrillators are disqualifying due to risk of syncope. Coumadin is a medical treatment which can improve the health and safety of the driver and should not, by its use, medically disqualify the commercial driver. The emphasis should be on the underlying medical condition(s) which require treatment and the general health of the driver. The FMCSA should be contacted at (202) 366-1790 for additional recommendations regarding the physical qualification of drivers on coumadin.

(See Cardiovascular Advisory Panel Guidelines for the Medical examination of Commercial Motor Vehicle Drivers at: http://www.fmcsa.dot.gov/rulesregs/medreports.htm)

Respiratory Dysfunction
§391.41(b)(5)
A person is physically qualified to drive a commercial motor vehicle if that person:

Has no established medical history or clinical diagnosis of a respiratory dysfunction likely to interfere with ability to control and drive a commercial motor vehicle safely.

Since a driver must be alert at all times, any change in his or her mental state is in direct conflict with highway safety. Even the slightest impairment in respiratory function under emergency conditions (when greater oxygen supply is necessary for performance) may be detrimental to safe driving.

There are many conditions that interfere with oxygen exchange and may result in incapacitation, including emphysema, chronic asthma, carcinoma, tuberculosis, chronic bronchitis and sleep apnea. If the medical examiner detects a respiratory dysfunction, that in any way is likely to interfere with the driver's ability to safely control and drive a commercial motor vehicle, the driver must be referred to a specialist for further evaluation and therapy. Anticoagulation therapy for deep vein thrombosis and/or pulmonary thromboembolism is not unqualifying once optimum dose is achieved, provided lower extremity venous examinations remain normal and the treating physician gives a favorable recommendation.

(See Conference on Pulmonary/Respiratory Disorders and Commercial Drivers at: http://www.fmcsa.dot.gov/rulesregs/medreports.htm

Hypertension
§391.41(b)(6)
A person is physically qualified to drive a commercial motor vehicle if that person:

Has no current clinical diagnosis of high blood pressure likely to interfere with ability to operate a commercial motor vehicle safely.

Hypertension alone is unlikely to cause sudden collapse; however, the likelihood increases when target organ damage, particularly cerebral vascular disease, is present. This regulatory criteria is based on FMCSA's Cardiovascular Advisory Guidelines for the Examination of CMV Drivers, which used the Sixth Report of the Joint National Committee on Detection, Evaluation, and Treatment of High Blood Pressure (1997).

Stage 1 hypertension corresponds to a systolic BP of 140-159 mmHg and/or a diastolic BP of 90-99 mmHg. The driver with a BP in this range is at low risk for hypertension-related acute incapacitation and may be medically certified to drive for a one-year period. Certification examinations should be done annually thereafter and should be at or less than 140/90. If less than 160/100, certification may be extended one time for 3 months.

A blood pressure of 160-179 systolic and/or 100-109 diastolic is considered Stage 2 hypertension, and the driver is not necessarily unqualified during evaluation and institution of treatment. The driver is given a one time certification of three months to reduce his or her blood pressure to less than or equal to 140/90. A blood pressure in this range is an absolute indication for anti-hypertensive drug therapy. Provided treatment is well tolerated and the driver demonstrates a BP value of 140/90 or less, he or she may be certified for one year from date of the initial exam. The driver is certified annually thereafter.

A blood pressure at or greater than 180 (systolic) and 110 (diastolic) is considered Stage 3, high risk for an acute BP-related event. The driver may not be qualified, even temporarily, until reduced to 140/90 or less and treatment is well tolerated. The driver may be certified for 6 months and biannually (every 6 months) thereafter if at recheck BP is 140/90 or less.

Annual recertification is recommended if the medical examiner does not know the severity of hypertension prior to treatment.

An elevated blood pressure finding should be confirmed by at least two subsequent measurements on different days.

Treatment includes nonpharmacologic and pharmacologic modalities as well as counseling to reduce other risk factors. Most antihypertensive medications also have side effects, the importance of which must be judged on an individual basis. Individuals must be alerted to the hazards of these medications while driving. Side effects of somnolence or syncope are particularly undesirable in commercial drivers.

Secondary hypertension is based on the above stages. Evaluation is warranted if patient is persistently hypertensive

on maximal or near-maximal doses of 2-3 pharmacologic agents. Some causes of secondary hypertension may be amenable to surgical intervention or specific pharmacologic disease.

(See Cardiovascular Advisory Panel Guidelines for the Medical Examination of Commercial Motor Vehicle Drivers at: http://www.fmcsa.dot.gov/rulesregs/medreports.htm)

Rheumatic, Arthritic, Orthopedic, Muscular, Neuromuscular or Vascular Disease §391.41(b)(7)
A person is physically qualified to drive a commercial motor vehicle if that person:

Has no established medical history or clinical diagnosis of rheumatic, arthritic, orthopedic, muscular, neuromuscular or vascular disease which interferes with the ability to control and operate a commercial motor vehicle safely.

Certain diseases are known to have acute episodes of transient muscle weakness, poor muscular coordination (ataxia), abnormal sensations (paresthesia), decreased muscular tone (hypotonia), visual disturbances (paresthesia) and pain which may be suddenly incapacitating. With each recurring episode, these symptoms may become more pronounced and remain for longer periods of time. Other diseases have more insidious onsets and display symptoms of muscle wasting (atrophy), swelling and paresthesia which may not suddenly incapacitate a person but may restrict his/her movements and eventually interfere with the ability to safely operate a motor vehicle. In many instances these diseases are degenerative in nature or may result in deterioration of the involved area.

Once the individual has been diagnosed as having a rheumatic, arthritic, orthopedic, muscular, neuromuscular or vascular disease, then he/she has an established history of that disease. The physician, when examining an individual, should consider the following: (1) the nature and severity of the individual's condition (such as sensory loss or loss of strength); (2) the degree of limitation present (such as range of motion); (3) the likelihood of progressive limitation (not always present initially but may manifest itself over time); and (4) the likelihood of sudden incapacitation. If severe functional impairment exists, the driver does not qualify. In cases where more frequent monitoring is required, a certificate for a shorter period of time may be issued. (See Conference on Neurological Disorders and Commercial Drivers at: http://www.fmcsa.dot.gov/rulesregs/medreports.htm)

Epilepsy
§391.41(b)(8)
A person is physically qualified to drive a commercial motor vehicle if that person:

Has no established medical history or clinical diagnosis of epilepsy or any other condition which is likely to cause loss of consciousness or any loss of ability to control a motor vehicle.

Epilepsy is a chronic functional disease characterized by seizures or episodes that occur without warning, resulting in loss of voluntary control which may lead to loss of consciousness and/or seizures. Therefore, the following drivers cannot be qualified: (1) a driver who has a medical history of epilepsy; (2) a driver who has a current clinical diagnosis of epilepsy; or (3) a driver who is taking antiseizure medication.

If an individual has had a sudden episode of a nonepileptic seizure or loss of consciousness of unknown cause which did not require antiseizure medication, the decision as to whether that person's condition will likely cause loss of consciousness or loss of ability to control a motor vehicle is made on an individual basis by the medical examiner in consultation with the treating physician. Before certification is considered, it is suggested that a 6 month waiting period elapse from the time of the episode. Following the waiting period, it is suggested that the individual have a complete neurological examination. If the results of the examination are negative and antiseizure medication is not required, then the driver may be qualified.

In those individual cases where a driver has a seizure or an episode of loss of consciousness that resulted from a known medical condition (e.g., drug reaction, high temperature, acute infectious disease, dehydration or acute metabolic disturbance), certification should be deferred until the driver has fully recovered from that condition and has no existing residual complications, and not taking antiseizure medication.

Drivers with a history of epilepsy/seizures off antiseizure medication **and** seizure-free for 10 years may be qualified to drive a CMV in interstate commerce. Interstate drivers with a history of a single unprovoked seizure may be qualified to drive a CMV in interstate commerce if seizure-free **and** off antiseizure medication for a 5-year period or more.

(See Conference on Neurological Disorders and Commercial Drivers at:

http://www.fmcsa.dot.gov/rulesregs/medreports.htm)

Mental Disorders
§391.41(b)(9)
A person is physically qualified to drive a commercial motor vehicle if that person:

Has no mental, nervous, organic or functional disease or psychiatric disorder likely to interfere with ability to drive a motor vehicle safely.

Emotional or adjustment problems contribute directly to an individual's level of memory, reasoning, attention, and judgment. These problems often underlie physical disorders. A variety of functional disorders can cause drowsiness, dizziness, confusion, weakness or paralysis that may lead to incoordination, inattention, loss of functional control and susceptibility to accidents while driving. Physical fatigue, headache, impaired coordination, recurring physical ailments and chronic "nagging" pain may be present to such a degree that certification for commercial driving is inadvisable. Somatic and psychosomatic complaints should be thoroughly examined when determining an individual's overall fitness to drive. Disorders of a periodically incapacitating nature, even in the early stages of development, may warrant disqualification.

Many bus and truck drivers have documented that "nervous trouble" related to neurotic, personality, or emotional or adjustment problems is responsible for a significant fraction of their preventable accidents. The degree to which an individual is able to appreciate, evaluate and adequately respond to environmental strain and emotional stress is critical when assessing an individual's mental alertness and flexibility to cope with the stresses of commercial motor vehicle driving.

When examining the driver, it should be kept in mind that individuals who live under chronic emotional upsets may have deeply ingrained maladaptive or erratic behavior patterns. Excessively antagonistic, instinctive, impulsive, openly aggressive, paranoid or severely depressed behavior greatly interfere with the driver's ability to drive safely. Those individuals who are highly susceptible to frequent states of emotional instability (schizophrenia, affective psychoses, paranoia, anxiety or depressive neuroses) may warrant disqualification. Careful consideration should be given to the side effects and interactions of medications in the overall qualification determination. See Psychiatric Conference Report for specific recommendations on the use of medications and potential hazards for driving.

(See Conference on Psychiatric Disorders and Commercial Drivers at:

http://www.fmcsa.dot.gov/rulesregs/medreports.htm)

Vision
§391.41(b)(10)
A person is physically qualified to drive a commercial motor vehicle if that person:

Has distant visual acuity of at least 20/40 (Snellen) in each eye with or without corrective lenses or visual acuity separately corrected to 20/40 (Snellen) or better with corrective lenses, distant binocular acuity of at least 20/40 (Snellen) in both eyes with or without corrective lenses, field of vision of at least 70 degrees in the horizontal meridian in each eye, and the ability to recognize the colors of traffic signals and devices showing standard red, green, and amber.

The term "ability to recognize the colors of" is interpreted to mean if a person can recognize and distinguish among traffic control signals and devices showing standard red, green and amber, he or she meets the minimum standard, even though he or she may have some type of color perception deficiency. If certain color perception tests are administered, (such as Ishihara, Pseudoisochromatic, Yarn) and doubtful findings are discovered, a controlled test using signal red, green and amber may be employed to determine the driver's ability to recognize these colors.

Contact lenses are permissible if there is sufficient evidence to indicate that the driver has good tolerance and is well adapted to their use. Use of a contact lens in one eye for distance visual acuity and another lens in the other eye for near vision is not acceptable, nor telescopic lenses acceptable for the driving of commercial motor vehicles.

If an individual meets the criteria by the use of glasses or contact lenses, the following statement shall appear on the Medical Examiner's Certificate: "Qualified only if wearing corrective lenses."

CMV drivers who do not meet the Federal vision standard may call (202) 366-1790 for an application for a vision exemption.

(See Visual Disorders and Commercial Drivers at:
http://www.fmcsa.dot.gov/rulesregs/medreports.htm)

Hearing
§391.41(b)(11)
A person is physically qualified to drive a commercial motor vehicle if that person:

First perceives a forced whispered voice in the better ear at not less than 5 feet with or without the use of a hearing aid, or, if tested by use of an audiometric device, does not have an average hearing loss in the better ear greater than 40 decibels at 500 Hz, 1,000 Hz, and 2,000 Hz with or without a hearing aid when the audiometric device is calibrated to American National Standard (formerly ADA Standard) Z24.5-1951.

Since the prescribed standard under the FMCSRs is the American Standards Association (ANSI), it may be necessary to convert the audiometric results from the ISO standard to the ANSI standard. Instructions are included on the Medical Examination report form.

If an individual meets the criteria by using a hearing aid, the driver must wear that hearing aid and have it in operation at all times while driving. Also, the driver must be in possession of a spare power source for the hearing aid.

For the whispered voice test, the individual should be stationed at least 5 feet from the examiner with the ear being tested turned toward the examiner. The other ear is covered. Using the breath which remains after a normal expiration, the examiner whispers words or random numbers such as 66, 18,

23, etc. The examiner should not use only sibilants (s sounding materials). The opposite ear should be tested in the same manner. If the individual fails the whispered voice test, the audiometric test should be administered.

If an individual meets the criteria by the use of a hearing aid, the following statement must appear on the Medical Examiner's Certificate "Qualified only when wearing a hearing aid."
(See Hearing Disorders and Commercial Motor Vehicle Drivers at: http://www.fmcsa.dot.gov/rulesregs/medreports.htm)

Drug Use
§391.41(b)(12)
A person is physically qualified to drive a commercial motor vehicle if that person:

Does not use a controlled substance identified in 21 CFR 1308.11, Schedule I, an amphetamine, a narcotic, or any other habit-forming drug. Exception: A driver may use such a substance or drug, if the substance or drug is prescribed by a licensed medical practitioner who is familiar with the driver's medical history and assigned duties; and has advised the driver that the prescribed substance or drug will not adversely affect the driver's ability to safely operate a commercial motor vehicle.

This exception does not apply to methadone. The intent of the medical certification process is to medically evaluate a driver to ensure that the driver has no medical condition which interferes with the safe performance of driving tasks on a public road. If a driver uses a Schedule I drug or other substance, an amphetamine, a narcotic, or any other habit-forming drug, it may be cause for the driver to be found medically unqualified. Motor carriers are encouraged to obtain a practitioner's written statement about the effects on transportation safety of the use of a particular drug. A test for controlled substances is not required as part of this biennial certification process. The FMCSA or the driver's employer should be contacted directly for information on controlled substances and alcohol testing under Part 382 of the FMCSRs.

The term "uses" is designed to encompass instances of prohibited drug use determined by a physician through established medical means. This may or may not involve body fluid testing. If body fluid testing takes place, positive test results should be confirmed by a second test of greater specificity. The term "habit-forming" is intended to include any drug or medication generally recognized as capable of becoming habitual, and which may impair the user's ability to operate a commercial motor vehicle safely.

The driver is medically unqualified for the duration of the prohibited drug(s) use and until a second examination shows the driver is free from the prohibited drug(s) use. Recertification may involve a substance abuse evaluation, the successful completion of a drug rehabilitation program, and a negative drug test result. Additionally, given that the certification period is normally two years, the examiner has the option to certify for a period of less than 2 years if this examiner determines more frequent monitoring is required.
(See Conference on Neurological Disorders and Commercial Drivers and Conference on Psychiatric Disorders and Commercial Drivers at: http://www.fmcsa.dot.gov/rulesregs/medreports.htm)

Alcoholism
§391.41(b)(13)
A person is physically qualified to drive a commercial motor vehicle if that person:

Has no current clinical diagnosis of alcoholism.

The term "current clinical diagnosis of" is specifically designed to encompass a current alcoholic illness or those instances where the individual's physical condition has not fully stabilized, regardless of the time element. If an individual shows signs of having an alcohol-use problem, he or she should be referred to a specialist. After counseling and/or treatment, he or she may be considered for certification.

MEDICAL EXAMINER'S CERTIFICATE

I certify that I have examined _____ In accordance with the Federal Motor Carrier Safety Regulations (49 CFR 391.41–391.49) and with knowledge of the driving duties, I find this person is qualified; and, if applicable, only when:

☐ wearing corrective lenses ☐ driving within an exempt intracity zone (49 CFR 391.62)

☐ wearing hearing aid ☐ accompanied by a Skill Performance Evaluation Certificate (SPE)

☐ accompanied by a _____ waiver exemption ☐ Qualified by operation of 49 CFR 391.64

The information I have provided regarding this physical examination is true and complete. A complete examination form with any attachment embodies my findings completely and correctly, and is on file in my office.

SIGNATURE OF MEDICAL EXAMINER	TELEPHONE	DATE

MEDICAL EXAMINER'S NAME (PRINT)	☐ MD ☐ DO ☐ Chiropractor ☐ Physician Assistant ☐ Advanced Practice Nurse

MEDICAL EXAMINER'S LICENSE OR CERTIFICATE NO./ISSUING STATE

SIGNATURE OF DRIVER	DRIVER'S LICENSE NO.	STATE

ADDRESS OF DRIVER

MEDICAL CERTIFICATE EXPIRATION DATE

and exiting of the cab, and the ability to climb ladders on the tractor and/or trailer(s).

In addition, a driver must have the perceptual skills to monitor a sometimes complex driving situation, the judgment skills to make quick decisions, when necessary, and the manipulative skills to control an oversize steering wheel, shift gears using a manual transmission, and maneuver a vehicle in crowded areas.

Instructions to the Medical Examiner

General Information   The purpose of this examination is to determine a driver's physical qualification to operate a commercial motor vehicle (CMV) in interstate commerce according to the requirements in 49 CFR 391.41-49. Therefore, the medical examiner must be knowledgeable of these requirements and guidelines developed by the FMCSA to assist the medical examiner in making the qualification determination. The medical examiner should be familiar with the driver's responsibilities and work environment and is referred to the section on the form, The Driver's Role.

In addition to reviewing the Health History section with the driver and conducting the physical examination, the medical examiner should discuss common prescriptions and over-the-counter medications relative to the side effects and hazards of these medications while driving. Educate driver to read warning labels on all medications. History of certain conditions may be cause for rejection, particularly if required by regulation, or may indicate the need for additional laboratory tests or more stringent examination perhaps by a medical specialist. These decisions are usually made by the medical examiner in light of the driver's job responsibilities, work schedule, and potential for the condition to render the driver unsafe.

Medical conditions should be recorded even if they are not cause for denial, and they should be discussed with the driver to encourage appropriate remedial care. This advice is especially needed when a condition, if neglected, could develop into a serious illness that could affect driving.

If the medical examiner determines that the driver is fit to drive and is also able to perform non-driving responsibilities as may be required, the medical examiner signs the medical certificate which the driver must carry with his/her license. The certificate must be dated. **Under current regulations, the certificate is valid for two years, unless the driver has a medical condition that does not prohibit driving but does require more frequent monitoring.** In such situations, the medical certificate should be issued for a shorter length of time. The physical examination should be done carefully and at least as complete as is indicated by the attached form.

Contact the FMCSA at (202) 366-1790 for further information (a vision exemption, qualifying drivers under 49 CFR 391.64, etc.).

Interpretation of Medical Standards

Since the issuance of the regulations for physical qualifications of commercial drivers, the Federal Motor Carrier Safety Administration (FMCSA) has published recommendations called Advisory Criteria to help medical examiners in determining whether a driver meets the physical qualifications for commercial driving. These recommendations have been condensed to provide information to medical examiners that (l) is directly relevant to the physical examination and (2) is not already included in the medical examination form. The specific regulation is printed in italics and its reference by section is highlighted.

Federal Motor Carrier Safety Regulations—
Advisory Criteria—

Loss of Limb - 391.41(b)(1)

A person is physically qualified to drive a commercial motor vehicle if that person:

Has no loss of a foot, leg, hand, or arm, or has been granted a Skill Performance Evaluation (SPE) Certificate pursuant to Section 391.49, and

Limb Impairment - 391.41(b)(2)

A person is physically qualified to drive a commercial motor vehicle if that person has no impairment of:

(i) *A hand or finger which interferes with prehension or power grasping.*

(ii) *An arm, foot, or leg which interferes with the ability to perform normal tasks associated with operating a commercial motor vehicle.*

(iii) *Any other significant limb defect or limitation which interferes with the ability to perform normal tasks associated with operating a commercial motor vehicle.*

(iv) *Has been granted a Skill Performance Evaluation (SPE) certificate pursuant to Section 391.49.*

A person who suffers loss of a foot, leg, hand or arm or whose limb impairment in any way interferes with the safe performance of normal tasks associated with operating a commercial motor vehicle is subject to the SPE Certification Program pursuant to Section 391.49, assuming the person is otherwise qualified.

With the advancement of technology, medical aids and equipment, modifications have been developed to compensate for certain disabilities. The SPE Certification Program (formerly the Limb Waiver Program) was designed to allow persons with the loss of a foot or limb or with functional impairment to qualify under the Federal Motor Carrier Safety Regulations (FMCSRs) by use of prosthetic devices or equipment modifications which enable them to safely operate a commercial motor vehicle. Since there are no medical aids equivalent to the original body or limb, certain risks are still present, and thus restrictions may be included on individual SPE certificates when a State Director for the FMCSA determines they are necessary to be consistent with safety and public interest.

If the driver is found otherwise medically qualified (391.41(b)(3) through (13)), the medical examiner must check on the medical certificate that the driver is qualified only if accompanied by a SPE certificate. The driver and the employing motor carrier are subject to appropriate penalty if the driver operates a motor vehicle in interstate or foreign commerce without a current SPE certificate for his/her physical disability.

Diabetes - 391.41(b)(3)

A person is physically qualified to drive a commercial motor vehicle if that person: Has no established medical history or clinical diagnosis of diabetes mellitus currently requiring insulin for control.

Diabetes mellitus is a disease which, on occasion, can result in a loss of consciousness or disorientation in time and space. Individuals who require insulin for control have conditions which can get out of control by the use of too much or too little insulin, or food intake not consistent with the insulin dosage. Incapacitation may occur from symptoms of hyperglycemic or hypoglycemic reactions (drowsiness, semiconsciousness, diabetic coma, or insulin shock).

The administration of insulin is within itself, a complicated process requiring insulin, syringe, needle, alcohol sponge, and a sterile technique. Factors related to long-haul commercial motor vehicle operations such as fatigue, lack of sleep, poor diet, emotional conditions, stress, and concomitant illness, compound the diabetic problem. Because of these inherent dangers, the FMCSA has consistently held that a diabetic who uses insulin for control does not meet the minimum physical requirements of the FMCSRs.

Hypoglycemic drugs, taken orally, are sometimes prescribed for diabetic individuals to help stimulate natural body production of insulin. If the condition can be controlled by the use of oral medication and diet, then an individual may be qualified under the present rule. CMV drivers who do not meet the Federal diabetes standard may call (202) 366-1790 for an application for a diabetes exemption.

See Conference Report on Diabetic Disorders and Commercial Drivers and Insulin-Using Commercial Motor Vehicle Drivers at: www.fmcsa.dot .gov/rulesregs/medreports.htm.

Cardiovascular Condition - 391.41(b)(4)

A person is physically qualified to drive a commercial motor vehicle if that person:

Has no current clinical diagnosis of myocardial infarction, angina pectoris, coronary insufficiency, thrombosis.

or

Any other cardiovascular disease of a variety known to be accompanied by syncope, dyspnea, collapse, or congestive cardiac failure.

The term "has no current clinical diagnosis of" is specifically designed to encompass (1) a current cardiovascular condition; or (2) a cardiovascular condition which has not fully stabilized regardless of the time limit. The term "known to be accompanied by" is designed to include a clinical diagnosis of a cardiovascular disease (1) which is accompanied by symptoms of syncope, dyspnea, collapse, or congestive cardiac failure; and or (2) which is likely to cause syncope, dyspnea, collapse, or congestive cardiac failure.

It is the intent of the Federal Motor Carrier Safety Regulations to render unqualified, a driver who has a current cardiovascular disease which is accompanied by and/or likely to cause symptoms of syncope, dyspnea, collapse, or congestive cardiac failure. However, the subjective decision of whether the nature and severity of an individual's condition will likely cause symptoms of cardiovascular insufficiency is on an individual basis and qualification rests with the medical examiner and the motor carrier. In those cases where there is an occurrence of cardiovascular insufficiency (myocardial infarction, thrombosis, etc.), it is suggested that, before a driver is certified, he/she have a normal resting and stress ECG, no residual complications, no physical limitations, and is taking no medication likely to interfere with safe driving.

Coronary artery bypass surgery and pacemaker implantation are remedial procedures and thus not unqualifying. Implantable cardioverter defibrillators are disqualifying due to risk of syncope.

Coumadin is a medical treatment which can improve the health and safety of the driver and should not, by its use, medically disqualify the commercial driver. The emphasis should be on the underlying medical condition(s) which require treatment and the general health of the driver. FMCSA should be contacted at (202) 366-1790 for additional recommendations regarding the physical qualification of drivers on Coumadin.

See Cardiovascular Advisory Panel Guidelines for the Medical Examination of Commercial Motor Vehicle Drivers at www.fmcsa.dot.gov/rulesregs/ medreports.htm.

Respiratory Dysfunction - 391.41(b)(5)

A person is physically qualified to drive a commercial motor vehicle if that person:

Has no established medical history or clinical diagnosis of a respiratory dysfunction likely to interfere with the ability to control and drive a commercial motor vehicle safely.

Since a driver must be alert at all times, any change in his or her mental state is in direct conflict with highway safety. Even the slightest impairment in respiratory function under emergency conditions (when greater oxygen supply is necessary for performance) may be detrimental to safe driving.

There are many conditions that interfere with oxygen exchange and may result in incapacitation, including emphysema, chronic asthma, carcinoma, tuberculosis, chronic bronchitis and sleep apnea. If the medical examiner detects a respiratory dysfunction, that in any way is likely to interfere with the driver's ability to safely control and drive a commercial motor vehicle, the driver must be referred to a specialist for further evaluation and therapy.

Anticoagulation therapy for deep vein thrombosis and/or pulmonary thromboembolism is not unqualifying once optimum dose is achieved, provided lower extremity venous examinations remain normal and the treating physician gives a favorable recommendation.

See Conference on Pulmonary/Respiratory Disorders and Commercial Drivers at www.fmcsa.dot.gov/rulesregs/medreports.htm.

Hypertension - 391.41(b)(6)

A person is physically qualified to drive a commercial motor vehicle if that person:

Has no current clinical diagnosis of high blood pressure likely to interfere with the ability to operate a commercial motor vehicle safely.

Hypertension alone is unlikely to cause sudden collapse; however, the likelihood increases when target organ damage, particularly cerebral vascular disease is present. This advisory criteria is based on FMCSA's Cardiovascular Advisory Guidelines for the Examination of CMV Drivers, which used the Sixth Report of the Joint National Committee on Prevention, Detection, Evaluation, and Treatment of High Blood Pressure (1997).

Stage 1 hypertension corresponds to a systolic BP of 140–159 mm Hg and/or a diastolic BP of 90–99 mm Hg. The driver with a BP in this range is at low risk for hypertension-related acute incapacitation and may be medically certified to drive for a one-year period. Certification examinations should be done annually thereafter and should be less than 140/90. If less than 160/100, certification may be extended one time for 3 months.

A blood pressure of 160–179 systolic and/or 100–109 diastolic is considered **Stage 2** hypertension, and the driver is not necessarily unqualified during evaluation and institution of treatment. The driver is given a one time certification of three months to reduce his or her blood pressure to less than 140/90. A blood pressure in this range is an absolute indication for antihypertensive drug therapy. Provided treatment is well tolerated and the driver demonstrates a BP value of less than 140/90, he or she may be certified for one year from the date of the initial exam. The driver is certified annually thereafter.

A blood pressure at or greater than 180 (systolic) and 110 (diastolic) is considered **Stage 3**, high risk for an acute BP-related event. The driver may **not** be qualified, even temporarily, until reduced to less than 140/90 and treatment is well tolerated. The driver may be certified for 6 months and biannually (every 6 months) thereafter if at recheck BP is less than 140/90.

Annual recertification is recommended if the medical examiner does not know the severity of hypertension prior to treatment.

An elevated blood pressure finding should be confirmed by at least two subsequent measurements on different days.

Treatment includes non-pharmacologic and pharmacologic modalities as well as counseling to reduce other risk factors. Most antihypertensive medications also have side effects, the importance of which must be judged on an individual basis. Individuals must be alerted to the hazards of these medications while driving. Side effects of somnolence or syncope are particularly undesirable in commercial drivers.

Secondary hypertension is based on the above stages. Evaluation is warranted if patient is persistently hypertensive on maximal or near-maximal doses of 2–3 pharmacologic agents. Some causes of secondary hypertension may be amenable to surgical intervention or specific pharmacologic therapy.

See Cardiovascular Advisory Panel Guidelines for the Medical Examination of Commercial Motor Vehicle Drivers at www.fmcsa.dot.gov/rulesregs/medreports.htm.

Rheumatic, Arthritic, Orthopedic, Muscular, Neuromuscular or Vascular Disease: - 391.41(b)(7)

A person is physically qualified to drive a commercial motor vehicle if that person:

Has no established medical history or clinical diagnosis of a rheumatic, arthritic, orthopedic, muscular, neuromuscular or vascular disease which interferes with the ability to control and operate a commercial motor vehicle.

Certain diseases are known to have acute episodes of transient muscle weakness, poor muscular coordination (ataxia), abnormal sensations (paresthesia), decreased muscle tone (hypotonia), visual disturbances and pain which may be suddenly incapacitating. With each recurring episode, these symptoms may become more pronounced and remain for longer periods of time. Other diseases have more insidious onsets and display symptoms of muscle wasting (atrophy), swelling and paresthesia which may not suddenly incapacitate a person but may restrict his/her movements and eventually interfere with the ability to safely operate a motor vehicle. In many instances these diseases are degenerative in nature or may result in deterioration of the involved area.

Once the individual has been diagnosed as having a rheumatic, arthritic, orthopedic, muscular, neuromuscular or vascular disease, then he/she has an established history of that disease. The physician, when examining an individual, should consider the following:

(1) The nature and severity of the individual's condition (such as sensory loss or loss of strength);
(2) The degree of limitation present (such as range of motion);
(3) The likelihood of progressive limitation (not always present initially but manifests itself over time);
(4) The likelihood of sudden incapacitation.

If severe functional impairment exists, the driver does not qualify. In cases where more frequent monitoring is required, a certificate for a shorter period of time may be issued.

See Conference on Neurological Disorders and Commercial Drivers at www.fmcsa.dot.gov/rulesregs/medreports.htm.

Epilepsy - 391.41(b)(8)

A person is physically qualified to drive a commercial motor vehicle if that person:
   Has no established medical history or clinical diagnosis of epilepsy;
   or
   Any other condition which is likely to cause the loss of consciousness, or any loss of ability to control a commercial motor vehicle.

Epilepsy is a chronic functional disease characterized by seizures or episodes that occur without warning, resulting in loss of voluntary control which may lead to loss of consciousness and/or seizures. Therefore, the following drivers cannot be qualified:

(1) a driver who has a medical history of epilepsy;
(2) a driver who has a current clinical diagnosis of epilepsy; or
(3) a driver who is taking antiseizure medication.

If an individual has had a sudden episode of a nonepileptic seizure or loss of consciousness of unknown cause which did not require antiseizure medication, the decision as to whether that person's condition will likely cause the loss of consciousness or loss of ability to control a commercial motor vehicle is made on an individual basis by the medical examiner in consultation with the treating physician. Before certification is considered, it is suggested that a 6-month waiting period elapse from the time of the episode. Following the waiting period, it is suggested that the individual have a complete neurological examination. If the results of the examination are negative and antiseizure medication is not required, then the driver may be qualified.

In those individual cases where a driver had a seizure or an episode of loss of consciousness that resulted from a known medical condition (e.g., drug reaction, high temperature, acute infectious disease, dehydration, or acute metabolic disturbance), certification should be deferred until the driver has fully recovered from that condition, has no existing residual complications, and is not taking antiseizure medication.

Drivers with a history of epilepsy/seizures off antiseizure medication and seizure-free for 10 years may be qualified to operate a CMV in interstate commerce. Interstate drivers with a history of a single unprovoked seizure may be qualified to drive a CMV in interstate commerce if seizure-free and off antiseizure medication for a 5-year period or more.

See Conference on Neurological Disorders and Commercial Drivers at www.fmcsa.dot.gov/rulesregs/medreports.htm.

Mental Disorders 391.41(b)(9)

A person is physically qualified to drive a commercial motor vehicle if that person:

Has no mental, nervous, organic, or functional disease or psychiatric disorder likely to interfere with the driver's ability to drive a commercial motor vehicle safely.

Emotional or adjustment problems contribute directly to an individual's level of memory, reasoning, attention, and judgment. These problems often underlie physical disorders. A variety of functional disorders can cause drowsiness, dizziness, confusion, weakness, or paralysis that may lead to incoordination, inattention, loss of functional control and susceptibility to crashes while driving. Physical fatigue, headache, impaired coordination, recurring physical ailments, and chronic "nagging" pain may be present to such a degree that certification for commercial driving is inadvisable. Somatic and psychosomatic complaints should be thoroughly examined when determining an individual's overall fitness to drive. Disorders of a periodically incapacitating nature, even in the early stages of development, may warrant disqualification.

Many bus and truck drivers have documented that "nervous trouble" related to neurotic, personality, emotional or adjustment problems is responsible for a significant fraction of their preventable crashes. The degree to which an individual is able to appreciate, evaluate and adequately respond to environmental strain and emotional stress is critical when assessing an individual's mental alertness and flexibility to cope with the stresses of commercial motor vehicle driving.

When examining the driver, it should be kept in mind that individuals who live under chronic emotional upsets may have deeply ingrained maladaptive or erratic behavior patterns. Excessively antagonistic, instinctive, impulsive, openly aggressive, paranoid or severely depressed behavior greatly interfere with the driver's ability to drive safely. Those individuals who are highly susceptible to frequent states of emotional instability (schizophrenia, affective psychoses, paranoia, anxiety or depressive neurosis) may warrant disqualification.

Careful consideration should be given to the side effects and interactions of medications in the overall qualification determination. See Psychiatric Conference Report for specific recommendations on the use of these medications and potential hazards for driving.

See Conference on Psychiatric Disorders and Commercial Drivers at www.fmcsa.dot.gov/rulesregs/medreports.htm.

Vision - 391.41 (b)(10)

A person is physically qualified to drive a commercial motor vehicle if that person:

Has a distant visual acuity of at least 20/40 (Snellen) in each eye with or without corrective lenses, or visual acuity separately corrected to 20/40 (Snellen) or better with corrective lenses; **and** *distant binocular acuity of at least 20/40 (Snellen) in both eyes with or without corrective lenses;* **and** *field of vision of at least 70 degrees in the horizontal meridian in each eye;* **and** *the ability to recognize the colors of traffic control signals and devices showing standard red, green, and amber.*

The term "ability to recognize the colors of" is interpreted to mean if a person can recognize and distinguish among traffic control signals and devices showing standard red, green, and amber, he or she meets the minimum standard, even though he or she may have some type of color perception deficiency. If certain color perception tests are administered (such as Ishihara, Pseudoisochromatic, Yarn, etc.), and doubtful findings are discovered, a controlled test using signal red, green, and amber may be employed to determine the driver's ability to recognize these colors.

Contact lenses are permissible if there is sufficient evidence to indicate that the driver has good tolerance and is well adapted to their use. Use of a contact lens in one eye for distant visual acuity and another lens in the other eye for near vision is not acceptable, nor are telescopic lenses acceptable for driving commercial motor vehicles.

If an individual meets the criteria by the use of glasses or contact lenses, the following statement shall appear on the Medical Examiner's Certificate: "Qualified only if wearing corrective lenses." CMV drivers who do not meet the Federal vision standards may call (202) 366-1790.

See Visual Disorders and Commercial Drivers at www.fmcsa.dot.gov/ rulesregs/medreports.htm.

Hearing 391.41(b)(11)

A person is physically qualified to drive a commercial vehicle if that person:

First perceives a forced whispered voice in the better ear at not less than five feet with or without the use of a hearing aid **or** *If tested by use of an audiometric device, does not have an average hearing loss in the better ear greater than 40 decibels at 500 Hz, 1,000 Hz and 2,000 Hz with or without a hearing aid when the audiometric device is calibrated to the American National Standard [formerly American Standard Association (ASA)] Z24.5-1951.*

Since the prescribed standard under the FMCSRs is the American National Standards Institute (ANSI), it may be necessary to convert the audiometric results from the International Standards Organization (ISO) standard to the ANSI standard. Instructions are included on the Medical Examination Report form.

If an individual meets the criteria by using a hearing aid, the driver must wear that hearing aid and have it in operation at all times while driving. Also, the driver must be in possession of a spare power source for the hearing aid.

For the whispered voice test, the individual should be stationed at least 5 feet from the examiner with the ear being tested turned toward the examiner. The other ear is covered. Using the breath which remains after a normal expiration, the examiner whispers words or random numbers such as 66, 18, 23, etc. The examiner should not use only sibilants (s-sounding test materials). If the individual fails the whispered voice test, the audiometric test should be administered.

If an individual meets the criteria by the use of a hearing aid, the following statement must appear on the Medical Examiner's Certificate "Qualified only when wearing a hearing aid."

See Hearing Disorders and Commercial Motor Vehicle Drivers at www.fmcsa.dot.gov/rulesregs/medreports.htm.

Drug Use - 391.41(b)(12)

A person is physically qualified to drive a commercial vehicle if that person:

Does not use a controlled substance identified in 21 CFR 1308.11, Schedule I, an amphetamine, a narcotic, or any other habit-forming drug.

Exception: A driver may use such a substance or drug, if the substance or drug is prescribed by a licensed medical practitioner who is familiar with the driver's medical history and assigned duties; and has advised the driver that the prescribed substance or drug will not adversely affect the driver's ability to safely operate a commercial motor vehicle.

This exception does not apply to the use of methadone. The intent of the medical certification process is to medically evaluate a driver to ensure that the driver has no medical condition which interferes with the safe performance of driving tasks on a public road. If a driver uses a Schedule I drug or other substance, amphetamine, a narcotic, or any other habit-forming drug, it may be cause for the driver to be found medically unqualified. Motor carriers are encouraged to obtain a practitioner's written statement about the effects on transportation safety of the use of a particular drug.

A test for controlled substances is not required as part of this biennial certification process. The FMCSA or the driver's employer should be contacted directly for information on controlled substances and alcohol testing under Part 382 of the FMCSR.

The term "uses" is designed to encompass instances of prohibited drug use determined by a physician through established medical means. This may or may not involve body fluid testing. If body fluid testing takes place, positive test results should be confirmed by a second test of greater specificity. The term "habit forming" is intended to include any drug or medication generally recognized as capable of becoming habitual, and which may impair the user's ability to operate a commercial motor vehicle safely.

The driver is medically unqualified for the duration of the prohibited drug(s) use and until a second examination shows the driver is free from the prohibited drug(s) use. Recertification may involve a substance abuse evaluation, the successful completion of a drug rehabilitation program, and a negative drug test result. Additionally, given that the certification period is normally 2 years, the examiner has the option to certify for a period of less than 2 years if this examiner determines more frequent monitoring is required.

See Conference on Neurological Disorders and Commercial Drivers and Conference on Psychiatric Disorders and Commercial Drivers at www.fmcsa .dot.gov/rulesregs/medreports.htm.

Alcoholism - 391.41(b)(13)

A person is physically qualified to drive a commercial motor vehicle if that person:
   Has no current clinical diagnosis of alcoholism.

The term "current clinical diagnosis" is specifically designed to encompass a current alcoholic illness or those instances where the individual's physical condition has not fully stabilized, regardless of the time element. If an individual shows signs of having an alcohol-use problem, he or she should be referred to a specialist. After counseling and/or treatment, he or she may be considered for certification.

§391.45   Persons who must be medically examined and certified.

Except as provided in §391.67, the following persons must be medically examined and certified in accordance with §391.43 as physically qualified to operate a commercial motor vehicle:

   (a) Any person who has not been medically examined and certified as physically qualified to operate a commercial motor vehicle;

   (b)(1) Any driver who has not been medically examined and certified as qualified to operate a commercial motor vehicle during the preceding 24 months; or (b)(2) Any driver authorized to operate a commercial motor vehicle only with an exempt intracity zone pursuant to §391.62, or only by operation of the exemption in §391.64, if such driver has not been medically examined and certified as qualified to drive in such zone during the preceding 12 months; and

(c) Any driver whose ability to perform his/her normal duties has been impaired by a physical or mental injury or disease.

§391.47   Resolution of conflicts of medical evaluation.

(a) **Applications.** Applications for determination of a driver's medical qualifications under standards in this part will only be accepted if they conform to the requirements of this section.

(b) **Content.** Applications will be accepted for consideration only if the following conditions are met.

(b)(1) The application must contain the name and address of the driver, motor carrier, and all physicians involved in the proceeding.

(b)(2) The applicant must submit proof that there is a disagreement between the physician for the driver and the physician for the motor carrier concerning the driver's qualifications.

(b)(3) The applicant must submit a copy of an opinion and report including results of all tests of an impartial medical specialist in the field in which the medical conflict arose. The specialist should be one agreed to by the motor carrier and the driver.

(b)(3)(i) In cases where the driver refuses to agree on a specialist and the applicant is the motor carrier the applicant must submit a statement of his/her agreement to submit the matter to an impartial medical specialist in the field, proof that he/she has requested the driver to submit to the medical specialist, and the response, if any, of the driver to his/her request.

(b)(3)(ii) In cases where the motor carrier refuses to agree on a medical specialist, the driver must submit an opinion and test results of an impartial medical specialist, proof that he/she has requested the motor carrier to agree to submit the matter to the medical specialist and the response, if any, of the motor carrier to his/her request.

(b)(4) The applicant must include a statement explaining in detail why the decision of the medical specialist identified in paragraph (b)(3) of this section is unacceptable.

(b)(5) The applicant must submit proof that the medical specialist mentioned in paragraph (b)(3) of this section was provided, prior to his/her determination, the medical history of the driver and an agreed upon statement of the work the driver performs.

(b)(6) The applicant must submit the medical history and statement of work provided to the medical specialist under paragraph (b)(5) of this section.

(b)(7) The applicant must submit all medical records and statements of the physicians who have given opinions on the driver's qualifications.

(b)(8) The applicant must submit a description and a copy of all written and documentary evidence upon which the party making application relies in the form set out in 49 CFR §386.37.

(b)(9) The application must be accompanied by a statement of the driver that he/she intends to drive in interstate commerce not subject to the commercial zone exemption or a statement of the carrier that he/she has used or intends to use the driver for such work.

(b)(10) The applicant must submit three copies of the application and all records.

(c) **Information.** The Director, Office of Bus and Truck Standards and Operations (MC-PSD), may request further information from the applicant if he/she determines that a decision cannot be made on the evidence submitted. If the applicant fails to submit the information requested, the Director, Office of Bus and Truck Standards and Operations (MC-PSD), may refuse to issue a determination.

(d)(1) **Action.** Upon receiving a satisfactory application the Director, Office of Bus and Truck Standards and Operations (MC-PSD), shall notify the parties (the driver, motor carrier, or any other interested party) that the application has been accepted and that a determination will be made. A copy of all evidence received shall be attached to the notice.

(d)(2) **Reply.** Any party may submit a reply to the notification within 15 days after service. Such reply must be accompanied by all evidence the party wants the Director, Office of Bus and Truck Standards and Operations (MC-PSD), to consider in making his/her determination. Evidence submitted should include all medical records and test results upon which the party relies.

(d)(3) **Parties.** A party for the purposes of this section includes the motor carrier and the driver, or anyone else submitting an application.

(e) **Petitions to review, burden of proof.** The driver or motor carrier may petition to review the Director's determination. Such petition must be submitted in accordance with §386.13(a) of this chapter. The burden of proof in such a proceeding is on the petitioner.

(f) **Status of driver.** Once an application is submitted to the Director, Office of Bus and Truck Standards and Operations (MC-PSD), the driver shall be deemed disqualified until such time as the Director, Office of Bus and Truck Standards and Operations (MC-PSD), makes a determination, or until the Director, Office of Bus and Truck Standards and Operations (MC-PSD), orders otherwise.

§391.49   Alternative physical qualification standards for the loss or impairment of limbs.

(a) A person who is not physically qualified to drive under §391.41(b)(1) or (b)(2) and who is otherwise qualified to drive a commercial motor vehicle, may drive a commercial motor vehicle, if the Division Administrator, FMCSA, has granted a Skill Performance Evaluation (SPE) Certificate to that person.

(b) *SPE certificate.* —(1) *Application.* A letter of application for an SPE certificate may be submitted jointly by the person (driver applicant) who seeks an SPE certificate and by the motor carrier that will employ the driver applicant, if the application is accepted.

(b)(2) *Application address.* The application must be addressed to the applicable field service center, FMCSA, for the State in which the co-applicant motor carrier's principal place of business is located. The address of each, and the States serviced, are listed in §390.27 of this chapter.

(b)(3) *Exception.* A letter of application for an SPE certificate may be submitted unilaterally by a driver applicant. The application must be addressed to the field service center, FMCSA, for the State in which the driver has legal residence. The driver applicant must comply with all the requirements of paragraph (c) of this section except those in (c)(1)(i) and (iii). The driver applicant shall respond to the requirements of paragraphs (c)(2)(i) to (v) of this section, if the information is known.

(c) A letter of application for an SPE certificate shall contain:

(c)(1) Identification of the applicant(s):

(c)(1)(i) Name and complete address of the motor carrier coapplicant;

(c)(1)(ii) Name and complete address of the driver applicant;

(c)(1)(iii) The U.S. DOT Motor Carrier Identification Number, if known; and

(c)(1)(iv) A description of the driver applicant's limb impairment for which SPE certificate is requested.

(c)(2) Description of the type of operation the driver will be employed to perform:

(c)(2)(i) State(s) in which the driver will operate for the motor carrier coapplicant (if more than 10 States, designate general geographic area only);

(c)(2)(ii) Average period of time the driver will be driving and/or on duty, per day;

(c)(2)(iii) Type of commodities or cargo to be transported;

(c)(2)(iv) Type of driver operation (*i.e.*, sleeper team, relay, owner operator, etc.); and

(c)(2)(v) Number of years experience operating the type of commercial motor vehicle(s) requested in the letter of application and total years of experience operating all types of commercial motor vehicles.

(c)(3) Description of the commercial motor vehicle(s) the driver applicant intends to drive:

(c)(3)(i) Truck, truck tractor, or bus make, model, and year (if known);

(c)(3)(ii) Drive train;

(c)(3)(ii)(A) Transmission type (automatic or manual—if manual, designate number of forward speeds);

(c)(3)(ii)(B) Auxiliary transmission (if any) and number of forward speeds; and

(c)(3)(ii)(C) Rear axle (designate single speed, 2 speed, or 3 speed).;

(c)(3)(iii) Type of brake system;

(c)(3)(iv) Steering, manual or power assisted;

(c)(3)(v) Description of type of trailer(s) (i.e., van, flatbed, cargo tank, drop frame, lowboy, or pole);

(c)(3)(vi) Number of semitrailers or full trailers to be towed at one time;

(c)(3)(vii) For commercial motor vehicles designed to transport passengers, indicate the seating capacity of commercial motor vehicle; and

(c)(3)(viii) Description of any modification(s) made to the commercial motor vehicle for the driver applicant; attach photograph(s) where applicable.

(c)(4) Otherwise qualified:

(c)(4)(i) The coapplicant motor carrier must certify that the driver applicant is otherwise qualified under the regulations of this part;

(c)(4)(ii) In the case of a unilateral application, the driver applicant must certify that he/she is otherwise qualified under the regulations of this part.

(c)(5) Signature of applicant(s):

(c)(5)(i) Driver applicant's signature and date signed;

(c)(5)(ii) Motor carrier official's signature (if application has a coapplicant), title, and date signed. Depending upon the motor carrier's organizational structure (corporation, partnership, or proprietorship), the signer of the application shall be an officer, partner, or the proprietor.

(d) The letter of application for an SPE certificate shall be accompanied by:

(d)(1) A copy of the results of the medical examination performed pursuant to §391.43;

(d)(2) A copy of the medical certificate completed pursuant to §391.43(h);

(d)(3) A medical evaluation summary completed by either a board qualified or board certified physiatrist (doctor of physical medicine) or orthopedic surgeon. The coapplicant motor carrier or the driver applicant shall provide the physiatrist or orthopedic surgeon with a description of the job-related tasks the driver applicant will be required to perform;

(d)(3)(i) The medical evaluation summary for a driver applicant disqualified under §391.41(b)(1) shall include:

(d)(3)(i)(A) An assessment of the functional capabilities of the driver as they relate to the ability of the driver to perform normal tasks associated with operating a commercial motor vehicle; and

(d)(3)(i)(B) A statement by the examiner that the applicant is capable of demonstrating precision prehension (*e.g.*, manipulating knobs and switches) and power grasp prehension (*e.g.*, holding and maneuvering the steering wheel) with each upper limb separately. This requirement does not apply to an individual who was granted a waiver, absent a prosthetic device, prior to the publication of this amendment.

(d)(3)(ii) The medical evaluation summary for a driver applicant disqualified under §391.41(b)(2) shall include:

(d)(3)(ii)(A) An explanation as to how and why the impairment interferes with the ability of the applicant to perform normal tasks associated with operating a commercial motor vehicle;

(d)(3)(ii)(B) An assessment and medical opinion of whether the condition will likely remain medically stable over the lifetime of the driver applicant; and

(d)(3)(ii)(C) A statement by the examiner that the applicant is capable of demonstrating precision prehension (*e.g.*, manipulating knobs and switches) and power grasp prehension (*e.g.*, holding and maneuvering the steering wheel) with each upper limb separately. This requirement does not apply to an individual who was granted an SPE certificate, absent an orthotic device, prior to the publication of this amendment.

(d)(4) A description of the driver applicant's prosthetic or orthotic device worn, if any;

(d)(5) Road test:

(d)(5)(i) A copy of the driver applicant's road test administered by the motor carrier coapplicant and the certificate issued pursuant to §391.31(b) through (g); or (d)(5)(ii) A unilateral applicant shall be responsible for having a road test administered by a motor carrier or a person who is competent to administer the test and evaluate its results.

(d)(6) Application for employment:

(d)(6)(i) A copy of the driver applicant's application for employment completed pursuant to §391.21; or

(d)(6)(ii) A unilateral applicant shall be responsible for submitting a copy of the last commercial driving position's employment application he/she held. If not previously employed as a commercial driver, so state.

(d)(7) A copy of the driver applicant's SPE certificate of certain physical defects issued by the individual State(s), where applicable; and

(d)(8) A copy of the driver applicant's State Motor Vehicle Driving Record for the past 3 years from each State in which a motor vehicle driver's license or permit has been obtained.

(e) *Agreement.* A motor carrier that employs a driver with an SPE certificate agrees to:

(e)(1) File promptly (within 30 days of the involved incident) with the Medical Program Specialist, FMCSA service center, such documents and information as may be required about driving activities, accidents, arrests, license suspensions, revocations, or withdrawals, and convictions which involve the driver applicant. This applies whether the driver's SPE certificate is a unilateral one or has a coapplicant motor carrier;

(e)(1)(i) A motor carrier who is a coapplicant must file the required documents with the Medical Program Specialist, FMCSA for the State in which the carrier's principal place of business is located; or

(e)(1)(ii) A motor carrier who employs a driver who has been issued a unilateral SPE certificate must file the required documents with the Medical Program Specialist, FMCSA service center, for the State in which the driver has legal residence.

(e)(2) Evaluate the driver with a road test using the trailer the motor carrier intends the driver to transport or, in lieu of, accept a certificate of a trailer road test from another motor carrier if the trailer type(s) is similar, or accept the trailer road test done during the Skill Performance Evaluation if it is a similar trailer type(s) to that of the prospective motor carrier. Job tasks, as stated in paragraph (e)(3) of this section, are not evaluated in the Skill Performance Evaluation;

(e)(3) Evaluate the driver for those nondriving safety related job tasks associated with whatever type of trailer(s) will be used and any other nondriving safety related or job related tasks unique to the operations of the employing motor carrier; and (c)(4) Use the driver to operate the type of commercial motor vehicle defined in the SPE certificate only when the driver is in compliance with the conditions and limitations of the SPE certificate.

(f) The driver shall supply each employing motor carrier with a copy of the SPE certificate.

(g) The State Director, FMCSA, may require the driver applicant to demonstrate his or her ability to safely operate the commercial motor vehicle(s) the driver intends to drive to an agent of the State Director, FMCSA. The SPE certificate form will identify the power unit (bus, truck, truck tractor) for which the SPE certificate has been granted. The SPE certificate forms will also identify the trailer type used in the Skill Performance Evaluation; however, the SPE certificate is not limited to that specific trailer type. A driver may use the SPE certificate with other trailer types if a successful trailer road test is completed in accordance with paragraph (e)(2) of this section. Job tasks, as stated in paragraph (e)(3) of this section, are not evaluated during the Skill Performance Evaluation.

(h) The State Director, FMCSA, may deny the application for SPE certificate or may grant it totally or in part and issue the SPE certificate subject to such terms, conditions, and limitations as deemed consistent with the public interest. The SPE certificate is valid for a period not to exceed 2 years from date of issue, and may be renewed 30 days prior to the expiration date.

(i) The SPE certificate renewal application shall be submitted to the Medical Program Specialist, FMCSA service center, for the State in which the driver has legal residence, if the SPE certificate was issued unilaterally. If the SPE certificate has a coapplicant, then the renewal application is submitted to the Medical Program Specialist, FMCSA field service center, for the State in which the coapplicant motor carrier's principal place of business is located. The SPE certificate renewal application shall contain the following:

(i)(1) Name and complete address of motor carrier currently employing the applicant;

(i)(2) Name and complete address of the driver;

(i)(3) Effective date of the current SPE certificate;

(i)(4) Expiration date of the current SPE certificate;

(i)(5) Total miles driven under the current SPE certificate;

(i)(6) Number of accidents incurred while driving under the current SPE certificate, including date of the accident(s), number of fatalities, number of injuries, and the estimated dollar amount of property damage;

(i)(7) A current medical examination report;

(i)(8) A medical evaluation summary pursuant to paragraph (d)(3) of this section, if an unstable medical condition exists. All handicapped conditions classified under §391.41(b)(1) are considered unstable. Refer to paragraph (d)(3)(ii) of this section for the condition under §391.41(b)(2) which may be considered medically stable.

(i)(9) A copy of driver's current State motor vehicle driving record for the period of time the current SPE certificate has been in effect;

(i)(10) Notification of any change in the type of tractor the driver will operate;

(i)(11) Driver's signature and date signed; and

(i)(12) Motor carrier coapplicant's signature and date signed.

(j)(1) Upon granting an SPE certificate, the State Director, FMCSA, will notify the driver applicant and co-applicant motor carrier (if applicable) by letter. The terms, conditions, and limitations of the SPE certificate will be set forth. A motor carrier shall maintain a copy of the SPE certificate in its driver qualification file. A copy of the SPE certificate shall be retained in the motor carrier's file for a period of 3 years after the driver's employment is terminated. The driver applicant shall have the SPE certificate (or a legible copy) in his/her possession whenever on duty.

(j)(2) Upon successful completion of the skill performance evaluation, the State Director, FMCSA, for the State where the driver applicant has legal residence, must notify the driver by letter and enclose an SPE certificate substantially in the following form:

Skill Performance Evaluation Certificate

Name of Issuing Agency: _____

Agency Address: _____

Telephone Number: ( ) _____

Issued Under 49 CFR 391.49, subchapter B of the Federal Motor Carrier Safety Regulations

Driver's Name: _____

Effective Date: _____

SSN: _____

DOB: _____

Expiration Date: _____

Address: _____

_____

_____

Driver Disability: _____ _____

Check One: __New __Renewal

Driver's License: _____
(State)   (Number)

In accordance with 49 CFR 391.49, subchapter B of the Federal Motor Carrier Safety Regulations (FMCSRs), the driver application for a skill performance evaluation (SPE) certificate is hereby granted authorizing the above-named driver to operate in interstate or foreign commerce under the provisions set forth below. This certificate is granted for the period shown above, not to exceed 2 years, subject to periodic review as may be found necessary. This certificate may be renewed upon submission of a renewal application. Continuation of this certificate is dependent upon strict adherence by the above-named driver to the provisions set forth below and compliance with the FMCSRs. Any failure to comply with provisions herein may be cause for cancellation.

CONDITIONS: As a condition of this certificate, reports of all accidents, arrests, suspensions, revocations, withdrawals of driver licenses or permits, and convictions involving the above-named driver shall be reported in writing to the Issuing Agency by the EMPLOYING MOTOR CARRIER within 30 days after occurrence.

LIMITATIONS:

1. Vehicle Type (power unit):* _____

2. Vehicle modification(s): _____

   _____

3. Prosthetic or Orthotic device(s) (Required to be Worn While Driving): _____

4. Additional Provision(s): _____

NOTICE: To all MOTOR CARRIERS employing a driver with an SPE certificate. This certificate is granted for the operation of the power unit only. It is the responsibility of the employing motor carrier to evaluate the driver with a road test using the trailer type(s) the motor carrier intends the driver to transport, or in lieu of, accept the trailer road test done during the SPE if it is a similar trailer type(s) to that of the prospective motor carrier. Also, it is the responsibility of the employing motor carrier to evaluate the driver for those non-driving safety-related job tasks associated with the type of trailer(s) utilized, as well as any other non-driving safety-related or job-related tasks unique to the operations of the employing motor carrier.

The SPE of the above named driver was given by a Skill Performance Evaluation Program Specialist. It was successfully completed utilizing the above named power unit and _____ (trailer, if applicable)

The tractor or truck had a _____ transmission.

Please read the NOTICE paragraph above.

Name: _____

Signature: _____

Title: _____

Date: _____

(k) The State Director, FMCSA, may revoke an SPE certificate after the person to whom it was issued is given notice of the proposed revocation and has been allowed a reasonable opportunity to appeal.

(l) Falsifying information in the letter of application, the renewal application, or falsifying information required by this section by either the applicant or motor carrier is prohibited.

Complete information and applications for Skill Performance Evaluation Certificates can be found at www.fmcsa.dot.gov/rules-regulations/topics/ medical/spepackage.htm.

Subpart F—Files and Records

§391.51   General requirements for driver qualification files.

(a) Each motor carrier shall maintain a driver qualification file for each driver it employs. A driver's qualification file may be combined with his/her personnel file.

(b) The qualification file for a driver must include:

(b)(1) The driver's application for employment completed in accordance with §391.21;

(b)(2) A copy of the response by each State agency concerning a driver's driving record pursuant to §391.23(a)(1);

(b)(3) The certificate of driver's road test issued to the driver pursuant to §391.31(e), or a copy of the license or certificate which the motor carrier accepted as equivalent to the driver's road test pursuant to §391.33;

(b)(4) The response of each State agency to the annual driver record inquiry required by §391.25(a);

(b)(5) A note relating to the annual review of the driver's driving record as required by §391.25(c)(2);

(b)(6) A list or certificate relating to violations of motor vehicle laws and ordinances required by §391.27;

(b)(7) The medical examiner's certificate of his/her physical quali-fication to drive a commercial motor vehicle as required by §391.43(f) or a legible photographic copy of the certificate; and

(b)(8) A letter from the Field Administrator, Division Administra-tor, or State Director granting a waiver of a physical disqualification, if a waiver was issued under §391.49.

(c) Except as provided in paragraph (d) of this section, each driv-er's qualification file shall be retained for as long as a driver is em-ployed by that motor carrier and for three years thereafter.

(d) The following records may be removed from a driver's qualifi-cation file three years after the date of execution:

(d)(1) The response of each State agency to the annual driver record inquiry required by §391.25(a);

(d)(2) The note relating to the annual review of the driver's driving record as required by §391.25(c)(2);

(d)(3) The list or certificate relating to violations of motor vehicle laws and ordinances required by §391.27;

(d)(4) The medical examiner's certificate of the driver's physical qualification to drive a commercial motor vehicle or the photographic copy of the certificate as required by §391.43(f); and

(d)(5) The letter issued under §391.49 granting a waiver of a phys-ical disqualification.

§391.53　　Driver Investigation History File.

(a) After October 29, 2004, each motor carrier must maintain records relating to the investigation into the safety performance history of a new or prospective driver pursuant to paragraphs (d) and (e) of §391.23. This file must be maintained in a secure location with con-trolled access.

(a)(1) The motor carrier must ensure that access to this data is lim-ited to those who are involved in the hiring decision or who control ac-cess to the data. In addition, the motor carrier's insurer may have access to the data, except the alcohol and controlled substances data.

(a)(2) This data must only be used for the hiring decision.

(b) The file must include:

(b)(1) A copy of the driver's written authorization for the motor carrier to seek information about a driver's alcohol and controlled sub-stances history as required under §391.23(d).

(b)(2) A copy of the response(s) received for investigations required by paragraphs (d) and (e) of §391.23 from each previous employer, or documentation of good faith efforts to contact them. The record must include the previous employer's name and address, the date the previous employer was contacted, and the information received about the driver from the previous employer. Failures to contact a previous employer, or of them to provide the required safety performance history information, must be documented.

(c) The safety performance histories received from previous employers for a driver who is hired must be retained for as long as the driver is employed by that motor carrier and for three years thereafter.

(d) A motor carrier must make all records and information in this file available to an authorized representative or special agent of the Federal Motor Carrier Safety Administration, an authorized State or local enforcement agency representative, or an authorized third party, upon request or as part of any inquiry within the time period specified by the requesting representative.

§391.55   LCV Driver-Instructor qualification files.

(a) Each motor carrier must maintain a qualification file for each LCV driver-instructor it employs or uses. The LCV driver-instructor qualification file may be combined with his/her personnel file.

(b) The LCV driver-instructor qualification file must include the information in paragraphs (b)(1) and (b)(2) of this section for a skills instructor or the information in paragraph (b)(1) of this section for a classroom instructor, as follows:

(b)(1) Evidence that the instructor has met the requirements of 49 CFR 380.301 or 380.303;

(b)(2) A photographic copy of the individual's currently valid CDL with the appropriate endorsements.

Subpart G — Limited Exemptions

§391.61   Drivers who were regularly employed before January 1, 1971.

The provisions of §391.21 (relating to applications for employment), §391.23 (relating to investigations and inquiries), and §391.33 (relating to road tests) do not apply to a driver who has been a single-employer driver (as defined in §390.5 of this subchapter) of a motor carrier for a continuous period which began before January 1, 1971, as long as he/she continues to be a single-employer driver of that motor carrier.

§391.62   Limited exemptions for intra-city zone drivers.

The provisions of §§391.11(b)(1) and 391.41(b)(1) through (b)(11) do not apply to a person who:

(a) Was otherwise qualified to operate and operated a commercial motor vehicle in a municipality or exempt intracity zone thereof throughout the one-year period ending November 18, 1988;

(b) Meets all the other requirements of this section;

(c) Operates wholly within the exempt intracity zone (as defined in 49 CFR 390.5);

(d) Does not operate a vehicle used in the transportation of hazardous materials in a quantity requiring placarding under regulations issued by the Secretary under 49 U.S.C. chapter 51; and

(e) Has a medical or physical condition which:

(e)(1) Would have prevented such person from operating a commercial motor vehicle under the Federal Motor Carrier Safety Regulations contained in this subchapter;

(e)(2) Existed on July 1, 1988, or at the time of the first required physical examination after that date; and

(e)(3) The examining physician has determined this condition has not substantially worsened since July 1, 1988, or at the time of the first required physical examination after that date.

§391.63 Multiple-employer drivers.

(a) If a motor carrier employs a person as a multiple-employer driver (as defined in §390.5 of this subchapter), the motor carrier shall comply with all requirements of this part, except that the motor carrier need not—

(a)(1) Require the person to furnish an application for employment in accordance with §391.21;

(a)(2) Make the investigations and inquiries specified in §391.23 with respect to that person;

(a)(3) Perform the annual driving record inquiry required by §391.25(a);

(a)(4) Perform the annual review of the person's driving record required by §391.25(b); or

(a)(5) Require the person to furnish a record of violations or a certificate in accordance with §391.27.

(b) Before a motor carrier permits a multiple-employer driver to drive a commercial motor vehicle, the motor carrier must obtain his/her name, his/her social security number, and the identification number, type and issuing State of his/her commercial motor vehicle operator's license. The motor carrier must maintain this information for 3 years after employment of the multiple-employer driver ceases.

§391.64 Grandfathering for certain drivers participating in vision and diabetes waiver study programs.

(a) The provisions of §391.41(b)(3) do not apply to a driver who was a participant in good standing on March 31, 1996, in a waiver study program concerning the operation of commercial motor vehicles by insulin-controlled diabetic drivers; provided:

(a)(1) The driver is physically examined every year, including an examination by a board-certified/eligible endocrinologist attesting to the fact that the driver is:

(a)(1)(i) Otherwise qualified under §391.41;

(a)(1)(ii) Free of insulin reactions (an individual is free of insulin reactions if that individual does not have severe hypoglycemia or hypoglycemia unawareness, and has less than one documented, symptomatic hypoglycemic reaction per month);

(a)(1)(iii) Able to and has demonstrated willingness to properly monitor and manage his/her diabetes; and

(a)(1)(iv) Not likely to suffer any diminution in driving ability due to his/her diabetic condition.

(a)(2) The driver agrees to and complies with the following conditions:

(a)(2)(i) A source of rapidly absorbable glucose shall be carried at all times while driving;

(a)(2)(ii) Blood glucose levels shall be self-monitored one hour prior to driving and at least once every four hours while driving or on duty prior to driving using a portable glucose monitoring device equipped with a computerized memory;

(a)(2)(iii) Submit blood glucose logs to the endocrinologist or medical examiner at the annual examination or when otherwise directed by an authorized agent of the FMCSA;

(a)(2)(iv) Provide a copy of the endocrinologist's report to the medical examiner at the time of the annual medical examination; and

(a)(2)(v) Provide a copy of the annual medical certification to the employer for retention in the driver's qualification file and retain a copy of the certification on his/her person while driving for presentation to a duly authorized Federal, State or local enforcement official.

(b) The provisions of §391.41(b)(10) do not apply to a driver who was a participant in good standing on March 31, 1996, in a waiver study program concerning the operation of commercial motor vehicles by drivers with visual impairment in one eye; provided:

(b)(1) The driver is physically examined every year, including an examination by an ophthalmologist or optometrist attesting to the fact that the driver:

(b)(1)(i) Is otherwise qualified under §391.41; and

(b)(1)(ii) Continues to measure at least 20/40 (Snellen) in the better eye.

(b)(2) The driver provides a copy of the ophthalmologist or optometrist report to the medical examiner at the time of the annual medical examination.

(b)(3) The driver provides a copy of the annual medical certification to the employer for retention in the driver's qualification file and retains a copy of the certification on his/her person while driving for presentation to a duly authorized federal, state or local enforcement official.

Interpretations for 49 CFR 391 – *Current as of May 21, 2007*

§391.41   Physical Qualifications for Drivers

Question 1: Who is responsible for ensuring that medical certifications meet the requirements?

Guidance: Medical certification determinations are the responsibility of the medical examiner. The motor carrier has the responsibility to ensure that the medical examiner is informed of the minimum medical requirements and the characteristics of the work to be performed. The motor carrier is also responsible for ensuring that only medically qualified drivers are operating CMVs in interstate commerce.

Question 2: Do the physical qualification requirements of the FMCSRs infringe upon a person's religious beliefs if such beliefs prohibit being examined by a licensed doctor of medicine or osteopathy?

Guidance: No. To determine whether a governmental regulation infringes on a person's right to freely practice his religion, the interest served by the regulation must be balanced against the degree to which a person's rights are adversely affected. *Biklen v. Board of Education,* 333 F. Supp. 902 (N.D.N.Y. 1971) aff'd 406 U.S. 951 (1972).

If there is an important objective being promoted by the requirement and the restriction on religious freedom is reasonably adapted to achieving that objective, the requirement should be upheld. *Burgin v. Henderson,* 536 F.2d 501 (2d Cir. 1976).

Based on the tests developed by the courts and the important objective served, the regulation meets Constitutional standards. It does not deny a driver his First Amendment rights.

Question 3: What are the physical qualification requirements for operating a CMV in interstate commerce?

Guidance: The physical qualification regulations for drivers in interstate commerce are found at §391.41. Instructions to medical examiners performing physical examinations of these drivers are found at

§391.43. Interpretive guidelines are distributed upon request.

The qualification standards cover 13 areas which directly relate to the driving function. All but four of the standards require a judgment by the medical examiner. A person's qualification to drive is determined by a medical examiner who is knowledgeable about the driver's functions and whether a particular condition would interfere with the driver's ability to operate a CMV safely. In the case of vision, hearing, insulin-using diabetes, and epilepsy, the current standards are absolute, providing no discretion to the medical examiner.

Question 4: Is a driver who is taking prescription methadone qualified to drive a CMV in interstate commerce?

Guidance: Methadone is a habit-forming narcotic which can produce drug dependence and is not an allowable drug for operators of CMVs.

Question 5: May the medical examiner restrict a driver's duties?

Guidance: No. The only conditions a medical examiner may impose upon a driver otherwise qualified involve the use of corrective lenses or hearing aids, securement of a waiver or limitation of driving to exempt intracity zones (see §391.43(g)). A medical examiner who believes a driver has a condition not specified in §391.41 that would affect his ability to operate a CMV safely should refuse to sign the examiner's certificate.

Question 6: If an interstate driver tests positive for alcohol or controlled substances under part 382, must the driver be medically re-examined and obtain a new medical examiner's certificate to drive again?

Guidance: The driver is not required to be medically re-examined or to obtain a new medical examiner's certificate provided the driver is seen by an SAP who evaluates the driver, does not make a clinical diagnosis of alcoholism, and provides the driver with documentation allowing the driver to return to work. However, if the SAP determines that alcoholism exists, the driver is not qualified to drive a CMV in interstate commerce. The ultimate responsibility rests with the motor carrier to ensure the driver is medically qualified and to determine whether a new medical examination should be completed.

Question 7: Are drivers prohibited from using CB radios and earphones?

Guidance: No. CB radios and earphones are not prohibited under the regulations, as long as they do not distract the driver and the driver is capable of complying with §391.41(b)(11).

Question 8: Is the use of Coumadin, an anticoagulant, an automatic disqualification for drivers operating CMVs in interstate commerce?

Guidance: No. Although the FHWA 1987 "Conference on Cardiac Disorders and Commercial Drivers" recommended that drivers who arc taking anticoagulants not be allowed to drive, the agency has not adopted a rule to that effect. The medical examiner and treating specialist may, but are not required to, accept the Conference recommendations. Therefore, the use of Coumadin is not an automatic disqualification, but a factor to be considered in determining the driver's physical qualification status.

§391.43   Medical Examination; Certificate of Physical Examination

Question 1: May a motor carrier, for the purposes of §391.41, or a State driver licensing agency, for the purposes of §383.71, accept the results of a medical examination performed by a foreign medical examiner?

Guidance: Yes. Foreign drivers operating in the U.S. with a driver's license recognized as equivalent to the CDL may be medically certified in accordance with the requirements of part 391, subpart E, by a medical examiner in the driver's home country who is licensed, certified, and/or registered to perform physical examinations in that country. However, U.S. drivers operating in interstate commerce within the U.S. must be medically certified in accordance with part 391, subpart E, by a medical examiner licensed, certified, and/or registered to perform physical examinations in the U.S.

Question 2: May a urine sample collected for purposes of performing a subpart H test be used to test for diabetes as part of a driver's FHWA-required physical examination?

Guidance: In general, no. However, the DOT has recognized an exception to this general policy whereby, after 60 milliliters of urine have been set aside for subpart H testing, any remaining portion of the sample may be used for other nondrug testing, but only if such other nondrug testing is required by the FHWA (under part 391, subpart E) such as testing for glucose and protein levels.

Question 3: Is a chest x-ray required under the minimum medical requirements of the FMCSRs?

Guidance: No, but a medical examiner may take an x-ray if appropriate.

Question 4: Does §391.43 of the FMCSRs require that physical examinations of applicants for employment be conducted by medical examiners employed by or designated by the carrier?

Guidance: No.

Question 5: Does a medical certificate displaying a facsimile of a medical examiner's signature meet the "signature of examining health care professional" requirement?

Guidance: Yes.

Question 6: The driver's medical exam is part of the Mexican Licencia Federal. If a roadside inspection reveals that a Mexico-based driver has not had the medical portion of the Licencia Federal re-validated, is the driver considered to be without a valid medical certificate or without a valid license?

Guidance: The Mexican Licencia Federal is issued for a period of 10 years but must be re-validated every 2 years. A condition of re-validation is that the driver must pass a new physical examination. The dates for each re-validation are on the Licencia Federal and must be stamped at the completion of each physical. This constitutes documentation that the driver is medically qualified. Therefore, if the Licencia Federal is not re-validated every 2 years as specified by Mexican law, the driver's license is considered invalid.

Question 7: If a motor carrier sends a potential interstate driver to a medical examiner to have both a pre-employment medical examination and a pre-employment controlled substances test performed, how must the medical examiner conduct the medical examination including the certification the driver meets the physical qualifications of §391.41(b)?

Guidance: The medical examiner must complete the physical examination first without collecting the Part 382 controlled substances urine specimen. If the potential driver meets the requirements of Part 391, Subpart E [especially §391.41(b)] and the medical examiner chooses to certify the potential driver as qualified to operate commercial motor vehicles (CMV) in interstate commerce, the medical examiner may prepare the medical examiner's certificate.

After the medical examiner has completed the medical examiner's certificate and provided a copy to the potential driver and to the motor carrier who will use the potential driver's services, the medical examiner may collect the specimen for the 49 CFR Part 382 pre-employment controlled substances test. The motor carrier is held fully responsible for ensuring the potential driver is not used to operate CMVs until the carrier receives a verified negative controlled substances test result from the medical review officer. A Department of Transportation pre-employment controlled substances test is not a medical examination test.

§391.45   Persons Who Must Be Medically Examined and Certified

Question 1: Is it intended that the words "person" and "driver" be used interchangeably in §391.45?

Guidance: Yes.

Question 2: Do the FMCSRs require applicants, possessing a current medical certificate, to undergo a new physical examination as a condition of employment?

Guidance: No. However, if a motor carrier accepts such a currently valid certificate from a driver subject to part 382, the driver is subject to additional controlled substance testing requirements unless otherwise excepted in subpart H.

Question 3: Must a driver who is returning from an illness or injury undergo a medical examination even if his current medical certificate has not expired?

Guidance: The FMCSRs do not require an examination in this case unless the injury or illness has impaired the driver's ability to perform his/her normal duties. However, the motor carrier may require a driver returning from any illness or injury to take a physical examination. But, in either case, the motor carrier has the obligation to determine if an injury or illness renders the driver medically unqualified.

§391.47   Resolution of Conflicts of Medical Evaluation

Question 1: Does the FHWA issue formal medical decisions as to the physical qualifications of drivers on an individual basis?

Guidance: No, except upon request for resolution of a conflict of medical evaluations.

§391.49   Waiver of Certain Physical Defects

Question 1: Since 49 CFR 391.49 does not mandate a Skill Performance Evaluation, does the term "performance standard" mean that the State must give a driving test or other Skill Performance Evaluation to the driver for every waiver issued or does this term mean that, depending upon the medical condition, the State may give some other type of performance test? For example, in the case of a vision waiver, would a vision examination suffice as a performance standard?

Guidance: Under the Tolerance Guidelines, Appendix C, Paragraph 3(j), each State that creates a waiver program for intrastate drivers is responsible for determining what constitutes "sound medical judgment," as well as determining the performance standard. In the example used above, a vision examination would suffice as a performance standard. It is the responsibility of each State establishing a waiver program to determine what constitutes an appropriate performance standard.

Frequently Asked Questions - Medical—
current as of May 21, 2007

www.fmcsa.dot.gov/rules-regulations/topics/medical/faq.asp

1. If the driver admits to regular alcohol use, and based on responses on the driver history, further questioning or additional tools such as CAGE, AUDIT or TWEAK assessments, may the examiner require further evaluation prior to signing the medical certificate?

Yes. Except where absolute criteria exist, the final determination as to whether the driver meets the FMCSA medical standards is to be made by the medical examiner. The examiner should use whatever tools or additional assessments they feel are necessary. Under 391.43, Instructions to the Medical Examiner -Laboratory and "Other Testing," support is provided to the examiner if they believe that "Other test(s) may be indicated based upon the medical history or findings of the physical examination."

Further supporting the need for additional evaluation is the medical advisory criteria for 391.41(b)13 which notes that "if an individual shows signs of having an alcohol-use problem, he or she should be referred to a specialist. After counseling and / or treatment, he or she may be considered for certification."

While not regulation, the medical advisory criteria are provided by the FMCSA to assist the Medical Examiner determine if a person is physically qualified to operate a CMV. The Medical Examiner may or may not choose to use these guidelines. These guidelines are based on expert review and considered practice standards. The examiner should document the reason(s) for not following the guidelines.

2. Can CMV drivers be qualified while being prescribed Provigil (Modafinil)?

Provigil (Modafinil) is a medication used to treat excessive sleepiness caused by certain sleep disorders. These sleep disorders are narcolepsy, obstructive sleep apnea / hypopnea syndrome and shift work sleep disorders. Provigil has several concerning side effects such as chest pain, dizziness, difficulty breathing, heart palpitations, irregular and / or fast heartbeat, increased blood pressure, tremors or shaking movements, anxiety, nervousness, rapidly changing mood, problems with memory, blurred vision or other vision changes to name a few. Many drugs interact with Provigil which include over-the-counter medications, prescription medications, nutritional supplements, herbal products, alcohol containing beverages and caffeine. The use of Provigil needs careful supervision. Provigil may affect concentration, function or may hide signs that an individual is tired. It is recommended that until an individual knows how Provigil affects him / her, they may not drive, use machinery or do any activity that requires mental alertness.

Drivers being prescribed Provigil should not be qualified until they have been monitored closely for at least 6 weeks while taking Provigil. The treating physician and the Medical Examiner should agree that the Provigil is effective in preventing daytime somnolence and document that no untoward side effects are present. Commercial motor vehicle drivers taking Provigil should be re-certified annually.

3. Is the certification limited to current employment or job duties?

When a Medical Examiner grants medical certification, he/she certifies the driver to perform any job duty required of a commercial driver, not just the driver's current job duties.

4. What medical conditions disqualify a commercial bus or truck driver?

The truck driver must be medically qualified to not only drive the vehicle safely, but also to do pre- and post-trip safety inspections, secure the load and make sure it has not shifted. Bus drivers have different demands.

By regulation, Specific Medically Disqualifying Conditions Found Under 49 CFR 391.41 are Hearing Loss, Vision Loss, Epilepsy and Insulin Use.

Drivers who require a Diabetes or Vision exemption to safely drive a commercial motor vehicle (CMV) in addition to those pre-printed on the certification form are disqualified until they receive such an exemption.

5. Is a release form required to be completed in order for the employer to legally keep the medical certification card on file?

No. The Medical Examiner is required to provide a copy of the Medical Examiner's Certificate (49 Code of Federal Regulations (CFR) 391.43(g)) to the motor carrier that employs the driver. A release form is not required. The motor carrier is required to keep a copy of the certificate in the driver qualification file. (49 CFR 391.51(b)(7))

6. What is the age requirement for operating a CMV in interstate commerce?

A person must be at least 21 years old to drive a CMV in interstate commerce.

7. Is getting a medical certificate mandatory for all CMV drivers in the United States?

In general, all CMV drivers driving in interstate commerce within the United States must obtain medical certification from a Medical Examiner. CMV drivers from Canada and Mexico can be medically qualified in their countries.

8. Are CMV drivers who operate in interstate commerce required to have a medical certificate?

Drivers are required to have a DOT Medical Certificate:

If they operate a motor vehicle with a gross vehicle weight rating (GVWR), gross combination weight rating (GCWR), gross vehicle weight (GVW), or gross combination weight (GCW) of 4,536 kilograms or more in interstate commerce.

If they operate a motor vehicle designed or used to transport more than 15 passengers (including the driver) in interstate commerce.

If they operate a motor vehicle designed or used to transport between 9 and 15 passengers, for direct compensation, beyond 75 air miles from the driver's normal work-reporting location, in interstate commerce.

If they transport hazardous materials, in a quantity requiring placards, in interstate commerce.

CFR 49 Part 391.41

CFR 49 Part 390.5

9. What is the protocol if the Medical Examiner's Certificate gets damaged, lost or unreadable?

A copy of the Medical Examiner's Certificate should be kept on file in the Medical Examiner's office. The driver may request a replacement copy of the certificate from the Medical Examiner or get a copy of the certificate from the motor carrier.

10. What are the hearing requirements for CMV drivers?

A person is physically qualified to drive a CMV if that person: First perceives a forced whispered voice in the better ear at not less than five feet with or without the use of a hearing aid or if tested by use of an audiometric device, does not have an average hearing loss in the better ear greater than 40 decibels at 500 Hz, 1,000 Hz, and 2,000 Hz with or without a hearing aid when the audiometric device is calibrated to the American National Standard Z24.5-1951.

11. Can a driver receive a hearing waiver?

Currently, there is no waiver program for hearing.

12. When is audiometry required?

A medical examiner may require a driver to have an audiometry test. If the driver fails the whisper test, the driver must pass an audiometer test to be qualified to drive a CMV.

Office audiometry is not able to test a person with a hearing aid. The person needs to be referred for accurate testing.

13. What is a waiver? An exemption?

A waiver is temporary regulatory relief from one or more of the FMCSRs given to a person subject to the regulations, or a person who intends to engage in an activity that would be subject to the regulations. A waiver provides the person with relief from the regulation for up to three months. 49 CFR 391.64 provides waivers to CMV drivers who were in the initial vision and insulin programs in the early 1990s.

An exemption is a temporary regulatory relief from one or more of the FMCSRs given to a person or class of persons subject to the regulations, or who intend to engage in an activity that would make them subject to the regulation. An exemption provides the person or class of persons with relief from the regulations for up to two years, but may be renewed.

14. Will my employer have access to my medical evaluation?

Although the FMCSRs do not require the Medical Examiner to give a copy of the Medical Examination Report to the employer, the FMCSA does not prohibit employers from obtaining copies of the medical examination form (long form). Medical Examiners should have a release form signed by the driver if the employer wishes to obtain a copy of the medical examination form (long form).

Employers must comply with applicable State and Federal laws regarding the privacy and maintenance of employee medical information. For information about the provisions of the Standards for Privacy of Individually Identifiable Health Information (the Privacy Rule) that was mandated by the Health Insurance Portability & Accountability Act of 1996 (HIPAA) (Public Law 104-191), contact the U.S. Department of Health & Human Services at the HIPAA Website of the Office of Civil Rights. Their toll-free information line is: 1-866-627-7748.

15. What will the FMCSA do after the agency receives my request for a waiver?

After the application is complete, the FMCSA will review the request and make a recommendation to the Administrator. The final decision whether to grant or deny the application for waiver is made by the Administrator.

16. Who signs the medical certificate?

The Medical Examiner who performs the medical examination must sign the Medical Certificate.

17. Who is required to have a copy of the Medical Certificate?

Section 391.43(g) requires the Medical Examiner to give a copy of the medical certificate to the driver and the motor carrier (employer), if the driver passes the medical examination.

18. Why are the diagnosis and treatment of hypertension important?

These criteria are important because there is strong prospective, randomized clinical-trial evidence that hypertension markedly increases the risk of cardiovascular disease and that effective treatment reduces cardiovascular morbidity and mortality. To be certified to drive, the driver should have ongoing hypertension management and be free of side effects that may impair safe driving.

19. Is Narcolepsy disqualifying?

The guidelines recommend disqualifying a CMV driver with a diagnosis of Narcolepsy, regardless of treatment because of the likelihood of excessive daytime somnolence.

20. Is Proteinuria disqualifying?

Depending on the amount, protein in the urine (proteinuria) may indicate significant renal disease. The Medical Examiner may certify, time limit, or disqualify a commercial driver with proteinuria. The decision is based on whether the examiner believes that proteinuria may adversely affect safe driving regardless of the examiner's decision. The driver should be referred for follow-up.

21. Who can serve as a Medical Examiner and perform DOT physical exams?

Federal Motor Carrier Safety Regulations define Medical Examiner as a person who is licensed, certified and/or registered in accordance with applicable State laws and regulations to perform physical examinations. The term includes but is not limited to doctors of medicine, doctors of osteopathy, physician assistants, advanced practice nurses and doctors of chiropractic.

22. Can a driver be qualified if he is taking Methadone?

No. CMV drivers taking Methadone cannot be qualified.

23. Can I apply for an exemption from the hypertension standard?

A CMV driver may apply for an exemption from any of the standards. Exemptions are granted only in those instances where the driver can show that safety would not be diminished by granting the exemption.

49 CFR 381.300

24. What if the certifying doctor is no longer available?

If the original Medical Examiner is not available, the physician or Medical Examiner in the office may sign the replacement certificate. The advisory criteria states that the original may be copied and given to the driver. Some physicians may require the driver to undergo a new physical examination.

25. If a driver had a Myocardial Infarction (MI), followed by coronary artery bypass graft (CABG) several months ago, should he have an ETT (exercise tolerance test) as recommended in the MI guidelines but not in the CABG guidelines?

Medical Examiners should follow the most current clinical guidelines; therefore after an MI, drivers should obtain an ejection fraction and ETT before returning to work and because of the CABG keeping the driver off work 3 months (not 2 as for MI) to allow time for sternal wound healing.

26. Is Sleep Apnea disqualifying?

Drivers should be disqualified until the diagnosis of sleep apnea has been ruled out or has been treated successfully. As a condition of continuing qualification, it is recommended that a CMV driver agree to continue uninterrupted therapy such as CPAP, etc./monitoring and undergo objective testing as required. *Excessive daytime sleepiness*

A driver with a diagnosis of (probable) sleep apnea or a driver who has EDS should be temporarily disqualified until the condition is either ruled out by objective testing or successfully treated.

Narcolepsy and sleep apnea account for about 70% of EDS. EDS lasting from a few days to a few weeks should not limit a driver's ability in the long run. However, persistent or chronic sleep disorders causing EDS can be a significant risk to the driver and the public. The examiner should consider general certification criteria at the initial and follow-up examinations:

Severity and frequency of EDS
Presence or absence of warning of attacks
Possibility of sleep during driving
Degree of symptomatic relief with treatment
Compliance with treatment.

27. May I request reconsideration if I am found not qualified for a medical certificate?

The decision to qualify a driver to operate a CMV in interstate commerce is the sole responsibility of the Medical Examiner. The driver may discuss the basis for the disqualification with the Medical Examiner and explore options for reconsideration.

28. Where may I obtain an application for an epilepsy waiver?

A CMV driver may apply for an exemption from any of the standards. Exemptions are granted only in those instances where the driver can show that safety would not be diminished by granting the exemption.

49 CFR 381.300

29. Is the Medical Examiner required to repeat the entire physical examination if the driver is only returning for blood pressure check? How is the new blood pressure documented?

This is at the discretion of the Medical Examiner; if the driver returns to the same Medical Examiner within the time required (3 months), the CMV driver is not required to repeat the entire physical examination. The Medical Examiner should write the date and new blood pressure reading on the original form and the qualification status.

30. Can a driver who takes nitroglycerine for angina be certified?

Yes. Nitroglycerine use is not disqualifying. The Medical Examiner may require an evaluation by the treating Cardiologist to make sure that the driver's angina is stable.

31. How soon may a driver be certified after CABG surgery?

The driver should not return to driving sooner than 3 months after CABG, to allow the sternal incision to heal. The driver should meet all the following criteria:

Clearance by physician (usually cardiologist)

Resting echocardiogram with an LVEF >40% after CABG

Asymptomatic status with no angina

32. Can a driver be qualified if he/she is having recurring episodes of ventricular tachycardia?

Drivers with sustained ventricular tachycardia (lasting >15 seconds) should be disqualified. Drivers experiencing non-sustained V-TACH should be evaluated by a cardiologist to determine the effect on the driver's ability to drive safely, treatment, and if the underlying cause of the ventricular tachycardia is disqualifying (see cardiovascular guidelines for complete review).

33. Are Medical Examiners who perform FMCSA CMV driver physical examinations required to be certified?

Medical Examiners are not currently required to be certified by FMCSA. Medical Examiners are required to be licensed, registered or certified to perform physical examinations by their state. FMCSA is developing the National Registry of Certified Medical Examiners (NRCME) program. When the NRCME program is established, all Medical Examiners who intend to perform examinations and issue medical certificates for drivers to meet the requirements of Section 391.41 of the FMCSRs would have to trained, certified, and listed on the FMCSA's National Registry. In order to be certified, Medical Examiners would have to pass a test demonstrating comprehensive understanding of the medical standards in Section 391.41 of the FMCSRs and how they relate to the medical and physical demands of driving a CMV. For more information on the NRCME program, see *www.nrcme .fmcsa.dot.gov.*

34. If I am a medically certified pilot, can I legally operate a CMV?

No. Operators of CMV in interstate commerce must be qualified according to the regulations in 49 CFR 391.41(b)(1-13)

35. What is the Federal Motor Carrier Safety Administration?

The Motor Carrier Safety Improvement Act of 1999 created the Federal Motor Carrier Safety Administration (FMCSA) as a separate administration within the U.S. Department of Transportation on January 1, 2000. The primary mission of FMCSA is to reduce crashes, injuries, and fatalities involving large trucks and buses. FMCSA is headquartered in Washington, D.C., and employs more than 1,000 individuals in all 50 States, the District of Columbia, and Puerto Rico. For more information, go to About Us section on the FMCSA Website.

36. Can a driver on oxygen therapy be qualified to drive in interstate commerce?

In most cases, the use of oxygen therapy while driving is disqualifying. Concerns include oxygen equipment malfunction, risk of explosion, and the presence of significant underlying disease that is disqualifying, such as pulmonary hypertension. The driver must be able to pass a Pulmonary Function Test (PFT).

37. How can I get a copy of my medical evaluation file?

You can contact the Medical Examiner that conducted your evaluation for a copy of your medical certification examination.

38. Are the DOT medical examinations covered by HIPAA?

Regulatory requirements take precedence over the Health Insurance Portability and Accountability Act (HIPAA) of 1996. There are potential subtle interpretations that can cause significant problems for the Medical Examiner. What information must or can be turned over to the carrier is a legal issue, and if in doubt, the examiner should obtain a legal opinion. Federal Motor Carrier Safety Regulation 391.43 does not address or prohibit the sharing of medical information by Medical Examiners. *www.hhs.gov/ocr/hipaa.*

39. Why is the DOT physical examination important?

The FMCSA physical examination is required to help ensure that a person is medically qualified to safely operate a CMV. In the interest of public safety, CMV drivers are held to higher physical, mental and emotional standards than passenger car drivers.

40. Who can give a waiver or exemption?

The Medical Examiner cannot grant waivers or exemptions. Only the FMCSA grants waivers or exemptions for certain medical conditions if the individual is otherwise qualified to drive. Section 381.205 of the FMCSRs allow the driver to request a waiver if one or more of the FMCSRs prevent the driver from operating a CMV or make it unreasonably difficult to do so, during a unique, non-emergency event that will take no more than three months to complete.

41. What should I do if I have an idea or suggestion for a pilot program?

You may send a written statement to the Federal Motor Carrier Safety Administration, U.S. Department of Transportation, Office of Bus & Truck Standards and Operations, 400 7th Street SW Room 8301, Washington, DC 20590. 381.400

42. If a driver with hypertension has lowered his blood pressure to normal range, lost weight, and is off medications, can he/she be certified for 2 years?

This is the Medical Examiner's decision.

43. What information should the Medical Examiner have available to decide if a driver is medically qualified?

Medical Examiners who perform FMCSA medical examinations should understand: (1) Specific physical and mental demands associated with operating a CMV, (2) Physical qualification standards specified by 49 CFR 391.41 (b) (1-13), (3) FMCSA advisory criteria and other criteria prepared by the FMCSA, and (4) FMCSA medical guidelines to assess the CMV driver's medical condition.

44. Are there duties related to the FMCSA medical certification?

No, the FMCSA does not have duties. The Medical Examiner is required to know the FMCSA driver physical qualification standards, medical guidelines, and advisory criteria. The examiner should understand the mental and physical demands of operating a CMV.

45. For how long is my medical certificate valid?

The certificate is valid for 2 years. In addition, drivers with specific medical conditions require more frequent certification:

Hypertension (high blood pressure) stable on treatment 1 year

Heart disease 1 year

Qualified under 391.64 the original diabetes and vision waiver program 1 year

New insulin and vision exemption program 1 year

Driving in exempt intra-city zone 1 year

Determination by examiner that condition requires more frequent monitoring, such as diabetes mellitus or sleep disorders.

46. What am I required to do if the FMCSA grants my exemption?

You must comply with the terms and conditions of the exemption. This information is provided to you.

47. May a Medical Examiner qualify a driver who has blood in his urine?

The Medical Examiner decides to certify, time-limit or disqualify. The decision to certify a driver is determined by whether the examiner believes that the blood in the urine affects the ability of the commercial driver to safely. Regardless of whether the CMV driver is certified, the Medical Examiner should document referral to a specialist or the driver's Primary Care Provider.

48. How do Medical Examiners differ from Medical Review Officers?

A Medical Review Officer (MRO) is a licensed physician responsible for receiving and reviewing laboratory results generated by an employer's drug testing program and evaluating medical explanations for test results. More information on MROs is available online at *www.dot.gov/ost/dapc/mro.html*. Medical Examiner means a person who is licensed, certified, or registered, in accordance with applicable State laws and regulations to perform physical examinations. This includes but is not limited to doctors of medicine, doctors of osteopathy, physician assistants, advanced practice nurses and doctors of chiropractic.

49. Are holders of Class 3 pilot licenses required to have another physical for commercial driving?

Drivers of CMVs who operate in interstate commerce must be medically qualified in accordance with 49 CFR 391.41.

50. What medical criteria are required to obtain a medical certificate?

The physical qualification regulations for CMV drivers in interstate commerce are found at Section 391.41(b) of the FMCSRs. Instructions to Medical Examiners performing physical examinations are found at Section 391.43. Advisory criteria under 391.41 are recommendations. They are accessible on the FMCSA's Website at *www.fmcsa.dot.gov/rules-regulations/administration/medical.htm*. FMCSA has published medical conference reports as recommendations to assist Medical Examiners determine whether a driver is qualified under Section 391.41(b). The conference reports may be accessed on the FMCSA Website.

51. How long will it take the agency to respond to my request for a waiver?

The agency will issue a final decision within 180 days of the date it receives your completed application. However, if you leave out required information, it takes longer to complete your application.

52. Can I get a waiver if I have had a single unprovoked seizure?

Drivers who have had one unprovoked seizure by definition do not have epilepsy (2 or more unprovoked seizures). Drivers who are seizure-free and off anticonvulsant medication(s) for at least 5 years after a single unprovoked seizure can be certified. Earlier return to work may be considered for drivers with a normal EEG who have no epileptic-form activity and normal examination by a neurologist specializing in epilepsy.

53. What does the medical examination involve?

The driver must be medically examined and certified in accordance with Section 391.43 of the FMCSRs.

54. Does the FMCSA set any guidelines for Medical Examiner fees associated with conducting medical examinations?

No. There is no fee schedule.

55. Is Meniere's Disease disqualifying?

Meniere's Disease—a condition associated with severe and unpredictable bouts of dizziness (vertigo) is disqualifying. This recommendation can be found in the Conference on Neurological Disorders and Commercial Drivers.

56. Can carriers set their own standards for CMV drivers who operate in interstate commerce?

49 CFR Section 390.3(d) gives employers the right to adopt stricter medical standards. Motor Carriers (companies) cannot set less restrictive standards. In addition, the employer can require the driver to perform ancillary duties as a condition of employment.

57. What is the effect on driver certification based on FMCSA hypertension stages?

A driver with a diagnosis of hypertension on treatment should have at least an annual certification.

A CMV driver with a Blood pressure (BP) 140/90 may be certified for 2 years.

First time blood BP elevated:

Stage 1—BP 140–159/90–99 Certification Period 1 year

Stage 2—BP 160–179/100–109 Certification Period 3 months as one time certification. Within the 3 months, if the blood pressure is below 140/90, the driver may receive 1 year certification.

Stage 3—BP Reading >180/110 Disqualified. When the blood pressure is less than 140/90, the driver can be certified at 6 month intervals.

58. What are the criteria used to determine if a driver with lung disease can be certified?

At the initial and follow-up examination, the Medical Examiner can use general certification criteria:

What are the effects of the lung disease on pulmonary function?

Is the disease contagious?

Can the driver safely use therapy while working?

Can the driver safely perform both driving and ancillary duties?

Is the disease progressive? A driver with a pulmonary disease that may progress or affect their ability to drive safely should be certified at least annually.

Additional criteria for the specific respiratory problem:

Certification for most chronic lung diseases is based on the clinical course. The examiner must decide if additional testing is required. The medical certification form states that the examiner may need to order a chest x-ray or pulmonary function tests.

59. What are the differences between the medical standards and the medical advisory criteria and the medical guidelines?

The Medical Examiner must follow the standards found in 49 CFR 391.41. In the case of vision, hearing, epilepsy and diabetes requiring any use of insulin, the FMCSRs standards are absolute and allow no discretion by the Medical Examiner.

FMCSA also provides medical advisory criteria and medical guidelines to assist the Medical Examiner determine if a person is physically qualified to operate a commercial bus or truck. The Medical Examiner may or may not choose to use these guidelines. These guidelines are based on expert review and considered practice standards. The examiner should document the reason(s) for not following the guidelines.

60. How long does it take to get my medical certificate once my medical examination is complete?

The FMCSRs do not specify that the Medical Examiner must give a copy of the Medical Examiner's Certificate to the driver immediately following the examination. The Medical Examiner may require additional medical tests or reports from your treating physician.

61. Can a driver who has a condition that causes excessive daytime sleepiness be certified?

Narcolepsy and sleep apnea account for about 70% of EDS. EDS lasting from a few days to a few weeks should not limit a driver's ability in the long run. However, persistent or chronic sleep disorders causing EDS can be a significant risk to the driver and the public. While most of these diseases are usually disqualifying, the examiner should consider these general certification criteria at the initial and follow-up examinations:

Underlying condition causing the EDS

Severity of and frequency of EDS

Presence or absence of warning of attacks

Possibility of sleep during driving

Degree of symptomatic relief with treatment

Compliance with treatment

After the initial evaluation, the examiner can decide if additional testing is required. Generally, drivers with excessive EDS need further evaluation to determine the cause and certification.

62. My medical certificate is still valid. Am I prohibited from operating a CMV if I have a medical condition that developed after my last medical certificate was issued?

FMCSA regulations prohibit a driver from beginning or continuing to drive if their ability and/or alertness is impaired by: fatigue, illness, or any cause that makes it unsafe to begin (continue) to drive a commercial vehicle.

Even if a driver currently has a valid medical certificate, the driver is prohibited from driving a CMV with any medical condition that would be disqualifying or may interfere with the safe operation of a CMV. Once a disqualifying medical condition is resolved, and before resuming operation of CMV, a driver is responsible for obtaining re-certification from a Medical Examiner. 391.45

63. What is a satisfactory exercise tolerance test?

A satisfactory ETT requires exercising to a workload capacity of at least six METS (through Bruce Stage II or equivalent) attaining a heart rate of >85% of predicted maximum (unless on beta blockers), a rise in SBP >20 mm Hg without angina, and having no significant ST segment depression or elevation.

Stress radionuclide or exercise echocardiogram should be performed for symptomatic individuals, individuals with an abnormal resting electrocardiogram, or individuals who fail to meet the ETT requirements.

64. Can I still get a medical certificate if I have a medical condition that is being treated by a physician?

The decision is made by the Medical Examiner. The examiner may request information about the driver's condition from their treating doctor. In general, certification is permitted if the driver does not have a condition, use medication or receive treatment that impairs safe driving.

65. As a Medical Examiner, can I disclose the results of my medical evaluation to a CMV driver's employer?

49 CFR 391.43 "Instructions to the Medical Examiner" do not address or prohibit the sharing of medical information. Refer to the HIPAA regulations for guidance.

www.hhs.gov/ocr/hipaa

66. Where can I find the FMCSRs?

All of the FMCSRs are listed numerically on the FMCSA's Website at *www.fmcsa.dot.gov/rules-regulations/administration/fmcsr/fmcsrguide .asp?section_type=A.*

67. May a driver who has non-insulin treated diabetes mellitus (treated with oral medication) be certified for 2 years?

In all cases, clinical judgment is required. The Medical Examiner decides if the driver's diabetes is adequately controlled, which determines certification, length of certification or disqualification. FMCSA guidelines recommend performing annual examination for vision, neurological function and cardiovascular disease, including hypertension. In general, the diabetic driver should have annual re-certification examinations.

68. Do drivers need to carry the medical certification when driving a CMV?

Yes. Drivers must carry a current copy of a medical examination certificate.

69. Is the driver required to provide a copy to the employer?

Yes, the motor carrier (employer) is required to keep a copy of the medical card (certificate) on file and the driver is required to keep the medical certificate (and supporting documents as required) with him while driving.

70. Can I report a driver operating without a medical certificate? What protection can I expect as a whistleblower and to whom would I report it?

Yes. Guidelines for reporting a driver operating a CMV without a medical certificate issued by a Medical Examiner and whistleblower protections, i.e., Motor Carrier Employee Whistle Blower Protection, (49 United States Code 31105 and 29 Code of Federal Regulations 1978).

71. Am I required to have a medical certificate if I only operate a CMV in my home State (intrastate commerce)?

Intrastate drivers are subject to the physical qualification regulations of their States. All 50 States have adapted their regulations based on some of the Federal requirements. Many states grant waivers for certain medical conditions.

NOTE: FedEx, UPS and DHL drivers usually do not leave the state but are subject to interstate regulations.

72. Who determines if a pilot program should be initiated?

Generally, pilot programs are initiated by the FMCSA when the agency determines that there may be an effective alternative to one or more of the requirements in the FMCSRs, but does not have sufficient research data to support the development of a notice of proposed rulemaking to change the regulation. 381.400

73. What is the basis of FMCSA's recommendations regarding high blood pressure?

FMCSA medical guidelines for hypertension are based on the Sixth Report of the Joint National Committee on Prevention, Detection, Evaluation and Treatment of High Blood Pressure (JNC 6–1997). The prior cardiovascular guidelines were based on an earlier JNC report.

The medical standard (49 CFR 391.41(b)(6)) permits qualification of CMV drivers if the driver has no current clinical diagnosis of high blood pressure likely to interfere with his/her ability to operate a motor vehicle safely. FMCSA provides guidelines to assist the Medical Examiner in determining if a person is physically qualified to operate a motor vehicle.

74. How do I request a waiver/exemption?

For exemptions from Federal standards other than Diabetes or Vision, please refer to the FMCSRs in Sections 381.210 and 391.310.

75. Does my driving record affect my eligibility for a medical certificate?

No.

76. What is a pilot program?

A pilot program collects specific data to evaluate alternatives to the regulations or innovative approaches to safety while ensuring that the safety performance goals of the regulations are satisfied.

In a pilot program, temporary regulatory relief from one or more FMCSR is given to a person or class of persons subject to the regulations or to a person or class of persons who intend to engage in an activity that would be subject to the regulations.

The number of participants in the pilot program must be large enough to ensure statistically valid findings. 381.400

NOTE: FMCSA is not conducting medical pilot programs at the time.

77. Are CMV drivers required to be CPR certified?

No. There is no regulation that requires CMV drivers to be CPR certified.

78. What medications disqualify a CMV driver?

A driver cannot take a controlled substance or prescription medication without a prescription from a licensed practitioner.

If a driver uses a drug identified in 21 CFR 1308.11 (391.42(b)(12)) or any other substance such as amphetamine, a narcotic, or any other habit forming drug, the driver is medically unqualified.

There is an exception: the prescribing doctor can write that the driver is safe to be a commercial driver while taking the medication. In this case, the Medical Examiner may, but does not have to certify the driver.

Any anti-seizure medication used for the prevention of seizures is disqualifying.

Methadone use is disqualifying.

The Medical Examiner has two ways to determine if any medication a driver uses will adversely affect safe operation of a CMV:

1. Review each medication—prescription, non-prescription and supplement
2. Request a letter from the prescribing doctor

79. What is the ANSI Standard?

When the audiometric device is calibrated to the American National Standard (formerly the American Standard Association (ASA) Z24.5-11951. Since the prescribed standard under the FMCSRs is the American National Standards Institute (ANSI), it may be necessary to convert the audiometric results from the ISO standard to the ANSI standard. Instructions are included on the Medical Examination Report form.

80. If a driver has had surgery for Meniere's Disease, is the condition disqualifying?

There is surgery for Meniere's Disease. The FMCSA is now reviewing this issue in relation to certification.

81. Who should I contact if I have questions about the status of my application for a Vision or Diabetes exemption?

You should contact the Office of Bus And Truck Standards and Operations, Federal Motor Carrier Safety Administration, 400 Seventh Street SW, Washington, DC 20590.

The telephone number is 1-703-448-3094.

82. Can a CMV driver be disqualified for using a legally prescribed drug?

Although the driver has a legal prescription, he/she may be disqualified if the medication could adversely affect the driver's ability to drive a CMV safely.

83. When may I request a waiver/exemption?

You may request a waiver if one or more of the FMCSRs would prevent you from using or operating CMVs or make it unreasonably difficult to do so, during a unique, non-emergency event that will take no more that three months to complete. You may apply for an exemption if one or more FMCSRs prevent you from implementing more efficient or effective operations that would maintain a level of safety equivalent to or greater than the level achieved without the exemption.

84. Can I drive a commercial vehicle after having angioplasty/ stents inserted into my heart?

Yes. Drivers who have uncomplicated, elective Percutaneous Coronary Intervention (PCI), with or without stenting, to treat stable angina may return to work as soon as one week after the procedure. Criteria for return to work after PCI include:

Examination and approval by the treating cardiologist;

Asymptomatic;

No injury to the vascular access site;

ETT three to six months post PCI. In the CMV driver this requires exercising to workload capacity of at least six METS (through Bruce Stage II or equivalent), attaining a heart rate >85% of predicted maximum (unless on beta blockers), a rise in SBP >20 mm Hg without angina, and having no significant ST segment depression or elevation. Stress radionuclide or echocardiography imaging should be performed for symptomatic individuals, individuals with an abnormal resting echocardiogram, or those drivers who fail to obtain the minimal standards required from the standard ETT;

Annual medical qualification examination;

Negative ETT at least every other year (criteria above) and tolerance of all cardiovascular medication. The driver should not experience orthostatic symptoms, including light-headedness; a resting SBP <95 mm Hg systolic; or a systolic blood pressure decline >20 mm Hg upon standing.

85. Is it possible to get exemptions for some medical conditions?

Under 49 United States Code 31315 and 31136(e), the FMCSA may grant an exemption from the FMCSRs if the agency determines it is in the public interest and would likely achieve a level of safety equivalent to, or greater than, the level that would be achieved by complying with the safety regulation. Sections 381.300 through 381.330 of the FMCSRs describe procedures applicants must follow to apply for exemptions and can be viewed at 49 CFR 381.330. FMCSA currently has exemption programs for vision and insulin-treated diabetes mellitus, and offers a certificate program for drivers with limb impairments. FMCSA also has a special certification program for drivers with missing and/or impaired limbs (49 CFR 391.41(b)(1)).

86. Are government employees exempt from routine/yearly physical examinations?

Transportation performed by the Federal government, a State, or any political subdivision of a State, or an agency established under a compact between states that has been approved by the Congress of the United States are exempt from the FMCSRs, if the political entity chooses.

87. I operate a CMV in the United States but reside outside of the United States. Can I use my foreign medical certificate?

Yes, if you are a resident of Mexico or Canada. Drivers certified in Canada are certified to drive in the United States, providing they meet U.S. requirements. For Mexican drivers, the medical examination is part of the Licencia Federal. It is not necessary for Mexican drivers to carry a separate medical certifying document.

A CMV operator from Canada or Mexico who has been issued a valid commercial driver's license by a Canadian Province or the Mexican Licencia Federal is no longer required to have a medical certificate. The driver's medical exam is part of the driver's license process and is proof of medical fitness to drive in the United States. However, Canadian and Mexican drivers who are insulin-using diabetics, who have epilepsy, or who are hearing-and-vision impaired are not qualified to drive CMVs in the United States. Furthermore, Canadian drivers who do not meet the medical fitness provisions of the Canadian National Safety Code for Motor Carriers but who have been issued a waiver by one of the Canadian Provinces or Territories are not qualified to drive

CMVs in the United States. Similarly, Mexican drivers who do not meet the medical fitness provision of the Licencia Federal de Conductor but who have been issued a waiver by the Licencia Federal de Conductor are not qualified to drive CMVs in the United States.

88. Who should I contact if I have questions about the information I am required to submit to the FMCSA to obtain a waiver or exemption?

You should contact the Office of Bus and Truck Standards and Operations, Federal Motor Carrier Safety Administration, 400 7th Street SW, Room 8301, Washington, DC 20590.

The telephone number is 703-448-3094.

89. Can a driver be qualified if taking prescribed medical marijuana?

No. Drivers taking medical marijuana cannot be certified.

90. Is a driver on kidney dialysis disqualified?

At this time, there is no guidance from FMCSA. At the least, the examiner should require a letter from the treating doctor (nephrologist) outlining the condition, medications, and recommendation regarding certification. The examiner may or may not accept this recommendation. The driver must meet all criteria for certification. Restrictions other than those on the pre-printed form are disqualifying.

91. Is there a "grandfathering" provision for the Vision and Diabetes standards?

Section 391.41(b)(10) do not apply to a driver who was a participant in good standing on March 31, 1996, in a waiver study program concerning the operation of CMVs by drivers with visual impairment in one eye; provided: (1) The driver is physically examined every year, including examination by an ophthalmologist or optometrist attesting to the fact that the driver: (i) Is otherwise qualified under 391.41; and (ii) Continues to measure at least 20/40 (Snellen) in the better eye. (2) The driver provides a copy of the ophthalmologist or optometrist report to the Medical Examiner at the time of the annual medical examination. (3) The driver provides a copy of the annual medical certification to the employer for retention in the driver's qualification file and retains a copy of the certification on his/her person while driving for presentation to an authorized federal, state or local law enforcement official. The grandfathering provision is no longer available.

92. Can a driver be certified who tests positive for a controlled substance on the urine test, but claims that the prescription was legally prescribed 5 years before?

No. Controlled substances expire no later than one year after the date of the original prescription.

93. What tests are used to determine if a driver has adequate hearing to drive safely?

The tests are either the forced whisper test or audiometry. For the whispered voice test, the driver should be 5 feet from the examiner with the ear being tested turned toward the examiner. The other ear is covered. Using the breath which remains after a forced expiration, the examiner whispers words or random numbers such as 66, 18, 23. The examiner should not use only sibilants (s-sounding test materials). If the individual fails the whisper test, the audiometric test should be administered.

94. Can a Canadian driver apply for a Skill Performance Evaluation (SPE) certificate to drive in the United States?

The reciprocity agreement between the United States and Canada does not permit drivers who do not meet the medical fitness requirements of Canada to drive in the United States. Both countries agree that Canadian drivers who do not meet the medical provisions in the National Safety Code of Canada but have a waiver by one of the Canadian Provinces or territories would not be qualified to operate a CMV in the United States. The National Safety Code states that a driver must wear a prosthesis and demonstrate his/her ability in an on-road test. Some of the Canadian provinces have not adopted the National Safety Code. If a driver has no prosthesis when entering the United States, the driver is not qualified to operate here.

It is not necessary for a Canadian driver to apply for a Skill Performance Evaluation certificate to drive in the United States. A valid commercial driver's license issued by a Canadian Province or Territory is proof of medical fitness to drive. If a Canadian driver is required to wear a prosthesis, the driver must wear the prosthesis while operating a commercial vehicle in the United States. If a driver has no prosthesis when entering the United States, the driver is not qualified to operate here.

95. Is the employer legally responsible for paying for the DOT medical examination?

The FMCSRs do not address this issue.

96. Are motor carriers legally obligated to provide air conditioning in commercial motor vehicles?

The FMCSRs do not address this issue.

97. As a Medical Examiner, can I disclose the results of my medical evaluation to a commercial motor vehicle driver's employer?

391.43 "Instructions to the Medical Examiner" do not address or prohibit the sharing of medical information. Refer to the HIIPA regulations for guidance.

www.hhs.gov/ocr/hipaa

98. How can I get more information or apply to serve on the Medical Review Board (MRB)?

Contact the MRB staff at (202) 366-4001 or *fmcsamrb@fmcsa.dot.gov.*

99. What is the Medical Review Board?

The Medical Review Board (MRB) is a nationally recognized standing board of licensed physicians established by FMCSA to provide expert advice to the Secretary of Transportation on matters related to physical qualifications of drivers, medical standards and guidelines, materials for training medical examiners, functional tests for drivers with multiple disabilities and identifying risks of sudden incapacitation.

100. What happens if a driver is not truthful about his/her health history on the medical examination form?

The FMCSA medical certification process is designed to ensure drivers are physically qualified to operate commercial vehicles safely. Each driver is required to complete the Health History section on the first page of the examination report and certify that the responses are complete and true. The driver must also certify that he/she understands that inaccurate, false or misleading information may invalidate the examination and medical examiner's certificate.

FMCSA relies on the medical examiner's clinical judgment to decide whether additional information should be obtained from the driver's treating physician. Deliberate omission or falsification of information may invalidate the examination and any certificate issued based on it. A civil penalty may also be levied against the driver under 49 U.S.C. 521(b)(2)(b), either for making a false statement of for concealing a disqualifying condition.

II
Specific Medical Conditions

Natalie P. Hartenbaum, MD, MPH

Most of the regulations that are used to determine whether a commercial driver should be medically qualified can be easily interpreted in several ways. Although there are four criteria that are not open to interpretation—vision, hearing, use of insulin, and use of medications to control seizures—the others are intentionally left to the discretion of the medical examiner. When the regulations state that a person should not be certified if a disease "of a variety known to be accompanied by . . ." is present, should the examiner refuse to qualify anyone with a medical diagnosis for which one of the possible outcomes is listed? Or should certification be acceptable unless the risk of sudden incapacitation is almost inevitable?

The intent of these regulations is to balance risk to the public and the driver with the likelihood of a specific event—the inability to operate a commercial motor vehicle safely. Many medical conditions can have an impact on driving ability, but usually drivers have sufficient warning to pull their vehicles to the side of the road and prevent an accident.

One component of risk is exposure. Although noncommercial drivers often spend less than 3 hours per day behind the wheel, the individuals we are asked to evaluate under 49 CFR 391.41 may be on the road more than 10 hours daily. A neurologic event that has a one in ten chance of occurring during the time a driver of a private vehicle is behind the wheel may have three to four times the likelihood of occurring while a commercial driver is driving. The Canadian Cardiovascular Society uses a 1 percent annual risk of an accident as the defining point at which a commercial driver should not be medically qualified [1].

Although the functional status resulting from a chronic disease may not increase the risk for a noncommercial driver, a commercial driver has additional stressors with which to contend (see Part III). Chronic medical problems also may interfere with many of the non-driving tasks of a commercial driver. Musculoskeletal or neurologic impairments may impede the driver's ability to manipulate load-securement devices or maneuver the steering wheel. Most important is the fact that the medical condition may not be present in isolation. A driver with currently stable heart disease and noninsulin-requiring diabetes should be evaluated differently than one with only a single disease process. It also is very important to obtain information from all the treating physicians to assess compliance with treatment and stability of the medical condition(s). If the examiner believes that the driver currently meets the criteria and is safe to operate a commercial vehicle but is uncertain of long-term status, he or she would be well advised to certify the driver for less than 2 years to monitor medical status.

Several references are available to guide the examiner in the decision-making process. The first resource must be the regulations and instructions to examiners, both of which are reproduced in this book (see Chapter 3). The Federal Motor Carrier Safety Administration's advisory criteria provide valuable guidance and are included on the examination form. While many examiners argue that the conferences sponsored by the Federal Highway Administration (FHWA) are out of date, the recommendations contained in those reports are useful for guidance. More recent guidance, such as from the Cardiovascular Advisory Panel and even more recent recommendations from the FMCSA's Medical Review Board, also should be reviewed.

In this section, we have attempted to compile information on specific medical conditions that can be used in evaluating commercial drivers. Much of the information is derived from the FHWA or FMCSA conference reports, as well as the advisory criteria, FAQs, and MRB reports. Non-U.S. guidelines are included for comparison. Where they exist, conclusions from recent medical literature also are included. Examiners must remember that theirs is the final decision and that good medical judgment, knowledge of disease processes, and an understanding of the driver's roles and responsibilities are all necessary components of the final qualification decision. The information presented is to be used for guidance only. Final decisions, as always, should be based on all available medical information, recent literature, and, most important, good medical judgment.

Reference

1. Brennan FJ, Davies RA, MacDonald RG, et al. Assessment of the cardiac patient for fitness to drive. *Can J Cardiol* 1992;8:406–412.

4

Cardiovascular Disorders

Natalie P. Hartenbaum, MD, MPH

The CDME processes are currently undergoing substantial changes. The FMCSA Medical Expert Panel on the Cardiovascular Disease and the Commercial Driver presented their findings and recommendations at an April 2007 medical review board meeting. The medical review board accepted most of their recommendations and these are included in this chapter. Although it is likely these will be adopted by the FMCSA, as of publication date, there has been no formal announcement although the FMCSA has indicated that examiners may begin to use new guidance once it is available. Please be aware of these updating processes.

Cardiovascular conditions may be one of the most likely medical reasons for sudden incapacitation of a commercial driver. In a 1989 study of 189 fatal-to-driver heavy truck accidents, 10 percent of the accidents were at least in part attributed to medical problems. Of those, 90 percent were cardiac in origin [1]. Studies evaluating the actual increased risk of an accident in drivers with cardiovascular disease are inconsistent. Some [2–3] have found no increased risk, whereas others [4–6] suggest an increased likelihood of a crash in some drivers with cardiovascular disease. Many of these studies focused on the general population and not on commercial drivers. Disease in these individuals may be exacerbated by the long hours, irregular schedules, and physical demands of the job. Many drivers do not perceive driving as stressful, although electrocardiographic (ECG) changes in drivers with heart disease while driving compared with controls have been demonstrated [7–8]. Although some drivers with medical conditions that may impair driving skills will limit their driving voluntarily, most do not [9]. In addition to the possibility that cardiovascular disease impairs safe driving in some individuals, some studies suggest that commercial drivers have an increased risk of cardiovascular disease compared with the general population [10–13], although this may be due to individual risk factors and the driver's lifestyle, rather than just the occupations.

The regulations covering cardiovascular diseases and hypertension are contained in 49 CFR 391.41(b)(4 and 6):

A person is physically qualified to drive a commercial motor vehicle if that person;

(4) Has no current clinical diagnosis of myocardial infarction, angina pectoris, coronary insufficiency, thrombosis, or any other cardiovascular disease of a variety known to be accompanied by syncope, dyspnea, collapse, or congestive cardiac failure;

(6) Has no current clinical diagnosis of high blood pressure likely to interfere with his/her ability to operate a motor vehicle safely.

Primary care physicians and specialists who are unfamiliar with the Federal Motor Carrier Safety Administration (FMCSA) regulations and other resource information can create conflict and confusion for both patients and examiners. Many examiners have been asked to evaluate a driver whose blood pressure (BP) always runs "just a little high" at 180/105 mm Hg and has been medically qualified by his or her family doctor for the past 20 years. Other examiners have had to explain criteria and conference recommendations to cardiologists who see no reason why a trucker cannot return to work 4 weeks after a myocardial infarction (MI) without further objective testing. There have been studies addressing the knowledge of both cardiologists and family practitioners in local regulations regarding a cardiac patient's ability to drive. In most cases, less than 50 percent were aware of existing regulations [14].

Even examiners who are well versed in the issues involved in commercial driver medical certification may interpret the guidelines differently. This is due in part to the vagueness of the advisory criteria and the inconsistency in training and understanding of the issues involved among examiners. The National Transportation Safety Board (NTSB) in 1989 recommended that the Federal Highway Administration (FHWA) develop a clear set of standards for cardiac risk assessment that would be used by medical examiners in evaluating older commercial drivers and all commercial drivers with cardiac conditions. The NTSB also recommended more extensive and frequent evaluations for this group of drivers (NTSB Recommendations H-90-024 and H-90-025) [1].

The advisory criteria for the evaluation of commercial drivers are found on the medical examination reporting form. It explains that the intent of the U.S. Department of Transportation (DOT) is to disqualify those drivers whose medical conditions may predispose them to sudden incapacitation. The criteria suggest that before they are certified those drivers with a history of coronary insufficiency should have a normal resting and stress ECG, no residual complications, no physical limitations, and are taking no medication likely to interfere with safe driving.

Coronary artery bypass grafting (CABG) and pacemakers need not automatically be underlying but implantable cardioverter defibrillators are disqualifying due to risk of syncope. With Coumadin, the focus should be on the underlying condition, and the examiner is directed to contact FMCSA at 202-366-1970 for additional information. Examiners are referred to the Cardiovascular Advisory Panel Guidelines for the Medical Examination of Commercial Motor Vehicle Drivers [15].

There are a few frequently asked questions [16] that address cardiac conditions. They mostly respond to issues addressed in the Cardiovascular Advisory Panel's Report [15] such as the ability to be medically qualified after percutaneous coronary intervention or what would constitute an acceptable stress test. One question indicates that medical certificates should only be valid 1 year for those drivers with heart disease or hypertension who are stable on medication. Another response indicates that it is up to the examiner whether to certify a driver for 2 years who had hypertension but has now lost weight, is off medication, and blood pressure is now in an acceptable range. It is also at the discretion of the examiner whether the entire examination needs to be repeated if the driver is returning within 3 months after initial examination. If the examiner does not require a new examination, he or she can write the new blood pressure and qualification status on the examination form.

A detailed diagram on determining the qualification of the commercial driver with hypertension is included on the examination form. This was based on the Sixth Report of the Joint National Committee (JNC VI) [17] but will likely be updated to be consistent with JNC VII [18] as per the Medical Expert Panel (MEP) on Cardiovascular Disease's recommendations to the medical review board [19] as discussed later. The main differences between JNC VI and JNC VII are that the normal and borderline categories in JNC VI are combined into prehypertension in JNC VII, and Stage 2 and Stage 3 hypertension are combined into Stage 2 in JNC VII. There were additional changes recommended by the MEP that are discussed in the recommendation section. The current recommendations for BP can be found in Table 4-1.

The advisory criteria explains that it is understood that hypertension itself is unlikely to cause collapse; however, there is concern regarding potential end-organ damage and its consequences. Prior to identifying a driver as hypertensive, the blood pressure should be confirmed by two separate readings on subsequent days.

Drivers with Stage 1 hypertension are at low risk for hypertension-related acute incapacitation and could be medically certified to drive

Table 4-1. Recommendations for the Commercial Driver with Hypertension

Reading	Category	Expiration Date	Recertification
140–159/90–99	Stage 1	1 year	1 year if < 140/90 One-time certificate for 3 months if 140–159/90–99
160–179/100–109	Stage 2	One-time certificate for 3 months	1 year from date of exam if < 140/90
≥ 180/110	Stage 3	Disqualified	6 months from date of exam if < 140/90, then every 6 months if < 140/90

for a 1-year period with annual recertification if the blood pressure is < 140/90. If less than 160/100, certification may be extended one time for 3 months. Drivers with Stage 2 hypertension can be given one 3-month certification to reduce his or her blood pressure to < 140/90. After that 3-month period, if the driver can show that therapy is well tolerated and the BP value is < 140/90, he or she may be certified for 1 year from the date of the initial exam and then recertified annually.

A blood pressure ≥ 180 (systolic) and 110 (diastolic) is considered Stage 3, high risk for an acute BP-related event. The driver may not be qualified, even temporarily, until reduced to < 140/90 and treatment is well tolerated. The driver may be certified for 6 months and biannually (every 6 months) thereafter if at recheck, BP is < 140/90.

Evaluation is warranted if patient is persistently hypertensive on maximal or near-maximal doses of two to three pharmacologic agents. Some causes of secondary hypertension may be amenable to surgical intervention or specific pharmacologic therapy.

Recommendations

The major purpose in evaluating the medical fitness of a commercial driver is to limit potential harm to the general public. The acceptable risk is based on several factors as well as perception. It is difficult to quantify the acceptable risk exactly, but for commercial drivers, exposure, the number of hours on the road, and the severity of the adverse consequence, fatality, or injury, must be considered. In most fatal truck accidents, the occupants of passenger vehicles are more likely to be more seriously injured, and, for these reasons, the acceptable risk for commercial drivers should be less than that for drivers of private vehicles [1]. The Canadian Cardiovascular Society suggested that for cardiac disease, the yearly risk for sudden cardiac incapacitation for commercial drivers should be < 1 percent [20].

When performing a commercial driver medical examination, the medical examiner should ask the same cardiac questions as for any other patient. Responses on the history portion of the examination form should be reviewed with the driver. Questions asked should include

Do you have chest pain?
Do you have shortness of breath? With activity? At rest?
Do you have difficulty lying flat at night?
Do you have episodes of dizziness or light-headedness?
Do you have palpitations?

For many years, examiners also relied on the report from the Conference on Cardiac Disorders and Commercial Drivers [21]. In 2002, this was replaced by the Cardiovascular Advisory Panel Guidelines for the Medical Examination of Commercial Motor Vehicle Drivers [15]. There were several changes from the 1987 recommendations including shortening the waiting period after an MI and directing that, for many conditions, the ejection fraction (EF) should be determined. Implantable defibrillators had not been discussed in earlier guidance and in the advisory panel report were recommended to be disqualifying. This document is very well written and researched and contains recommendation tables for ease of use. Many of these tables are adapted for use in this chapter. Examiners should review the full report, because the background information is both interesting and useful.

This chapter does not cover all of the details or diagnoses but focuses on those that the medical examiner is most likely to encounter. It is explained in the guidelines that although these are recommendations from the advisory panel and are not law, they should be followed. They are intended as standards of practice for medical examiners.

In April 2007, the Medical Expert Panel on Cardiovascular Disease and Commercial Motor Vehicle Safety presented their finding and recommendations to the medical review board [19]. These recommendations were mostly accepted by the board and it is anticipated that many if not all of these recommendations will become incorporated into the medical examination process by the FMCSA.

The expert panel suggested that examiners expand the physical examination when coronary heart disease (CHD) disease is present or suspected. Occasionally, the history as offered may not be accurate. Examiners have learned of patients who denied having heart disease on the form, only to reveal on further questioning that they are taking multiple cardiac medications or on examination are found to have prominent chest scars. The Canadian Cardiovascular Society noted that "symptoms may change when some privilege or economic benefit is involved" [20]. While in some cases drivers may be trying to conceal their medical problems, in other cases they may believe that the medications or the surgery corrected their problem and therefore consider the diagnosis no longer current. The new physical examination form requires the driver to sign and certify that the history is accurate.

A thorough physical examination often will yield more information than the history. Some of the physical findings that may suggest cardiac disease include abnormal BP, irregular pulse, distended neck veins, rales, ascites, peripheral edema, and abnormal heart sounds such as gallops or a murmur.

The remainder of this chapter presents the recommendations of the advisory panel guidelines and the recommendations from the 2007 Medical Expert Panel unless otherwise noted. Examiners may wish to review criteria from other countries or organizations for comparison [22–26].

Ischemic Heart Disease

Next to hypertension, one of the most common cardiovascular conditions encountered in FMCSA examinations is ischemic heart disease (IHD). It is difficult to determine the exact relationship between IHD and motor vehicle accidents. In one study of 2,000 motor vehicle accidents, IHD accounted for 8 percent of accidents caused by driver incapacity [27]. Although 41 percent of deaths from coronary artery disease are sudden, in most cases, the driver would have enough warning to pull over to the side of the road to avert an accident [28]. However, one concern would be the occurrence of an arrhythmia in conjunction with the ischemic event, which could be suddenly incapacitating. Although most cases of sudden cardiac incapacitation were not associated with serious injury, the consequence of such an event depends on traffic density and the speed of vehicle travel [29].

The evaluation of a driver with coronary artery disease should take into account his or her functional reserve and the risk for arrhythmias. A complete medical history and physical examination must be performed, with special attention given to heart size, rhythm, and rate and the presence or absence of abnormal murmurs, gallops, or pulses. EKGs are no longer routinely recommended and should be obtained only if clinically indicated. There is some suggestion that commercial drivers have an increased number of risk factors for CHD [10,30–33].

It was recommended that the examiner obtain information about risk factors by taking a history, from the driver's physician, or through additional testing. Risk factors to be considered are given in Table 4-2. Multiple risk factors alone should not drive the certification decision. Drivers older than 40 years with a Framingham CHD risk for nonfatal MI or CHD death of ≥ 20 percent for 10 years, diabetes mellitus, or peripheral vascular disease (considered to be CHD-risk equivalents) are recommended to be evaluated the same as drivers with known CHD. Tables 4-3 and 4-4 are the National Heart, Lung, and Blood Institute Risk Factors tables [34]. It is important to remember that major cardiovascular risk factors (e.g., smoking, elevated BP, elevated serum total cholesterol and low-density lipoprotein cholesterol levels, low-serum high-density lipoprotein cholesterol level, diabetes mellitus, and advancing age) are additive. The other major risk factors (i.e., obesity and physical inactivity) also are associated with an increase risk, although

Table 4-2. Cardiovascular Risk Factors

Modifiable	Nonmodifiable
Hypertension (systolic BP >140 mm Hg or diastolic BP > 90 mm Hg)	History of premature heart disease in first-degree relative
Tobacco smoking	Increasing age (> 60 years)
Hypercholesterolemia	Sex (men and postmenopausal women)
Low high-density lipoprotein cholesterol	
Diabetes mellitus	
Overweight or obesity	
Physical inactivity	

BP = blood pressure.
Source: Adapted from Blumenthal R, Braunstein J, Connolly H, Epstein A, Gersh BJ, Wittels EH. *Cardiovascular Advisory Panel Guidelines for the Medical Examination of Commercial Motor Vehicle Drivers.* FMCSA-MCP-02-002. Washington: U.S. Department of Transportation, Federal Motor Carrier Safety Administration.

Table 4-3. Estimate of 10-Year Risk of Myocardial Infarction and Coronary Death in Men

Age	Points
20–34	−9
35–39	−4
40–44	0
45–49	3
50–54	6
55–59	8
60–64	1o
65–69	11
70–74	12
75–79	13

Total Cholesterol	Points				
	Age 20–39	Age 40–49	Age 50–59	Age 60–69	Age 70–79
<160	0	0	0	0	0
161–199	4	3	2	1	0
200–239	7	5	3	1	0
240–279	9	6	4	2	1
≥280	11	8	5	3	1

	Points				
	Age 20–39	Age 40–49	Age 50–59	Age 60–69	Age 70–79
Nonsmoker	0	0	0	0	0
Smoker	8	5	3	1	1

HDL (mg/dL)	Points
≥60	−1
50–59	0
40–49	1
< 40	2

Systolic BP (mm Hg)	If Untreated	If Treated
<120	0	0
120–129	0	1
130–139	1	2
140–159	1	2
≥160	2	3

Point Total	10 Year Risk %
<0	<1
0	1
1	1
2	1
3	1
4	1
5	2
6	2
7	3
8	4
9	5
10	6
11	8
12	10
13	12
14	16
15	20
16	25
≥17	≥30

Source: Executive Summary of the Third Report of the National Cholesterol Education Program (NCEP) Expert Panel on the Detection, Evaluation, and Treatment of High Blood Cholesterol in Adults (Adult Treatment Panel III).

Table 4-4. Estimate of 10-Year Risk of Myocardial Infarction and Coronary Death in Women

Age	Points
20–34	−7
35–39	−3
40–44	0
45–49	3
50–54	6
55–59	8
60–64	10
65–69	12
70–74	14
75–79	16

Total Cholesterol	Points				
	Age 20–39	Age 40–49	Age 50–59	Age 60–69	Age 70–79
<160	0	0	0	0	0
161–199	4	3	2	1	1
200–239	8	6	4	2	1
240–279	11	8	5	3	2
≥280	13	10	7	4	2

	Points				
	Age 20–39	Age 40–49	Age 50–59	Age 60–69	Age 70–79
Nonsmoker	0	0	0	0	0
Smoker	9	7	4	2	1

HDL (mg/dL)	Points
≥60	−1
50–59	0
40–49	1
< 40	2

Systolic BP (mm Hg)	If Untreated	If Treated
<120	0	0
120–129	1	3
130–139	2	4
140–159	3	5
≥160	4	6

Point Total	10 Year Risk %
<9	<1
9	1
10	1
11	1
12	1
13	2
14	2
15	3
16	4
17	5
18	6
19	8
20	11
21	14
22	17
23	22
24	27
≥25	≥30

Source: Executive Summary of the Third Report of the National Cholesterol Education Program (NCEP) Expert Panel on the Detection, Evaluation, and Treatment of High Blood Cholesterol in Adults (Adult Treatment Panel III).

their individual and quantitative contributions are not as well defined [35].

The advisory panel did not recommend for or against an exercise tolerance test (ETT) in asymptomatic individuals based on risk factors alone. An examiner still may determine that an ETT is appropriate. The U.S. Preventive Services Task Force does not recommend routine screening by exercise testing for all individuals. In the discussion, however, they acknowledge that for individuals in "certain occupations, such as pilots and heavy equipment operators, where sudden death or incapacitation would endanger the safety of others, considerations other than benefit to the individual patients may favor screening. Although screening cannot reliably identify all persons at risk of an acute event, it may increase the margin of safety for the public" [36]. Each driver should be evaluated on an individual basis, and additional testing should be recommended for those who seem to be at higher risk, and those with the highest risk should be evaluated the same as a driver with CHD.

For those drivers in whom an ETT is appropriate, in those with and without known heart disease, the panel recommended that the driver be able to attain at least 6 METs (through Bruce Stage II or equivalent), have no ischemic changes on exercise ECG, or no ischemic segments on myocardial imaging if performed. They should be able to attain ≥ 85 percent maximum predicted heart rate (unless on beta-blockers), have a rise in systolic BP of ≥ 20 mm Hg without angina, and no significant ST-segment depression or elevation.

The 2007 panel [19] recommended that the definition of abnormal ETT be an inability to exceed 6 METs without reference to the protocol used. They also recommended that all drivers with known heart disease have their medications titrated to the optimal dose.

After an MI, there should be a 2-month wait and an evaluation by a cardiologist prior to returning to commercial driving. After an MI, the driver should be examined annually and be asymptomatic. An echocardiogram, measuring ejection fraction (EF) is recommended to assess ventricular function. This could be performed while still in the hospital, but it should demonstrate an EF of ≥ 40 percent. An ETT should be performed 4 to 6 weeks after the MI, and it should be repeated at least every 2 years, more often if indicated. The driver also should not have any side effects from medication, including orthostatic symptoms.

A definition of MI was published by the Joint European Society/ American College of Cardiology Committee in 2000 [37]. The new criteria include those patients with elevated troponin I levels but no elevation of the peak creatinine kinase–MB fraction. More patients who were not considered to have had an MI now meet the criteria. Those who published the new criteria acknowledged that the increased accuracy in diagnosing acute MI may result in consequences for patients, including professional careers. In one study [38], those who were diagnosed by an elevated troponin I level, regardless of ECG changes or creatinine kinase–MB levels, had similar rates of in-hospital events and mortality. They also had a worse, although not statistically significant, 6-month mortality than those diagnosed by the old criteria. This group of patients would not have been identified as having had an acute MI by the old criteria. Even if there is an issue of whether the driver is diagnosed as having had an MI, in this context, they would at least be considered to have unstable angina. If not determined to have had an MI, the certification determination should follow the recommendations for unstable angina.

Angina pectoris usually is caused by narrowing or spasm in one or more coronary arteries. It can either be stable or unstable. If there has not been angina at rest and symptoms have been stable without a change in the pattern of the angina for at least 3 months, the driver can be qualified after examination and approved to drive by a driver's physician, usually a cardiologist. He or she should have an annual qualification examination and an ETT performed at least every 2 years. In addition, it is recommended that he or she be asymptomatic both from the disease and from the medications (no light-headedness); no resting systolic BP < 95 mm Hg and no systolic BP decline > 20 mm Hg upon standing. The MEP recommended that a driver with a stable pattern of angina could be certified rather than the current criteria of asymptomatic.

Percutaneous coronary interventions (PCIs) can be performed in either the acute (MI or unstable angina) or chronic coronary insufficiency setting. If the PCI is performed electively to treat stable angina, the driver could return to work after 1 week with examination and approval of the treating cardiologist. There should be no damage to the vascular site. An ETT is recommended 3 to 6 months after the procedure, with an appropriate result as defined previously. Those drivers who are symptomatic, have an abnormal resting ECG, or are unable to meet the minimum ETT standards should have stress radionuclide or echocardiogram performed. Drivers who have undergone PCIs should have annual medical qualification examinations and a negative ETT at least every 2 years. In addition, it is recommended that they be asymptomatic both from the disease and from the medications (no light-headedness); no resting systolic BP < 95 mm Hg and no systolic BP decline > 20 mm Hg upon standing. If the PCI is performed because of an MI or unstable angina, the recommended waiting period for those conditions should apply.

The American College of Cardiology, American Heart Association, and Society for Cardiovascular and Angiography Interventions [39–40] no longer recommend testing 6 to 9 months after PCI and therefore the MEP recommended eliminating the requirement for an ETT 3 to 6 months following a PCI.

A waiting period of 3 months still is recommended prior to returning to work as a commercial motor vehicle operator after CABG. This is to allow for sufficient time for sternal wound healing. Examination and approval by a cardiologist should precede return to work, and the driver should undergo annual medical certification examinations. ETTs were not recommended prior to return to work, and there was no specific recommendation as to the frequency of ETTs within 5 years of CABG. When an ETT is performed, the driver should be able to meet the earlier criteria and should not have any ventricular dysrhythmias. The examiner should have a low threshold for requiring radionuclide stress testing or echocardiographic myocardial imaging in these individuals. These are indicated if the driver cannot meet the ETT criteria, has a dysrhythmia, or has an abnormal ECG. A resting echocardiogram is recommended at or prior to the first qualifying examination after the procedure (in-hospital after CABG is acceptable), and the driver's EF should not be < 40 percent. Orthostatic symptoms or other side effects from medications also would be cause for disqualification.

For consistency, the MEP recommended that after annual recertification examinations for the first 5 years after a CABG, rather than an ETT every year, it be performed every 2 years as is recommended for drivers who have had an MI or have angina pectoris.

Table 4-5 summarizes the recommendations from the 2002 report for drivers with ischemic heart disease.

Hypertension

It appears likely that drivers with hypertension may have an increased risk of motor vehicle crashes, especially with the presence of end-organ damage and that that hypertension is not an all-or-nothing diagnosis and that with increasing arterial pressure, the rates of coronary heart disease and death from all causes increase [41]. It is important to measure blood pressure accurately and in those cases where white-coat hypertension may be a concern, 24-hour ambulatory monitoring may be useful and may also be a better predictor of risk [42].

The hypertension recommendations from the advisory panel were reviewed earlier in this chapter. The MEP made several significant

Table 4-5. Recommendations for the Commercial Driver with Ischemic Heart Disease

Diagnosis	Certification	Recertification
Post-MI	Yes if ≥ 2 months post-MI No recurrent anginal symptoms Cleared by a cardiologist Post-MI EF ≥ 40 percent, ETT 4–6 weeks post-MI (completes Stage II of Bruce Protocol—6 METs, 85 percent maximal predicted heart rate, rise in systolic BP ≥ 20 mm Hg without angina, no significant ST-segment depression, tolerance to medication)	Annual with ETT at least every 2 years If ETT is positive or inconclusive, imaging test recommended Cardiologist evaluation recommended
Angina pectoris	Yes if asymptomatic No if change in anginal pattern within 3 months or rest angina, abnormal ETT, ischemic changes on rest ECG, intolerance to medications	Annual, with ETT at least every 2 years If ETT is positive or inconclusive, imaging test recommended Cardiologist evaluation recommended
Post-PCI	Yes if not in the setting of MI or unstable angina, at least 1 week after procedure, clearance by a cardiologist and tolerance to medication, no complication at vascular access-site, and no ischemic changes on ECG ETT 3–6 months post-PCI	Annual ETT at least every 2 years if ET is positive or inconclusive, imaging test recommended Cardiologist evaluation recommended

Source: Adapted from Blumenthal R, Braunstein J, Connolly H, Epstein A, Gersh BJ, Wittels EH. *Cardiovascular Advisory Panel Guidelines for the Medical Examination of Commercial Motor Vehicle Drivers.* FMCSA-MCP-02-002. Washington: U.S. Department of Transportation, Federal Motor Carrier Safety Administration.

recommendations to modify these. First they recommended that the following general principles be included:

a. Certification and recertification of individuals with hypertension should be based on blood pressure, the presence of target organ damage, and comorbidities.
b. Blood pressure recorded at the certification (or recertification) examination should be used to determine blood pressure stage.

   1. The certifying examiner may decide on the length of certification for drivers with elevated blood pressure despite treatment.

c. All CMV drivers should be referred to their personal physician for therapy, education, and long-term management.
d. It should be expected that blood pressure have been measured appropriately.

It was clarified that target blood pressure should be < 140 / < 90 and that blood pressure medication has been appropriately titrated. Additional recommendations are that drivers be properly educated about proper lifestyle and compliance with medication and that the hypertension stages be consistent with JNC VII [18].

Valvular Heart Disease

Individuals with valvular heart disease will have degrees of disability ranging from none to severe impairment. The advisory panel drew many of their recommendations from the American College of Cardiology (ACC)/American Heart Association (AHA) Guidelines for the Management of Patients with Valvular Heart Disease [43]. Evaluation should be by a cardiologist and with initial evaluation including a history, physical examination, and ECG, and in many patients a chest X-ray. Depending on the specific diagnosis, ECG or ETT may be indicated. The 2007 MEP did not suggest any changes to these guidelines.

Mitral Stenosis. In addition to the standard initial evaluation, two-dimensional Doppler echocardiography should be performed. Stress testing may be indicated to assess effort tolerance and the effect of the stenosis on functional capacity. The normal mitral valve area is 4 to 6 cm^2, with severe mitral stenosis defined as a valve area of $\leq$ 1.0 cm^2, a resting mean pressure gradient $\geq$ 10 mm Hg, or a pressure half-time of $\geq$ 220 msec. Symptoms, the presence of atrial fibrillation, or systolic embolization also should be considered in addition to valve area. Drivers with either mild or moderate mitral stenosis can be certified annually if they are asymptomatic. They should be evaluated annually by a cardiologist, and a two-dimensional Doppler echocardiography usually would be appropriate. Drivers should be disqualified if their symptoms place them in New York Heart Association Class II or higher (Table 4-6), they have paroxysmal or established atrial fibrillation, or they have a history of systolic embolization. If the pulmonary artery pressure is ≥ 50 percent of systemic pressure or the driver is unable to exercise for > 6 METs on Bruce protocol ETT, he or she also should not be certified. If a percutaneous balloon valvuloplasty is performed, the driver could be certified after at least a 4-week wait or after at least a 3-month wait for a surgical commissurotomy provided there are no thromboembolic complications after surgery, and pulmonary

Table 4-6. New York Heart Association Functional Capacity

Functional Capacity	Objective Assessment
Class I. Patients with cardiac disease but without resulting limitation of physical activity. Ordinary physical activity does not cause undue fatigue, palpitation, dyspnea, or anginal pain.	**A.** No objective evidence of cardiovascular disease.
Class II. Patients with cardiac disease resulting in slight limitation of physical activity. They are comfortable at rest. Ordinary physical activity results in fatigue, palpitation, dyspnea, or anginal pain.	**B.** Objective evidence of minimal cardiovascular disease.
Class III. Patients with cardiac disease resulting in marked limitation of physical activity. They are comfortable at rest. Less-than-ordinary activity causes fatigue, palpitation, dyspnea, or anginal pain.	**C.** Objective evidence of moderately severe cardiovascular disease.
Class IV. Patients with cardiac disease resulting in inability to carry on any physical activity without discomfort. Symptoms of heart failure or the anginal syndrome may be present even at rest. If any physical activity is undertaken, discomfort is increased.	**D.** Objective evidence of severe cardiovascular disease.

Source: American Heart Association.
www.americanheart.org/presenter.jhtml?identifier=4569. Accessed June 5, 2007.

artery pressure is not ≥ 50 percent of systemic BP. In either circumstance, the driver should be recertified annually with an annual evaluation by a cardiologist.

Mitral Regurgitation. The standard initial evaluation is a chest X-ray and a two-dimensional Doppler echocardiogram. Stress testing should be obtained if needed to assess effort tolerance and symptomatic status if unclear. In some cases, transesophageal echocardiography may be appropriate. Drivers with severe mitral regurgitation who are symptomatic or have reduced effort tolerance (≤ 6 METs or ≤ 6 minutes on a Bruce protocol), ruptured chordae or flail leaflet, atrial fibrillation, or thromboembolism should be disqualified. Other recommendations for disqualification include left ventricular dysfunction (EF < 60 percent or left ventricular end systolic dimension > 45 mm or left ventricular end diastolic dimension ≥ 70 mm) or pulmonary hypertension (pulmonary artery pressure > 50 percent systemic arterial pressure). Those with severe mitral regurgitation who are asymptomatic and do not meet the previously mentioned disqualifying criteria can be medically qualified but should be recertified annually with an echocardiogram every 6 to 12 months and stress testing to assess effort tolerance. Those with mild or moderate mitral regurgitation can be qualified if they are asymptomatic, have normal left ventricular size and function, and have normal pulmonary artery pressure. They should be recertified annually. Annual echocardiography is not required with mild regurgitation but is indicated annually for those with moderate disease.

If the individual has undergone surgical repair of the mitral valve, there should be at least a 3-month waiting period after the procedure. For follow-up certifications, drivers should be asymptomatic.

Aortic Stenosis. Patients with aortic stenosis tend to do well during a latent period, during which they may be asymptomatic. Once symptoms of angina, syncope, or congestive heart failure develop, prognosis is poor, with survival of < 3 years. Sudden death also has been seen in patients with aortic stenosis who were asymptomatic but with a positive stress test and a valve area of ≤ 0.6 cm^2 [44]. The initial evaluation should include the history and physical examination, ECG, and two-dimensional Doppler echocardiography to assess gradient, valve area, and severity of left ventricular hypertrophy. Cardiac catheterization and coronary angiography may be needed, and ETT is occasionally required to assess symptoms, effort tolerance, and prognosis. Table 4-7 contains the recommendations for the commercial driver with aortic stenosis.

Aortic Regurgitation. In addition to the standard evaluation, chest X-ray and two-dimensional echocardiography should be obtained. ETT may be useful for those who are sedentary or if symptoms are

Table 4-7. Recommendations for the Commercial Driver with Aortic Stenosis

Diagnosis	Certification	Recertification
Mild aortic stenosis (AVA ≥ 1.5 cm²)	Yes, if asymptomatic	Annual Echocardiogram every 5 years
Moderate aortic stenosis (AVA ≥ 1.0–1.5 cm²)	Yes if asymptomatic	Annual Echocardiogram every 1–2 years
	Yes if ≥ 3 months after surgery	Annual
	No if: Angina; heart failure; syncope; atrial fibrillation; LV dysfunction with EF < 50 percent; thromboembolism	
Severe aortic stenosis (AVA < 1.0 cm²)	No, irrespective of symptoms or LV function	Annual
	Yes, if ≥ 3 months after surgery	

AVA = aortic valve area; EF = ejection fraction; LV = left ventricular.
Source: Adapted from Blumenthal R, Braunstein J, Connolly H, Epstein A, Gersh BJ, Wittels EH. *Cardiovascular Advisory Panel Guidelines for the Medical Examination of Commercial Motor Vehicle Drivers.* FMCSA-MCP-02-002. Washington: U.S. Department of Transportation, Federal Motor Carrier Safety Administration, October 2002.

equivocal. Drivers with severe aortic regurgitation should be disqualified if they are symptomatic or unable to obtain > 6 METs on ETT, have a reduced EF of ≤ 50 percent, or if they have an end systolic dimension > 55 mm or end diastolic dimension 70 mm with normal EF or if they are in atrial fibrillation. A second examination by a cardiologist is recommended 2 to 3 months after the initial evaluation to determine whether there has been progression of the condition. Drivers who are asymptomatic with mild or moderate aortic regurgitation should be recertified annually with an echocardiogram every 2 to 3 years. For severe disease refer to Table 4-8. After valve repair, there should be a 3-month waiting period, clearance by a cardiologist, and no thromboembolic complications.

   Prosthetic Valve Repair. After valve repair with a mechanical prosthetic valve, commercial drivers can return to work after at least a

Table 4-8. Recommendations for the Commercial Driver with Aortic Regurgitation

Diagnosis	Certification	Recertification
Mild aortic regurgitation	Yes if asymptomatic	Annual Echocardiogram every 2–3 years
Moderate aortic regurgitation	Yes if: Normal LV function No or mild LV enlargement	Annual Echocardiogram every 2–3 years
Severe aortic regurgitation	Yes if: Asymptomatic Normal LV function (EF ≥ 50 percent) LV dilatation LVEDD < 60 mm LVESD < 50 mm	Every 6 months Echocardiogram every 6–12 months
	If LVEDD ≥ 60 mm or LVESD ≥ 50 mm: No if: Symptoms Unable to complete Stage II of Bruce protocol Reduced EF < 50 percent LV dilatation LVEDD > 70 mm or LVESD > 55 mm Yes if: Valve surgery and ≥ 3 months since surgery	Every 4–6 months Echocardiogram every 4–6 months if no surgery performed
	Asymptomatic and cleared by cardiologist	Annual

EF = ejection fraction; LV = left ventricular; LVEDD = LV end diastolic dimension; LVESD = LV end systolic dimension.
Source: Adapted from Blumenthal R, Braunstein J, Connolly H, Epstein A, Gersh BJ, Wittels EH. *Cardiovascular Advisory Panel Guidelines for the Medical Examination of Commercial Motor Vehicle Drivers.* FMCSA-MCP-02-002. Washington: U.S. Department of Transportation, Federal Motor Carrier Safety Administration, FMCSA-MCP-02-002. October 2002.

3-month wait and clearance by a cardiologist provided they are asymptomatic. They should not be qualified if they have left ventricular dysfunction (EF < 40 percent), thromboembolic complications postprocedure, or pulmonary hypertension or if they are unable to maintain adequate anticoagulation. The international normalized ratio (INR) should be monitored monthly. If a biologic prosthetic valve is used, the same criteria should be used except that anticoagulation is not necessary if there is no history of emboli or a hypercoagulable state. Those drivers who have atrial fibrillation after valve repair can be certified after the appropriate waiting period and if they are adequately anticoagulated for at least 1 month and monitored monthly by INR. The rate should be controlled and they should be cleared by a cardiologist.

Myocardial Disease

Since the publication of the Cardiovascular Advisory Panel Report [15], the classifications of cardiomyopathies have changed [45]. A new definition for cardiomyopathy was recommended:

> *Cardiomyopathies are a heterogeneous group of diseases of the myocardium associated with mechanical and/or electrical dysfunction that usually (but not invariably) exhibit inappropriate ventricular hypertrophy or dilatation and are due to a variety of causes that frequently are genetic. Cardiomyopathies either are confined to the heart or are part of generalized systemic disorders, often leading to cardiovascular death or progressive heart failure–related disability.*

The authors recommended that cardiomyopathies be classified into two major categories, based on predominant organ involvement. Primary cardiomyopathies (genetic, nongenetic, acquired) are those solely or predominantly confined to heart muscle while secondary cardiomyopathies have myocardial involvement as part generalized systemic disorders. Although many of the recommendations based on category of cardiomyopathy are still applicable, the MEP recommended updating the classifications to reflect the new guidelines.

In 2002, it was recommended that drivers with echocardiographically diagnosed hypertrophic cardiomyopathy (HCM) not be qualified. Those with borderline hypertrophic cardiomyopathy, hypertensive hypertrophic cardiomyopathy, or other similar diagnoses could be qualified but should be reevaluated after 1 year. With the current recognition that not all patients with HCM are at high risk of sudden incapacitation, the MEP recommended that since the individuals who meet the following criteria are at lower risk [46] they could be medically certified.

- No history of cardiac arrest
- No spontaneous sustained ventricular tachycardia (VT)
- Normal exercise blood pressure (e.g., no decrease at maximal exercise)
- No nonsustained VT
- No family history of premature sudden death
- No syncope
- Left ventricular septum thickness < 30 mm

Current guidelines on drivers with congestive cardiac failure or idiopathic dilated cardiomyopathy state that those with an EF of < 40 percent should be disqualified. If a subsequent evaluation demonstrates an improved EF ≥ 40 percent or more, the driver can be recertified if asymptomatic. Evaluation should include two-dimensional Doppler echocardiography to assess EF, left ventricular size, and/or valvular heart disease. Radionuclide ventriculography or ETT may be indicated in some patients. Drivers should not be qualified if they have symptomatic congestive cardiac function. If they are asymptomatic with an EF of ≤ 50 percent but with either sustained or nonsustained ventricular tachycardia or symptomatic palpitations, they should not be qualified. Drivers can be considered for certification after disqualification if symptoms resolve, they do not have ventricular arrhythmia, and the EF improves to ≥ 40 percent. If certified, these drivers should be evaluated annually with echocardiography and Holter monitoring.

New recommendations suggest modifying the criteria to disqualifying those drivers who have sustained ventricular arrhythmia for 30 seconds or more if intervention is required or if the LVEF is ≤ 40 percent.

There was no change to the recommendation that due to a poor prognosis, drivers with restrictive cardiomyopathy should be disqualified.

Cardiac Arrhythmias, Pacemakers, and Implantable Defibrillators

Arrhythmias are the cardiac disorders most likely to suddenly impair a driver. Driving generally is safe for most individuals with arrhythmias, but incapacitation can occur suddenly and unpredictably. The initial evaluation should include a medical history and a review of records, physical examination, and additional testing as indicated. In addition to the advisory panel report, one of the best reviews on the effect of arrhythmias on consciousness and the impact on public safety is by the AHA and the North American Society of Pacing and Electrophysiology (NAS) and their recent update [25–26].

Atrial fibrillation generally is seen in older patients and usually is associated with some type of cardiovascular or metabolic diseases (e.g., thyrotoxicosis). In healthy young individuals, atrial fibrillation may occur with no identifiable underlying disease, lone atrial fibrillation. Those individuals could be certified with annual recertification.

Some patients are at increased risk of stroke with atrial fibrillation. The 2007 MEP [19] recommended providing details on how examiners should evaluate risk of stroke from embolization from atrial fibrillation. The CHADS$_2$ (Cardiac Failure, Hypertension, Age, Diabetes, Stroke and Transient Ischemic Attack) [47] model is the most appropriate. In this model, two points are assigned for those with a history of stroke or TIA and one point for age over 75, history of hypertension, diabetes, or heart failure. Those with scores of about one to three are at intermediate risk and some will suggest anticoagulation while others will recommend anticoagulation for those with higher risk [48]. The American College of Cardiology, American Heart Association, and European College of Cardiology offered the recommendations in Table 4-9 [48]. They indicated previous stroke, TIA or embolism, mitral

Table 4-9. ACC/AHA/ESC Recommendation for Antithrombotic Therapy for Patients with Atrial Fibrillation

Risk Category	Recommended Treatment
No risk factors	Aspirin, 81 to 325 mg daily
One moderate-risk factor	Aspirin, 81 to 325 mg daily, or warfarin
Any high-risk factor or more than 1 moderate-risk factor	Warfarin

Source: Adapted from Fuster V, Ryden LE, Cannom DS, et al. ACC/AHA/ESC 2006 Guidelines for the Management of Patients with Atrial Fibrillation—Executive Summary: A Report of the American College of Cardiology/American Heart Association Task Force on Practice Guidelines and the European Society of Cardiology Committee for Practice Guidelines (Writing Committee to Revise the 2001 Guidelines for the Management of Patients with Atrial Fibrillation): Developed in Collaboration with the European Heart Rhythm Association and the Heart Rhythm Society. *Circulation* 2006;114:700–752.

stenosis, or a prosthetic heart valve would be high-risk factors and age ≥ 75 years, hypertension, heart failure, LV EF ≤ 35 percent, or diabetes should be considered moderate-risk factors. If warfarin is used, the INR should be between 2.0 and 3.0 with the target 2.5 except in those with a mechanical valve in whom the target should be greater than 2.5. Those patients, who are anticoagulated, should be adequately anticoagulated for at least 1 month and be monitored monthly by INR, with annual recertification. Their rate and rhythm should be adequately controlled, determined preferably by a cardiologist.

If the fibrillation occurs following thoracic surgery, the drivers also should be controlled on anticoagulants for at least 1 month and be followed monthly by INR, with clearance by a cardiologist. Recertification should be annually. Drivers with Wolf-Parkinson-White syndrome and atrial fibrillation should not be medically qualified. In general, atrial flutter should be handled in the same manner as atrial fibrillation. If isthmus ablation is performed, the driver can return to work at least 1 month after the procedure provided the arrhythmia is successfully treated. Clearance should be by an electrophysiologist, with annual recertification.

Drivers with multifocal atrial tachycardia can be medically qualified provided they are asymptomatic or the symptoms are controlled and the multifocal atrial tachycardia is not associated with another condition that is disqualifying, such as severe pulmonary disease. Recertification should be annual.

Ventricular arrhythmias carry a higher risk of sudden incapacitation and may be the cause of the majority of sudden cardiac deaths. Drivers with CHD and sustained ventricular tachycardia, nonsustained ventricular tachycardia (NSVT) with an EF < 40 percent, or symptomatic NSVT with an EF of ≥ 40 percent should not be certified. If the driver has NSVT with an EF ≥ 40 percent and is currently asymptomatic, he or she can be certified at least 1 month after successful drug or other treatment, with clearance by a cardiologist. Recertification should be annual, with examination by a cardiologist.

With a diagnosis of dilated cardiomyopathy, the driver should not be certified if sustained ventricular tachycardia, NSVT with an EF ≤ 40 percent, or episodes of syncope or near syncope occur.

Drivers with long QT interval syndrome or Brugada syndrome should not be medically certified. Bundle branch block can progress, leading to third-degree heart block. Drivers who are symptomatic should not be certified. If the individual is asymptomatic and the risk from any underlying heart disease is acceptable, he or she can be certified for up to 2 years. If the driver is currently under treatment for a disease that has been symptomatic, has no underlying cardiac disease, and is cleared by a cardiologist, he or she can be certified but should be recertified annually.

With sinus node dysfunction or atrioventricular block, the driver should not be certified until at least 1 month after pacemaker insertion, provided that underlying heart disease is not disqualifying. Recertification should be annual, with documented pacemaker checks.

Although the regulations clearly state that a driver with a cardiovascular condition that may be accompanied by syncope should not be qualified to drive, the 2002 Cardiovascular Advisory Panel did not provide specific guidance on a driver who experienced a single episode of syncope. In many cases, the etiology of the event will remain unknown. Some recommend that for drivers in whom a clearly identified, nonrecurring cause can be shown (i.e., fainting from the sight of blood, prolonged standing, or fear), there be no restriction. However, for those in whom the cause is not so obvious, further testing should be done [49]. This may include evaluations by neurologists or cardiologists. One study reviewed the approaches of arrhythmia specialists in nine countries on determining when an individual could return safely to driving [50] and found that the majority used the tilt-table test to substantiate the diagnosis of vasovagal syncope yet overused it to evaluate treatment efficiency. Participants in this study also suggested that syncope that occurred in a sitting position should be more of a concern than if it occurred in a standing position. The average suggested wait was a minimum of 2 months after successful treatment, with a range of no restriction to never returning the individual to driving. Almost all would be more conservative when dealing with a commercial driver.

The MEP [19] recommended that examiner should be provided with sufficient documentation to distinguish cardiogenic syncope from syncope due to other causes. Evaluation of the patient with syncope should begin with a detailed history and physical examination, EKG, and review of medications. In the majority of cases, the cause can be identified but in about 40 percent of cases, it remains unexplained [51]. History should focus on factors that can differentiate cardiac from noncardiac causes such as an aura, prodrome, postictal confusion, or focal neurologic deficits. Tonic-clonic movement can be seen with both cardiac and neurologic syncopal episodes. The presence or absence of orthostatic hypotension, carotid bruits, or neurologic abnormalities should be noted. If these are normal, the next steps should be an echocardiogram, exercise test, and evaluation for ischemia. Further evaluation was not recommended for a single episode of syncope. For frequent episodes, a Holter or event monitor or implantable loop recorder was recommended and for further evaluation of infrequent events, an implantable loop recorder should be used [51].

The 2002 report recommended that drivers with symptoms from neurocardiogenic syncope or hypersensitive carotid sinus with syncope should not be certified unless a pacemaker has been inserted and after a 3-month wait. That was recommended as the cardioinhibitory (slowing of heart rate) will be treated by the pacemaker while the pacemaker may not entirely correct the vasodepressor (drop in BP) component of the syndrome. Absence of symptom recurrence and documentation of correct pacemaker function should be required prior to certification. Recertification should be annual, with pacemaker checks and no recurrence of symptoms. Based on more recent studies, a pacemaker should no longer be accepted as definitive treatment for neurocardiogenic syncope [52–54].

Implantable cardioverter defibrillators (ICDs) are now increasingly being used in patients for both primary and secondary prevention. They do not prevent the arrhythmias but attempt to terminate the arrhythmia once it occurs. After a ventricular arrhythmia occurs, it may take 20 seconds for an ICD to discharge; during this time, a driver may lose consciousness. Drivers who have had an ICD implanted after cardiac arrest or hemodynamically significant ventricular tachycardia should not be certified. Drivers who have an ICD placed for primary prevention are believed to be at sufficient risk of sudden death that they should not be operating commercial motor vehicles [25–27,54,55]. In the majority of these patients, the cardiac function, LVEF will be < 40 percent, which by itself is a disqualifying condition. The 2007 MEP recommended upholding the prohibition of the medical certification of drivers with ICDS.

Congenital Heart Disease

Most drivers with symptom-limiting congenital heart disease will select themselves out of the commercial driver pool. With improvements in medical and surgical treatment, the examiner may see an increasing number of drivers with congenital heart disease. The decision to qualify should be based on the specific diagnosis, current symptoms, and the natural history of the disease, including early and late complications. The evaluation should include a medical history and a complete review of all pertinent medical records, a complete history and physical examination, a chest X-ray, and a comprehensive two-dimensional Doppler echocardiogram. In drivers in whom cardiac arrhythmias are a concern, ambulatory monitoring at rest and during exercise should be done. In some cases, an ETT also would be useful. For drivers who had recently undergone surgery, at least a 3-month wait and clearance by a cardiologist knowledgeable in adult congenital heart disease is recommended. Drivers with congenital heart disease, whether having undergone surgical repair or followed medically, should be recertified annually with evaluation by a cardiologist knowledgeable in adult congenital heart disease. For recommendations on specific conditions, refer to the advisory panel guidelines.

Vascular Disease

Examiners should ensure that drivers with a history of vascular disease do not also have associated coronary artery or cerebrovascular disease.

The advisory panel recommended that all abdominal aortic aneurysms > 5 cm should be disqualifying due to the high risk of rupture. The 2007 MEP recommended that this be increased to 5.5 cm for men [19]. Based on current literature [56], they also recommended that if the AAA is between 4.0 and 5.4 cm, drivers could be certified if asymptomatic and cleared by a vascular surgeon who indicates that surgery is not indicated. If surgery is not planned and there are no symptoms, the driver could be qualified annually and the size of the aneurysm followed by ultrasound. It had been recommended that drivers with aneurysms of the thoracic aorta be disqualified if the aneurysm diameter is > 3.5 cm; this was recommended to be increased to 5.0 cm.

Drivers who have undergone surgery for repair of abdominal aortic aneurysm, thoracic aortic aneurysm, or aneurysm of another vessel should not be cleared for commercial driving for at least 3 months and should obtain clearance from a cardiovascular specialist. Guidance was recommended to be added that drivers who have undergone endovascular AAA repair must comply with accepted follow-up protocol with their annual examinations. The risk of leaks at 1 year ranges from 17–31 percent and there is a 10–20 percent risk of need for second surgery and risk of rupture of 0.4–1 percent. For these reasons, annual contrast CT of the abdomen is recommended [57].

Peripheral vascular disease may present with intermittent claudication. If there are no other disqualifying cardiovascular conditions, the driver can be certified but should be recertified annually. It had been recommended that the driver with pain at rest be disqualified from operating commercial vehicles. There should be at least a 3-month wait after surgery or angioplasty for peripheral vascular disease, and these drivers should also be recertified annually. The 2007 MEP recommended that drivers with DVT should only be disqualified if it occurs at rest [19].

Deep venous thrombosis (DVT) can result in local complications as well as pulmonary emboli, a cause of sudden incapacitation. DVTs should be disqualifying until the driver is adequately treated. This includes no residual acute DVT, and if on Coumadin, regulated for at least 1 month, with the INR monitored at least monthly.

The MEP [19] recommended clarifying this to include the following:

1. Active DVT should disqualify an individual from driving a CMV.
2. Individuals who have experienced DVT that has resolved should be maintained on anticoagulation with a vitamin K antagonist for a minimum of 3 months (preferably 6 months) following resolution.
3. If on a vitamin K antagonist such as warfarin (Coumadin), drivers need to be regulated at least 1 month prior to certification (or recertification) and have their INR monitored at least monthly thereafter.
4. International normalized ratio should be maintained within the target range: 2.0–3.0.
5. Individuals treated with subcutaneous heparin or low molecular weight heparin may be certified (or recertified) to drive a CMV as soon as the DVT has resolved.

If there were pulmonary emboli, drivers should not be certified for at least 3 months from a pulmonary embolus. They should be on appropriate long-term therapy, and if Coumadin is used, the dosage should be regulated for at least 1 month, with follow-up INR at least monthly. These drivers should be recertified as least annually.

The advisory panel recommended that the Coumadin dosage be regulated for at least 1 month prior to returning to commercial driving, not just on the medication for 1 month. In July 1996, the FHWA responded to the question of whether warfarin is an automatic disqualifier by issuing recommendations on the use of anticoagulants in commercial drivers. They stated that the use of warfarin should be one factor in deciding whether an individual can operate a commercial motor vehicle safely. The following recommendations for evaluating a driver on anticoagulants also were issued by the FHWA at that time. Aside from the recommended 3-month wait, the examiner should consider the other issues described.

1. Warfarin is a medical treatment that can improve the health and safety of a driver by its use and should not be automatically dis-

qualifying. The emphasis should be on the underlying medical condition and the general health of the driver.
2. The examiner is responsible for making the decision and should consult with other physicians who have been treating the driver.
3. The INR should be used to monitor the effect of warfarin.
4. The driver on warfarin should be educated about the interaction of warfarin and other medications and about the increased risk of bleeding with trauma. He or she also should be counseled on the need for regular monitoring.
5. Because of increased sensitivity to warfarin and the risk for significant bleeding, careful consideration should be given prior to qualifying drivers using warfarin who are older than 65 years.
6. Drivers on warfarin with cerebrovascular disease are not recommended to be medically qualified due to the increased risk of intracranial hemorrhage with resulting sudden loss of consciousness.
7. Individuals should not be qualified during the first 3 months of treatment because the risk of side effects is highest during this period.
8. Individuals qualified under 49 CFR 391.41 and on warfarin should be examined yearly to monitor both the effect of warfarin and the underlying disease process.

Varicose veins and superficial thrombophlebitis do not carry a significant risk of embolism. Individuals with these problems can be medically qualified if no other disqualifying abnormalities are found.

Heart Transplantation

Commercial drivers who have had a heart transplantation and want to return to work can be considered after a 1-year wait. They should be asymptomatic, cleared by a cardiologist, and stable on medications. In addition, there should be no signs of rejection. Drivers should be recertified every 6 months after an evaluation by a cardiologist.

Cardiovascular Medications

This area is not covered in the current guidelines but the medical examiner still must review medications and any potential side effects. Reviewing the medication also can provide the examiner with information on a diagnosis that may not have been identified on the history questions. When it is discovered that a driver is on a cardiovascular medication, two main issues need to be addressed. First, what condition is the medication treating, and, second, are there significant side effects from the medication? Frequently, an individual will deny medical problems, and when the use of a medication is discovered, he or she will explain that because of the medication, he or she no longer has the medical problem.

Some of the side effects that should be addressed by an examiner performing a commercial driver medical examination are somnolence, fatigue, impaired judgment, impaired reflexes, neurologic dysfunction, and orthostatic changes.

Conclusion

It is important not to evaluate the cardiovascular condition in isolation. A driver with multiple medical problems, all with borderline control, may be at greater risk than a driver with only one condition at the same level of stability.

The most important aspect of evaluating a cardiac patient's ability to operate a commercial motor vehicle safely is his or her underlying cardiac status. Will such a driver's heart allow him or her to perform the tasks required safely without ischemia or arrhythmia? Is the driver likely to have his or her level of alertness impaired owing to cardiac conditions or medications? Assessment of most drivers with cardiac disease should include an ECG, echocardiogram, and ETT and, depending on the diagnosis, 24-hour ambulatory monitoring. In select cases, cardiac catheterization or electrophysiologic studies may be indicated.

References

1. National Transportation Safety Board. *Fatigue, Alcohol, Other Drugs and Medical Factors in Fatal-to-Driver Heavy Truck Crashes*. PB90-917992, NTSB/SS-90/01. Washington: NTSB, 1990.
2. Dionne G, Desjarding D, Laberge-Nadeau C, Maaz U. Medical conditions, risk exposure, and truck drivers' accidents: An analysis with count data regression models. *Accid Anal Prev* 1995;27:295–305.
3. Guibert R, Duarte-Franco E, Ciampi A, et al. Medical conditions and the risk of motor vehicle crashes in men. *Arch Fam Med* 1998;7:554–558.
4. Medgyesi M, Koch D. Medical impairments to driving: Cardiovascular disease, in 39th Annual Proceedings of the Association for the Advancement of Automotive Medicine, October 1995:483–499.

5. Stewart RB, Moore MT, Marks RG, et al. *Driving Cessation and Accidents in the Elderly: An Analysis of Symptoms, Diseases, Cognitive Dysfunction and Medications.* New York: AAA Foundation for Traffic Safety, 1993.

6. Diller E, Cook L, Leonard D, et al. Evaluating drivers with medical conditions in Utah 1992–1996. NHSTA technical reports, contract DTNH22-96-H-59017, 1996.

7. Bellet S, Roman L, Kostis J, Slater A. Continuous electrocardiographic monitoring during automobile driving: Studies in normal subjects and patients with coronary disease. *Am J Cardiol* 1968;22:856–862.

8. Cocco G, Iselin HU. Cardiac risk of speed traps. *Clin Cardiol* 1992;15:441–444.

9. Dhala A, Bremner S, Blanck Z, et al. Impairment of driving abilities in patients with supraventricular tachycardia. *Am J Cardiol* 1995;75:516–518.

10. Belkic K, Savic C, Theorell T, et al. Mechanisms of cardiac risk among professional drivers. *Scand J Work Environ Health* 1994;20:73–86.

11. Aronson KL, Howe GR, Carpenter M, Fair ME. Surveillance of potential associations between occupations and causes of death in Canada, 1965–1991. *Occupational and Environmental Medicine* 1999;56:265–269.

12. Hannerz H, Tuschen F. Hospital admissions among male drivers in Denmark. *Occupational and Environmental Medicine* 2001;59:253–260.

13. Bigert C, Gustavsson P, Hallqvist J, Hogstedt C, Lewne M, Plato N, Reuterwall C, Scheele P. Myocardial infarction among professional drivers. *Epidemiology* 2003;14(3):333–339.

14. King D, Benbow SJ, Barrett JA. The law and medical fitness to drive: A study of doctor's knowledge. *Postgrad Med J* 1992;68:624–628.

15. Blumenthal R, Braunstein J, Connolly H, Epstein A, Gersh BJ, Wittels EH. *Cardiovascular Advisory Panel Guidelines for the Medical Examination of Commercial Motor Vehicle Drivers.* FMCSA-MCP-02-002. Washington: U.S. Department of Transportation, Federal Motor Carrier Safety Administration, October 2002. www.fmcsa.dot.gov/facts-research/research-technology/publications/medreports.htm. Accessed June 4, 2007.

16. FMCSA Medical Frequently Asked Questions. www.fmcsa.dot.gov/rules-regulations/topics/medical/faq.asp. Accessed June 4, 2007.

17. The Sixth Report of the Joint National Committee on the Prevention, Detection, Evaluation and Treatment of High Blood Pressure. *Arch Intern Med* 1997;157:2413–2446.

18. Seventh Report of the Joint National Committee on Prevention, Detection, Evaluation, and Treatment of High Blood Pressure. National Heart, Blood and Lung Institute. www.nhlbi.nih.gov/guidelines/hypertension/jnc7full.pdf. Accessed June 5, 2007.

19. Draft Summary for the April 25, 2007, MRB Public Meeting. www.mrb.fmcsa.dot.gov/042507_meeting.htm. Accessed June 4, 2007.

20. Canadian Cardiovascular Society. Assessment of the cardiac patient for fitness to drive. *Can J Cardiol* 1992;8:406–412.

21. U.S. Department of Transportation, Federal Highway Administration. Conference on Cardiac Disorders and Commercial Drivers. Publication No. FHWA-MC-88-040. Washington: U.S. DOT, Federal Highway Administration, Office of Motor Carriers, 1987.

22. Canadian Medical Association. *Determining Medical Fitness to Operate Motor Vehicles CMA Driver's Guide*, 7th ed. Ottawa: CMA, 2006. www.cma .ca/index.cfm/ci_id/18223/la_id/1.htm. Accessed May 25, 2007.

23. Drivers Medical Group. *For Medical Practitioners, At-a-Glance Guide to the Current Medical Standards of Fitness to Drive.* Swansea, England: Driver and Vehicle Licensing Agency, February 2007. www.dvla.gov.uk/at_a_glance/ content.htm. Accessed May 25, 2007.

24. Assessing Fitness to Drive. Interim Review Report. Austroads, National Transportation Commission, Melbourne, Australia, 2005. www.austroads .com.au/cms/AFTD%20web%20Aug%202006.pdf. Accessed May 27, 2007.

25. Epstein AE, Miles WM, Benditt DG, et al. Personal and public safety issues related to arrhythmias that may affect consciousness: Implications for regulation and physician recommendations. *Circulation* 1996;94:1147–1166.

26. Epstein AE, Baessler CA, Curtis AB, Estes NA 3rd, Gersh BJ, Grubb B, Mitchell LB; American Heart Association; Heart Rhythm Society. Addendum to "Personal and public safety issues related to arrhythmias that may affect consciousness: Implications for regulation and physician recommendations: A medical/scientific statement from the American Heart Association and the North American Society of Pacing and Electrophysiology": Public safety issues in patients with implantable defibrillators: A scientific statement from the American Heart Association and the Heart Rhythm Society. *Circulation* 2007;6;115(9):1170–1176.

27. Petch MC. Driving and heart disease. *Eur Heart J* 1998;19:1165–1177.

28. Antecol DH, Roberts WC. Sudden death behind the wheel from natural disease in drivers of four-wheeled motorized vehicles. *Am J Cardiol* 1990;66:1329–1335.

29. Anderson MA, Camm AJ. Legal and ethical aspects of driving and working in patients with an implantable cardioverter defibrillator. *Am Heart J* 1994;127:1185–1193.24.

30. Rosengren A, Anderson K, Wilhelmsen L. Risk of coronary heart disease in middle-aged male bus and tram drivers compared to men in other occupations: A prospective study. *Int J Epidemiol* 1991;20:82–87.

31. Robinson CF, Burnett CA. Truck drivers and heart disease in the United States 1979–1990. *Am J Ind Med* 2005;47:113–119.

32. Van Amelsvoort LG. Coronary heart disease among truck drivers. Report of the International Workshop on the epidemiology of coronary heart disease among European truck drivers. Bilthoven: European Commission 1995.

33. Alfredsson L, Hammar N, Hogstedt C. Incidence of myocardial infarction and mortality from specific causes among bus drivers in Sweden. *Int J Epidemiol* 1993;22:57–61.

34. Executive Summary of the Third Report of the National Cholesterol Education Program (NCEP) Expert Panel on the Detection, Evaluation, and Treatment of High Blood Cholesterol in Adults (Adult Treatment Panel III). www.nhlbi.nih.gov/guidelines/cholesterol/atp_iii.htm. Accessed June 4, 2007.

35. Grundy SM, Pasternak R, Greenland P, et al. Assessment of cardiovascular risk by use of multiple risk factor assessment equations: A statement for healthcare professionals from the American Heart Association. *Circulation* 1999;100:1481–1492.

36. *U.S. Preventive Services Task Force (USPSTF) in the Guide to Clinical Preventive Services*, 2nd ed. Baltimore: Williams & Wilkins, 1996.

37. The Joint European Society/American College of Cardiology Committee. Myocardial infarction redefined: A consensus document of the Joint European Society of Cardiology/American College of Cardiology Committee for the redefinition of myocardial infarction. *Eur Heart J* 2000;21:1502–1513.

38. Meier MA, Al-Badr WH, Cooper JV, Kline-Rogers EM, Smith DE, Eagle KA, Mehta RH. The new definition of myocardial infarction: Diagnostic and prognostic implications in patients with acute coronary syndromes. *Arch Intern Med* 2002;162:1585–1589.

39. Smith SC Jr, Feldman TE, Hirshfeld JW Jr, Jacobs AK, Kern MJ, King SB III, Morrison DA, O'Neill WW, Schaff HV, Whitlow PL, Williams DO. ACC/AHA/SCAI 2005 guideline update for percutaneous coronary intervention: A report of the American College of Cardiology/American Heart Association Task Force on Practice Guidelines ACC/AHA/SCAI Writing Committee to Update the 2001 Guidelines for Percutaneous Coronary Intervention.

40. Gibbons RJ, Balady GJ, Bricker JT, et al. ACC/AHA 2002 guideline update for exercise testing—summary article: A report of the American College of Cardiology/American Heart Association Task Force on Practice Guidelines (Committee to Update the 1997 Exercise Testing Guidelines). *Circulation* 2002;106:1883–1892.

41. Poulter N, Marmot MG. Hypertension and the probability of an incapacitating event over a defined period: Impact of treatment. *Eur Heart J* 1992;13(suppl H):39–44.

42. Pickering RG, Hall JE, Appel LJ, Falkner BE, Graves J, Hill MN, Jones DW, Kurtz T, Sheps SG, and Roccella EJ. Recommendations for blood pressure measurement in humans and experimental animals: Part 1: Blood pressure measurement in humans: A statement for professionals from the Subcommittee of Professional and Public Education of the American Heart Association Council on High Blood Pressure Research. *Hypertension* 2005;45:142–161.

43. Bonow RO, ACC/AHA Task Force Report. Guidelines for the management of patients with valvular heart disease. *J Am Coll Cardiol* 1998;32:1486–1588.

44. Amato MCM, Moffa PJ, Werner KE, Ramires JA. Treatment decision in asymptomatic aortic valve stenosis: Role of exercise testing. *Heart* 2001;86:381–386.

45. Maron BJ, Towbin JA, Thiene G, Antzelevitch C, Corrado D, Arnett D, Moss AJ, Seidman CE, Young JB; American Heart Association; Council on Clinical Cardiology, Heart Failure and Transplantation Committee; Quality of Care and Outcomes Research and Functional Genomics and Translational Biology Interdisciplinary Working Groups; Council on Epidemiology and Prevention. Contemporary definitions and classification of the cardiomyopathies: An American Heart Association Scientific Statement from the Council on Clinical Cardiology, Heart Failure and Transplantation Committee; Quality of Care and Outcomes Research and Functional Genomics and Translational Biology Interdisciplinary Working Groups; and Council on Epidemiology and Prevention. *Circulation* 2006;113:1807–1816.

46. McKenna WJ, Behr ER. Hypertrophic cardiomyopathy: Management, risk stratification and prevention of sudden death. *Heart* 2002;87:168–176.

47. van Walraven WC, Hart RG, Wells GA, et al. A. clinical prediction rule to identify patients with atrial fibrillation and a low risk for stroke while taking aspirin. *Arch Intern Med* 2003;163:936–43.

48. Fuster V, Ryden LE, Cannom DS, et al. ACC/AHA/ESC 2006 Guidelines for the Management of Patients With Atrial Fibrillation—Executive Summary: A Report of the American College of Cardiology/American Heart Association Task Force on Practice Guidelines and the European Society of Cardiology Committee for Practice Guidelines (Writing Committee to Revise the 2001 Guidelines for the Management of Patients With Atrial Fibrillation): *Circulation* 2006;114:700-752. http://circ.ahajournals.org/cgi/reprint/CIRCULATIONAHA.106.177031. Accessed June 8, 2007.

49. Linzer M, Yang EH, Estes NAM, et al. Diagnosing syncope: I. Value of history, physical examination and electrocardiography. *Ann Intern Med* 1997;126:989–996.

50. Lurie KG, Iskos D, Sakaguchi S, et al. Resumption of motor vehicle operations in vasovagal fainters. *Am J Cardiol* 1999;83:604–606.

51. Strickberger SA, Benson DW, Biaggioni I, et al. AHA/ACCF Scientific Statement on the evaluation of syncope: From the American Heart Association Councils on Clinical Cardiology, Cardiovascular Nursing, Cardiovascular Disease in the Young, and Stroke, and the Quality of Care and Outcomes Research Interdisciplinary Working Group; and the American College of Cardiology Foundation: In collaboration with the Heart Rhythm Society: Endorsed by the American Autonomic Society. *Circulation* 2006;113:316–327.

52. Brignole M, Alboni P, Benditt DG, et al. Guidelines on management (diagnosis and treatment) of syncope—Update 2004. *Europace* 2004;6:467–537.

53. Raviele A, Giada F, Menozzi C, et al. Vasovagal syncope and pacing trial investigators: A randomized double-blind, placebo-controlled study of permanent cardiac pacing for the treatment of recurrent tilt-induced vasovagal syncope. The vasovagal syncope and pacing trial (SYNPACE). *Eur Heart J* 2004;25:1741–1748.

54. Connolly SJ, Sheldon R, Thorpe KE, et al. VPS III Investigators. Pacemaker therapy for prevention of syncope in patients with recurrent severe vaso-

vagal syncope. Second vasovagal pacemake study (VPS II): A randomized trial. *JAMA* 2003;289:2224–2229.

55. Simpson C, Dorian P, Gupta A, et al. Canadian Cardiovascular Society Consensus Conference. Assessment of the cardiac patient for fitness to drive: Drive subgroup executive summary. *Can J Cardiol* 2004;20:1314–1320.

56. Creager MA, Jones DW, Easton JD, et al. Atherosclerotic Vascular Disease Conference: Writing Group V: Medical decision making and therapy. *Circulation* 2004;109:2634–2642.

57. Bettmann MA, Dake MD, Hopkins LN, et al. Atherosclerotic Vascular Disease Conference: Writing Group VI: Revascularization. *Circulation* 2004;109:2643–2650.

5

Pulmonary Disorders

NATALIE P. HARTENBAUM, MD, MPH

The respiratory system is responsible for providing adequate oxygen to the tissues and removing carbon dioxide from the bloodstream. The brain and heart are particularly sensitive to oxygen deprivation. Acute or chronic abnormalities in oxygen content or carrying capacity of the blood may result either directly or indirectly in confusion, dizziness, or loss of consciousness.

Respiratory problems are not as likely as cardiac or neurologic dysfunction to suddenly incapacitate a driver. As pulmonary function declines, it becomes more difficult for a driver to perform required tasks aside from driving. It is estimated that truck driving itself requires 3.0 metabolic equivalents [METs, defined as the energy demand in liters of oxygen consumption per minute of basal oxygen consumption (3.5 mL/kg per minute)], whereas lifting and carrying 60 to 80 lb requires 7.5 METs [1]. With mild impairment, pulmonary function test (PFT) abnormalities may not correlate well with complaints of dyspnea. As respiratory function declines, there is a direct correlation. The more abnormal the PFT, the less likely it is that the individual will be able to work as a commercial driver.

Obstructive sleep apnea (OSA), and its resulting daytime somnolence or decreased alertness, has been recognized as a potential cause of motor vehicle accidents. The new Medical Examination Reporting Form includes a question on sleep apnea and other sleep disorders, requiring drivers to indicate whether they have a "sleep disorder, pauses in breathing while sleeping, daytime sleepiness, loud snoring."

Many medications used to treat respiratory conditions such as allergies or cough have potentially serious side effects. These side effects must be taken into account during the decision-making process.

The standard addressing respiratory function [49 CFR 391.41(b)(5)] states that

A person is physically qualified to drive a commercial motor vehicle if that person:

(5) Has no established medical history or clinical diagnosis of a respiratory dysfunction likely to interfere with his/her ability to control and drive a motor vehicle safely.

The intent of the Federal Motor Carrier Safety Administration (FMCSA) regarding pulmonary disqualification is widely open to interpretation. The medical advisory criteria explain that impairment in respiratory function, especially when there is greater oxygen demand, as in emergency situations, may be "detrimental to safe driving." The medical examiner is advised to refer to a specialist if any abnormality that may interfere with safe operation of the commercial motor vehicle is detected. If the driver is on anticoagulation therapy for deep venous thrombosis (DVT) or pulmonary embolus (PE), he or she can be qualified once the lower extremity vascular studies are normal and the optimal dose of anticoagulation has been reached. The advisory criteria refer the driver to the Conference on Pulmonary/Respiratory Disorders and Commercial Drivers [2]. Guidance on the driver with DVT or PE also can be found in the Cardiovascular Panel Guidelines [3]. The cardiac advisory criteria also offer that the examiner may contact the Federal Motor Carrier Safety Administration (FMCSA) at 202-366-1790 for additional information on qualifying drivers on Coumadin.

Several of the Frequently Asked Questions (FAQs) address pulmonary issues [4]. In one, examiners are reminded that they can use general certification criteria in evaluating the driver with pulmonary disease:

What are the effects of the lung disease on pulmonary function?
Is the disease contagious?
Can the driver safely use therapy while working?
Can the driver safely perform both driving and ancillary duties?
Is the disease progressive?

As with any condition that may progress or affect the ability to drive safely, drivers with pulmonary disease should be certified at least annually for chronic pulmonary disease, the examiner should determine if additional testing such as a chest X-ray, pulmonary function, or arterial blood gases is needed.

Another FAQ reviewed the use of modafinil in obstructive sleep disorder, narcolepsy, or shift work sleep disorder. It noted that modafinil has several concerning side effects such as chest pain, dizziness, difficulty breathing, heart palpitations, irregular and/or fast heartbeat, increased blood pressure, tremors or shaking movements, anxiety, nervousness, rapidly changing mood, problems with memory, and blurred vision or other vision changes. There was also concern that many medications may interact with modafinil and that its use requires close supervision and may hide signs that an individual is tired. A recent update indicated that drivers being prescribed Provigil should be closely monitored for 6 weeks before they are certified. Both the treating physician and the Medical Examiner should agree that the Provigil is effective in preventing daytime somnolence and document that no untoward side effects are present. Drivers on modafinil should be recertified annually. Although the original FAQ on modafinil reminded examiners that drivers with narcolepsy should not be medically qualified, the update does not include that statement. A specific FAQ on narcolepsy does indicate that guidelines recommend disqualifying a CMV driver with a diagnosis of narcolepsy, regardless of treatment because of the likelihood of excessive daytime somnolence.

Recommendations

The qualification recommendations in the remainder of this chapter are from the FHWA pulmonary conference [2], except where indicated. Additional information on some conditions is included, and the reference source noted.

Evaluation

In screening drivers for pulmonary disease, questions that should be asked include:

> Do you smoke? If so, how much? For how many years?
> Do you feel short of breath with activity or while driving?
> Do you cough? If so, is your cough productive of sputum?
> Do you have tightness in your chest during exercise or at rest?
> Do you snore? If so, do you feel sleepy during the day?
> Do you wheeze?

In addition to obvious signs of shortness of breath (e.g., a patient becomes short of breath just getting onto the examining table), other physical signs of pulmonary disease may include clubbing; cyanosis; slowing of expiration; tachypnea at rest; diffuse rhonchi, wheezes, or rales; decreased or absent breath sounds; pleural rubs; significant kyphosis; or use of accessory muscles of ventilation at rest. Obesity and falling asleep on the examination table may raise the question of OSA.

Pulmonary Function Tests (PFTs).   Although few examiners routinely obtain PFTs, participants in the Pulmonary/Respiratory Disorders Conference recommended PFTs as an integral part of lung function evaluation. They suggest PFTs for any driver with a history of lung disease or symptoms of shortness of breath, cough, chest tightness, or wheezing. PFTs were also recommended for all cigarette smokers older than 35 years. Although this may identify all drivers with suboptimal lung function, the cost and number of normal tests will make this cost prohibitive. However, many of the drivers with lung function below the levels recommended likely will have some physical signs to suggest impairment.

Recommendations from the report for certification are based on PFTs where indicated. For drivers who have normal PFTs, no further evaluation is needed. For drivers with obstructive disease, if the PFTs are abnormal, forced expiratory volume in 1 second (FEV_1) <65% of predicted, forced vital capacity (FVC) <60% of predicted, or FEV_1/FVC ratio <65%, arterial blood gases (ABGs) or pulse oximetry was recommended. The criterion for performing ABGs or pulse oximetry in patients with restrictive diseases is an FVC <60% of predicted. If the screening pulse oximetry is <92%, then ABGs should be reviewed. A partial pressure of arterial oxygen (PaO_2) of <65 mm Hg or a partial pressure of carbon dioxide ($PaCO_2$) of >45 mm Hg should cause the driver to not be medically qualified. One method of evaluating the efficiency of gas exchange is through diffusing lung capacity of carbon monoxide (DLco). If the results here are <60% of predicted, further studies also should be obtained.

Chronic Obstructive Pulmonary Disease (COPD)

A thorough history and physical examination are essential for drivers with COPD. Lung status should be evaluated through the PFTs, chest X-rays, and ABGs, if indicated. In some patients, it may be desirable to assess O_2 saturation response to exercise. Decisions as to certification should be individualized but based on PFTs or O_2 saturation response to exercise. When exercise testing is chosen as part of the evaluation for pulmonary disease, the driver should be able to reach at least 4.3 METs. If the driver is unable to do so, or if there is a drop in O_2 saturation, he or she should not be qualified.

Many individuals with COPD will have minimal physical findings. As lung function deteriorates, work ability also declines. The risk of COPD increases with increasing years of smoking, and, therefore, PFTs were recommended for all smokers older than 35 years.

COPD also carries the risk of cough syncope. Drivers with COPD and cough syncope should not be qualified because cough syncope can be unpredictable and incapacitating. Cystic fibrosis may present with end-stage COPD. In the past, many cystic fibrosis patients did not survive into adulthood. Now, however, with numerous medical advances, many do, and those who wish to enter the commercial driver pool should be evaluated with the same criteria as others with COPD. Depending on the driver's current status, evaluation more frequently than every 2 years may be desirable.

The American Medical Association (AMA) guidelines, which are now almost 2 decades old and have not been updated, base their recommendation on drivers with COPD on clinical findings, in addition to the standard physiologic studies [5]. The AMA suggests that individuals with moderate to severe respiratory impairment be restricted from commercial vehicle driving. Such impairment includes dyspnea while walking on level ground or up one flight of stairs. The FEV_1 in such individuals would be <59% of predicted, and the FVC <60% of predicted.

More recent guidelines from the Canadian Medical Association (CMA) [6] also base recommendations on level of impairment. Drivers with COPD and no or only mild impairment would be permitted to operate commercial vehicles. The CMA recommends that those commercial drivers with moderate impairment, shortness of breath when walking for a few minutes, or after 100 m walking on level ground be assessed on the level of activity required. Those drivers with moderate or severe impairment and who use oxygen at rest should be disqualified. Great Britain's Driver and Vehicle Licensing Agency (DVLA) recommends that if the driver has any chronic respiratory disease, commercial driving should be suspended until free from syncope/presyncope for 5 years. If coughing causes asystole, commercial driving could be considered once a pacemaker has been implanted [7].

Pneumothoraces

A pneumothorax may be idiopathic or due to trauma. Traumatic pneumothoraces often are easily treated and unlikely to recur. In a commercial driver, complete resolution should be documented by chest X-ray, and if no other abnormalities are present, the driver may be qualified. There is a 25% risk of recurrence of spontaneous pneumothoraces in the first 2 years, increasing to 85% in individuals with a history of three prior spontaneous pneumothoraces. Spontaneous pneumothoraces usually are associated with underlying lung disease. Drivers with a history of two or more spontaneous pneumothoraces on the same side should not be qualified. After successful pleurodesis, a driver with recurrent pneumothoraces can be qualified if other pulmonary parameters are within acceptable ranges. Drivers with a single spontaneous pneumothorax and no associated pulmonary disease can be qualified if they have no chest pain or shortness of breath and if resolution of the pneumothorax has been confirmed.

Allergies and Asthma

Allergies are very common and, in and of themselves, are unlikely to cause a problem for commercial drivers. Studies have evaluated the effect of antihistamines on driving and have concluded that they do have a significant effect on performance [8,9]. Some states have laws against driving under the influence of any agent that impairs performance, including antihistamines [10]. Drivers with allergic rhinitis should be advised to use the nonsedating antihistamines or local steroid sprays. Those with severe symptoms, such as uncontrollable sneezing or impaired vision due to ophthalmic involvement, should refrain temporarily from driving.

Asthmatics can be certified, but their pulmonary function should meet the recommended criteria. Some tasks associated with commercial driving may exacerbate asthma, such as exposure to nonspecific irritants or cold temperatures. Recurrent hospitalizations or a frequent need for high-dose steroids should prompt further evaluation. If a driver is severely symptomatic, or if there is significant pulmonary impairment (FEV$_1$ <65% or PaO$_2$ <65 mm Hg) that cannot be reversed by treatment, the driver should not be medically qualified.

Hypersensitivity pneumonitis can be associated with dyspnea, cough, or fever. However, drivers with hypersensitivity pneumonitis can be qualified, but they should avoid the causative agent, and, if possible, they should take preventive precautions.

Drivers with a history of allergy to stinging insects not only may be incapacitated from a sting but also may panic at the sight of an insect. Immunotherapy may be indicated depending on the severity of reactions, and injectable epinephrine must be available.

Hereditary or acquired angioedema can be controlled with treatment, and if it is, commercial driving is acceptable. Recurrent episodes of idiopathic anaphylaxis may be difficult to control. If such episodes are due to a recognized allergen that can be avoided or if the symptoms can be managed, driver qualification may be acceptable. When such a driver is unable to prevent the sudden onset of dyspnea or loss of consciousness, he or she should be medically disqualified.

Obstructive Sleep Apnea (OSA)

A great deal has changed with respect to OSA since the pulmonary/respiratory report. The current form includes a specific question on OSA and sleep apnea is mentioned in the advisory criteria as a respiratory condition that may "result in incapacitation."

There is evidence that drivers with sleep disorders have as much as a seven-fold increased risk of accidents [11–15]. It is estimated that 1% to 3% of U.S. motor vehicle crashes are caused by driver sleepiness; of those, about 3% involve commercial drivers [12].

Powell et al. [16] found reaction times worse in individuals with sleep-disordered breathing than in subjects with a blood alcohol concentration of 0.057 g/dL. Although drivers may be aware that they are sleepy, they may not take action to stop driving and prevent accidents.

This condition, which commonly affects obese, middle-aged males, is characterized by episodes of nocturnal apnea or hypopnea, with brief episodes of waking, snoring, and resultant excessive daytime somnolence. The hypersomnolence that occurs during waking hours is seen most frequently during monotonous activities such as driving. Drivers with sleep apnea also tend to underestimate their level of daytime sleepiness, so reliance on subjective report of somnolence may be unreliable [17] and health care providers are also poor at identifying those who should be evaluated for OSA [18,19]. The use of alcohol or sedatives, shift work, and sleep deprivation can further exacerbate the degree of impairment. Physical finding to suggest OSA may include obesity (body mass index [BMI] >28), increased neck circumference (≥16 inches in women and 17 inches in men), craniosynostosis, mandibular hypoplasia, and retrognathia. Other findings may include elongated soft palate and uvula, high arched palate, and enlarged tonsils. There also is a relationship between hypertension, metabolic syndrome, and other medical conditions and OSA [20–23].

In a project [24] sponsored by the FMCSA and the American Transportation Research Institute of the American Trucking Association, among their sample of commercial driver's license holders, 17.6% had mild sleep apnea, 5.8% had moderate sleep apnea, and 4.7% had severe sleep apnea, a prevalence similar to the general population. An earlier study found a much higher incidence in commercial drivers [25]. The prevalence of sleep apnea depended on the relationship between age and obesity. Daytime performance depended not only on the severity of sleep apnea but also on the average duration of sleep of the driver.

One of the challenges is in identifying those drivers with OSA at highest risk of being involved in a motor vehicle crash [26]. Among 448 patients with OSA in one study [27], almost 9% had been involved in an automobile accident, mainly caused by falling asleep at the wheel, within the preceding 5 years. In this group, excessive sleepiness was associated with an ESS of >11 and an Apnea/Hypopnea Index (AHI) of >15. In another study, drivers found to have an AHI of 10 or higher had an odds ratio of 6.3 for having a traffic accident [11]. Increased risk remained even after controlling for confounders. The risk of accidents has been shown to decrease with adequate treatment [28].

The polysomnogram is considered the gold standard in the diagnosis of OSA. It simultaneously measures electroencephalography, respiration, electrocardiography, and oxygenation, assessing apneic episodes and sleep stages. One of the measures reported is the AHI. This is calculated by adding the total number of apneas to the total number of hypopneas and dividing it by the total number of sleep hours. Because of variability in scoring, there is no consensus for what constitutes disease. Generally accepted criteria are that an AHI between 5 and 15 constitute mild disease, between 15 and 30 moderate, and greater than 30 represents severe disease.

There does not appear to be a definite correlation between AHI and the degree of sleepiness or crash risk but there is a relationship between AHI and cardiovascular disease [20]. It can be challenging to determine which patients should undergo the expensive and not conveniently available polysomnogram. There are several algorithms and questionnaires that attempt to stratify risk. Examples include a two-step algorithm [29] utilizing nocturnal pulse oximetry and the Multivariable Apnea Prediction questionnaire [30]. These allowed the researchers to stratify patients referred to a sleep disorder clinic into low- and higher-risk groups. Other methods include screening on history, physical findings or history of previous sleep related motor vehicle crash [20].

A consensus document from 1999 recommended treating with CPAP those patients with OSA and an AHI ≥30 events per hour for those with an AHI between 5 and 30 if they have excessive daytime somnolence, cognitive impairment, or documented cardiovascular disease [31]. A more recent practice parameter from the American Academy of Sleep Medicine recommends treatment with PAP for individuals with AHI ≥15 or between 5 and 14 with excessive daytime somnolence [32].

The most recent guidance from the FMCSA on evaluating the commercial driver with OSA is from the 1991 respiratory conference report. That panel recommended that if there is any suspicion that sleep apnea exists, the driver should be evaluated and the condition successfully treated prior to returning to work. They acknowledged that treatment may consist of CPAP, uvulopalatopharyngoplasty, weight loss, and/or tracheostomy.

The conference participants recommended at least a 1-month waiting period after initiating treatment before returning to commercial driving. A major concern is compliance only about half the patients using it as prescribed [33].

The conference participants also advised evaluation of the effectiveness of treatment through either multiple sleep-latency testing (MSLT) or polysomnographs. MSLT is able to evaluate the ease with which an individual can fall asleep during normal waking hours. Another test that is used by the FAA in evaluating pilots with OSA is the maintenance-of-wakefulness test (MWT), which measures the ability of an individual to remain awake. It was advised in the conference report that drivers with sleep apnea who are medically qualified to drive commercial motor vehicles be reevaluated annually by sleep studies or MSLT. Many examiners have been using the MWT because it measures the ability to stay awake rather than how quickly an individual can fall asleep. Neither test however, has been consistently shown to predict risk of crashes [20].

The American Thoracic Society (ATS) [34] discussed the importance of OSA's role in vehicle accidents and suggests use of a higher level of caution in commercial drivers. The ATS defined a high-risk individual as one who has excessive daytime sleepiness as well as a prior motor vehicle accident.

Some states, such as California and Texas, address sleep apnea in their medical criteria for drivers [15], so it is important to also be aware of both the state where the driver is licensed and where the driver has obtained his or her commercial driver's license.

A task force composed of members from the American College of Occupational and Environmental Medicine, American College of Chest Physicians, and the National Sleep Foundation prepared an extensive review of the commercial driver with OSA including recommendations on screening, diagnosis, treatment, and follow up [20]. (See Tables 5-1 and 5-2.) These recommendations have not been adopted by the FMCSA but they will be convening an expert panel on sleep disorders in late 2007 to review and update the current guidelines.

Infectious Diseases

Acute respiratory infections such as influenza, bronchitis, or the common cold generally will not have long-term safety implications. During an acute infection, the symptoms may interfere with the ability to perform heavy work and with alertness. Regulating these short-term

Table 5-1. Screening Recommendations for Commercial Drivers with Possible or Probable Sleep Apnea

Medically qualified to drive commercial vehicles if either of the following:	In-Service Evaluation recommended (ISE) if driver falls into one of the following five major categories (*3 months max. certification*):	Out-of-Service Immediate Evaluation (OSE) recommended if driver meets any one of the following factors:
1. No positive findings or only one of the numbered in-service evaluation factors	1. Sleep history suggestive (snoring, excessive daytime sleepiness, witnessed apneas)	1. Observed unexplained excessive daytime sleepiness (sleeping in exam or waiting room); confessed excessive sleepiness
2. Diagnosis of OSA with CPAP compliance documented	2. Two or more of the following: a. BMI $\geq$35, b. Neck circumference greater than 17 inches in men, 16 inches in women c. Hypertension (new, uncontrolled, or unable to control with less than two medications)	2. Motor vehicle accident (run off road, at fault rear-end collision) likely related to sleep disturbance unless evaluated for sleep disorder in the interim
	3. ESS greater than >10	3. ESS $\geq$16 or FOSQ<18
	4. Previously diagnosed sleep disorder: Compliance claimed but no recent medical visits/compliance data available for review (must be reviewed within 3-month period). If not compliant, should be removed from service. (Includes surgical treatment)	4. Previously diagnosed sleep disorder: a. Noncompliant (CPAP treatment not tolerated) b. No recent follow-up c. Any surgical approach with no objective follow-up
	5. AHI .5 but less than 30 in a prior sleep study and no excessive daytime somnolence (ESS <11), no motor vehicle accidents and no hypertension requiring two or more agents to control	5. AHI greater than 30

Source: Adapted from Hartenbaum et al. with permission of ACOEM.

Table 5-2. Recommendations for the Evaluation for Fitness for Duty for Commercial Drivers with Possible or Probably Obstructive Sleep Apnea

Category	Recommendation
Diagnosis	1. Diagnosis should be determined by a physician and confirmed by polysomnography, preferably in an accredited sleep laboratory or by a certified sleep specialist.
	2. A full-night study should be done unless a split-night study is indicated (severe OSA identified after at least 2 hours of sleep).
Treatment	1. First-line treatment for commercial drivers with OSA should be delivered by positive airway pressure (CPAP, BPAP).
	2. All commercial drivers on PAP must use a machine that is able to measure time on pressure.
	3. A minimum acceptable average use of CPAP is 4 hours within a 24-hour period, but drivers should be advised that longer treatment would be more beneficial.
	4. Treatment should be started as soon as possible but within 2 weeks of the sleep study.
	5. Follow-up by a sleep specialist should be done after between 2–4 weeks of treatment.
Return to work after treatment Treatment with PAP	1. After about 1 week of treatment, contact between the patient and personnel from either the DME supplier or sleep specialist.
	2. AHI ≤5 documented with CPAP at initial titration or after surgery or with use of oral appliance. AHI ≤10 depending on clinical findings.
	3. Query driver on fit, compliance, and reminded to bring card (if used) or machine to next visit.
	4. At a minimum of 2 weeks but within 4 weeks, the driver should be reevaluated by the sleep specialist where compliance and blood pressure are assessed.
	5. If compliant and blood pressure are controlled, the driver can return to work but should be certified for no longer than 3 months.

Table 5-2. Recommendations for the Evaluation for Fitness for Duty for Commercial Drivers with Possible or Probably Obstructive Sleep Apnea *(continued)*

Category	Recommendation
Return to work after treatment Treatment with Oral Appliances	1. Oral appliance should only be used as primary therapy if initial AHI <30. 2. Prior to returning to service, must have follow-up sleep study demonstrating ideally AHI <5 but ≤10 while wearing oral appliance. 3. All reported symptoms of sleepiness must be resolved and blood pressure must be controlled.
Return to work after treatment Treatment with surgery or weight loss	1. Follow-up sleep study, AHI ideally <5 but ≤10 is required to document efficacy.
Follow-up	1. Drivers with OSA should be certified annually. 2. Annual evaluation by sleep specialist. 3. At least annual assessment of compliance and documentation of compliance provided to the commercial driver medical examiner for review.

diseases is not practical. Pneumonia should preclude commercial driving until the infection has been adequately treated.

The respiratory status of individuals with underlying chronic but stable conditions such as asthma or chronic bronchitis may decompensate significantly with respiratory infections or influenza. When evaluating drivers with chronic pulmonary disorders, it is important to determine whether their status may change significantly with acute exacerbations. Drivers who are able to do so may take sick or vacation time, but the long-haul trucker may be at the other end of the United States when symptoms occur and may have no choice but to continue working. Medications may be taken to treat the congestion, runny nose, or cough, but some can have potentially dangerous side effects. All drivers should be warned at the time of the medical evaluation to exercise caution when using any medication while working, including those available over the counter.

Infection and hemoptysis may occur in individuals with bronchiectasis, a disease characterized by inflammatory destruction of the bronchioles. For them, pulmonary function should be evaluated, and drivers not meeting the criteria listed earlier should not be qualified. Drivers with a recent episode of hemoptysis of >250 mL or with recurrent exacerbations also should be disqualified.

Clinical manifestation of tuberculosis can range from a positive tuberculin test to advanced disease. If chest X-rays do not indicate recent infection or a change from earlier evaluations, there is no reason to deny certification. Recent tuberculin test conversion should prompt the initiation of treatment, but the driver can continue to work once treatment has been initiated. If streptomycin is required as the drug of choice, the driver should not be medically qualified until the treatment is completed because of streptomycin's effect on hearing and balance. Individuals with severe disease, as determined through PFTs and chest X-rays, or those with inadequately treated disease or chronic tuberculosis should be disqualified.

Atypical tuberculosis is generally not a contagious disease. The driver should be allowed to work if pulmonary function is adequate. If coexistent medical conditions or the infection itself causes fatigue, weakness, or other interfering symptoms, the driver should not be medically qualified.

Secondary Pulmonary Conditions

Pneumonectomy is usually done to remove a cancerous growth; it also may be performed to remove a diseased portion of tissue in otherwise healthy lungs. Certification of drivers who have undergone pneumonectomy should be based on the underlying disease process and pulmonary function. Most individuals without other pulmonary disease will do well after surgery. If such individuals meet PFT and ABG criteria, they should be medically qualified.

A tracheostomy does not itself present a danger, but as in several other situations, concern focuses on the disease that necessitated the procedure. When the tracheostomy is done because of surgery for cancer of the head or neck, the functional status and progression of the disease should guide the driver qualification decision. If the tracheostomy was performed because of acute but reversible respiratory disease, the stoma usually is permitted to heal once the acute episode has resolved. Occasionally, sleep apnea is treated with a tracheostomy, and in such a circumstance, the sleep apnea should be controlled, prior to driver qualification.

Long-haul drivers who go for long periods of time without changing position may be at risk for deep venous thrombosis (DVT) and possible resulting pulmonary embolism (PE), with shortness of breath, cardiac insufficiency, or collapse. An increased risk of recurrence may exist for several months after the initial incident. In 1992, at the time of the pulmonary conference, the FHWA recommended against the use of oral anticoagulants in commercial drivers. Guidance was issued in 1996 that drivers could be certified if on Coumadin with specific criteria. The Cardiovascular Advisory Panel provided the most current guidance on drivers with DVT or pulmonary emboli. They advised that DVTs should be disqualifying until the driver is adequately treated, no residual acute DVT, and if on Coumadin, regulated for at least 1 month, with the INR monitored at least monthly.

If the driver had a PE, they should not be certified for at least 3 months and be on appropriate long-term therapy. If Coumadin is used, the dosage should be regulated for at least 1 month, with follow-up INR at least monthly. Drivers on Coumadin should be recertified as least annually. (See Chapter 4 for recommendations of 2007 Cardiac Medical Expert Panel.)

Despite symptoms that may occur with either primary or secondary lung carcinoma, some of these individuals can be qualified as commercial drivers. Individuals not currently receiving treatment who do not have severe cough, dyspnea, or brain involvement and have a PaO_2 >65 mm Hg could be medically qualified. However, they should be reevaluated every 3 months for 2 years and then yearly for 5 years. If such individuals are currently receiving treatment; have no severe side effects of the treatment such as nausea, vomiting, or weakness; and meet other criteria, they should be medically qualified but evaluated monthly. Great Britain's DVLA recommends a 2-year cessation from commercial driving after treatment for carcinoma of the lung. Such drivers also should be free from evidence of cerebral metastasis before resuming driving [7].

Cor pulmonale is a right ventricular dysfunction caused by pulmonary hypertension, usually as a result of pulmonary disease. Pulmonary hypertension also can be caused by left ventricular dysfunction. Patients with pulmonary hypertension or cor pulmonale may experience shortness of breath, chest pain, dizziness, or syncope. Abnormalities such as distended neck veins, liver enlargement, or peripheral edema may be found on physical examination. Cardiac findings may include a P_2, right-sided S_3, or murmur of tricuspid insufficiency. Electrocardiographic or chest X-ray abnormalities also are possible, but the diagnosis is confirmed by right heart catheterization. Vasodilators may be used to treat this disease, and they can produce hypotension, dizziness, or syncope. ABG criteria must be met for such a driver to be qualified. The driver also should be free from dyspnea at rest, dizziness, or hypotension.

After lung transplantation, most patients will return to adequate pulmonary function within 3 to 6 months. Return of cardiac function to normal generally is not seen in heart-lung transplant patients, and maximal O_2 response to exercise usually is impaired. If such a driver is able to return to work, his or her status should be evaluated by the standard methods. The medications used to prevent rejection, such as cyclosporine, prednisone, or azathioprine, can present risks of their own. Drug levels, blood chemistries, and blood cell counts must be monitored regularly, and the driver must not miss any doses. Such drivers should limit their geographic range so that compliance with treatment and testing regimens can be met. They also should have access to nearby tertiary centers capable of handling emergencies such as rejection so that appropriate treatment can be obtained within a few hours.

Pulmonary Medications

With respiratory disorders, the medications used to treat the diseases and symptoms may be more dangerous than the disease itself. The sympathomimetics elevate blood pressure and can cause rapid heart rates or arrhythmias. Older antihistamines may produce drowsiness. Narcotics in cough medication also can cause sedation. The pulmonary/respiratory report recommended avoiding sedating medications for at least 12 hours prior to driving although a recent recommendation from the National Transportation Safety Board [35] suggested a two half-life wait after taking a sedating medication. Drivers, especially those subject to random drug and alcohol testing, also should be cautioned against taking a family member's narcotic-containing cough medication.

Conclusion

The bottom line with pulmonary disorders and medical certification is that regardless of the disease, the decision should be based on lung function. If indicated, PFTs should be obtained first, followed by ABGs or, if clinically indicated, exercise studies. In the competitive market for occupational health services, obtaining all recommended studies may be difficult and costly. There is always an examiner willing to cut costs when pushed, especially if the testing is not mandated.

Medications and accompanying side effects are relevant and should be evaluated and the driver counseled on the potential safety hazards of certain medications.

OSA is the pulmonary condition that examiners will encounter most frequently. At the time this is being written, the most recent guidance is from the OSA and Commercial Driver Task Force of the ACCP, ACOEM, and NSF. These recommendations have been endorsed by each of the participating medical organizations but have not been adopted by the FMCSA. A medical expert panel of the FMCSA is planned and examiners should watch for updated guidance from the FMCSA.

References

1. Harber P, Fedoruk MJ. Work placement and worker fitness: Implications of the Americans with Disabilities Act for pulmonary medicine. *Chest* 1994;105:1564–1571.
2. U.S. Department of Transportation, Federal Highway Administration. *Conference on Respiratory/Pulmonary Disorders and Commercial Drivers.* Publication No. FHWA-MC-91-004. Washington: U.S. DOT, Federal Highway Administration, Office of Motor Carriers, 1991.
3. Blumenthal R, Braunstein J, Connolly H, Epstein A, Gersh BJ, Wittels EH. *Cardiovascular Advisory Panel Guidelines for the Medical Examination of Commercial Motor Vehicle Drivers.* FMCSA-MCP-02-002. Washington: U.S. Department of Transportation, Federal Motor Carrier Safety Administration, October 2002.
4. FMCSA Frequently Asked Questions. www.fmcsa.dot.gov/rules-regulations/topics/medical/faq.asp. Accessed April 13, 2007.

5. American Medical Association. *Medical Conditions Affecting Drivers.* Chicago: AMA, 1986.

6. Canadian Medical Association. *Determining Medical Fitness to Operate Motor Vehicles CMA Driver's Guide,* 7th ed. Ottawa: CMA, 2006. www .cma.ca/index.cfm/ci_id/18223/la_id/1.htm. Accessed April 16, 2007.

7. Drivers Medical Group. *For Medical Practitioners, At-a-Glance Guide to the Current Medical Standards of Fitness to Drive.* Swansea, England: Driver and Vehicle Licensing Agency, February 2007. www.dvla.gov.uk/at_a_glance/ content.htm. Accessed April 16, 2007.

8. O'Hanlon JF, Ramaekers JG. Antihistamine effects on actual driving performance in a standard test: A summary of Dutch experience, 1989–1994. *Allergy* 1995;50:234–242.

9. Reidel WJ, Schoenmakers EAJM, O'Hanlon JF. Sedation and performance impairment with antihistamines. In: Kalinger MA, ed. *Management of Allergy in the 1990s.* Toronto: Hans Huber, 1989:38–49.

10. U.S. Department of Transportation. *Digest of State Alcohol-Related Highway Safety Legislation,* 14th ed. Washington: U.S. DOT, 1996.

11. Teran-Santos J, Jimenez-Gomez A, Cordero-Guevara J. The association between sleep apnea and the risk of traffic accidents. *N Engl J Med* 1999; 340:847–851.

12. Lyznicki JM, Doege TC, Davis RM, Williams MA. Sleepiness, driving, and motor vehicle crashes. *JAMA* 1998;279:1908–1913.

13. Pack AI, Pack AM, Rodgman E, et al. Characteristics of crashes attributed to the driver having fallen asleep. *Accid Anal Prev* 1995;27:769–775.

14. Horstman S, Hess CW, Bassetti C, Gugger M, Mathis J. Sleepiness related accidents in sleep apnea patients. *Sleep* 200;23:283–289.

15. Pakola SJ, Dinges DF, Pack AI. Driving and sleepiness: Review of regulations and guidelines for commercial and noncommercial drivers with sleep apnea and narcolepsy. *Sleep* 1995;18(9):787–796.

16. Powell NB, Riley RW, Schechtman KB, Blumen MB, Dinges DF, Guilleminault C. A comparative model: Reaction time performance in sleep-disordered breathing versus alcohol-impaired controls. *Laryngoscope* 1999;109: 1648–1654.

17. Engelman HM, Hirst WS, Douglas NJ. Underreporting of sleepiness and driving impairment in patients with sleep apnea/hypopnea syndrome. *J Sleep Res* 1997;6:272–275.

18. Philip P. Sleepiness of occupational drivers. *Ind Health.* 2005;43(1):30–33.

19. Reuveni H, Tarasiuk A, Wainstock T, Ziv A, Elhayany A, Tal A. Awareness level of obstructive sleep apnea syndrome during routine unstructured interviews of a standardized patient by primary care physicians. *Sleep* 2004;27(8):1518–1525.

20. Hartenbaum N, Collop N, Rosen IM, Phillips B, George CF, Rowley JA, Freedman N, Weaver TE, Gurubhagavatula I, Strohl K, Leaman HM, Moffitt GL, Rosekind MR. Sleep apnea and commercial motor vehicle operators: Statement from the Joint Task Force of the American College of Chest Physicians, American College of Occupational and Environmental Medi-

cine, and the National Sleep Foundation. *J Occup Environ Med* 2006;48(9 Suppl):S4–S37.

21. Attarian HP, Sabri AN. When to suspect obstructive sleep apnea syndrome: Symptoms may be subtle, but treatment is straightforward. *Postgrad Med* 2002;111:70–76.

22. Davies RJ, Stradling JR. The relationship between neck circumference, radiographic pharyngeal anatomy, and the obstructive sleep apnoea syndrome. *Eur Respir J* 1990;3:509–514.

23. Dagan Y, Doljansky JT, Green A, Weiner A. Body mass index (BMI) as a first-line screening criterion for detection of excessive daytime sleepiness among professional drivers. *Traffic Inj Prev* 2006;7:44–48.

24. Pack AI, Dinges DF, Maislin G. A study of prevalence of sleep apnea among commercial truck drivers. FMCSA Publication No. DOT-RT-02-030. Washington: FMCSA, 2002.

25. Stoohs RA, Bingham LA, Itoi A, Guilleminault C, Dement WC. Sleep and sleep-disordered breathing in commercial long-haul truck drivers. *Chest* 1995;107(5):1275–1282.

26. George CF. Reduction in motor vehicle collisions following treatment of sleep apnea with nasal CPAP. *Thorax* 2001;56(7):508–512.

27. Shiomi T, Arita AT, Banno K, et al. Falling asleep while driving and automobile accidents among patients with obstructive sleep apnea-hypopnea syndrome. *Psychiatry Clin Neurosci* 2002;56:333–334.

28. Findley L, Smith C, Hooper J, Dineen M, Suratt PM. Treatment with nasal CPAP decreases automobile accidents in patients with sleep apnea. *Am J Respir Crit Care Med* 2000;161:857–859.

29. Gurubhagavatula I, Maislin G, Pack AI. An algorithm to stratify sleep apnea risk in a sleep disorders clinic population. *Am J Respir Crit Care Med* 2001;164:1904–1909.

30. Maislin G, Pack A, Kribbs N, Smith P, Schwab R, Dinges D. A survey screen for prediction of apnea. *Sleep* 1995;18:158–166.

31. Loube D, Gay P, Strohl K, Pack A, White D, Collop N. Indications for positive airway pressure treatment of adult obstructive sleep apnea patients. *Chest* 1999;115:863–866.

32. Kushida CA, Littner MR, Hirshkowitz M, et al. Practice parameters for the use of continuous and bilevel positive airway pressure devices to treat adult patients with sleep-related breathing disorders. *Sleep* 2006;29(3):375–380.

33. Weaver TE, Kribbs NB, Pack AI, et al. Night-to-night variability in CPAP use over the first three months of treatment. *Sleep* 1997;20(4):278–283.

34. American Thoracic Society. Sleep apnea, sleepiness, and driving risk. *Am J Respir Crit Care Med* 1994;150:1463–1473.

35. National Transportation Safety Board Recommendation I-00-3, January 13, 2000. www.ntsb.gov/Recs/letters/2000/I00_1_4.pdf. Accessed April 16, 2007.

6

Musculoskeletal Disorders

ERIC WOOD, MD, MPH

The CDME processes are currently undergoing substantial changes. The FMCSA has a planned Medical Expert Panel on Musculoskeletal Conditions in 2008 for presentation to the Medical Review Board (MRB). After the MRB reviews a subject, the FMCSA may be advised of suggested changes in the CDME processes by the MRB, after which rule-making may or may not commence. Please be aware of these updating processes.

Operation of commercial vehicles requires musculoskeletal capabilities that extend well beyond the routine demands of noncommercial driving. Despite advances in electronics and power-assisted devices, the forces and frequencies of manual activities performed by commercial drivers requires a high level of both fine and gross motor control and skill. The medical examiner must be able to address strength, dexterity, endurance, and overall musculoskeletal function of the driver in order to assess their capabilities for safe operation of commercial vehicles.

With respect to motor vehicle crash risk and musculoskeletal disorders (MSDs), unfortunately, little data have been collected, especially for commercial drivers. Despite the paucity of data, there exists some literature to suggest that drivers with MSDs are at increased risk for crashes. In a retrospective study of truck drivers involved in crashes in Australia from 1988–2000, MSDs were the most common cause for hospitalization with 27 percent of the cohort ever admitted for MSDs [1]. Data from a population-based 5-year retrospective study from the general driving population showed that the risk for at-fault motor vehicle crashes among noncommercial drivers with licensing restrictions owing to MSDs was quite elevated (relative risk [RR] = 11.3, 95% confidence interval [CI] 2.39, 53.3), as was that among drivers without restrictions (RR = 1.84, 95% CI 1.14, 2.98). The RRs for all motor vehicle crashes for those with MSDs but not restricted were elevated (RR = 1.59, 95% CI = 1.10, 2.29), as were those for restricted drivers (RR = 4.51, 95% CI = 1.01, 20.1) [2].

An additional concern for the medical examiner relates to possible risks associated with self treatment for pain related to MSDs. Prescription medications to treat musculoskeletal pain may include narcotic analgesics, muscle relaxers, benzodiazepines, and other potentially sedating medications. Over-the-counter medications such as nonsteroidal anti-inflammatory drugs (NSAIDS), antihistamines, and others are often used by themselves, or in combination with other medications to alleviate pain as well [3–6]. A case-control study from Europe showed an increased risk of crash in users of NSAIDS (Odds Ratio [OR] = 1.7, 95% CI 1.0, 2.6). Benzodiazepine use also was found to be associated with an increased risk of at fault crash in this study (OR = 5.2, 95% CI: 0.9, 30.0) [7]. At the same time, altered levels of attention and alertness due to the distraction of pain from MSDs may also affect driving safety.

Musculoskeletal Disorders and the Commercial Driver Medical Examiner Certification Process

In addition to the regulations that address musculoskeletal conditions, the FMCSA has issued interpretations, and advisory criteria for musculoskeletal disorders. There is also a process for those drivers with a loss of limb, limb impairment, or diseases of the musculoskeletal system to be granted a variance from the medical standard [8]. To date, no medical advisory panel has been convened to address MSDs, and accordingly, no medical conference report exists to provide additional support for medical decision making. Importantly, with the establishment of the FMCSA Medical Review Board, a schedule has been proposed for review of MSDs by an expert medical advisory panel in the near future [9].

Regulations

The regulations that address musculoskeletal conditions are:

Loss of Limb

§391.41(b)(1) A person is physically qualified to drive a commercial motor vehicle if that person:
Has no loss of a foot, leg, hand, or arm, or has been granted a Skill Performance Evaluation (SPE) Certificate pursuant to Section 391.49.

Limb Impairment

§391.41(b)(2) A person is physically qualified to drive a commercial motor vehicle if that person:

Has no impairment of: (i) A hand or finger which interferes with prehension or power grasping; or (ii) An arm, foot, or leg which interferes with the ability to perform normal tasks associated with operating a commercial motor vehicle; or (iii) Any other significant limb defect or limitation which interferes with the ability to perform normal tasks associated with operating a commercial motor vehicle; or (iv) Has been granted a Skill Performance Evaluation (SPE) Certificate pursuant to Section 391.49.

Rheumatic, Arthritic, Orthopedic, Muscular, Neuromuscular, or Vascular Disease:

§391.41(b)(7) A person is physically qualified to drive a commercial motor vehicle if that person:

Has no established medical history or clinical diagnosis of rheumatic, arthritic, orthopedic, muscular, neuromuscular, or vascular disease which interferes with his/her ability to control and operate a commercial motor vehicle safely.

The Federal Motor Carrier Safety Regulations (FMCSRs) and Advisory Criteria provide guidance for evaluation of commercial drivers with respect to loss of limb, limb impairment, and diseases of the musculoskeletal system. The guidance is directed at an assessment of performance in tactile, manipulative, range of motion, and strength capabilities of the upper and lower extremities. Although explicit criteria for evaluating these capabilities have not been described, an examination directed toward these functions can provide a basis for rendering an appropriate recommendation by the medical examiner.

Implicit in determining *"the ability to perform normal tasks associated with operating a commercial motor vehicle"* or in determining what *"interferes with his/her ability to control and operate a commercial motor vehicle safely"* is an understanding by the medical examiner of the work environment of the commercial driver, and the essential job functions performed by the commercial driver. Although no two drivers may have the same vehicle or duties, certain factors are common to this role.

The primary worksite of the commercial driver is their vehicle, and the area immediately surrounding that vehicle. A commercial driver medical certificate allows a driver to operate any commercial vehicle as defined by 49 CFR 390.5. These vehicles may weigh from 10,000 lbs to upwards of 80,000 lbs or more when fully loaded. They may be of a straight (one-piece) vehicle design, or a tractor-trailer design. Straight trucks include vans, panel trucks, flatbeds, and dump-bodies. Tractor-trailers consist of the tractor power unit that may include a sleeping compartment, and from one to three trailers [10,11]. In the course of routine operations, drivers are required to climb in and out of their truck cabs, perform safety inspections, and respond to emergency situations in variable weather, lighting, and surface conditions. Drivers also may be required to load and unload material or equipment from their vehicles, couple and uncouple the trailer units, affix tire chains for travel over snow and ice, fix tarps and straps over loads to secure the loads in transit, and climb onto and over the vehicle or trailer units. These activities often are physically demanding, and the driver may be required to perform them in isolated settings without opportunity for assistance.

At a minimum, FMCSA has determined that all drivers must have the capability "to not only drive the vehicle safely, but also to do pre- and post-trip safety inspections, secure the load and make sure it has not shifted. Bus drivers have different demands" [12].

Advisory Criteria

Loss of Limb

The medical evaluation of an individual with loss of limb is a relatively straightforward exercise for the medical examiner. During the course of the medical examination, should the examiner observe the loss or absence of a foot, leg, hand, or arm, FMCSRs direct the examiner to disqualify the individual for medical clearance. The exception to this is when the individual is *"granted a Skill Performance Evaluation (SPE) Certificate pursuant to Section §391.49."*

The SPE Certification Program (formerly known as the Limb Waiver Program) was designed to allow persons with the loss of a foot or limb or with functional impairment to qualify under the FMCSRs by demonstrating adequate function or by use of prosthetic devices or equipment modifications if they are to safely operate a commercial motor vehicle. Certain risks still may be present, and therefore restrictions may be included on individual SPE certificates when a state director for the FMCSA determines they are necessary to be consistent with safety and public interest.

If the examiner finds the driver otherwise qualified, he or she may sign the medical certificate and mark on the medical certificate that the driver is qualified only if accompanied by a SPE certificate. This is different than for exemptions from any of the diabetes or vision exemptions, where the examiner would not sign the medical certificate until the exemption has been granted. The driver or the driver jointly with the motor carrier then is responsible for applying for the

SPE and both are subject to appropriate penalty if the driver operates a motor vehicle in interstate or foreign commerce without a current SPE certificate.

The medical examiner who observes or acknowledges a loss of limb for the first time in an individual seeking a commercial driver medical evaluation certification should be knowledgeable about the application process for obtaining an SPE certificate in order to appropriately complete the certification requirements, and to facilitate the application process for the driver applicant [8].

The certification process for an SPE certificate includes completion of a formal application submitted to the regional service center, for the state in which the coapplicant motor carrier's principal place of business is located, or if submitted unilaterally by a driver applicant, the application must be addressed to the field service center, FMCSA, for the state in which the driver has legal residence. The driver also is responsible for submission of appropriate medical documentation.

The medical evaluation and documentation specific to the requirements of the SPE certification process is a formal evaluation that must be completed by either a board-qualified or board-certified physiatrist (doctor of physical medicine) or orthopedic surgeon. In order to successfully complete this evaluation, the physiatrist or orthopedic surgeon must be provided by the coapplicant motor carrier or the driver applicant a description of the job-related tasks the driver applicant will be required to perform. The medical evaluation summary is required to include the following:

> §391.49(d)(3)(i)(A) An assessment of the functional capabilities of the driver as they relate to the ability of the driver to perform normal tasks associated with operating a commercial motor vehicle; and
>
> (d)(3)(i)(B) A statement by the examiner that the applicant is capable of demonstrating precision prehension (*e.g.*, manipulating knobs and switches) and power grasp prehension (*e.g.*, holding and maneuvering the steering wheel) with each upper limb separately. This requirement does not apply to an individual who was granted a waiver, absent a prosthetic device, prior to the publication of this amendment.

If the letter of application is accepted by the state director, FMCSA, then the state director may require the driver applicant to demonstrate his or her ability to safely operate the commercial motor vehicle(s) the driver intends to drive to the state agency, or an agent authorized by the state agency. Demonstration of these abilities may be accomplished by an evaluation of necessary skill sets including safety checks, skill specific driving tasks, and an over-the-road driving test.

Limb Impairment

Evaluating an individual with limb impairment poses additional challenges to the medical examiner. Although in some cases these impairments may be frankly obvious, in other cases, they may be rather subtle, and may even escape notice from the less-experienced or less-observant examiner. Examples of limb impairments may include conditions such as posttraumatic changes resulting in loss of range of motion or strength; neurodegenerative disorders with accompanying decreased sensory or motor function; or other organic impairments that prevent normal functional use of limbs.

As with loss of limb, FMCSA has developed a mechanism for individuals with limb impairment who meet specific criteria to qualify as a commercial driver. For the most part, this process is identical to that for loss of limb. A person whose limb impairment in any way interferes with the safe performance of normal tasks associated with operating a commercial motor vehicle is subject to the SPE Certification Program pursuant to Section 391.49, assuming the person is otherwise qualified. Application to this program is identical to that outlined for loss of limb.

Again, similar to requirements in loss of limb, the medical evaluation and documentation for limb impairment includes a formal evaluation that must be completed by either a board-qualified or board-certified physiatrist or orthopedic surgeon. In addition to the requirements of the loss of limb, the physiatrist or orthopedic surgeon must also provide the following:

§391.49(d)(3)(ii)(A) An explanation as to how and why the impairment interferes with the ability of the applicant to perform normal tasks associated with operating a commercial motor vehicle;

(d)(3)(ii)(B) An assessment and medical opinion of whether the condition will likely remain medically stable over the lifetime of the driver applicant; and

(d)(3)(ii)(C) A statement by the examiner that the applicant is capable of demonstrating precision prehension (*e.g.*, manipulating knobs and switches) and power grasp prehension (*e.g.*, holding and maneuvering the steering wheel) with each upper limb separately. This requirement does not apply to an individual who was granted an SPE Certificate, absent an orthotic device, prior to the publication of this amendment.

(d)(4) A description of the driver applicant's prosthetic or orthotic device worn, if any.

Rheumatic, Arthritic, Orthopedic, Muscular, Neuromuscular, or Vascular Disease

Evaluation of the individual with rheumatic, arthritic, orthopedic, muscular, neuromuscular, or vascular disease has the potential to pose even more challenges to the medical examiner. Even subtle manifestations of some of these disorders have the potential to pose significant risk for sudden incapacitation to drivers. Evaluation of some of these conditions warrants careful attention to appropriate screening instruments, and use of expert consultation when warranted.

The Advisory Criteria for this section states the following:

§391.41(b)(7) A person is physically qualified to drive a commercial vehicle if that person:

Has no established medical history or clinical diagnosis of rheumatic, arthritic, orthopedic, muscular, neuromuscular or vascular disease which interferes with ability to control and operate a commercial motor vehicle safely.

Certain diseases are known to have acute episodes of transient muscle weakness, poor muscular coordination (ataxia), abnormal sensations (paresthesia), decreased muscle tone (hypotonia), visual disturbances, and pain that suddenly may be incapacitating. With each recurring episode, these symptoms may become more pronounced and remain for longer periods of time. Other diseases have more insidious onsets and display symptoms of muscle wasting (atrophy), swelling, and paresthesia which may not suddenly incapacitate a person but may restrict his or her movements and eventually interfere with the ability to safely operate a motor vehicle. In many instances these diseases are degenerative in nature or may result in deterioration of the involved area.

Once the individual has been diagnosed as having a rheumatic, arthritic, orthopedic, muscular, neuromuscular, or vascular disease, then he or she has an established history of that disease. The physician, when examining an individual, should consider the following:

(1) The nature and severity of the individual's condition (such as sensory loss or loss of strength)
(2) The degree of limitation present (such as range of motion)
(3) The likelihood of progressive limitation (not always present initially but manifests itself over time)
(4) The likelihood of sudden incapacitation

If severe functional impairment exists, the driver does not qualify. In cases where more frequent monitoring is required, a certificate for a shorter period of time may be issued.

In general, as §391.41(b)(7) implies, this subpart includes an enormously broad class of diseases and disorders. The various conditions may have temporary, stable, progressive, or relapsing courses over their natural history. Because of this, the medical examiner needs to be aware of the natural history of these conditions in order to make appropriate recommendations regarding the capability of the individual to operate a commercial vehicle safely. When evaluating these drivers, the medical examiner should certify only those drivers whose current status is unlikely to interfere with the safe operation of the commercial vehicle. If there is any question of deterioration that would pose a risk for safe operation of the commercial vehicle, the medical examiner may qualify the driver for a period less than 2 years.

Conditions encountered among individuals seeking a commercial driver's license reflect those seen in the general working population. Although a comprehensive review of disorders included within §391.41(b)(7) is not possible in a text of this nature, a brief review of some of the more commonly encountered, or problematic disorders can provide a working framework for the medical examiner. Additional rare or uncommon conditions may certainly be encountered, and the medical examiner should bear in mind that these will likely require further review and/or specialty consultation.

Individuals may present for a CDME with a diagnosis of these related musculoskeletal disorders or they may have symptoms and/or findings suggestive of subclinical disease that has yet to be diagnosed. These conditions may cause pain, deformity, and functional limitations of the musculoskeletal system. Many of these disorders, particularly the rheumatic and neuromuscular diseases, can be exacerbated by conditions of commercial driving. These factors include lifestyle limitations of diet, exercise, and sleep; cyclic periods of relative inactivity interspersed with high-exertional activities; mechanical stress and trauma associated with vibration during driving and idling; and mental stressors associated with driving under time pressures or variable weather and traffic conditions.

The natural history of these related musculoskeletal disorders must be considered when making decisions for qualifying of drivers, or for assigning duration of the medical certificate. In coming to this decision, the examiner will need to consider the individual's report of history, medication usage, the physical examination, and additional ancillary information including medical records from treating physicians, and available laboratory and imaging studies. Often, direct communication with the individual's treating physician will be required to better gauge current limitations, potential complications from medication regimens, and ultimate near- and long-term prognosis.

The following is a brief review of some common rheumatic, arthritic, orthopedic, muscular, neuromuscular, and vascular diseases the medical examiner may encounter when evaluating individuals. Diagnostic criteria for many of these conditions are based on classification by the American College of Rheumatology [13].

- **Osteoarthritis** is typically a progressive disease often associated with aging, or prior history of trauma. It affects upwards of 21 million Americans with an equal sex ratio. Joint surfaces are affected as cartilage wears or thins. Individuals suffer with variable degrees of functional limitations as a result of the cartilaginous damage. Most commonly weight-bearing joints are involved, but any joint can be affected. Neurological structures also can be affected, particularly in areas of the spine where nerve roots come in contact with associated bone lesions. In one general population-based study, arthritis was found to be associated with increased risk of crash among females (OR = 1.8, 95% CI: 1.1, 2.9) [7]. Medical examiners must address range of motion, strength and deconditioning, and any potential neurological impairment associated with this condition that may affect essential job functions and safety.
- **Rheumatoid arthritis (RA)** is a chronic progressive autoimmune disease affecting joints as well as other organ systems. It affects upwards of 2 million Americans with female-to-male ratio of 3:1. Diagnosis of RA can be challenging, so many individuals with RA often go undiagnosed. Classic features include morning stiffness, and involvement of the small joints of the hands and feet. Constitutional symptoms may include fatigue, malaise, weakness, low-grade fevers, and loss of appetite. Dry eyes and mouth often are associated with Sjogren's syndrome, a condition often seen in association with RA or systemic lupus erythematosus. RA also is associated with elevated risk for heart disease and stroke. Common complications of RA include joint pain, limitation of motion, flexion contractures, hyperextensibility, subluxation, peripheral swelling, entrapment neuropathies, and loss of function.
- **Psoriatic arthritis** is an autoimmune disease affecting approximately 15 percent of people with psoriasis. The usual age of onset is between ages 30 to 50. Although generally considered mild and nonprogressive in nature, individuals can suffer permanent joint damage. Psoriatic arthritis can include spondylitis (affecting the neck and back), and enthesopathies (affecting any tendinous or lig-

amentous attachment) and thus has broad potential to affect function.

- **Spondyloarthritis** includes several disorders that affect the spine, peripheral joints, and tendon and ligamentous attachments. Usual age of onset is in the teens and twenties with a male-to-female ratio of 2 to 3:1. Most patients share the HLA-B27 genetic marker. This class of disorders includes ankylosing spondylitis, reactive arthritis (formerly known as Reiter's syndrome), psoriatic arthritis, and psoriatic spondylitis, and the arthritis or spondylitis associated with the inflammatory bowel diseases, ulcerative colitis and Crohn's disease. Uveitis may occur in upwards of 40 percent of patients, and inflammation of the aortic valve is not uncommon.

- **Reactive arthritis** is a condition associated with an infectious agent, usually of the gastrointestinal or genital tract. Approximately 15 percent to 20 percent of individuals suffering from infections of the gastrointestinal or genital tract will develop reactive arthritis. Although generally self-limiting, people who suffer from this condition have a tendency for recurrence with subsequent infections.

- **Myopathies** are rare idiopathic disorders and include diseases such as polymyositis and dermatomyositis. Prevalence rates are estimated to be 1 per 100,000 with bimodal peak incidences between ages 5–10 and 40–50 years. Women are affected twice as frequently as men. Inclusion body myositis, a more rare disorder, affects men more frequently than women. These disorders tend to be progressive with time. Myopathies tend to affect the proximal muscle groups, and are not generally associated with pain. Functional capacity, specifically related to strength limitations, may directly impact safe operation of motor vehicles, so adequate screening of individuals with known or suspected myopathic disorders requires appropriate assessment of strength.

- **Paget's disease** is an uncommon progressive chronic idiopathic disorder affecting approximately 1 percent of people in the United States. It primarily affects people greater than 40 years of age, and has a 3:2 male-to-female ratio. Individuals with Paget's disease experience abnormal bone metabolism resulting in areas of rapid bone growth, typically in the pelvis, spine, hips, extremities, and skull. These changes can lead to bone pain, pathological fractures, and arthritic changes.

- **Gout** is a result of excess uric acid accumulation and deposition of uric acid crystals between joint surfaces causing acute painful episodic flares. Gout affects approximately 1 percent of people in the United States and as many as 6 percent to 7 percent of older males. Gout is strongly associated with obesity, hypertension, hyperlipidemia, and diabetes. Appropriate treatment including medications and dietary modification can reduce frequency of episodes when gout is recurrent. Lifestyle risk factors in commercial drivers have potential to adversely impact control of this condition.

- **Osteoporosis** develops as bone resorption exceeds bone formation, typically as a result of aging, use of certain medications such as corticosteroids, or specific pathological processes such as Cushing's disease. It is more common over age 50, and in non-Hispanic Caucasian and Asian populations. Additional risk factors include smoking, excess alcohol intake, sedentary lifestyle, inadequate intake of calcium and vitamin D, and decreased production of sex hormones. Individuals with osteoporosis are subject to increased risk from bone fracture. Treatment for osteoporosis including medications such as bisphosphonates can pose challenges for the demands of commercial drivers.

- **Systemic connective disorders** include a broad group of autoimmune disorders that can affect multiorgan systems, most notably the musculoskeletal system.

  - **Systemic lupus erythematosus (SLE)** is a chronic inflammatory disease that can affect the skin, joints, kidneys, lungs, nervous system, and other organ systems. It affects women 10 times more frequently than men. The clinical course varies from mild to severe, and it has a pattern of relapse and remission.

  - **Scleroderma** is a relatively uncommon disorder affecting upwards of 100,000 Americans with a female-to-male ratio of 3:1. Two forms exist with localized scleroderma primarily affecting skin structures, and systemic sclerosis affecting skin and other organ systems. Scleroderma causes thickening and fibrosis of tissue with resultant limitations on range of motion and strengths.

  - **Polymyalgia rheumatica** is a common cause of joint pain in older adults with a typical onset after age 50. It primarily affects the shoulders, back, neck, and hips. It can limit ambulation, and lifting ability. Giant cell arteritis (or temporal arteritis) may occur in 5 percent to 15 percent of people with polymyalgia rheumatica.

- **Entrapment neuropathies** may affect nerve and muscle function and limit capacity to adequately perform prehension and fine motor control. Carpal tunnel syndrome (CTS) is the most common entrapment neuropathy and reportedly affects between 3 percent to 7 percent of people in the United States. CTS results in slowed nerve transmission along the median nerve. This may cause paresthesia in the thumb, index, middle, and radial aspect of the ring fingers. Over time, progressive and untreated cases may go on to develop muscular atrophy. CTS can diminish tactile sensation and motor control which can impair ability to manipulate gauges, and knobs, as well as prehension to grip steering wheels and engage gear mechanisms. Driving is also recognized to aggravate symptoms of this condition [14], although whether driving causes CTS has not been determined. Ulnar neuropathy at the elbow, including cubital tunnel syndrome, affects the ulnar nerve which can result in sensory and motor findings in the ring and fifth finger. It also has the potential to impair function similarly to CTS. Tarsal tunnel syndrome involves entrapment of the tibial nerve at the medial malleolus. This may affect sensation and motor function of the foot that in turn can affect safe operation of the brake, clutch, and gas pedal.

- **Tendinitis** and **bursitis**, particularly of the upper extremities, can significantly impair necessary function in commercial drivers. Tendinitis may arise from trauma, high-force activities, repetition, postural issues, or merely arising through normal aging and other nonoccupational factors. Commercial drivers have been shown to be at elevated risk for shoulder tendinitis [15]. Bursitis may arise under similar conditions, however, it is important to recognize that infectious causes, or septic bursitis, require more careful management. Certain safety sensitive driving tasks like steering, shifting, and operation of switches, knobs, and gauges may be severely limited by active tendinitis or bursitis.

- **Back disorders** including low back pain (LBP), sciatica, discogenic disease, and history of back surgery are extremely common among commercial drivers. A multicenter study from the United States and Sweden found that 50 percent of commercial drivers reported low back pain. The highest risk factors for low back pain were long-term vibration exposure (OR = 2.0, 95% CI 0.98–4.1), heavy lifting (OR = 1.86, 95% CI 1.2–2.8), and frequent lifting (OR = 1.55, 95% CI 1.01–2.39) [15]. Work loss from low back pain was influenced by perceived job stress. Prolonged sitting, intervals of heavy lifting, vibration, and lifestyle factors such as lack of physical activity, and poor dietary patterns have all been cited as factors associated with this high prevalence of back pain among commercial drivers [16–18]. The medical examiner needs to be aware of functional limitations associated with these conditions, and will need to assess range of motion of the spine, as well as perform appropriate neurological evaluation. It also may be necessary to review medical records including surgeries, injections, functional capacity evaluations, imaging studies, and nerve conduction studies to better assess functional limitations and safety concerns.

- **Neck disorders** including neck pain, radiculopathy, discogenic disease, and history of cervical neck surgery are also common in the commercial driving population [15]. The medical examiner should carefully assess neck range of motion, especially the ability to rotate the neck. Adequate visualization by the driver requires the ability to rotate the neck in order to adequately assess road and traffic conditions, gauges and other electronic devices in the tractor unit, load stability, and other critical safety features of the vehicle and its surroundings.

- **Neuromuscular disorders** were reviewed by the Conference on Neurological Disorders and Commercial Drivers in 1988 [19]. At that time, the consensus of the participants in the conference was that the content of the commercial driver medical examination was insufficient for assessing individuals with neurological disorders. The report recommended that any driver with signs or symptoms of neurological disorder be referred to a neurologist for evaluation. Within the body of the report, neurological disorders were separated into two categories for consideration of disqualification (Table 6-1). Drivers with disease in the first category were to be disqualified automatically. Drivers with disease in the second category also would likely be disqualified, but consideration of appeals was possible.

Table 6-1. Recommended Categories for Neurologic Disqualification*

Automatic Disqualification	Disqualification with Possible Appeal
Dementia	Multiple sclerosis
Motor neuron disease	Peripheral neuropathy
Malignant tumors of the central nervous system	Myopathy
Huntington's disease	Neuromuscular junction disorder
Wilson's disease	Benign brain tumor Dyskinesia Treatable dementia Cerebellar ataxia

*Categories recommended by the Conference on Neurologic Disorders and Commercial Drivers, August 1988 [19].

The appeals process proposed in the conference report included an evaluation by a board-certified neurologist, neurosurgeon, or physiatrist. If a driver were to complete such an evaluation successfully, an on-the-road driving test would be required. Annual examination was recommended if such a driver was deemed medically qualified after the complete assessment. Although the appeals process has not been implemented in law, this process offers a foundation and guidance to assist the medical examiner with evaluation and management of drivers with neuromuscular disorders.

- **Acute and subacute conditions** also may have potential to affect the function of the musculoskeletal system. Individuals may frequently present in some phase of recovery from acute conditions with or without self-limiting natural histories. These may include a range of conditions from minor first aid–type injuries with little medical consequence to more serious traumatic injuries that may lead to permanent functional impairment. Commonly encountered conditions include strains, sprains, fractures, wounds, burns, and other posttraumatic changes. Although many of these conditions will resolve without need for further medical evaluation, it is always possible for complications to arise that could eventuate permanent impairment of function. For example, even minor conditions such as superficial wounds may lead to infection with further potential to impair soft tissue, joint, bone or nerve structures [20].

Of greater challenge for the examiner are more complicated traumatic injuries. Deep-tissue injuries, wounds over joint surfaces, infections of skin, bursa, tendons or bones, tendon lacerations, complex fractures, postoperative repairs, and other complications of trauma make it difficult to predict outcome. The examiner must recognize that permanent limitations of function may exist following a traumatic injury that would preclude safe operation of a commercial vehicle. Therefore, when an individual presents with an acute condition that either limits function, or could possibly limit function upon recovery, then the examiner should consider not qualifying the individual for medical certification until an evaluation at the point of maximum medical improvement has been reached. At that time, the examiner should focus on functional recovery of the affected system or limb including range of motion, strength, sensation and ability to perform the routine tasks of the commercial driver as noted previously. Any limitations noted may require application for certification through the limb impairment SPE process.

Musculoskeletal History and Examination

The musculoskeletal examination of the commercial driver needs to be both focused and comprehensive. The medical examiner must be able to provide an assessment that the individual has adequate function, and lack of any significant impairment to allow safe operation of a commercial vehicle.

The self report of history provided by the individual on the written medical form may provide assistance in understanding preexisting musculoskeletal problems, but it is not in itself adequate to determine prior or existing musculoskeletal problems. The medical examiner should query the individual directly with a focused musculoskeletal history. This line of inquiry should include questions about prior medical care, surgeries, trauma, or other problems. Specific questions regarding subjective symptoms of pain, paresthesia, weakness, or limitations in range of motion or other limitations in function also should be addressed.

In addition to direct questions regarding potential musculoskeletal problems, the medical examiner, as well as ancillary office staff, needs to be observant of behavior and activities prior to the formal examination. Gait disturbances, behavior suggestive of pain (e.g., grimaces, guarding, verbalization or vocalization of pain, etc.), or other abnormalities should be noted and followed up with appropriate questions and examination.

The examination should be comprehensive to include all aspects of the musculoskeletal system, and focused to specific areas intrinsic to the demands of commercial driving. Specifically the medical examiner must pay attention to the back and extremities. The examination must ensure that the individual has adequate strength, range of motion, and intact sensory and proprioceptive responses to perform the essential job functions and assure safe operation of the commercial vehicle. The examination should be methodical to assure that each component is adequately assessed. It also must be focused to more carefully assess specific areas identified in the history, or that otherwise might merit more careful attention (e.g., past surgical problems, complaints of pain, noted asymmetries, etc.).

The examination should include a thorough evaluation of the back and neck for range of motion, posture, and appropriate neurological responses of reflexes, sensation, and motor function. Upper and lower extremities should be examined for symmetry, range of motion, strength, sensation, and other neurovascular parameters. Suspected abnormalities may be referenced to accepted normal values such as those published in the *Guides to the Evaluation of Permanent Impairment*

[21], or other accepted standard references [22–24]. In some cases, specific tests or examination maneuvers might be warranted. This might include strength testing (e.g., hand-grip dynamometer or other objective measures), range of motion testing (e.g., goniometer or other objective measures), sensory testing (e.g., two-point discrimination, filament sensation, or other objective measures), and/or provocative physical examination tests for ligamentous or joint stability. Specific abnormalities found on examination or subjective symptoms may at times require further evaluation such as laboratory tests, radiological imaging, nerve conduction testing, or specialty referral.

Ultimately, the medical examiner must be able to provide an assessment that the individual has the functional capability to perform the essential job functions of a commercial driver, and to do so in a manner consistent with safe operation of a commercial vehicle. Anything short of this objective requires that the medical examiner fail to qualify the individual on medical grounds.

References

1. Meuleners LB, Lee AH, Legge M, Cercarelli R. Health conditions of heavy vehicle drivers involved in a crash in western Australia: A retrospective study using linked data. *Health Promotion Journal Australia* 2005;Apr; 16(1):37–40.
2. Diller E, Cook L, Leonard D, Reading J, Dean JM, Vernon D. Evaluating drivers licensed with medical conditions in Utah, 1992–1996. Technical Report No. DOT HS 809 023. Washington: National Highway Traffic Safety Administration, June 1999.
3. Mantyselka P, Ahonen R, Viinamaki H, Takala J, Kumpusalo E. Drug use by patients visiting primary care physicians due to nonacute musculoskeletal pain. *Eur J Pharm Sci* 2002;17(4–5):201–206.
4. van Tulder MW, Touray T, Furlan AD, Solway S, Bouter LM. Muscle relaxants for non-specific low-back pain. Cochrane Database Syst Rev. Art. No.: CD004252. DOI: 10.1002/14651858.CD004252.
5. Peloso P, Gross A, Haines T, Trinh K, Goldsmith CH, Aker P, Cervical Overview Group. Medicinal and injection therapies for mechanical neck disorders. Cochrane Database Syst Rev. Art. No.: CD000319. DOI: 10.1002/14651858.CD000319.pub3.
6. Gagnier JJ, vanTulder M, Berman B, Bombardier C. Herbal medicine for low back pain. Cochrane Database Syst Rev. Art. No.: CD004504. DOI: 10.1002/14651858.CD004504.pub3.
7. McGwin G, Sims RV, Yulley L, Roseman JM. Relations among chronic medical conditions, medications, and automobile crashes in the elderly: A population-based case-control study. *American Journal of Epidemiology* 2000;152(5):424–431.

8. Skill Performance Evaluation Application Information. www.fmcsa.dot .gov/rules-regulations/topics/medical/spepackage.htm. Accessed June 1, 2007.

9. Federal Motor Carrier Medical Review Board. www.mrb.fmcsa.dot.gov/meeting.htm. Accessed June 1, 2007.

10. .49 CFR Part 658, Truck Size and Weight, Route Destinations. Length, Width, and Weight Limitations. www.fmcsa.dot.gov/rules-regulations/administration/fmcsr/fmcsrguidedetails.asp?rule_toc=778&section_toc=778. Accessed May 21, 2007.

11. The Truckers Report—Facts about Trucks—Eighteen-Wheelers. www.thetruckersreport.com/truck_facts.shtml. Accessed May 21, 2007.

12. Federal Motor Carrier Safety Administration, Frequently Asked Questions. www.fmcsa.dot.gov/rules-regulations/topics/medical/faq.asp.Accessed May 21, 2007.

13. The American College of Rheumatology. www. rheumatology.org/. Accessed March 30, 2007.

14. Clinical evaluation and management of work-related carpal tunnel syndrome. *American Journal of Industrial Medicine*: 1999;37(1): 62–74.

15. Magnusson ML, Pope MH, Wilder DG, Areskoug B. Are occupational drivers at an increased risk for developing musculoskeletal disorders? *Spine* 1996;21(6):710–717.

16. Lyons J. Factors contributing to low back pain among professional drivers: A review of current literature and possible ergonomic controls. *Work* 2002;19(1):95–102.

17. Biering-Sörensen F, Thomsen CE, Hilden J. Risk indicators for low back trouble. *Scand J Rehab Med* 1989;21:151–157.

18. Frymoyer JW, Pope MH, Clements JH. Risk factors in LBP. An epidemiological survey. *J Bone Joint Surg* 1983;65:213–218.

19. U.S. Department of Transportation, Federal Highway Administration. Conference on Neurologic Disorders and Commercial Drivers. Publication No. FHWA-MC-88-042. Washington: U.S. DOT, Federal Highway Administration, Office of Motor Carriers, 1988.

20. Trott AT. *Wounds and Lacerations: Emergency Care and Closure*, 3rd ed. St. Louis, MO: Mosby, 2005.

21. Andersson GJB, Cocchiarella L, editors. *Guides to the Evaluation of Permanent Impairment*, 5th ed. Chicago, IL: American Medical Association, 2000.

22. Griffin LY, editor. *Essentials of Musculoskeletal Care*, 3rd ed. Rosemont, IL: American Academy of Orthopaedic Surgeons, 2005.

23. Hoppenfeld S. *Physical Examination of the Spine and Extremities*. Norwalk, CT: Appleton-Century-Crofts, 1976.

24. Glass LS, Harris JS, editors. *Occupational Medicine Practice Guidelines: Evaluation and Management of Common Health Problems and Functional Recovery in Workers*, 2nd ed. Beverly Farms, MA: American College of Occupational and Environmental Medicine, 2004.

7

Neurologic Disorders

Kurt T. Hegmann, MD, MPH

The CDME processes are currently undergoing substantial changes. As of June 2007, the schedule for the FMCSA Medical Review Board (MRB) is to review seizure disorders in 2007, vision in late 2007, and other neurological disorders in 2008. After the MRB reviews a subject, the FMCSA may be advised of suggested changes in the CDME processes by the MRB, after which rule-making may or may not commence. Please be aware of these updating processes.

There are numerous common disorders affecting the nervous system and the capability for safe operation of commercial motor vehicles. Cerebrovascular disorders are the third leading cause of death in the United States [1]. Headaches, fatigue, vertigo, and dizziness are among common reasons to visit a physician in the United States. Data suggest that some of these disorders present an increased risk for motor vehicle crashes [2]. Thus, the high prevalence of nervous system disorders combined with increased motor vehicle crash risk results in the need to frequently deal with such issues in the context of the commercial driver medical examination process.

Regulations, Advisory Criteria, and Frequently Asked Questions

Several regulations either directly or indirectly address neurologic conditions in the commercial driver. They are:

(b)(7) Has no established medical history or clinical diagnosis of rheumatic, arthritic, orthopedic, muscular, neuromuscular, or vascular disease which interferes with his/her ability to control and operate a commercial motor vehicle safely;

(b)(8) Has no established medical history or clinical diagnosis of epilepsy or any other condition which is likely to cause loss of consciousness or any loss of ability to control a commercial motor vehicle;

(b)(9) Has no mental, nervous, organic, or functional disease or psychiatric disorder likely to interfere with his/her ability to drive a commercial motor vehicle safely;

(b)(10) Has distant visual acuity of at least 20/40 (Snellen) in each eye without corrective lenses or visual acuity separately corrected to 20/40 (Snellen) or better with corrective lenses, distant binocular acuity of at least 20/40 (Snellen) in both eyes with or without corrective lenses, field of vision of at least 70° in the horizontal meridian in each eye, and the ability to recognize the colors of traffic signals and devices showing standard red, green, and amber;

(b)(11) First perceives a forced whispered voice in the better ear at not less than 5 feet with or without the use of a hearing aid or, if tested by use of an audiometric device, does not have an average hearing loss in the better ear greater than 40 decibels at 500 Hz, 1,000 Hz, and 2,000 Hz with or without a hearing aid when the audiometric device is calibrated to American National Standard (formerly ASA Standard) Z24.5-1951.

Standards 391.41b(7) and b(9) will be discussed in greater detail in Chapters 6 and 9 respectively.

The advisory criteria on drivers with seizures or loss of consciousness clarify that drivers should not be qualified if they:

(1) have a medical history of epilepsy
(2) have a current clinical diagnosis of epilepsy
(3) are taking antiseizure medication to control or prevent seizure

After a 6-month waiting period for an individual with a nonepileptic seizure or other loss of consciousness of unknown cause that did not require use of antiseizure medication, the medical examiner in consultation with the treating provider should decide whether an individual's condition will likely cause loss of consciousness or loss of ability to control a commercial motor vehicle. Prior to certification, a complete neurologic evaluation should be performed if the evaluation is normal and antiseizure medication is not required, then the driver may be qualified.

When an identified condition led to a seizure or an episode of loss of consciousness such as a drug reaction, high temperature, dehydration, or acute metabolic disturbance, certification should be deferred until the driver has fully recovered from that condition, has no existing residual complications, and is not taking antiseizure medication.

Drivers with a history of epilepsy/seizures should be off anti-seizure medication and seizure free for 10 years before they are medically qualified. Those with a single unprovoked seizure should be seizure free and off antiseizure medication for at least 5 years before operating a commercial motor vehicle in interstate commerce.

Vision advisory criteria explains that an individual can have some type of color deficiency but will meet the standard if they are able to recognize and distinguish between traffic control signals and devices showing standard red, green, and amber. Contact lenses are permissible if there is sufficient evidence to indicate that the driver has good tolerance and is well adapted to their use. Use of a contact lens in one eye for distant visual acuity and another lens in the other eye for near vision is not acceptable, nor are telescopic lenses acceptable for driving commercial motor vehicles.

If a driver requires corrective lenses to meet the criteria, the examiner should indicate qualified "only when . . . wearing corrective lenses" on the medical examination form and the certificate. Drivers who do not meet the criteria may be eligible for a vision exemption. Additional information on the exemption can be found at www.fmcsa.dot.gov/rules-regulations/topics/medical/exemptions.htm.

For hearing, the examiner is instructed to perform the whisper test by standing at least 5 feet from the driver with the ear being tested turned toward the examiner and the other ear covered. Using the breath that remains after a normal expiration, the examiner whispers words or random numbers. If the individual fails the whispered voice test, the audiometric test should be administered. If the driver needs a hearing aid to meet the criteria, they must wear it at all times while driving. The examiner should indicate that the driver is qualified "only when . . . wearing a hearing aid" on the medical examination form and the medical certificate.

There are two frequently asked questions [3] on Ménière's disease. In one, Ménière's disease is noted to be disqualifying due to severe and unpredictable bouts of vertigo. The other acknowledges that there is now surgery for Ménière's and the issue is being reviewed. There is also one question indicating that a driver with epilepsy who is interested in applying for an exemption can do so, if safety would not be compromised. There have been four applications for exemptions from the epilepsy/loss of consciousness standard [4]; final determination has not yet been published.

Many other disorders and problems are recommended by the Conference on Neurologic Disorders and Commercial Drivers [5] as disqualifying due to diagnosis, prognosis, or complications of treatment. The remainder of this chapter focuses on recommendations from that conference report, noting recommendations from other countries where available. Remember that over the next few years, these recommendations are likely to be updated.

Recommendations

Neurologic and psychiatric disorders were addressed in separate conference reports that were recommendations of committees of experts to the U.S. Department of Transportation for dealing with these problems. The specific sets of recommendations were never implemented, yet they form the basis for handling these problems and approaching patients with various disorders.

Invariably, the first issue is to secure an accurate diagnosis [5]. Subsequently, it was recommended that three categories of risk be addressed:

1. The prognosis / risk of the disease itself
2. The risk of a complication or recurrence
3. The risk of a therapeutic complication

At any step during this proposed, sequenced evaluation, a commercial driver may be disqualified based on the information obtained at that step (Table 7-1). For example, a driver may have a diagnosis such as presumptive Alzheimer's disease, a condition recommended to be disqualifying by the conference report. In that case, the driver would not be allowed to drive. Conversely, a driver with a relatively benign disorder, such as a benign tremor not necessitating treatment, would likely be allowed to drive.

For relatively stable and benign conditions, such as a driver with a diagnosis of mild Parkinson's disease, easily managed by medication and without substantial potential for impairment while driving, an "appeals process" was proposed, though never implemented, that would allow the driver to retain certification.

This conceptual framework still is useful in evaluating the commercial driver. If one encounters drivers with some of these conditions, particularly in areas of uncertainty about driving risk, referrals to gain learned opinions are frequently helpful in this process.

Table 7-1. Commercial Driver Medical Examination Guidelines for Neurologic Disorders*

1. Diagnosis
2. Disability
3. Mental disability
4. Approved to drive

Note: Disqualification may occur at any step in the proposed process.
*Recommendation from the Conference on Neurologic Disorders and Commercial Drivers [5].

Proposed Cognitive Screen Components

The Conference on Neurologic Disorders and Commercial Drivers [5] recommended a cognitive-impairment screen to assess an individual's ability to perform mental functions. The proposed screen includes evaluation of

1. Orientation to person, place, and time
2. Verbal and nonverbal intellect
3. Visual and verbal memory
4. Visuoperceptive abilities, including visual resolution, fields, and visuospatial performance
5. Language ability, including comprehension, ability to repeat, and reading ability

For the basic commercial driver medical examination, it was recommended that the physician

1. Note the comportment and level of alertness, comprehension of questions, and insightfulness of responses.*
2. Have the applicant read a standard paragraph or sentence aloud and state what it means.
3. Have the applicant spontaneously write a sentence.*
4. Have the applicant copy a standard complex geometric figure.
5. Administer a standard Mini-Mental Status Examination whenever there is doubt about the capabilities.*
6. Test visual acuity with a Snellen chart.*
7. Assess visual fields separately in each ocular quadrant by finger counting to confrontational fields.*

8. Look for evidence of hemineglect of sensory stimuli by double simultaneous stimulation in the visual hemifields and in the tactile modality.

Doubtless, the commercial driver medical examination is not currently performed with all of the tests noted in this list. Still, several of these items are generally performed (as noted by the asterisk—*), and in those situations where further investigation is desired, the list may serve as a useful reminder of potential avenues for additional testing.

The task of writing is frequently assessed with the standard questionnaire. Particularly, all positive responses to the review of systems portion of the form should be further explained in the form's section following the checklist. One may consider observing the driver complete the form for those who failed to write additional, requisite information in this area of the form. A complete Mini-Mental Status Examination also is not generally performed because it would usually be of low yield in a setting outside of significant impairment, yet it may be of assistance in certain cases where questions particularly concerning global impairment arise. Should abnormalities be discovered or suspected through this process, then some or all of the items recommended by the conference report, as well as other clinical tests, may be needed. It should be noted that a systematic literature review concluded that for purposes of screening for cognitive predictors of fitness to drive in persons with dementia, "It is impossible to employ tests in a standardized fashion in front-line clinical settings" [6]. Separately, a prospective cohort study found that performance-based cognitive measures at motor vehicle administration field sites in Maryland were successful at identifying older adults at risk for at-fault motor vehicle crashes [7].

The physical examination recommendations in the conference report are detailed, time-consuming, and likely of low yield for routine implementation. However, they too may be of assistance for use in those situations where additional investigation seems to be needed. The conference report recommendations include the following tests:

1. Cranial nerves (CNs)—visual fields, presence of hemianopia or central scotopia, denial of any field, diplopia, or oscillopsia; significant hearing deficits
2. Sensory nerves—pain, paresthesias, or dysesthesias because these can distract the driver's attention; any hypesthesia or anesthesia likely to impair fine-skilled use of the hands, arms, or legs; disturbances in proprioception

3. Motor nerves—strength, range of motion, reflexes, skill, dexterity, and reaction time; involuntary movements or alterations in tone (spasticity, rigidity); gait (normal and tandem)

The following list of screening tests for neurologic disorders is recommended for routine use by this author for commercial driver medical examinations (with additional tests performed as indicated):

1. Snellen, Ishihara, depth perception, and peripheral visual fields (CN II)
2. Pupillary appearance, reactivity to light, and constriction (CN II)
3. Extraocular movements (CNs III, IV, and VI)
4. Facial expression and symmetry (CN VII)
5. Tympanic membranes and middle ear appearance (CN VIII)
6. Audiometry, or at least a forced whisper test (CN VIII)
7. Gag reflex (CN IX)
8. Palatal movement (CN X)
9. Tongue movement (CN XII)
10. Gait
11. Squat and standing strength, qualitative grip strength
12. Ranges of motion of the back (flexion), neck (all planes), shoulders, elbows, wrists, and phalanges; appearance of same
13. Deep-tendon reflexes (patellar)
14. Romberg
15. Babinski
16. Speech
17. Comprehension, understanding, communication, and interaction

Disqualifying Conditions

Tables 7-2 through 7-5 list those conditions that were recommended to be automatically disqualifying in the Conference on Neurologic Disorders and Commercial Drivers. Although the lists are fairly lengthy, they are not exhaustive, because there are many rare conditions. These lists provide a basis for dealing with nearly all drivers, since persons with rare conditions most commonly would be categorized in a disease group (e.g., motor neuron diseases) and the recommendation could be inferred from the recommendations for similar conditions. It should be remembered, however, that none of these conditions, with the exception of active seizure disorder, is considered to be absolutely "disqualifying" by the Federal Motor Carrier Safety Administration (FMCSA); rather, these were the recommended actions for each of these disorders by the panel of experts.

Table 7-2. Automatically Disqualifying Neurologic Disorders*

Legally incompetent	Construction apraxia
Major psychiatric disorder	Amnestic problems
Aphasia, alexia	Frontal-lobe disorders
Dementia	Chronic cluster headaches
Cranial neuralgia	Migraines with neurologic deficits
Diplopia, oscillopsia	Ménière's disease
Nonfunctioning labyrinth	Hemineglect, right to left disorientation
Labyrinthine fistula	Hemianopia/hemineglect of the visual field

*As recommended by the Conference on Neurologic Disorders and Commercial Drivers [5].

Table 7-3. Recommended as Automatically Disqualifying Dementias*

Alzheimer's disease	Antihypertensive use
AIDS	Creutzfeldt-Jakob disease
Pick's disease	Syphilis
Parkinson's disease	Metabolic encephalopathy
Huntington's chorea	Alcoholism
Progressive supranuclear palsy	Depression
Cerebrovascular accident(s)	Granulomatous meningitis
Encephalitis	Vitamin B_{12} deficiency
Hypothyroidism	Heavy-metal toxicity
Organic-solvent toxicity	Tranquilizer use
Sedative use (prescribed and over-the-counter)	

Structural lesions

Tumor

Subdural hematoma

Multiple sclerosis

Stroke

Hydrocephalus

*These were recommended as disqualifying even if only "entertained" as a diagnosis for the presentation of dementia [5].

Table 7-4. Recommended as Automatically Disqualifying Neuromuscular Diseases*

Motor neuron disease

Systemic peripheral neuropathy

Neuromuscular junction disease

Multiple dystrophy

Dermatomyositis

Metabolic muscle disease

Congenital myopathy

Myotonia

*As recommended by the Conference on Neurologic Disorders and Commercial Drivers [5].

Table 7-5. Tumor and Parkinson's Disease (Proposed Procedure)*

CNS tumors (primary or secondary)

1. Disqualify

2. Drivers with treated benign tumors may apply for an "appeal"

Parkinsonism

1. Disqualify

2. Drivers who are stable under treatment and compliant, with no on-off phenomena, no side effects, and no mental impairments, may "appeal"

*Conference on Neurologic Disorders and Commercial Drivers [5].

Acute Encephalitis and Meningitis

There are no specific criteria or guidance in the United States, although acute disorders are disqualifying. Chronic issues, including seizure-related potential, should be assessed prior to returning to driving. Other guidance may apply such as headaches and other impairments. In Great Britain, the driver is required to notify the DVLA [8]. If the driver has meningitis, he or she cannot drive for 5 years if they suffer seizures and during that 5-year interval they must be off antiepileptics and seizure free. For encephalitis, the same rule applies, except that the interval is 10 years.

Cerebellar Degeneration

This group of disorders includes hereditary degenerative disorders, alcoholism, hypothyroidism, multiple sclerosis, infections, and consequences of tumors. Individuals with cerebellar ataxia were recommended to be disqualified from commercial vehicle operation by the conference report. Generally, the same is true for the other disorders. However, it was believed that if the symptoms were mild or due to a treatable problem, then a second opinion from a neurologist was indicated.

Cerebrovascular Disease, Strokes, and Transient Ischemic Attacks

Cerebrovascular disease is the third leading cause of death in the United States, although 87 percent of deaths occur in persons over 65 years of age [9]. There also is a high prevalence of people affected by these problems, with an estimate of more than 4.4 million stroke survivors in the United States [10]. An elevated risk of accidents in affected drivers has been reported [11]. Because some problems occur at younger ages and the prevalence of these disorders is high, it is reasonable to infer that a commercial driver medical examiner will deal with this issue on a periodic basis. Although there are no studies evaluating the risks among commercial vehicle drivers, there are some studies among the elderly reporting that prior stroke is a risk for subsequent motor vehicle crash (Odds Ratio = 1.9) [12], Odds Ratio = 1.93 [13], and Relative Risk = 2.7 [14].

Transient ischemic attacks (TIAs) are often one of the first manifestations of cerebrovascular disease, and the conference report recommended that a person with a history of TIAs be disqualified from driving a commercial vehicle interstate for 1 year because of the high rate of recurrence and / or stroke within the first year. Subsequent clearance by a neurologist was recommended.

Drivers with thromboembolic strokes involving the brainstem or cerebellum were recommended to be handled the same as those with TIAs. However, strokes more commonly involve the middle / anterior cerebral distributions and have a worse prognosis. For such drivers, it was recommended that 5 years elapse prior to a neurology clearance examination to consider up to a 1-year certification, particularly if there is evidence of neurologic deficit. Drivers with deficits and stability such that a license can be granted should be recertified for no more than 1 year. Because most strokes involve areas such as the middle cerebral artery in those in their sixth or seventh decade, these are often career-ending events.

In Australia, drivers who have had a stroke are not believed to be qualified to continue driving a commercial vehicle [15]. A conditional license could be granted if the stroke was "caused by a condition which has now been satisfactorily treated. A satisfactory recovery from the stroke, including perceptual deficits, must also be demonstrated." Two or more TIAs preclude driving, but a conditional license may be granted if there is a 6-month TIA-free interval and the underlying cause has been "removed." For drivers with one TIA, referral to an approved specialist is required for certification.

In Canada, the CMA recommends that a driver not operate a vehicle for at least 1 month after a stroke [16]. They are not to drive if they have a TIA until a medical assessment is performed, even if there are no residua.

In Great Britain, the regulations recommend at least 12 months without driving a commercial vehicle after either a stroke or a TIA [8]: "Can be considered for licensing after this period if there is a full and complete recovery and there are no other significant risk factors. Licensing will also be subject to satisfactory medical reports including exercise ECG testing."

Dementias

Data on the motor vehicle crash risk for commercial drivers with dementia appear absent. This is not surprising because these individuals are mostly considered unqualified to drive. Relatively sparse data are available on crash risk for noncommercial drivers. Risks as high as 11-fold have been reported (odds ratio [OR] = 10.7, 95% confidence interval [CI] = 1.43–44.0) [17]. Similarly, a driver simulator study found 33 percent of those with Alzheimer disease sustained a simulated crash versus none of the controls [18]. However, another study found mildly increased crash risk unless the disease was more advanced [19].

The conference report recommended that dementias be considered disqualifying conditions, even if the diagnosis has only been "entertained" (see Table 7-3). Thus, a patient who is being evaluated for the possibility of Parkinson's disease theoretically should be disqualified. The presence of tumors (benign or malignant), significant depression, and Alzheimer's disease all warrant disqualification. If the diagnosis is of a progressive disorder, the conference believed that there were "unequivocal grounds for disqualification." In such instances, computed tomography and magnetic resonance imaging (MRI) were considered "mandatory." For such drivers with mild symptoms or a slow rate of progression, as is often found in early Parkinson's disease, it was recommended that the examinee follow the "appeals process" (Tables 7-5 and 7-6); the same appeals process was recommended for those with a treatable disorder, such as toxic dementia. If the neurologist and the examiner believe that the person can drive safely, then a shorter period of recertification, such as 6 months or 1 year, is recommended. As noted previously, however, this appeals process was never implemented. Nevertheless, the procedure for referring individuals with the potential to drive is logical and easily followed, except that education of the physician to whom the referral is made regarding driving requirements and regulations is often necessary.

Dementias are disqualifying conditions in Australia if the diagnosis or impairment is confirmed, although a conditional license is available if: (1) the cause is likely responsive to treatment, (2) there have been appropriate neuropsychological tests, (3) a practical driving test is completed, and (4) the IQ is over 70 [15]. In Canada, there is no guidance for commercial drivers, but it was felt that "People with mild dementia who are deemed fit to continue driving should be re-evaluated, and possibly retested, every 6–12 months."[16]. In Great Britain, the license must be revoked [8].

Extrapyramidal Disorders

These disorders are known to range in symptoms, severity, and prognoses. Common disorders include torsion dystonias (e.g., dystonia musculorum deformans, spasmodic torticollis, Meigs' syndrome, and blepharospasm), choreas (e.g., Huntington's, rheumatic fever, benign familial chorea, drug toxicities, or secondary to tumors and/or cerebrovascular accidents), myoclonus, tics, and benign essential (familial)

Table 7-6. Appeals Process for Neurologic Disorders*

1. Minor multiple sclerosis, mild dementia, some tumors, etc.

2. Magnetic resonance imaging

3. Neurology/physiatry examination

4. Simulated driving skills test

5. On-the-road driving test

Note: This process was proposed but never instituted. Disqualification could occur at any step in the process.
*Conference on Neurologic Disorders and Commercial Drivers [5].

tremor. Drivers with Wilson's disease or Huntington's chorea are recommended to have "unequivocal grounds for disqualification." Other disorders require a careful assessment of the driver's status and a comparison between the person's capabilities and the demands of the job. Drivers with milder problems such as essential tremor, myoclonus, and focal dystonias were thought to be possible candidates for continued driving. However, annual recertification and neurologic or physiatric evaluations were thought to be required.

Headaches

Although headaches are common, only rarely are they considered to be a disqualifying condition (Table 7-7). A history of any of the following were believed to warrant a more detailed history: tension headache, migraine with or without neurologic deficit, cluster headache, posttraumatic head injury syndrome, drug-related headache, cranial neuralgia, atypical facial pain, cough headache, or exertional headache. Chronic cluster headaches, a rare condition, tend to bother an individual for an extended period of time (in contrast to more usual cluster headaches) and are considered disqualifying. However, if any headache is severe and incapacitating, or if medications are being taken that impair the ability to drive, then the headaches may be disqualifying. Migraines with neurologic deficits and cranial neuralgia also were classified as disqualifying conditions. Some data do exist to suggest higher accident rates among drivers with migraine headaches [20].

When evaluating an individual with headaches, it is recommended that the following information be elicited:

1. Frequency and severity of the headache
2. Associated features

   a. Visual abnormalities: halos, scintillations, teichopsias, scotoma, quadrant anopsia, hemianopsia, diplopia, astereopsis, mosaic vision, visual distortion, or visual hallucinations
   b. Nausea and vomiting
   c. Dizziness, vertigo, dysequilibrium, and ataxia
   d. Mood swings from depression to agitation; transient psychosis
   e. Syncope
   f. Cognitive deficits: inattention, memory loss, confusion, disorientation, loss of concentration, speech disturbances, receptive deficits, or coma
   g. Motor deficits: ataxia, hemiparesis, hemiplegia, quadriparesis, or quadriplegia

Table 7-7. Headaches and Vertigo*
Headaches
Chronic or incapacitating, *may* be disqualifying
Medication use may be problematic
Vertigo
Benign positional vertigo may requalify after 2 months
Acute/chronic vestibulopathy may requalify after 2 months
Ménière's disease and other chronic vertiginous problems are disqualifying

*As recommended by the Conference on Neurologic Disorders and Commercial Drivers [4].

The conference report recommended automatic disqualification for any of the listed associated features. However, it seems that an individual who has a migraine once yearly, with nausea and vomiting, probably would be a reasonably good candidate for driving, provided there was reasonable warning prior to the emesis.

Special attention to the potential side effects from beta-blockers, antidepressants, and anticonvulsants used to treat headaches also is recommended.

Hearing Loss

Hearing acuity is obviously a less-important sense than vision for the purposes of driving. Relatively few high-quality studies have been performed regarding the risks for motor vehicle accidents in hearing-impaired drivers, and almost none had been performed in commercial drivers. However, some studies do report an elevated risk for motor vehicle accidents in hearing-impaired drivers [21].

The required commercial driver medical examination screening for hearing acuity is the forced whisper test. In practice, a substantial number of examinations are accomplished with audiometry.

The basic regulatory criterion for hearing is the perception of a forced whisper at not less than 5 ft. Frequently, this is accomplished by asking the driver to repeat a series of random numbers. One of the problems with this test is that the typical examination room does not have 5 ft of distance from the patient's ear without either placing the patient in the corner of the room or requesting that the patient rotate his or her head position to test each ear. Although some firms request that their drivers be given a minimal screening, it is recommended that a formal request be made to the companies to screen with audiometry owing to the crude measure with the forced whisper combined with typically inadequately sized examination rooms. Thus, it is the opinion of this author that either audiometry or a handheld audioscope is preferable to the forced whisper test.

If a driver fails the forced whisper examination, then audiometry is recommended, and the requirement is that the individual have a corrected threshold of no worse than 40 dB-A averaged at 500, 1,000, and 2,000 Hz in the better ear. Thus, it is acceptable either to be deaf in one ear (provided that the other ear functions at the required threshold) or to achieve the required threshold through the use of hearing aids.

In Australia, qualifications are somewhat more conservative, and disqualification occurs if the hearing threshold is better than 40 dB-A in the better ear averaged at 500, 1,000, 2,000, and 3,000 Hz [15]. Conditional licensure is granted for drivers who attain the hearing threshold requirements with hearing aids and upon review of an otolaryngologist and the driver licensing authority. The CMA recommendations are that hearing impaired individuals seeking a Class 2 or 4 license must undergo an audiogram and the criteria for driving are the same as those in the United States with the addition of a corrected word recognition score of at least 50 percent to 60 percent [16]. Those transporting dangerous goods must also meet these requirements, otherwise, there are no hearing requirements for driving in Canada. In Great Britain, those with profound deafness must be able to communicate in the event of an emergency by speech or by using a device, e.g., a MINICOM: "If unable so to do the license is likely to be refused or revoked" [8].

Multiple Sclerosis

Multiple sclerosis is one of the more common disorders encountered in the commercial driver certification process. The wide divergence in clinical course, treatment, impairment, cognitive involvement, and prognoses makes this disorder among the most challenging.

The risk of motor vehicle crashes has not been estimated in commercial drivers, however, one historical cohort register study of 197 multiple sclerosis patients found a relative risk (RR) of motor vehicle crashes requiring emergency department treatment of 3.4 (95% CI = 0.73–17.2); however, this failed to achieve statistical significance [22]. Another epidemiological study demonstrated increased crash risk among those with cognitive impairment [23]. Also, one driving simulator study [24] similarly found that those with cognitive deficits performed worse than those without cognitive deficits. Another simulator study found significantly increased crashes among relapsing-remitting multiple sclerosis patients [25].

The conference report recommended that multiple sclerosis be considered a disqualifying condition. However, it was recognized that the severity of the problem, variability in the clinical presentation, and differing prognoses warranted the proposed "appeals" process for those with intermittent symptoms, mild deficits, and/or a stable clinical course. The conference report recommended an appeal under the following circumstances:

1. No signs of relapse or progression
2. No or only functionally insignificant neurologic signs and symptoms as determined by a neurologist
3. An MRI and triple-evoked potential studies are normal or do not reveal new lesions compared with prior evaluations made at least 1 year apart
4. No history of excessive fatigability or periodic fluctuations in motor performance, especially in relation to heat, physical and emotional stress, and infections

Since that conference report, the treatment of multiple sclerosis has evolved. Although far from curative, it is believed that some of the therapies have delayed disease progression. When in remission and early in the course of the disease, it may be that a driver can safely drive for some time without unnecessary risk to others. Significant judgment and the opinions of the treating neurologist are generally required in these circumstances.

In Australia, a conditional license may be granted with annual reviews if: (1) it is responsive to treatment, (2) report of the driver assessor is favorable, and (3) any modifications to the vehicle are made [15]. The CMA recommends an evaluation of all drivers with disorders of coordination and muscle control to ascertain the degree of impairment [16]; for those "in the early stages of some of these conditions, no restriction on normal driving is necessary." In Great Britain, it is recommended that licensure not be granted if the disease is "progressive or disabling. If driving would not be impaired and [the] condition [is] stable, [drivers] can be considered for licensing subject to satisfactory reports and annual review" [8]. This is the same guidance as for other chronic neurologic disorders.

Narcolepsy

Narcolepsy is considered disqualifying in the United States. Narcolepsy is also a disqualifying condition in Australia if the diagnosis is confirmed, although a conditional license is available if the following are met: (1) clinical assessment by a sleep physician, (2) cataplexy has not been a feature in the past year, (3) medication is taken regularly, (4) absence of symptoms for 6 months, and (5) normal latency present on MWT on or off medication. Narcolepsy is believed to be incompatible with driving of commercial motor vehicles in Canada. In Great Britain, individuals with narcolepsy are considered to have a completely disqualifying condition unless "a long period of control has been established," and then "licensing may be considered on an individual basis."

Neuromuscular Diseases

Neuromuscular diseases are largely considered to be automatically disqualifying owing to interference with driving demands and poor prognoses. In the physical examination, particular attention should be paid to strength, sensory loss, and range of motion. Motor neuron diseases (e.g., spinal muscular atrophy, amyotrophic lateral sclerosis) should be disqualifying, as are systemic peripheral neuropathies (hereditary and acquired).

Myasthenia gravis is the main exception to automatic disqualification for the neuromuscular diseases. Although the conference report recommends that these neuromuscular junction diseases be considered disqualifying, most patients with myasthenia gravis, for example, likely can be completely managed. In such treated and stable individuals, recertification is generally justifiable.

Muscle diseases such as metabolic muscle diseases, muscular dystrophies, inflammatory myopathies (e.g., dermatomyositis, polymyositis, inclusion-body myositis), congenital myopathies, and diseases with abnormal muscle activity (e.g., myotonia, Isaac's syndrome, stiff-man syndrome) have disqualifying conditions. Confirmation of the diagnosis may be necessary; however, the conference report recommends that these be disqualifying conditions. It is recommended that any individual with a mild deficit from these types of diseases who is allowed to drive be given no more than a 1-year certification, and only after a careful evaluation.

In Australia, a conditional license may be granted if "the disability is limited to minor muscular weakness (subject to frequent reassessment because of the progressive nature of such disorders)" [15]. The CMA recommends that these problems be handled in the same manner as multiple sclerosis [16]. In Great Britain, these disorders are handled in the same manner as Parkinson's disease or multiple sclerosis [8].

Parkinsonism

Motor vehicle crash data are not available for commercial drivers with Parkinson's disease. However, those with Parkinson's disease have been reported to have significant daytime somnolence (51 percent). The Epworth Sleepiness Scale helped somewhat to identify individuals falling asleep at the wheel (OR = 1.14, 95% CI = 1.06–1.24); however, an additional sleep scale (the "Inappropriate Sleep Composite Score") was more predictive (OR = 2.54, 95% CI = 1.76–3.66) [26]. This disorder typically occurs in older individuals, and thus concomitant diseases that may be disqualifying in and of themselves are possible and should be evaluated.

The conference report recommended that Parkinson's disease be disqualifying—yet, presumably someone with mild, readily controlled Parkinson's symptoms and signs, no problems with dementia, no "on-off" phenomena, good compliance, and a lack of mental deficits may be considered for a shortened, time-limited certification.

In Australia, a conditional license may be granted with annual reviews if: (1) it is responsive to treatment, (2) report of the driver assessor is favorable, and (3) any modifications to the vehicle are made [15]. The CMA recommends that these problems be handled in the same manner as multiple sclerosis [16]. In Great Britain, it is recommended that licensure not be granted if the disease is "progressive or disabling. If driving would not be impaired and [the] condition [is] stable, [drivers] can be considered for licensing subject to satisfactory reports and annual review" [8]. This is the same guidance as for other chronic neurologic disorders.

Seizures

A history of epilepsy is one of the more common disorders (Table 7-8) encountered in the commercial driver certification process, because there is an approximately 3.0 percent cumulative incidence through age 74 years for epilepsy, 4.1 percent for unprovoked seizure, and almost 10 percent for any convulsive disorder [27]. Although an active seizure disorder has been generally considered disqualifying for commercial drivers, the general driving population contains many individuals on antiepileptic medications. Thus, there are no data for safety in the commercial driving population, yet there are many data from the general driving population.

Data consistently demonstrate that drivers with an epileptic disorder have an elevated risk for motor vehicle crash, with typical estimates of approximately twice the risk of the general population for

Table 7-8. Seizures and the Commercial Driver Certification Process*

Uncontrolled epilepsy is a disqualifier.

Controlled epilepsy is a disqualifier.

Remote history of seizures, on no medications, and seizure free for 10+ years: Recertify.

History of one seizure, no recurrence, on no seizure medications for 5+ years: Recertify.

History of febrile seizures as a child is *not* disqualifying.

*As recommended by the Conference on Neurologic Disorders and Commercial Drivers [5].

motor vehicle crashes [28–30]. A recent population-based study found similar estimates of risk; however, it found somewhat higher estimates for those involved in an at-fault accident whether on restrictions (RR = 2.39, 95% CI = 1.70–3.36) or not on restrictions (RR = 2.02, 95% CI = 1.08–2.27) [2]. A 10-year Danish study found a much higher risk estimate of sevenfold RR for motor vehicle crashes (RR = 7.0, 95% CI = 2.2–26.1) [31]. Severity of accidents also has been evaluated in a study evaluating emergency department treatment, with even stronger measures of risk (rate ratio = 7.01, 95% CI = 2.18–26.13), although the study was relatively small [31]. There also are data suggesting that those with epilepsy have experienced seizures while driving (33.3–39.2%) and report having experienced accidents while driving (17.3–26.7%) [32,33]. Seizure ablative therapy has not been found to be completely successful in those who also discontinue antiepileptic treatment, with reported 14 percent 2-year and 36 percent 5-year recurrence rates [34]. There are reported markers for reduced risk of motor vehicle crash from epilepsy and include prolonged seizure-free intervals, reliable auras, few prior nonseizure-related accidents and having had the antiepileptic drugs reduced or switched [35]. The majority of the crashes (54%) occurred among those "driving illegally, with seizure-free intervals shorter than legally permitted."

In the United States, a history of childhood febrile seizures is the sole exception to concerns about a seizure history. A history of febrile seizures is not considered disqualifying. All other histories of seizure disorders necessitate careful investigation of the condition. Controlled or uncontrolled epilepsy is considered to be a completely disqualifying condition. Although a history of any seizure disorder is a complete disqualifier, there are some exceptions.

When an individual has had only one seizure, has been off medications for 5 years, and has remained seizure free, that driver may be considered for qualification. Drivers with a seizure-disorder history, off medications for 10 years, and remaining seizure free may be considered for qualification as well.

It may be noteworthy that there is evidence that most of the recurrence of seizures occurs within the first 2 years after cessation of antiepileptic agents [36], although the best data are in children and there are few data for adults [37] and some reported risk factors for recurrence include numbers of medications used, duration, and age at onset [38,39].

In Australia, epilepsy precludes commercial vehicle driving, however, conditional licenses are available. Single provoked seizures are not believed to preclude commercial vehicle licensing, but requirements are (1) provocative factors are reliably avoidable, (2) seizure free for 1 year, (3) no antiepileptic medications, and (4) EEG shows no epileptiform activity. For those with a history of febrile seizures or benign childhood epilepsy, a conditional license is available for: (1) no antiepileptic medication and (2) EEG shows no epileptiform activity. For those with epilepsy, a conditional license also is available with the following requirements: (1) seizure free for 5 years, takes no epileptic medication and EEG shows no epileptiform activity; OR (1) takes mediation, (2) maintains at least annual reviews and compliance, (3) seizure free for 5 years, (4) no more than three seizures in the prior 10 years, and (5) EEG shows no epileptiform activity; OR (1) has had surgical treatment for epilepsy, (2) maintains annual reviews, (3) seizure free for 5 years, and (4) EEG shows no epileptiform activity; OR (1) limited or restricted vehicle use, (2) taking antiepileptic medication, (3) periodic reviews and compliance, (4) seizure free for 5 years, and (5) EEG shows no epileptiform activity; OR (1) limited or restricted vehicle use, (2) single provoked seizure, (3) provocative factors can be avoided, (4) seizure free for 1 year, (5) takes no antiepileptic medication, and (6) EEG shows no epileptiform activity. Recurrence of seizures requires immediate suspension of driving and the driver reporting to the driver licensing authority. Withdrawal of medication is not compatible with continued commercial vehicle driving. This standard now is being considered for early review after three incidents involving several deaths. One case involved the "non-reporting" of the epilepsy. The conditional license is to be granted such that the epilepsy is "so well controlled as to reduce the risk of a convulsion to that of any member of the general population," which seems to be virtually unattainable in nearly all cases.

The CMA recommends against allowing epileptic drivers to operate commercial vehicles [16]. Those with a solitary seizure are believed to be able to be certified if a work-up (evaluation, MRI, waking and sleep EEGs) is negative and they are seizure free for 1 year. For those with an epileptic history, they are considered able to drive if seizure free with or without medication, or after surgery to prevent seizures, for a 5-year epilepsy-free period. If medications are withdrawn or changed, they are not to drive for 6 months. If seizures recur after withdrawal and they resume treatment, they must wait 6 months prior to resuming commercial driving. For simple partial seizures, they may drive if the seizures remain benign for at least 3 years. Those with alcohol withdrawal seizures, commercial driving may be resumed if alcohol free and seizure free to at least 6 months, as well as a rehabilitation program is successfully completed.

In Great Britain, the criterion for commercial driving is a risk for seizure threshold that is less than 2 percent per year, regardless of cause. (Although this threshold approach appears admirable, the data for comparative purposes in a specific circumstance are generally limited to absent.) The regulations require that drivers remain free of seizures for 10 years without anticonvulsants to be considered for certification [8]. For an unprovoked seizure, 10 years without an additional seizure is required to resume commercial driving. If the solitary seizure is due to alcohol use or medications, 5 years without an additional seizure is required. The only exception is if the seizure occurred "immediately at the time of the acute head injury or intracranial surgery, and not thereafter and/or where no liability to seizure has been demonstrated. Following head injury or intracranial surgery, the risk of seizure must have fallen to no greater than 2% per annum before returning to vocational driving."

Sleep Apnea

Sleep apnea is dealt with in the conference report on neurologic disorders as well as the conference report on pulmonary disorders. See Chapter 5 for a thorough discussion of this topic.

Syncope

Syncope is dealt with in the cardiovascular chapter. However, it also is covered in neurological sections of standards and will be mentioned here, particularly syncope of unknown cause.

In Australia, syncope is considered to be incompatible with driving unless the cause is identified, treatment is successful, and compliance is confirmed [15]. Six months is to elapse prior to resumption of driving for unexplained loss of consciousness. It should be noted that the minimal nondriving time for cardiogenic syncope is 3 months.

The CMA [16] indicates that one syncopal episode that is explained and that is unlikely to recur may require no more than careful observation. Those with recurrent syncopal problems should not drive unless they have had successful treatment.

In Great Britain, individuals with syncope of unknown etiology, no injury at the time of syncope, with negative cardiovascular/neurological exams and normal electrocardiograph, and thought to be at low risk for recurrence may drive after 3 months after the event [8]. In cases where any of the previously mentioned work-up was positive and no cause remains identified, they cannot drive for 1 year after the event. If a seizure was suspected (e.g., amnesia over 5 minutes, injury, tongue biting, incontinence, remaining conscious but with confused behavior, and/or headache post attack) but no proven, they may drive if 5 years have passed since the event.

Transient Global Amnesia

Transient global amnesia is a condition believed to be due to cerebral ischemia that causes an episode of amnesia and confusion, with the patient recovering without sequelae. It is recommended that such a person be evaluated carefully with an electroencephalogram and psychiatric evaluation. If the evaluations are unremarkable, no restrictions are recommended, because the condition then is considered to be benign.

In Great Britain, driving should cease if there are two or more episodes [8]. After one episode, however, the driver is not required to surrender his or her license.

Traumatic Brain and Spinal Cord Injuries and Intracranial Bleeding

Problems related to traumatic brain injuries generally are due to lingering deficits (e.g., paresis or seizures) rather than the diagnosis, because they tend not to be progressive conditions. If there is no deficit, no special evaluations or time limits are recommended. However, the examiner may institute a different time frame for recertification if he or she believes that this is indicated. The conference report recommended that the evaluation be performed by a neurologist and include a physical examination, neurologic examination, neuro-ophthalmologic evaluation, and neuropsychological testing. If there is a deficit, annual follow-up evaluations are recommended. Spinal cord injuries resulting in paraplegia should result in disqualification. If weakness is present following a spinal cord injury, an assessment should be made to determine whether there is an impairment that would interfere with the safe operation of a motor vehicle. It is believed that the presence of a deficit should allow for no more than a 1-year certification, if at all.

In Australia, someone with more than 24 hours of altered consciousness or a serious head injury is not qualified to drive a commercial vehicle until assessed [15]. If there are chronic functional disturbances, a conditional license is available that includes: (1) a medical examination, (2) neuropsychological testing, (3) driver assessment, and (4) consideration of other disabilities.

The CMA believes that minor traumatic brain injuries would not impair driving capability for more than a few hours [16]. It recommends that drivers with a more serious injury "should be fully evaluated before driving is resumed." It also is noted that the immediate effects may not correlate well with longer term effects and there is great variability in recovery. Those with moderate to severe traumatic brain injury (TBI) were felt to often require comprehensive assessments. Regarding TBI, "The lack of consensus on measurement of cognitive indicators and ability indices continues to make this a problematic issue." Those with an untreated cerebral aneurysm are disqualified. After surgical treatment, they may be requalified if symptom free for 6 months.

In Great Britain, a specialist evaluation is recommended to assess such drivers [8]. The two primary complications to be addressed are epilepsy risk and driver performance. "Return to driving will depend on Specialist assessment (risk of seizure must have fallen to no greater than 2% per annum) with clinical recovery." For extradural intracranial hematomas requiring craniotomy but without cerebral damage, 6 months without personal car operation is recommended and the same criteria as noted earlier apply. For extradural intracranial hematomas requiring craniotomy and accompanied by craniotomy, for personal vehicle operation, 1 year without vehicle operation is recommended and for commercial drivers, the same criteria as noted earlier apply. For either acute subdural hematomas (or acute intracerebral bleeds) treated with burr holes or requiring craniotomy, 6 months or 1 year respectively without personal vehicle operation is recommended. For commercial drivers, the same criteria noted above apply. Chronic subdural hematomas treated surgically require 6 months to 1 year off depending on clinical features. Subarachnoid hemorrhage requires 6 months off and reinstatement only if an angiography is normal and the driver remains symptom free. If a craniotomy is required for a cerebral aneurysm, then 1 year without driving is recommended if the recovery is complete; revocation is recommended if recovery is incomplete. If the aneurysm producing the subarachnoid hemorrhage is in the middle cerebral artery distribution, however, then 18 to 24 months away from driving is required for those without a residual deficit. For those with a residual deficit, the same criteria noted apply regarding specialist evaluation and seizure potential. For those with subarachnoid hemorrhage treated with embolization or other noncraniotomy procedures, it is required that there be angiographic evidence of complete ablation and the seizure risk threshold applies; those without treatment are not qualified. For those with an incidental intracranial aneurysm, it is recommended that to be acceptable for commercial driving, anterior circulation aneurysms (excluding cavernous carotid) must be less than 13 mm in diameter and posterior circulation less than 7 mm. If the incidental aneurysm is operated on, then 1 year without driving is required. If an intracranial arteriovenous malformation (AVM) is diagnosed, the license is to be revoked and 10 years must pass without seizure since definitive treatment (craniotomy, embolization, or stereotactic radiotherapy) to be reconsidered for commercial driving. If untreated, they are permanently disqualified. For those with an incidental finding of an AVM and without treatment, the license is to be revoked and if treated, the criteria apply. For those with an intracerebral abscess or subdural empyema, they may be considered for commercial driving if 10 years have passed and they have not had seizures. Those with hydrocephalus may drive "if uncomplicated and no associated neurological problems." Intraventricular shunts, intracranial pressure monitoring devices, and neuroendoscopic procedures are to be assessed individually. Those with implanted electrodes implanted for movement disorders need an assessment to drive commercially provided there are no complications from surgery, they are seizure free, and the underlying condition is not progressive. Those with implanted motor cortex stimulator for pain relief are not qualified.

Tumors

There is a wide range in potential impairments from tumors, ranging from no impairment to permanent total disability. Treated, benign central nervous system (CNS) tumors generally provide no long-term certification limitations provided there is no neurologic deficit or seizure disorder.

However, malignant CNS tumors do present significant problems that generally necessitate disqualification. Individuals with metastases should be considered disqualified permanently because they are unlikely to have a good prognostic outcome. Occasionally, individuals with malignant primary CNS tumors may be recertified after adequate treatment, complete cure, and no untoward effects (e.g., seizures, paresis, coordination abnormalities). A waiting period of several years prior to recertification, however, seems wise. Clearance by a neurologist is recommended.

The CMA recommends that benign tumors that have been treated and without deficits do not usually require prohibition from driving [16]. If a seizure occurs in the process of treatment, then a 1-year seizure-free period is required. An individual assessment is believed to be needed after treatment for a malignant tumor.

In Great Britain, the license is to be surrendered, and a driver may be considered for reinstatement 5 years after surgery with successful removal or cure of benign supratentorial tumors [8]. Drivers with gliomas are recommended to be permanently disqualified. Those with histologically malignant tumors (e.g., medulloblastoma) are allowed to be considered if disease free and after passage of 5 years. If the problem is an acoustic neuroma or meningioma, then driving may be resumed provided there are no disabling symptoms. A 6-month disqualification from driving after craniotomy for pituitary tumors is recommended, provided there are no visual field defects.

Vertigo

Acute labyrinthitis is likely the most common type of vertigo. As it is an acute and self-limited disorder, it is unlikely to result in long-term impairment or crash risk. The conference report recommends disqualification for 2 months; however, some individuals are symptom free within a week.

Drivers with acute and chronic vestibulopathies are recommended for recertification after being symptom free for 2 months. Individuals with chronic progressive vestibular diseases or permanent dysfunction, such as Ménière's disease, labyrinthine fistulas, and nonfunctioning labyrinths, are considered to have completely disabling conditions. (In contrast, the CMA does not recommend withdrawing a commercial license for individuals with chronic progressive vestibulopathies [16]).

The conference report recommended evaluation by a neurologist and careful assessment of drivers having these disorders. However, it seems that an individual with a clear case of acute labyrinthitis and complete resolution of symptoms would be a good candidate for recertification by the commercial driver examiner without universal neurologic clearance. Nevertheless, a time-limited certification for 2 to 6 months may be indicated for the first certification period.

In Australia, a conditional license is available subject to periodic reviews if: (1) at least 12 months free of vertigo caused by Ménière's, (2) at least 6 months free of vertigo caused by acute labyrinthitis (deafness and vertigo), acute neurolabyrinthitis (vestibular neuronitis or other vertigo), or (3) at least 2 months free of vertigo and signs of benign positional vertigo. The CMA advises that those with acute labyrinthitis not drive "until their condition has subsided and the acute symptoms have resolved" [16]. Those with recurrent vertiginous problems such as Ménière's "should be advised to pull off the road at the first sign of an acute attack, until their symptoms subside. Those prone to severe or prolonged episodes should not drive any class of motor vehicle until their symptoms have been controlled." Great Britain has taken a similar approach that requires that the condition to not be sudden or disabling and "Consider underlying diagnosis and if likely to cause recurrent attacks, must be symptom free and completely controlled for at least 1 year before reapplication" [8].

Visual Impairment

Monocular commercial drivers have reported motor vehicle crash rates that compare favorably with those of the general population or commercial vehicle drivers [40].

However, a population-based study of motor vehicle drivers found elevated crash risks whether the driver was unrestricted (RR = 1.27, 95% CI = 1.04–1.55) or restricted (RR = 1.35, 95% CI = 1.25–1.46). At-fault accident risks were further elevated whether unrestricted (RR = 1.52, 95% CI = 1.38–1.68) or restricted (RR = 1.56, 95% CI = 1.25–1.94) [2]. Elderly drivers with cataracts seem to have problems driving with elevated crash risk [41]. Another study among the elderly reported increased crash risk for failing the useful field-of-view test [14]. A nonstatistically significant increased risk for motor vehicle collision was found in a case-control study of drivers with visual field defects from glaucoma (OR = 3.2, 95% CI 0.9–10.4 [42]). A small controlled study of diplopia generally failed to find significant differences in response and recognition times [43].

The commercial driver medical examination screens for vision with three screens: (1) the Snellen chart, (2) a color screen, and (3) a peripheral vision screen. The basic criterion to drive is that a driver have visual acuity of 20/40 or better in both eyes, whether corrected or not. The applicant must be able to discern the colors red, amber, and green. Last, peripheral vision must be at least 70 degrees laterally in each eye.

The capability to distinguish the three colors may not be waived, although owing to this fairly simple requirement, drivers with many types of color blindness are still able to drive commercial motor vehicles. The minimum requirement of 20/40 visual acuity in each eye also may not be waived. However, drivers who have at least 20/40 corrected visual acuity in the better eye may be eligible for a vision exemption.

A provisional waiver program for monocular drivers was begun in 1992 [44]. A total of 2,686 drivers were enrolled in the waiver program prior to a court injunction that stopped further enrollments in the mid-1990s. Nevertheless, these drivers were allowed to continue to operate commercial motor vehicles but were followed as part of an uncontrolled study. To be eligible for enrollment in the original program, drivers were required to have operated a commercial vehicle safely for 3 years prior to enrollment, to have no licensure suspensions/restrictions, and to have a doctor's approval that they could operate such a vehicle safely. (For more details of the waiver programs, see "Diabetes Mellitus Exemptions" in Chapter 8.) Drivers then were monitored for accident rates, fatality rates, and property damage estimates.

There were 2,234 drivers participating as of November 1995, a total dropout rate of approximately 16.8 percent [44]. All measures of accident rates were lower for the waived drivers compared with the national accident rate. The total accident rate was 1.706 per million vehicle miles traveled (VMTs) compared with the national rate of 2.605 per million VMTs. The property damage accident rate was 1.284 versus 2.048 per million VMTs. The accident rate with injury(ies) was 0.408 versus 0.534 per million VMTs. The fatal accident rate was 0.013 versus 0.026 million VMTs for the national rate. All achieved statistical significance, but these were calculated at 90 percent CIs.

Based in part on the preceding findings, drivers who were in the program after its termination were permitted to continue operating in interstate commerce provided the following conditions are met:

1. They receive an annual ophthalmologic/optometric examination.
2. The vision in the better eye is documented to be 20/40 or better.
3. Annual certification by a medical examiner indicates that the driver is otherwise physically qualified to drive a commercial vehicle for interstate commerce.
4. The driver provides a copy of the ophthalmologic/optometric evaluation to the medical examiner at the time of examination.
5. The driver provides a copy of the annual medical certification to his or her employer or retains it in his or her driver qualification file if self-employed.

Vision exemptions now are being considered provided the individual is able to demonstrate to the FMCSA that the degree of safety is at least equal to that which would be present were the exemption not needed. (See www.fmcsa.dot.gov/rules-regulations/topics/medical/exemptions .htm for more information.)

Monocular drivers may be conditionally certified in Australia [15]. The visual requirement is that the corrected visual acuity be at least 6/9 in the better eye and after considering the underlying disorder. Conditional licenses also may be granted for those with partial visual field defects if the loss does not result in less than 140 degrees within 10 degrees above and below the horizontal midline and there is no significant visual field loss and after considering the underlying disease. Those with diplopia when fixating objects within 20 degrees of the primary direction of gaze are disqualified. There is no color vision standard.

Canadian recommendations are at least 20/30 corrected with both eyes opened and examined together and not less than 20/400 in the worse eye [16]. Visual fields of 150 degrees in the horizontal plane and 20 degrees above and below fixation with both eyes examined together are required. There is no color standard requirement, although "all drivers should be able to discriminate among traffic lights."

Requirements in Great Britain are that a driver must have corrected visual acuity of at least 6/9 in the better eye and 6/12 in the worse eye [8]. Additionally, the uncorrected acuity must be at least 3/60 in both eyes. Those with cataracts must meet the visual acuity requirements and impairments from glare must be addressed. Monocular drivers may not be certified by law, although there is a grandfathering provision for previously licensed drivers. Diplopia is permanently disqualifying if inoperable and patching is not acceptable to meet the requirement. Night blindness may be considered on an individual basis provided acuity and field standards are met. Blepharospasm requires consultation for those with mild symptoms. Those treated with botulinum toxin may be acceptable provided there is no uncontrollable diplopia. The field of vision must be normal bilaterally and if there is a defect in any one eye, it must be completely compensated by the other eye. Color blindness is not disqualifying.

Two aspects of licensure for monocular drivers deserve further mention. The first is that a careful scrutiny of symptoms and problems with the remaining functional eye must be undertaken as part of the commercial driver medical examination. The second is that reliance on the neck range of motion to achieve a functional visual field is underrecognized. It is recommended that assessment of monocular drivers include an assessment of functional visual field by including a focused examination of the neck for axial rotation range of motion in the direction of the compromised eye.

References

1. National Center for Health Statistics. Health, United States, preliminary data 2004. www.cdc.gov/nchs/fastats/deaths.htm. Accessed May 29, 2007.
2. Diller E, Cook L, Leonard D, Reading J, Dean JM, Vernon D. Evaluating drivers licensed with medical conditions in Utah, 1992–1996. Technical Report DOT HS 809 023. Washington: National Highway Traffic Safety Administration, June 1999.
3. FMCSA Frequently Asked Questions. www.fmcsa.dot.gov/rules-regulations/topics/medical/faq.asp. Accessed May 30, 2007.
4. Federal Motor Carrier Safety Administration, U.S. Department of Transportation. Qualification of Drivers; Exemption Requests; Epilepsy and Seizure Disorders, Notice of applications for exemptions, request for comments. *Fed Reg* 2006;71(Oct. 13):60606–60607.
5. U.S. Department of Transportation, Federal Highway Administration. Conference on Neurologic Disorders and Commercial Drivers. Publication No. FHWA-MC-88-042. Washington: U.S. DOT, Federal Highway Administration, Office of Motor Carriers, 1988.
6. Molnar FJ, Patel A, Marshall SC, Man-Son-Hing M, Wilson KG. Clinical utility of office-based cognitive predictors of fitness to drive in persons with dementia: A systematic review. *J Am Geriatr Soc* 2006;54(12):1809–1824.
7. Ball KK, Roenker DL, Wadley VG, et al. Can high-risk older drivers be identified through performance-based measures in a Department of Motor Vehicles setting? *J Am Geriatr Soc* 2006;54(1):77–84.
8. Driver and Vehicle Licensing Agency. At-a-Glance Guide to the Current Medical Standards of Fitness to Drive. Swansea, England: Drivers Medical Unit, DVLA. www.dvla.gov.uk. Accessed May 27, 2007.
9. U.S. Preventive Services Task Force. *Guide to Clinical Preventive Services*, 2nd ed. Baltimore: Williams & Wilkins, 1996.
10. Effectiveness and Cost-Effectiveness of Echocardiography and Carotid Imaging in the Management of Stroke. Summary, Evidence Report/Technology Assessment: Number 49. AHRQ Publication Number 02-E021, July 2002. Agency for Healthcare Research and Quality, Rockville, MD. www.ahrq.gov/clinic/epcsums/strokemansum.htm. Accessed May 27, 2007.
11. Hansotia P. Seizure disorders, diabetes mellitus and cerebrovascular disease: Considerations for older drivers. *Clin Geriatr Med* 1993;9(2):323–339.
12. McGwin G Jr., Sims RV, Pulley L, Roseman JM. Relations among chronic medical conditions, medications, and automobile crashes in the elderly: A population-based case-control study. *Am J Epidemiol* 2000;152(5):424–431.

13. Sagberg F. Driver health and crash involvement: A case-control study. *Accid Anal Prev* 2006;38(1):28–34.

14. Sims RV, McGwin G Jr, Allman RM, Ball K, Owsley C. Exploratory study of incident vehicle crashes among older drivers. *J Gerontol A Biol Sci Med Sci* 2000;55(1):M22–M27.

15. Assessing Fitness to Drive. Interim Review Report. Austroads, National Transportation Commission, Melbourne, Australia, 2005. www .austroads.com.au/cms/AFTD%20web%20Aug%202006.pdf. Accessed May 27, 2007.

16. Canadian Medical Association. *Determining Medical Fitness to Operate Motor Vehicles CMA Driver's Guide*, 7th ed. Ottawa, Canada. www.cma.ca/index.cfm/ci_id/18223/la_id/1.htm. Accessed May 27, 2007.

17. Zuin D, Ortiz H, Boromei D, Lopez OL. Motor vehicle crashes and abnormal driving behaviors in patients with dementia in Mendoza, Argentina. *Eur J Neurol* 2002;9:29–34.

18. Rizzo M, McGehee DV, Dawson JD, Anderson SN. Simulated car crashes at intersections in drivers with Alzheimer disease. *Alzheimer Dis Assoc Disord* 2001;15(1):10–20.

19. Dubinsky RM, Stein AC, Lyons K. Practice parameter: Risk of driving and Alzheimer's disease (an evidence-based review): Report of the Quality Standards Subcommittee of the American Academy of Neurology. *Neurology* 2000;54:2205–2211.

20. Lerman Y, Matar M, Lavie B, Danon YL. Effect of valvular heart diseases, migraine headaches, and perianal diseases on the risk of involvement in motor vehicle crashes. *J Trauma* 1995;39(6):1058–1062.

21. Songer TJ, LaPorte RE, Palmer CV, et al. Hearing Disorders and Commercial Motor Vehicle Drivers. Report No. FHWA-MC-93-004. Washington: U.S. DOT, Federal Highway Administration, Office of Motor Carriers, 1992.

22. Lings S. Driving accident frequency increased in patients with multiple sclerosis. *Acta Neurol Scand* 2002;105:169–173.

23. Schultheis MT, Garay E, Millis S, DeLuca J. Motor vehicle crashes and violations among drivers with multiple sclerosis. *Arch Phys Med Rehabil* 2002;83:1175–1178.

24. Schultheis MT, Garay E, DeLuca J. The influence of cognitive impairment on driving performance in multiple sclerosis. *Neurology* 2001;56(8):1089–1094.

25. Kotterba S, Orth M, Eren E, Fangerau T, Sindern E. Assessment of driving performance in patients with relapsing-remitting multiple sclerosis by a driving simulator. *Eur Neurol* 2003;30(3):160–164.

26. Hobson DE, Lang AE, Martin WRW, Rasmy A, Rivest J, Fleming J. Excessive daytime sleepiness and sudden-onset sleep in Parkinson disease. *JAMA* 2002;287:455–463.

27. Hauser WA, Annegers JF, Rocca WA. Descriptive epidemiology of epilepsy: Contributions of population-based studies from Rochester, Minnesota. *Mayo Clin Proc* 1996;71:576–586.

28. Hansotia P, Broste S. The effects of epilepsy and diabetes mellitus on the risk of automobile accidents. *N Engl J Med* 1991;324:22–26

29. Hornio A. Does epilepsy mean higher susceptibility to traffic accidents? *Acta Psychiatr Scand* 1961;150(suppl):210–212.

30. Krumholz A, Fisher RS, Lesser RP, Hauser WA. Driving and epilepsy: A review and reappraisal. *JAMA* 1991;265(5):622–626.

31. Lings S. Increased driving accident frequency in Danish patients with epilepsy. *Neurology* 2001;57:435–439.

32. Berg AT, Vickery BG, Sperling MR, et al. Driving in adults with refractory localization-related epilepsy. *Neurology* 2000;54:625–630.

33. Gastaut H, Zifkin BG. The risk of automobile accidents with seizures occurring while driving: Relation to seizure type. *Neurology* 1987;37:1613–1616.

34. Schiller Y, Cascino GC, So EL, Marsh WR. Discontinuation of antiepileptic drugs after successful epilepsy surgery. *Neurology* 2000;54:346.

35. Krauss GL, Krumholz A, Carter RC, Li G, Kaplan P. *Neurology* 1999;52(7):1324-1329.

36. Emerson R, D'Souza BJ, Vining EP, Holden KR, Mellits ED, Freeman JM. Stopping medication in children with epilepsy: Predictors of outcome. *N Engl J Med* 1981;304:1125–1129.

37. Sirven JI, Sperling M, Wingerchuk DM. Early versus late antiepileptic drug withdrawal for people with epilepsy in remission (Cochrane Review). In: The Cochrane Library. Issue 4; 2001. Oxford.

38. Medical Research Council Antiepileptic Drug Withdrawal Study Group. Randomized study of antiepileptic drug withdrawal in patients in remission. *Lancet* 1991;337(8751):1175–1180.

39. Medical Research Council Antiepileptic Drug Withdrawal Study Group. Prognostic index for recurrence of seizures after remission of epilepsy. *BMJ* 1993;306(6889):1374–1378.

40. Decina LE, Breton ME, Staplin L. Visual Disorders and Commercial Drivers. Publication No. FHWA-MC-92-003. Washington: U.S. DOT, Federal Highway Administration, 1991.

41. Owsley C, Stalvey BT, Wells J, Sloane ME, McGwin G Jr. Visual risk factors for crash involvement in older drivers with cataract. *Arch Ophthalmol* 2001;119(6):881–887.

42. McGwin G Jr., Xie A, Mays A, Joiner W, DeCarlo DK, Hall TA, Owsely C. Visual field defects and the risk for motor vehicle collisions among patients with glaucoma. *Invest Ophthalmol Vis Sci* 2005;46(12):4437–4441.

43. White JF, Marshall SC, Diedrich-Closson KL, Burton AL. Evaluation of motor vehicle driving performance in patients with chronic diplopia. *J AAPOS* 2001;5:184–188.

44. Office of Motor Carrier Research and Standards. Qualification of Drivers: Vision and Diabetes. Technical Brief. Publication No. FHWA-MCRT-99-017. Washington: U.S. DOT, Federal Highway Administration, September 1999.

Additional References

Laux LF, Brelsford J. Age-Related Changes in Sensory, Cognitive, Psychomotor and Physical Functioning and Driving Performance in Drivers Aged 40 to 92. Washington: AAA Foundation for Traffic Safety, 1990:1–58.

Rehm CG, Ross SE. Syncope as etiology of road crashes involving elderly drivers. *Am Surg* 1995;61(11):1006–1008.

8

Endocrine Disorders

Kurt T. Hegmann, MD, MPH

The CDME processes are currently undergoing substantial changes. The FMCSA Medical Review Board reviewed diabetes mellitus in late 2006, and any recommendations to the FMCSA are pending as of this writing. After the MRB completes its review of the subject, the FMCSA may be advised of suggested changes in the CDME processes, after which rulemaking may or may not commence. Please be aware of these updating processes. An Advance Notice of Proposed Rulemaking already has been issued for diabetes.

Diabetes mellitus is the primary endocrine disorder of concern and has been a difficult problem for the commercial driver medical examiner since the inception of the commercial driver medical examiner processes some eight decades ago. Several recent major advances in treatment have reduced problems with hypoglycemia for many drivers. Still, other problems, particularly including intensive treatment, the increased propensity for those undergoing intensive treatment to sustain hypoglycemia, and questions concerning the fitness of insulin using drivers to operate commercial drivers involved in intrastate commerce continue to confront the examiner.

An estimated 20.8 million people have diabetes in the United States [1]. Approximately 40 percent remain undiagnosed. Type 1 diabetics are 5–10 percent of all diabetics; thus, Type 2 diabetics account for 90–95 percent of diabetics. Diabetes mellitus is one of the two most common disorders encountered in the commercial driver certification process (along with hypertension). Although the prevalence among commercial drivers is unclear, robust population-based estimates are available. The prevalence among those ages 40–74 years is 12–14 percent and is approximately 20 percent of males ages 60–74 years [2–5].

Elderly drivers who have diabetes but are not medicated have a 3.08 fold risk of a motor vehicle crash [6]. Increasing attention is being devoted to a problem closely related to diabetes, the "metabolic syndrome" (also known as dysmetabolic syndrome X) due to accompanying cardiovascular morbidity and mortality. See Table 8-1 for

Table 8-1. Metabolic Syndrome Diagnostic Criteria
(ICD-9-CM 277.7)

Major Criteria
- Acanthosis nigricans
- Waist circumference > 102 cm for men and > 88 cm for women
- Dyslipidemia (HDL cholesterol < 35 mg/dl for men and < 45 mg/dl for women, or triglycerides > 150 mg/dl)
- Hypertension
- Impaired fasting glucose or Type 2 diabetes mellitus
- Hyperuricemia

Minor Criteria
- Hypercoagulability
- Polycystic ovary syndrome
- Vascular endothelial dysfunction
- Microalbuminuria
- Coronary heart disease

Source: American Association of Clinical Endocrinologists.

diagnostic criteria. Additionally, recent reports indicate that those diabetics using rosiglitazone (Avandia) are at increased risk of cardiovascular events, thus raising concerns about still higher cardiovascular risks among some diabetics [7]. It is not clear whether those risks are replicable in other studies, apply to the entire class of medications, or merely one drug. In short, there are numerous concerns about diabetes and the risks for motor vehicle crash.

The trucking industry accounts for 12 percent of all worker deaths. In 2004, there were 4,862 large trucks involved in a total of 5,190 fatalities; 137,144 large truck crashes in 2005, with 59,405 crashes involving 89,681 injuries [8]. Considering the prevalence of diabetes in the trucking industry, combined with the statistics on elevated crash risk related to diabetes, it appears that diabetes likely has significant impacts on current truck crashes, injuries, and fatalities. Identifying the precise cause of those risks and minimizing the risks from diabetes mellitus would appear to be a major current and future challenge for the commercial driver medical examiner.

Regulations, Advisory Criteria, and Frequently Asked Questions

The regulation that directly addresses endocrine conditions in the commercial driver is:

391.41(h)(3) Has no established medical history or clinical diagnosis of diabetes mellitus currently requiring insulin for control

The advisory criteria explain that a diabetic who uses insulin for control does not meet the minimum physical requirements of the FMCSRs. Hypoglycemic agents are not disqualifying if the diabetes can be controlled. Examiners are referred to the Conference on Diabetic Disorders and Commercial Drivers for more information [9].

Thus, interstate commercial drivers currently are prohibited from using insulin, although there is an exemption program for insulin-using diabetic drivers meeting certain criteria (see additional information later). Other medical management of diabetes mellitus does not necessitate disqualification, however, a driver is to be under adequate control to be certified. The degree of control is not specified. Other complicating conditions may necessitate disqualification. All drivers must submit to urinalysis, although the thresholds for glucosuria demonstrate significant interindividual variation.

Other than insulin use, there are no specific, mandatory endocrine criteria for other endocrine disorders, such as thyroid diseases. However, there are many disorders, conditions, and medication uses that are recommended for disqualification by the conference report [9].

There are eight frequently asked questions (FAQs) posted on the FMCSA Website, addressing diabetes and related issues. One of particular interest dealing solely with diabetes addresses the recommended length of certification for diabetic drivers:

> In all cases, clinical judgment is required. The Medical Examiner decides if the driver's diabetes is adequately controlled, which determines certification, length of certification or disqualification. FMCSA guidelines recommend performing annual examination for vision, neurological function and cardiovascular disease, including hypertension. In general, the diabetic driver should have annual re-certification examinations.

Recommendations

There have been a series of three conference reports or reports of panels of experts to the U.S. Department of Transportation for dealing with diabetic drivers, with much of the attention on insulin-using diabetics [6,9,10].

The terms used to describe the different diabetic states are somewhat confusing, particularly since the older terms persist in common use and the conference reports mostly use the older terms [9,10]. Therefore, a brief review of the terms is presented. Type 1 and Type 2 diabetes mellitus are the terms that will be used primarily in this chapter because they communicate the physiology of the patients [1]. Patients with Type 1 diabetes mellitus are always insulin deficient and also are prone to ketoacidosis. For such individuals, insulin administration is a necessity for sustenance of life; they are truly insulin dependent. Patients with Type 2 diabetes mellitus have adequate to high levels of endogenous-circulating insulin but do not use it properly. They may or may not need to administer exogenous insulin to attain improved glycemic control. Insulin-using Type 2 diabetics are widely but somewhat misleadingly labeled as insulin dependent.

Insulin-dependent diabetes mellitus is the term that continues to be used in practice to describe anyone using insulin, whether Type 1 or Type 2. Noninsulin-dependent diabetes mellitus is the term used to describe a Type 2 diabetic, but only if he or she is not being treated with insulin. The other term used in the DOT conference reports, and thus necessarily used in this chapter, is insulin-taking diabetes mellitus (ITDM); a term technically denoting anyone using insulin, whether Type 1 or Type 2, but presumably primarily dealing with Type 2 insulin-using diabetics.

Commercial driver medical examinations involve two main screening elements for diabetes mellitus: one historical question ("diabetes or elevated blood sugar") and a urinalysis (glucosuria). However, many individuals who unknowingly have diabetes mellitus may go undetected by urinalysis performed for the commercial driver medical examination, due to variable thresholds for glucosuria.

The FMCSA regulations require that a diabetic driver must have the disease under "good control" and prohibit the use of insulin for interstate truck driving. There is neither a definition of good control for these purposes, nor regulatory guidance of same. However, in some states, such drivers could be considered qualified to drive school buses or intrastate trucks, and the physician may still have to deal with this issue in a local jurisdiction. If a person has Type 2 diabetes mellitus and the disease is controlled with diet and/or oral hypoglycemic agents, then the diabetes is not a disqualifying condition. Aspects to consider in making a determination of fitness for duty include the number and frequency of hypoglycemic reactions, the severity of the reactions, the driver's knowledge of diabetes mellitus (particularly regarding hypoglycemic risk factors and management of symptoms), and complications of the disorder. For example, for a person who has frequent hypoglycemic reactions without adequate warning of those reactions, the risk likely is too great to be allowed to drive. Thus the physician may still judge the diabetic on oral agents as unfit to drive.

Summary of the Evidence on Four Key Questions

In 2006, an expedited review of the evidence was conducted under the FMCSA's direction in part to address some of these issues confronted by the examiner [11]. This expedited review included a systematic review of the evidence. Four key questions were addressed concerning diabetes mellitus as part of this expedited review process. Although the implications of the findings from this systematic review have not yet been defined by the medical review board or the FMCSA, the answers to these questions are already of potential use for the examiner.

The four key questions and a summary of the answers to those questions follow:

1. *Are individuals with diabetes mellitus at increased risk for a motor vehicle crash when compared with comparable individuals who do not have diabetes?*

   This question was answered, "Yes, with qualifications."

   There is insufficient evidence whether CMV drivers are at increased risk of a motor vehicle crash because there are no high-quality studies. However, there is evidence from 13 studies that were combined in a fixed effects meta-analysis that drivers with diabetes are at increased risk of a motor vehicle crash RR = 1.19 (95% CI 1.08–1.31). It was felt that there was not sufficient evidence to determine whether Type 1 or Type 2 diabetics were overrepresented in populations who experienced a crash, although data suggested diabetics were overrepresented (OR = 1.41, 95% CI 0.86–2.29, p = 0.18). Whether insulin-using diabetics were overrepresented could similarly not be determined, although again they were overrepresented OR = 1.35, 95% CI 0.86–1.7, p = 0.17.

   Thus, although the evidence is strong that diabetics are at increased risk of a motor vehicle crash, the magnitude of the risk is not high. On an individual basis, this is not a particularly significant magnitude of risk, but on a population basis, it likely has major impacts due to the huge number of affected drivers.

   The other major conclusion is that the data that are relied upon for decision making are not robust. There are few studies and quality is not high. Available evidence implies that insulin-using diabetics are at increased risk of motor vehicle crashes, but statistical significance is lacking. The magnitude of the risk among insulin users appears likely to be modestly higher than that for all diabetics, but importantly it is not statistically significant.

2. *Is hypoglycemia an important risk factor for a motor vehicle crash among individuals with diabetes mellitus?*

This question was answered, "Yes with qualifications."

Simulated studies only included Type 1 diabetics. None included Type 2 diabetics. The strength of evidence was felt to be moderate for the effects of hypoglycemia on driving ability. Induced hypoglycemia (2.5–3.0 mmol/L; 45–54 mg/dL) also was found to have decrements in cognitive and psychomotor function.

3. *What treatment-related factors are associated with an increased incidence of severe hypoglycemia among individuals with diabetes mellitus?*

This question was answered, "Unclear."

It was noted that known treatment-related risk factors for increased incidence of severe hypoglycemia include lower hemoglobin A1c, use of insulin, and intensified insulin treatment. However, the focus of this question was to address whether different types of insulin, different types of oral hypoglycemic agents, or different treatment combinations influence the risk of severe hypoglycemia. It was concluded that available studies do not address this question.

4. *How effective is hypoglycemia awareness training in preventing the consequences of hypoglycemia?*

This question was answered, "Unclear."

There was moderate evidence that blood glucose awareness training improves the ability of individuals with Type 1 to accurately estimate their blood glucose levels. There was a paucity of evidence regarding whether blood glucose awareness training reduces the incidence of severe hypoglycemia.

The risks for severe hypoglycemia are believed to be higher for Type 1 diabetics than for Type 2 diabetics that require insulin for control [12,13]. Estimates of the magnitude or increased risks for severe hypoglycemia range from 2–3.3 fold [12–14].

Licensure Differences Between Jurisdictions

In a 1993 study, a variety of criteria for diabetic drivers were found between various jurisdictions. At that time, of 23 countries surveyed, 10 (43.5 percent), including Canada, Mexico, and the United States, prohibit insulin use in commercial motor vehicle drivers [15]. Since that time, Canada has altered that policy and the United States is considering allowing select insulin-using diabetics to driver commercial vehicles [16]. In Great Britain, insulin-using drivers may only drive light trucks [17]. The differences in evaluating risks of diabetic drivers highlight the lack of objective data upon which to base evidenced-based policies regarding diabetes mellitus [18].

Australia allows drivers controlled solely by diet to drive unrestricted. A conditional license and annual reviews are allowed for non-insulin-requiring Type 2 diabetics provided the condition is well controlled, the patient is compliant, there is an absence of hypoglycemia, there is no hypoglycemia unawareness, the patient is taking the agents with minimum risk for hypoglycemia, and there is an absence of end organ effects. A conditional license is similarly available for insulin-requiring Type 1 and Type 2 diabetics of recommended by a specialist in diabetes or endocrinology, and considering the nature of the driving task. These drivers are subject to annual review and must demonstrate control, compliance, absence of hypoglycemia, lack of hypoglycemic unawareness, the use of agents that provide the "minimum risk of hypoglycaemia," and an absence of end organ effects that may affect driving [19].

The Canadian Medical Association recommends annual examinations for commercial drivers who are insulin-using diabetics [20]. Those treated without medications or treated with metformin, acarbose, or thiazoledinediones are felt to be at very low risk for severe hypoglycemia. Those treated with sulfonylureas, repaglinide, and nateglinide are felt to be at low risk for severe hypoglycemia. For those without insulin for treatment, they are to have a good understanding of the diseases, comply with treatment and remain under "regular medical supervision." "Commercial drivers, especially those who operate heavy trucks over long distances, can have great difficulty maintaining the essential balance between insulin dose, food intake and physical exertion" due to long and irregular work schedules and labor. Detailed guidelines are in place, including requirements to undergo a complete assessment by an internist or diabetologist and have medical records available for review (prior 24 months), evidence of diabetes education program attendance, physical examination (including ophthalmology/optometry), glycosylated hemoglobin levels within the prior 3 months, and 6 months of twice daily glucose log results. Exclusions include no severe hypoglycemia in the prior 6 months, no hypoglycemia unawareness, no instability in the insulin treatment regimen (unable to drive for 1 month), and no significant new or worsening complications of diabetes [presumably, e.g., no visual impairment, no progressive proliferative retinopathy, no "obvious peripheral neuropathy with loss of function," no cardiovascular disease with dysrhythmias, and angina or myocardial infarction (prior year)]. Annual exams contain similar requirements, including 2 glycosylated hemoglobin measurements at 3-month intervals and 6 months of glucose logs. Drivers are not to drive if the glucose level falls below 108 mg/dL (6 mmol/L), are to measure glucose levels 1 hour prior to driving and every 4 hours while driving, and carry a rapidly absorbable source of glucose.

Currently, drivers who use insulin are prohibited from commercial vehicle licensing in Great Britain, with "grandfathering" of some insulin-using drivers who were licensed prior to January 4, 1991 [19]. There are tight exceptions for those driving small lorries (up to 12 tons). Those criteria include: (1) no hypoglycemia attacks requiring the assistance while driving in the prior 12 months, (2) at least 1 month of stability, (3) regular monitoring of glucose at least twice daily and at times relevant to driving with encouragement to use memory chip meters, (4) examination at least every 12 months with a diabetologist including review of glucose records over the prior 3 months, (5) no other conditions "which would render them a danger when driving C1 vehicles," and (6) a requirement to "sign an undertaking to comply with the directions of doctor(s) treating the diabetes and to report immediately to DVLA any significant change in their condition." Great Britain also requires satisfactory control, recognition of warning symptoms, and a lack of end-organ problems that would preclude safe driving. The drivers must report to the DVLA if their diabetes causes any of the following: insulin use, laser treatment for retinopathy, or circulation problems in the legs.

In a 1992 report, it was noted that some of the U.S. states permit drivers using insulin to operate commercial vehicles [10] (Table 8-2). Although some require additional monitoring if dietary management is initiated and some will allow insulin use for intrastate commercial vehicle operation, others prohibit use of insulin. Familiarity with local regulations is essential.

Table 8-2. License Status When an Existing CMV Driver Develops Diabetes

Treatment for Diabetes	Lose License	Restrictions/ Medical Exam	No Change	Don't Know or No Response
Begin insulin	9 (18%)	26 (52%)	14 (28%)	1 (2%)
Begin oral hypoglycemic	0 (0%)	22 (44%)	25 (50%)	3 (6%)
Begin dietary management	0 (0%)	14 (28%)	35 (70%)	1 (2%)

Source: U.S. Department of Transportation, Federal Highway Administration. Effect of limitation of various treatment protocols for diabetes mellitus on intrastate licenses in the 50 states. Washington: Office of Motor Carriers. Publication No. FHWA-MC-92-012, 1992.

Screening for Diabetes Mellitus

Diabetes mellitus is one of most important disorders in the commercial driver certification process due to prevalence [3–4], complications, and hazard potential to the public. With the sharply increasing prevalence of obesity, the prevalence of diabetes is expected to further increase. The U.S. Preventive Services Task Force indicates that the evidence is insufficient to recommend for or against screening for diabetes in the general population but it is recommended in those with hypertension or hyperlipidemia [21]. The American Diabetes Association recommends that screening be performed (Tables 8-3 and 8-4) in certain asymptomatic patients [22]. Population-based screening studies have shown elevated risks for retinopathy starting at and rising sharply from fasting glucose levels of approximately 110 to 120 mg/dL [2]. Due to significant evidence for efficacy of intensive glycemic control to pre-

---

Table 8-3. Criteria for the Diagnosis of Diabetes Mellitus

Diabetes Mellitus

1. Symptoms of diabetes and a casual plasma glucose ≥ 200 mg/dL (11.1 mmol/L).

   (Casual is defined as any time of day without regard to time since last meal.)

   Classic symptoms of diabetes include polyuria, polydipsia, and unexplained weight loss.

OR

2. FPG ≥ 126 mg/dL (7.0 mmol/L).

   (Fasting is defined as no caloric intake for at least 8 hours.)

   OR

   3.2-h plasma glucose ≥ 200 mg/dL (11.1 mmol/L) during an OGTT.

   (The test should be performed as described by the World Health Organization, using a glucose load containing the equivalent of 75-g anhydrous glucose dissolved in water.)

   Prediabetes—Impaired Fasting Glucose or Impaired Glucose Tolerance

   - IFG = FPG 100 mg/dL (5.6 mmol/L) to 125 mg/dL (6.9 mmol/L)

   - IGT = 2-h plasma glucose 140 mg/dL (7.8 mmol/l) to 199 mg/dL (11.0 mmol/L)

Source: American Diabetes Association. Standards of medical care in diabetes, 2007. *Diabetes Care* 2007;30:S4–S41.

Table 8-4. Screening Criteria for Diabetes Mellitus

---

1. Testing for diabetes should be considered in all individuals at age 45 years and above, particularly in those with a BMI $\geq$ 25 kg/m^2, and, if normal, should be repeated at 3-year intervals.

2. Testing should be considered at a younger age or be carried out more frequently in individuals who are overweight (BMI $\geq$ 25 kg/m^2) and have additional risk factors:

   - are habitually physically inactive
   - have a first-degree relative with diabetes
   - are members of a high-risk ethnic population (e.g., African American, Latino, Native American, Asian American, Pacific Islander)
   - have delivered a baby weighing > 9 lb or have been diagnosed with GDM
   - are hypertensive (140/90 mm Hg)
   - have an HDL cholesterol level < 35 mg/dL (0.90 mmol/L) and/or a triglyceride level > 250 mg/dL (2.82 mmol/L)
   - have PCOS
   - on previous testing, had IGT or IFG
   - have other clinical conditions associated with insulin resistance (e.g., PCOS or acanthosis nigricans)
   - have a history of vascular disease

Source: American Diabetes Association. Standards of medical care in diabetes, 2007. *Diabetes Care* 2007;30:S4–S41.

vent complications [23–24], further impetus to screen for diabetes mellitus likely will be given. Wider use of screening would likely significantly increase the numbers of commercial drivers known to have diabetes mellitus.

Diabetes Management Issues

The management of diabetes mellitus is continuing to undergo significant changes. The two basic changes are (1) the switch from traditional oral hypoglycemic agents to newer pharmaceutical agents with less hypoglycemic risk and (2) tightness of control. Long-acting sulfonylureas have been prescribed for many years. These have assisted patients in maintaining compliance with medication regimens because of the infrequent dosing intervals; however, they also may result in more frequent and prolonged hypoglycemic episodes. This presents a risk for a driver who is on an unusually long haul and cannot eat at the prescribed time, as might be precipitated by unanticipated traffic or adverse weather. Other medications have been introduced in the United States (Table 8-5) and include metformin [25], which decreases produc-

Table 8-5. Oral Medications for Type 2 Diabetes Mellitus

Sulfonylureas	Thiazolidinediones
First generation	Rosiglitazone (Avandia)
Acetohexamide (Dymelor)	Pioglitazone (Actos)
Chlorpropamide (Diabinese)	**Meglitinides**
Tolazamide (Tolinase)	
Tolbutamide (Orinase)	Nateglinide (Starlix)
Second generation	Repaglinide (Prandin)
Glimepiride (Amaryl)	**Incretin mimetic**
Glipizide (Glucotrol)	Exenatide (Byetta)
Glyburide (DiaBeta, Micronase,	
Glynase)	**Dipeptidyl-peptidase-4 Inhibitor**
Biguanide	Sitagliptin (Januvia)
Metformin (Glucophage)	**Combinations**
Alpha-glucosidase inhibitor	Glimepiride/Rosiglitazone
Acarbose (Precose)	(Avandaryl)
Miglitol (Glyset)	Metformin/Glyburide
	Pioglitazone/Glimepiride (Duetact)

Source: Adapted from *The Medical Letter* 2007;49(1251):1–3 and 2007;49(1253):9–11.

tion of glucose and increases uptake. Diabetic drivers who are required to do substantial manual unloading of trucks may not be good candidates for metformin use, however, because the medication infrequently causes potentially fatal lactic acidosis, and this risk is believed to be increased in the face of vigorous activity or renal insufficiency. Newer agents have been developed with either a lower probability of producing hypoglycemia, or no increased risk above a placebo. The most recent medication released, sitagliptin (Januvia), is in a new class of medications, dipeptidyl peptidase-4 inhibitor, which has no risk above that of a placebo. Alpha-glucosidase inhibitors have also been introduced, and they delay absorption of glucose from the gastrointestinal tract via enzymatic blockade. Use of the alpha-glucosidase inhibitors as monotherapy also is believed to have little risk for precipitating hypoglycemia. The thiazolidinediones assist in the management of diabetes mellitus by reducing a person's resistance to insulin. Repaglinide is thought to have less potential for precipitating hypoglycemia than the sulfonylureas. While the risk for hypoglycemia from the nonsulfonylureas is believed to range from none to low, these medications are being used in various combination therapies, and the risk for hypoglycemia in such circumstances is thought to be mildly elevated.

It is important that the examiner assess the medication regimen of the diabetic driver. The more intensive ("tight") the control with medications, the higher is the likelihood for hypoglycemia.

It was believed previously that intensive control of glucose levels did not result in improved clinical outcomes. However, there is now robust evidence from several controlled clinical trials that intensive control does result in fewer problems with diabetic peripheral neuropathy (60 percent reduction), diabetic proliferative retinopathy (75 percent reduction at 6.5 years), and diabetic nephropathy (60 percent reduction), as well as nerve conduction velocity [24–25]. Glycohemoglobin levels are being used as markers of quality of medical care, further accelerating the drive toward intensive control treatment strategies. Unfortunately, the major drawback of intensive control has been an increased risk for hypoglycemic reactions (threefold increased risk of severe hypoglycemic reactions). The evidence suggests that individuals with intensive control may be involved in more motor vehicle accidents, including deaths. Although these studies were of people utilizing insulin, it would seem likely that similar results, though less stark, would apply to people on oral hypoglycemic agents attempting intensive control of glucose levels and glycohemoglobin levels.

The conflict for a commercial driver between minimizing the risk for end-organ dysfunctions via intensive control versus the risk for hypoglycemic complications continues to grow, though the increasing use of newer oral agents helps to mitigate this for those drivers who can attain control with those medications.

Assessing the Diabetic Driver

In the performance of the CDME, it is recommended that applicants be asked questions about whether they have or had diabetes mellitus or "sugar problems." Any positive responses should result in many additional questions, including duration, medication(s), glycosylated hemoglobin results, diabetic education, end-organ complication(s), and frequency of physician examinations.

From these questions, the examiner then may draw conclusions regarding the intensity of diabetic control and the risks for severe hypoglycemic reactions and better ascertain whether the individual is able to drive safely. The tightness of control can be ascertained by asking questions about medication regimens, goals for treatment, and hypoglycemic symptoms. Ideally, this also should be combined with recall of glycohemoglobin measurement (or records). The current target for all patients is glycohemoglobin levels less than 7 percent (still there is an elevated risk for retinopathy in those with glycohemoglobin levels of 6–7%) [22]. The CDME should keep in mind however, that for drivers eligible for the diabetes exemption, the recommended range of glycohemoglobin is 7–10%. Ideally, most diabetics should know their glycohemoglobin measurement because it is a critical variable in assessing control. Yet, once they cannot address such a question, they are more likely to know the answer in the future if asked at serial examinations. These pieces of information assist the examiner in independently inferring the intensiveness of control and management of the condition. Knowledge of these issues also assists in gauging future risk for adverse events that are known to have dose-response relationships between glycemic levels and development of adverse conditions (e.g., myocardial infarction, neuropathy, retinopathy, and nephropathy). Hypoglycemic symptoms should be specifically ascertained during the commercial driver examination process. Severe hypoglycemic events include those during which there are (i) seizures, (ii) loss of consciousness, (iii) hospitalizations, or (iv) when the patient needs the help of another to recover (e.g., if someone else is required to retrieve a glucose source and place it in the patient's mouth).

Because of the great variability in the threshold for glucosuria, any nondiabetic individual who has glucose in the urine on dipstick urinalysis should necessitate further evaluation and at most should have a very short time-limited certification while undergoing further evaluation to ascertain whether the serum glucose level and/or glycohemoglobin is/are within the normal range, because the individual may well be completely out of control at the time of the screening test. Individuals who are thought to be in fair control probably should be certified for shorter time increments (e.g., 6 to 9 months) to allow for better surveillance of the situation and to encourage better control and compliance. Instead of examinations every 2 years, the FMCSA has recently recommended through the FAQs noted previously, that all diabetics undergo yearly commercial driver medical examinations.

It is recommended by the conference report on diabetic disorders and commercial drivers that the diabetic driver be evaluated by his or her personal physician at least every 6 months, although complete recertification at that time is not felt to be required [9]. Ophthalmologic examination, or at least a careful eye examination by the primary physician, also should be performed. Neurologic status should be assessed with the goal of ascertaining the presence or absence of a significant neuropathy. An electrocardiogram (ECG) is recommended at least every 2 years.

The following is a summary of the recommendations for the physical examination in a Type 2 diabetic driver:

1. A focused history asking these questions:
   a. Is a hypoglycemic agent being used? Is insulin being used?
   b. Are there hypoglycemic symptoms?
   c. Does the driver have a basic knowledge of diabetes, including the effects of missed meals, particularly while taking oral hypoglycemic agents?
   d. Does the driver carry a readily accessible glucose source in the vehicle?
   e. Is the glycemic control good or at least acceptable?
   f. Does the patient self-monitor glucose levels as recommended by the conference report?
2. Physical examination that includes
   a. Neurologic assessment searching for end-organ dysfunction
   b. Retinal examination, especially if eye care is suboptimal. A careful eye examination by the primary care physician was recommended by the conference report.
3. ECG every 2 years.
4. Evaluations by the primary care physician every 6 months.

Type 2 diabetics on insulin are handled differently and as of this writing, are not considered able to drive in interstate commerce in the United States without an exemption (see "Diabetes Mellitus Exemptions" on pages 215–228). An infrequent clinical problem that occurs is the patient who is taken off insulin just prior to the examination and then placed back on the insulin after the examination and is allowed to drive. It is recommended that such individuals be considered unfit to drive interstate commercial vehicles due to lack of good control of the diabetes.

Complications of hyperglycemia include fatigue and somnolence. An individual who is poorly controlled with an oral hypoglycemic agent at the time of evaluation for commercial driver recertification also should be considered unfit for duty. He or she should be told to see his or her personal physician to get the diabetes under better control, and the certification should be withheld pending better control.

Several factors are likely to increase the risk of hypoglycemia (Table 8-6). A number of these factors apply specifically to diabetic drivers of commercial vehicles, particularly age, erratic oral intake, variability in medication schedules, and irregular sleep schedules. There also are a number of medications that place the diabetic driver at greater risk for hypoglycemic events. It is recommended that these factors and agents be evaluated carefully in a diabetic truck driver under-

Table 8-6. Hypoglycemia Risk Factors

General	Medications
Age	Long-acting oral hypoglycemic agents
Renal disease	Aspirin
Hepatic disease	Sulfa medications
Congestive heart failure	Phenylbutazone
Alcohol	Dicumarol
Irregular exercise	Chloramphenicol
Irregular meals	Beta-blockers
	Irregular medication regimens

going a recertification examination.

An additional complication of diabetes mellitus is retinopathy. Diabetic retinopathy is estimated to be the most frequent cause of new cases of blindness among adults ages 20–74 years [22]. Incidence of diabetic retinopathy is strongly related to duration of diabetes. By 15 years, approximately 50 percent of both Type I and Type II diabetics have retinopathy [26]. Screening and laser treatment are estimated to significantly reduce the risk of blindness including at baseline for those with Type 2 diabetes mellitus [23,26–29]. These data suggest additional lines of inquiry during the certification process.

Diabetes Mellitus Exemptions

The driver who needs insulin is disqualified from interstate commercial vehicle operations at the current time, but eligible to apply for an exemption. As noted previously, this exemption program is under review by the MRB and the FMCSA.

The U.S. FHWA experimented with a waiver program for insulin-using commercial drivers [30–33]. No new drivers are being admitted into this program and under 100 such drivers remain in the program. The FHWA convened a panel of experts in the late 1980s and obtained an opinion that people who take insulin can and do drive safely as long as some fairly stringent requirements are met [10]. As a result, the FHWA began to enroll people in this waiver program and another waiver program for vision. Approximately 139 diabetics were initially certified before a court injunction that stopped further enrollment. It was argued that the program was not proven to be safe and that studies had shown diabetics to have an elevated risk for accidents. Information on the accident rates of the drivers operating with diabetic waivers to date has not shown an elevated risk in this select group. A recent publication from the Federal Motor Carrier Safety Administration [30] indicated that the accident rate in the waiver group was 2.31 per million vehicle miles traveled (n = 13) compared with the national rate of 2.61 (n = 444,000). The property damage rate was lower in the waiver group (1.78 versus 2.05), the injury rate was the same for both (0.53), and the fatality rate was lower (0.00 versus 0.03). Problems with these data are that they involve small numbers, the program was nonrandom/uncontrolled, the drivers with waivers were required to have had a good driving record for the prior 3 years, and the comparison population was not truly comparable. This last problem is probably an underrecognized problem with these data. The comparison population included people who likely have disqualifying or poorly controlled conditions but who have been given licenses by those who do not know the regulations. For a valid comparison to assess the hazards of insulin use in truck drivers, it would appear that the comparison population also should have been under similar scrutiny.

An exemption program for drivers on insulin was announced in 2003 [34]. Initially, the drivers had to demonstrate a 3-year safe driving record while on insulin but current requirements as a result of the Safe, Efficient and Flexible Transportation Equity Act—A Legacy for Users (SAFETEA-LU) [35], that requirement has been shorted to 1 month if changing to insulin from oral agents or 2 months if newly diagnosed, unless a longer period is recommended by the treating provider [36].

The current requirements for a driver wishing to apply for an exemption from the insulin-treated diabetes exclusion must complete a detailed application (Table 8-7) [37]. Parts of this must also be completed by an endocrinologist and optometrist/ophthalmologist. The driver must undergo an examination by a board-certified or board-eligible endocrinologist, including an examination specific for diabetes and have:

1. A current or past license that was not renewable due to the diabetes mellitus.
2. A safe driving record (e.g., no suspensions/revocations, no moving traffic violations while operating a CMV).
3. "No other disqualifying conditions" including those that are diabetic related.
4. No recurrent (≥ 2) severe hypoglycemic events (loss of consciousness, seizures, or hypoglycemic reactions requiring the help of an-

other, or hypoglycemic unawareness) from diabetes in the prior 5 years. One year of stability is needed after the first episode of each of these.

5. No recurrent hypoglycemic reactions with impaired cognitive function occurring without warning in the past 5 years. One year of stability is needed after the first of these events.

Once a driver obtains the exemption and is driving they must:

1. Carry a glucose meter with memory, and availability of insulin and rapidly absorbable glucose source.
2. Maintain a daily log of driving time to correlate with daily glucose measurements.
3. Perform frequent glucose checks (before driving and every 2–4 hours while driving).
4. Drive only when the glucose is between 100 and 400 mg/dL.

The monitoring of insulin-using drivers includes:

1. Provide written confirmation from the endocrinologist quarterly.
2. Include the make/model of the glucometer.
3. Review that the glucose measurements and glycosylated hemoglobin measures are in the "adequate" range (based on measures).
4. Undergo an annual comprehensive medical evaluation by an endocrinologist (similar to baseline).
5. If severe hypoglycemia has occurred, then the driver cannot drive until 1 year of stability has been achieved and cannot be a recurrent problem.

In addition the driver must report "all episodes of severe hypoglycemia, significant complications, or inability to manage diabetes" and all accidents/adverse events whether regardless of whether hypoglycemia related.

The FMCSA has indicated that it plans to pursue rulemaking that would permit the medical examiner to make the determination of whether a driver whose diabetes is being treated with insulin is safe to operate a commercial motor vehicle. Comments were sought on this in 2006 [38] and examiner should watch for changes in the medical certification of commercial drivers on insulin.

Table 8-7. Exemption Application, Diabetes Standard

Applicant Checklist

1. Driver Information

Name (First, Middle Initial, Last): _____

Street Address: _____

City: _____ State: _____ ZIP code: _____

Mailing Address, if different from above:

_____

City: _____ State: _____ ZIP code: _____

Telephone number: (____) _____-_____

Mobile phone number: (____) _____-_____

Fax number: (____) _____-_____

Sex (check one):   ☐ Male   ☐ Female

Date of birth (MM/DD/YYYY): _____

Social Security number: _____ -_____ -_____

2. Current Employment

Employer's name (If applicable): _____

Employer's address: _____

City: _____ State: _____ ZIP code: _____

Employer's telephone number: (____) _____-_____

Employer's DOT or ICC#: _____

Do you currently drive for this employer? (Check one):   ☐ YES   ☐ NO

Exemption Application, Diabetes Standard

3. Statement of Qualification

Prior to signing this statement, please review the Regulatory Criteria on Physical Qualifications for Commercial Drivers attached to the Endocrinologist Medical Evaluation Checklist.

Note: "otherwise qualified" or "hold a valid medical exemption" means that you meet the physical qualifications standards to drive a Commercial Motor Vehicle (CMV) (except for diabetes) or that you have an exemption or a skill performance evaluation certificate.

By signing below, I hereby certify that the following statement is true: "I acknowledge that I must be otherwise qualified under 49 CFR 391.41(b)(1-13) or hold a valid medical exemption before I can legally operate a CMV in interstate commerce."

Signature: _____

Do you have any waivers, exemptions, or Skill Performance Evaluation certificates? (check one)

 ☐ YES ☐ NO

If yes, list each, including date of issue, date of expiration, and identification number.

Name	**Issue Date**	**Expiration Date**	**ID#**

4. Driver License and Motor Vehicle Record

Please attach a readable copy of **both sides** of your current **VALID** driver's license. You must include your driving record, furnished by an official state agency on its letterhead, bearing the state seal or official stamp. *No other documentation will be accepted.* This request is to verify that you have a valid license and will not be used for any other purpose.

Exemption Application, Diabetes Standard

US Department Of Transportation   **400 Seventh St., SW**
Federal Motor Carrier   **Washington, DC   20590**
Safety Administration

Dear Sir/Madam:

The information and checklists enclosed are necessary to apply for an exemption from the
Federal regulation that prohibits insulin use by a diabetic commercial motor vehicle (CMV)
driver. The material in this packet includes:
1. Required applicant information;
2. Medical evaluation to be completed by a board-certified or board-eligible endocrinologist;
3. Medical evaluation to be completed by an ophthalmologist or optometrist;
4. Federal Register information about the Diabetes Exemption Program.

The CMV driver applying for the exemption—the applicant—is responsible for providing all
required checklists and information to the Diabetes Exemption Program.

**How Does a CMV Driver—the Applicant—Apply for an Exemption from the Diabetes
Standard?**

A. Endocrinologist Medical Evaluation Checklist
The applicant must be examined by a board-certified or board-eligible endocrinologist. The
applicant should take the Endocrinologist Medical Evaluation checklist to the appointment. The
endocrinologist must complete all parts of the checklist. When submitting a completed
application to the Diabetes Exemption Program, the applicant must ensure that the
endocrinologist's signed letterhead, a completed checklist, and any additional information
requested has been included.

B. Vision Medical Evaluation Checklist
The applicant must have an eye examination by an ophthalmologist or optometrist. An
applicant with **diabetic retinopathy MUST be evaluated by an ophthalmologist**. The
applicant should take the Vision Medical Evaluation Checklist to the appointment. The
ophthalmologist or optometrist must complete all parts of the checklist. When submitting a
completed application to the Diabetes Exemption Program, the applicant must ensure that the
ophthalmologist's or optometrist's signed letterhead, the completed checklist, and any additional
information requested has been included.

Both medical evaluations **MUST** be completed within **6 months** of submitting a completed
application to the Diabetes Exemption Program Office.

Exemption Application, Diabetes Standard

C. Additional Applicant Information

The applicant must provide all requested information as indicated on the applicant checklist and include a readable photocopy of both sides of his or her driver's license.

Additional medical information may be required, based on review of the information submitted. Prior to submitting the application, please review all information and make sure that each checklist is **completely filled out and that all required information is included.** Application review will be delayed if the information submitted is not current or if it is incomplete. Mail all information to:

> **Diabetes Exemption Program**
> **Room 8301**
> **400 Seventh Street, SW**
> **Washington, DC 20590-0001**

The application may be faxed to 703-448-3077. However, an original **must** be mailed to the address above.

What Happens After a Completed Application Is Submitted?

FMCSA will review the application and notify the applicant if additional information is needed. Please note that additional medical information may be required depending on any medical conditions outlined in the application. Once the application is complete, Federal Motor Carrier Safety Administration (FMCSA) will determine if the eligibility criteria have been met.

If the applicant is eligible for an exemption, a notice must be published in the *Federal Register* requesting public comment on the application. The comments help determine if granting the exemption would achieve a level of safety equivalent to or greater than the level of safety that would be achieved without the exemption. The notice discloses the applicant's full name, age, basic information related to the applicant's insulin use to control diabetes, and the type of driving license held; however, the notice does not include any detailed personal information, such as the applicant's address, employer, medical records, or driver's license number. The *Federal Register* notice usually includes several drivers eligible for an exemption. A 30-day comment period is provided for interested parties to respond.

If there are no comments that warrant denial of the application, FMCSA will publish a notice in the *Federal Register* announcing the decision to grant the exemption. The exemption is valid for operating a CMV within the United States and does not exempt the applicant from the physical qualifications of bordering countries.

Exemption Application, Diabetes Standard

If the Applicant Does Not Meet Eligibility Criteria
If FMCSA determines that the applicant does not meet one or more of the eligibility criteria, a denial letter will be mailed to the applicant outlining the reason that the Agency is unable to grant the exemption from the diabetes standard. Please note that the denial letter applies only to the portions of the application reviewed.

How Long Does the Process Take?
It may take up to 180 days from the date a preliminary decision is made to grant an exemption until the exemption is granted. This time is required to evaluation of the completed application and to complete the *Federal Register* notice process.

What Is Required After an Exemption Is Granted?
The exemption is sent to the applicant by certified mail. The exemption document outlines all requirements of the exemption. FMCSA can issue an exemption for a maximum of 2 years. At the end of the 2-year period, FMCSA may renew the exemption at its discretion. To retain the exemption and remain eligible for a renewal of the exemption, the driver must meet all requirements of the Diabetes Exemption Program.

If you have questions related to the application process outlined in this document, please call 703-448-3094.

Sincerely yours,

Mary D. Gunnels
Chief, Physical Qualifications Division

Regulatory Criteria on Physical Qualifications for Commercial Drivers

A person is physically qualified to drive a commercial motor vehicle if that person:

1. Has no loss of a foot, a leg, a hand, or an arm, or has been granted a skill performance evaluation certificate;

2. Has no impairment of: a hand or finger that interferes with prehension or power grasping; or an arm, foot, or leg that interferes with the ability to perform normal tasks associated with operating a commercial motor vehicle, or any other significant limb defect or limitation that interferes with the ability to perform normal tasks associated with operating a commercial motor vehicle, or has been granted a skill performance evaluation certificate.

3. Has no established medical history or clinical diagnosis of diabetes mellitus currently requiring insulin for control.

4. Has no current clinical diagnosis of myocardial infarction, angina pectoris, coronary insufficiency, thrombosis, or any other cardiovascular disease of a variety known to be accompanied by syncope, dyspnea, collapse, or congestive cardiac failure.

5. Has no established medical history or clinical diagnosis of a respiratory dysfunction likely to interfere with his/her ability to control and drive a commercial motor vehicle safely;

6. Has no current clinical diagnosis of high blood pressure likely to interfere with his/her ability to operate a commercial motor vehicle safely;

7. Has no established medical history or clinical diagnosis of rheumatic, arthritic, orthopedic, muscular, neuromuscular, or vascular disease that interferes with his/her ability to control and operate a commercial motor vehicle safely;

8. Has no established medical history or clinical diagnosis of epilepsy or any other condition likely to cause loss of consciousness or any loss of ability to control a commercial motor vehicle;

9. Has no mental, nervous, organic, or functional disease or psychiatric disorder likely to interfere with the driver's ability to drive a commercial motor vehicle safely.

10. Has distant visual acuity of at least 20/40 (Snellen) in each eye without corrective lenses or visual acuity separately corrected to 20/40 (Snellen) or better with corrective lenses, distant binocular acuity of at least 20/40 (Snellen) in both eyes with or without corrective lenses, field of vision of at least 70° in the horizontal Meridian in each eye, and the ability to recognize the colors of traffic signals and devices showing standard red, green, and amber.

Exemption Application, Diabetes Standard

11. First perceives a forced whispered voice in the better ear at not less than 5 feet with or without the use of a hearing aid or, if tested by use of an audiometric device, does not have an average hearing loss in the better ear greater than 40 decibels at 500 Hz, 1,000 Hz, and 2,000 Hz with or without a hearing aid.

12. Does not use a controlled substance identified in 21 CFR 1308.11 *Schedule I*, an amphetamine, narcotic, or any other habit-forming drug, unless prescribed by a licensed medical practitioner who is familiar with the driver's medical history and assigned duties; and has advised the driver that it will not adversely affect the driver's ability to safely operate a commercial motor vehicle.

13. Has no current clinical diagnosis of alcoholism.

Exemption Application, Diabetes Standard

Endocrinologist Medical Evaluation Checklist

Driver Information

Name: _____
     First   MI   Last

Address: _____

DOB (MM/DD/YYYY): _____

This individual is applying for a Federal diabetes exemption to operate a commercial motor vehicle (CMV), while taking insulin, in interstate commerce. Before receiving an exemption, an endocrinologist must thoroughly evaluate the driver. This evaluation is essential in determining if the person is able to drive safely. Therefore, this form must be filled out completely. If you have questions, please call 703-448-3094 and leave a message on our automated system for the diabetes exemption program. A specialist will return your call promptly. We appreciate your cooperation.

PLEASE CHECK / FILL IN REQUESTED INFORMATION.

1.   ☐ I am board-<u>certified</u> in endocrinology.

     ☐ I am board-<u>eligible</u> in endocrinology.
If neither, do not continue your assessment. Applicants must be evaluated by an endocrinologist who is board certified or board eligible.

2. Telephone number: _____

3. Fax number: _____

4. Date of examination (MM/DD/YYYY): _____

5. I am familiar with the patient's medical history for the past 5 years through treating the patient or consultation with the treating physician.
              ☐ YES   ☐ NO
A review of the patient's 5-year medical history is required. If the history for 5 years is not available please state the reason.

_____
_____
_____

6. Date of diabetes diagnosis: _____

    Treatment for diabetes prior to insulin use:
            ☐ None   ☐ Diet   ☐ Oral agent

Exemption Application, Diabetes Standard

7. Insulin Usage:
    Date insulin use began: _____
    Current insulin type: _____
    Current dose: _____
    If patient uses insulin pump, current average daily dose: _____
    Length of time on current dose: _____

8. FMCSA defines **a severe hypoglycemic reaction** as one that results in:
    Seizure, or
    Loss of consciousness, or
    Requiring assistance of another person, or
    Period of impaired cognitive function that occurred without warning.

In the last 5 years, while being treated for diabetes, has the patient had recurrent (2 or more) severe hypoglycemic episodes?   ☐ YES   ☐ NO

In the last 12 months, while being treated for diabetes, has the patient had a severe hypoglycemic episode?   ☐ YES   ☐ NO (**If no proceed to #9 below**)

If yes, provide information on each hypoglycemic episode:
       Date(s)
       _____
       Include additional information about each episode including symptoms of hypoglycemic reaction, treatment, and suspected cause:
       _____
       _____
       _____
       _____

Was the patient hospitalized?   ☐ YES   ☐ NO
If yes, provide details related to the hospitalization:
       _____
       _____
       _____

Has the patient's treatment regimen changed since the last hypoglycemic episode?
              ☐ YES   ☐ NO

Please explain changes:
       _____
       _____
       _____
       _____

Exemption Application, Diabetes Standard

After a severe hypoglycemic event, the driver is NOT qualified to operate a CMV for 1 year.

9. Does the patient have the ability and demonstrated willingness to properly monitor and manage his or her diabetes?   □ YES   □ NO

10. Since beginning insulin use, has the patient received education in the management of diabetes that includes diet, monitoring, recognition and treatment of hypoglycemia and hyperglycemia reactions?   □ YES   □ NO

11. Current Diet Used: _____

12. Additional Diabetes History: (If none, write *none.*)

_____
_____
_____
_____

13. List all medications taken: (*drug, name, dosage route, frequency*, to include *over-the-counter medications and herbal remedies*). If none, write none.

Name of Medication	**Dose**	**Diagnosis (Reason for taking medication)**

Medications listed above will not compromise the driver's ability to operate a CMV safely.
        □ YES   □ NO

14. Associated Medical Conditions (please check *yes* or *no*)

Cerebrovascular Disease	Carotid Artery Disease	□ YES	□ NO
	Transient Ischemic Attack (TIA)	□ YES	□ NO
	Stroke	□ YES	□ NO
Cardiovascular Disease	Hypertension	□ YES	□ NO
	Coronary Heart Disease	□ YES	□ NO
	Myocardial Infarction (MI)	□ YES	□ NO
	Angina Pectoris	□ YES	□ NO
	Congestive Heart Failure (CHF)	□ YES	□ NO
	Peripheral Vascular Disease	□ YES	□ NO

Exemption Application, Diabetes Standard

14. Associated Medical Conditions (Continued - please check *yes* or *no*)

Renal Disease	Renal insufficiency	☐ YES	☐ NO
	Proteinuria	☐ YES	☐ NO
	Nephrotic Syndrome	☐ YES	☐ NO
Neurologic Disease	Autonomic neuropathy (i.e., orthostatic hypotension)	☐ YES	☐ NO
	Peripheral Neuropathy (Please indicate degree)	☐ YES	☐ NO

If the applicant has been or is currently being treated for any of the above medical conditions, provide relevant additional information (consultant notes, special studies, follow-up reports, and hospital records).

15. Laboratory Reports/Stable Insulin Regimen

    A. Background and criteria

The driver should have stable control that decreases the health complications related to diabetes and does not increase the risk of hypoglycemia and hyperglycemia while operating a CMV.

An individual diagnosed with diabetes who was previously treated with oral medication and who now requires insulin should have at least a 1-month period on insulin to establish stable control.

An individual newly diagnosed with diabetes, not previously treated with oral medication, and who is now starting on insulin should have at least a 2-month period on insulin to establish stable control.

    B. Glycosylated hemoglobin A1C (A1C test) and blood glucose

Review of A1C test and blood glucose testing provides evidence of the driver's ability to manage his/her diabetes and drive safely. **Newly diagnosed patients and those converting from oral agents are required to provide an A1C test within 30 days of the date of application. Long-term insulin-treated diabetics must provide an A1C test within 6 months of the date of application.** FMCSA recognizes that an A1C test collected prior to beginning insulin may not reflect the individual's current control. In these cases, this information will be used as a baseline for monitoring. **Additional A1C test results are encouraged.**

FMCSA published the acceptable range of Hg A1C as 7% to 10%. This range was selected to acknowledge that individuals with A1C test levels <7% may be more

Exemption Application, Diabetes Standard

prone to hypoglycemic episodes. **Applicants with A1C test levels <7% are eligible for an exemption if they have no history of severe hypoglycemic episodes.**

Please provide a copy of the following:
☐ Laboratory reports reflecting A1C test result(s), to include lab reference normal range.

Glucose Measurements

FMCSA's major concern is that a driver can drive a CMV safely. A CMV driver **should not have large fluctuations in blood glucose levels.** Drivers should maintain blood glucose levels between 100 to 400 mg/dl prior to and while driving a CMV. This range is not intended to reflect stable medical control while taking insulin. **The determination of a patient's stable control is left to the treating endocrinologist.**

I have reviewed the patient's daily glucose monitoring logs while using insulin and the patient has no large fluctuations in results that are of concern.
☐ YES   ☐ NO

In my medical opinion, the patient is on a stable insulin regimen.
☐ YES   ☐ NO

Important: The criteria listed above, under 15A, relate to minimum guidelines for insulin use. If the treating endocrinologist concludes that the patient requires additional time to have the insulin dose adjusted, achieve stable control, or learn more about diabetes management, the time periods above should be extended, and the endocrinologist should note this when answering the following question.

16. I hereby certify that in my medical opinion, this applicant understands diabetes management and monitoring.
☐ YES   ☐ NO

17. The patient has stable control of his/her diabetes using insulin and is therefore able to drive a CMV safely.
☐ YES   ☐ NO

18. I have reviewed the attached Regulatory Criteria on Physical Qualifications for Commercial Drivers and I hereby certify that in my medical opinion this applicant has no disqualifying condition(s) other than diabetes.
☐ YES   ☐ NO

19. **PLEASE ATTACH COMPREHENSIVE PHYSICAL EXAMINATION. This exam must include vital signs, a brief medical/surgical history, and results of a full head-to-toe assessment at a minimum.**

20. **Please attach a copy of your office letterhead with your printed/typed name, signature, date, medical license number, and state of issue to this checklist.**

Exemption Application, Diabetes Standard

Diabetes Medical Evaluation Checklist
Optometrist/Ophthalmologist

Driver Information

Name: _____
             First   MI   Last
Address:

DOB (MM/DD/YYYY): _____

This applicant is applying for a Federal diabetes exemption to operate a commercial motor vehicle while using insulin in interstate commerce.

Before receiving an exemption, an ophthalmologist or optometrist must thoroughly evaluate the driver. This evaluation is essential in determining if the person is able to drive safely. Therefore, this form must be filled out completely. If you have questions, please call 703-448-3094 and leave a message on our automated system for the diabetes exemption program. A specialist will return your call promptly. We appreciate your cooperation.

The applicant's examination by an ophthalmologist or an optometrist must be within 6 months of submitting a completed application for a Federal diabetes exemption.

PLEASE CHECK / FILL IN REQUESTED INFORMATION.

An applicant with diabetic retinopathy must be evaluated by an ophthalmologist. The vision examination must be AFTER any eye surgery/procedures.

1.   ☐ I am an ophthalmologist   ☐ I am an optometrist

2.   Date of most recent examination: _____

3.   Distant visual acuity:
                         ☐ UNCORRECTED   ☐ CORRECTED
                                                                          ☐ Glasses
                                                                          ☐ Contact Lens

       Left eye: 20/_____   20/_____
       Right eye: 20/_____   20/_____

4.   Field of vision (FOV)*:
       Left eye: _____ degrees
       Right eye: _____ degrees

       Test used to determine: _____
*Note: If the patient has received laser treatment, and in your medical opinion you believe the patient's FOV could have been compromised, FMCSA recommends formal perimetry to determine if the patient meets the standard.

Exemption Application, Diabetes Standard

5. Color Vision
    The patient is able to identify correctly the standard red, green, and amber of traffic
    control signals.   ☐ YES   ☐ NO

Note: If certain color perception tests are administered (such as Ishihara, Pseudoisochromatic,
Yarn, etc.), and doubtful results are found, it is acceptable to administer a controlled test using a
traffic signal to determine the patient's ability to recognize red, green, and amber.

6. Does the patient have diabetic retinopathy?   ☐ YES   ☐ NO

    IF YES: ☐ Proliferative
                        O Stable   O Unstable
                   ☐ Nonproliferative
                        O Stable   O Unstable
    Treatment: _____
    Date diagnosed: _____
    Surgery/procedures: _____
    Requires recheck in ____ months

7. Does the patient have macular edema?   ☐ YES   ☐ NO

8. Does the patient have cataract(s)?
                        ☐ YES   ☐ NO

    If yes, is this condition stable?
                        ☐ YES   ☐ NO

    In your medical opinion, does this condition require monitoring more frequently than on
    an annual basis?
                        ☐ YES   ☐ NO
    If yes, how often?_____

9. Does the patient have any other diagnosis related to vision?
                        ☐ YES   ☐ NO
    If yes, what? _____

10. **Please attach a copy of your office letterhead with your printed/typed name,
    signature, date, medical license number, and state of issue to this checklist.**

Thyroid Disorders

Thyroid disorders are the most common endocrine system abnormalities. Increasing age and female gender are two prominent risk factors. The annual incidence of hypothyroid states is slightly higher than that for hyperthyroid states. Data on motor vehicle crash risks are absent. Generally, these problems are believed to be unlikely to interfere with an individual's ability to drive because they usually present in a mild state. However, there are some exceptions.

An individual with significant symptoms of thyrotoxicosis or "thyroid storm" would best be temporarily deferred from recertification. In addition, a driver with profound hypothyroidism should not be recertified until the disease manifestations are brought under reasonable control, often after a month or more. However, most patients with hypothyroidism develop the symptoms slowly and notice weight gain; recertification of such patients probably should not be withheld. If there is any concern about the patient's willingness or ability to maintain the prescribed medical regimen, a short recertification, for a few weeks to 3 months, can be given. On achieving a stable medical regimen, the driver can be returned to a standard 2-year recertification interval.

In Australia, there are no specific recommendations aside from being aware that visual fields may be affected by exophthalmos [19].

In Canada, the Canadian Medical Association recommends that those with "hyperthyroidism complicated by cardiac, neurologic or muscular symptoms that impair judgment or motor skills should not drive any type of motor vehicle until the condition has been controlled" [20]. Those with symptomatic hypothyroidism also are felt not to be candidates to drive until the condition is controlled successfully. Parathyroid disorders also are addressed, and it is recommended that "Patients with hypocalcemia with significant neurologic or muscular symptoms should not drive. If their symptoms respond well to treatment, they should be able to resume driving all vehicles without undue risk." Commercial drivers with diabetes insipidus should not drive until stabilized by treatment. Those with panhypopituitarism or other anterior pituitary hormone deficiencies should not drive until their condition is assessed and treated. Those with pituitary tumors or other space occupying lesions "should be regularly assessed for visual defects." Those with Cushing's disease who develop muscle weakness should not drive until after successful treatment. Those with Addison's may drive provided treatment is successful. Pheochromocytoma is felt to be a contraindication to the operation of any vehicle. "A grossly obese driver may not be able to respond rapidly enough to a sudden emergency situation and may not be able to operate vehicle controls properly. If the examining physician believes that an obese patient might have difficulty driving safely or maintaining a vehicle, the physician should recommend a road test."

In the United States, there are no detailed guidelines for thyroid disorders. Thus these situations are left to the examiner's judgment. It may be best for the examiner to ask him- or herself a question such as, "Is this person able to drive safely?" or "Would I like to have this person on the road next to me?" Because most people are reasonable, asking the driver such questions may prompt quick understanding and agreement that he or she should defer driving until better able to do so safely.

Hypothalamic-Pituitary-Adrenocortical Axis Disorders

These endocrine disorders parallel those of the thyroid in that they generally do not prevent recertification. Often, these disorders are slow in onset. If symptoms are severe, however, such as severe Addison's disease, then CDME recertification should be withheld until the disorder is brought under better control. In contrast, the Canadian Medical Examination appears to recommend that patients with diabetes insipidus, Addison's disease, acromegaly (with complicating factors), or untreated Cushing's syndrome not be allowed to drive commercial vehicles [26]. Similar to thyroid disorders, there is no specific guidance in Australia [27].

References

1. National Institute of Diabetes and Digestive and Kidney Diseases (NIDDK). National diabetes statistics fact sheet: General information and national estimates on diabetes in the United States, 2005 [NIH Pub. No. 06-3892]. US DHHS, NIH, 11/2005. http://diabetes.niddk.nih.gov/dm/pubs/statistics/Index/htm#7.
2. American Diabetes Association. Report of the expert committee on the diagnosis and classification of diabetes mellitus. *Diabetes Care* 2000; 23(Suppl. 1):S4–S19.
3. Harris MI et al. Prevalence of diabetes, impaired fasting glucose, and impaired glucose tolerance in U.S. adults. *Diabetes Care* 1998;21:518–524.
4. American Diabetes Association. Diabetes facts and figures, 1999. www.diabetes.org/ada/facts.asp.
5. Harris MI. Prevalence of non-insulin-dependent diabetes and impaired glucose tolerance. In National Diabetes Data Group, ed. *Diabetes in America: Diabetes Data Compiled 1984.* Washington: U.S. Department of Health and Human Services, 1985:VI1–VI31.

6. Sagberg F. Driver health and crash involvement: A case-control study. *Accid Anal Prev* 2006;38(1):28–34.

7. Psaty BM, Furberg CD. *N Engl J Med* May 21, 2007, Epub ahead of print.

8. National Large Truck Crash Facts. http://ai.volpe.dot.gov/CrashProfile/CrashProfileMainNew.asp?dy=2005. Accessed July 2, 2007.

9. U.S. Department of Transportation, Federal Highway Administration. Conference on Diabetic Disorders and Commercial Drivers. Publication No. FHWA-MC-88-041. Washington: Office of Motor Carriers, 1988.

10. U.S. Department of Transportation, Federal Highway Administration. Insulin-Using Commercial Motor Vehicle Drivers. Publication No. FHWA-MC-92-012. Washington: Office of Motor Carriers, 1992.

11. Diabetes Expert Panel Evidence Report Executive Summary. September 8, 2006. www.mrb.fmcsa.dot.gov/documents/Diabetes_Exec_Sum.pdf. Accessed June 7, 2007.

12. Heller S. Stratifying *Hypoglycaemic Event Risk in Insulin-Treated Diabetes.* London (UK): University of Sheffield, Department for Transport; 2006, p. 70.

13. Donnelly LA, Morris AD, Frier BM, et al. Frequency and predictors of hyoglycaemia in Type 1 and insulin-treated Type 2 diabetes: A population-based study. *Diabetes Med* 2005;22(6):749–755.

14. MacLeod KM, Hepburn DA, Frier BM. Frequency and morbidity of severe hypoglycaemia in insulin-treated diabetic patients. *Diabet Med* 1993;10(3): 238–245.

15. DiaMond Project Group on Social Issues. Global regulations on diabetics treated with insulin and their operation of commercial motor vehicles. *Br Med J* 1993;307(6898):250–253.

16. Federal Motor Carrier Safety Administration, DOT. Advance notice of proposed rulemaking request for comments. Qualifications of Drivers; Diabetes Standard. *Fed Reg* 2006;71(March 17):13801–13805.

17. Driver and Vehicle Licensing Agency. At a Glance Guide to the Current Medical Standards of Fitness to Drive. Swansea, England: Drivers Medical Unit, DVLA, www.dvla.gov.uk/medical/ataglance.aspx. Accessed June 7, 2007.

18. Gill G, Durston J, Johnston R, MacLeod K, Watkins P. Insulin-treated diabetes and driving in the UK. *Diabet Med* 2002;19:435–439.

19. Assessing Fitness to Drive. Interim Review Report. Austroads, National Transportation Commission, Melbourne, Australia, 2005. www.austroads.com.au/cms/AFTD%20web%20Aug%202006.pdf. Accessed May 27, 2007.

20. Canadian Medical Association. *Determining Medical Fitness to Operate Motor Vehicles CMA Driver's Guide,* 7th ed. www.cma.ca/index.cfm/ci_id/18223/la_id/1.htm. Accessed May 27, 2007.

21. Guide to Clinical Preventive Services. 2006. Recommendations of the U.S. Preventive Services Task Force. www.ahrq.gov/clinic/pocketgd.htm. Accessed June 7, 2007.

22. American Diabetes Associate. Standards of Medical Care in Diabetes, 2007. *Diabetes Care* 2007;30:S4–S41.

23. The Diabetes Control and Complications Trial Research Group. The effect of intensive treatment of diabetes on the development and progression of long-term complications in insulin-dependent diabetes mellitus. *N Engl J Med* 1993;329:977–986.

24. Reichard P, Nilsson B-Y, Rosenqvist U. The effect of long-term intensified insulin treatment on the development of microvascular complications of diabetes mellitus. *N Engl J Med* 1993;329:304–309.

25. Oral Medications for Type 2 Diabetes Mellitus. *Med Lett Drugs Therapeut* 2001;43(1102):29.

26. Kristinsson JK, Hauksdottir H, Stefánsson E, Jonasson F, Gislason I. Active prevention in diabetic eye disease. *Acta Ophthalmol Scand* 1997;75:249–254.

27. UKPDS: Intensive blood-glucose control with sulphonylureas or insulin compared with conventional treatment and risk of complications in patients with type 2 diabetes (UKPDS 33). UK Prospective Diabetes Study (UKPDS) Group. *Lancet* 1998;352:837–853.

28. UK Prospective Diabetes Study (UKPDS) Group. Effect of intensive blood-glucose control with metformin on complications in overweight patients with type 2 diabetes (UKPDS 34). *Lancet* 1998;352:854–865.

29. Stratton IM, Adler AI, Neil HA, Matthews DR, Manley SE, Cull CA, Hadden D, Turner RC, Holman RR. Association of glycaemia with macrovascular and microvascular complications of type 2 diabetes (UKPDS 35): Prospective observational study. *BMJ* 2000;321:405–412.

30. Federal Motor Carrier Safety Administration. An analysis of the risks associated with the operation of commercial motor vehicles by drivers with insulin-treated diabetes mellitus concluded that they were not at elevated risk. FMCSA-PPD-02-001; 2001.

31. Qualifications of drivers: Vision and diabetes—Limited exemptions. *Fed Reg* 1996;61(March 26):13338–13347.

32. Qualifications of drivers: Vision and diabetes—Proposed rule. *Fed Reg* 1996;61(Jan. 8):606–611.

33. Qualification of drivers: Waivers—Diabetes. *Fed Reg* 1993;58(July 29): 40690–40697.

34. Department of Transportation, Federal Motor Carrier Safety Administration. Qualification of drivers: Exemption applications: Diabetes. Notice of final dispositions. *Fed Reg* 2003;68(Sept. 3):52441–52452.

35. Safe, Efficient, Flexible and Efficient Transportation Equity Act: A Legacy for Users, 2005. www.fhwa.dot.gov/safetealu/legis.htm. Accessed July 3, 2007.

36. Federal Motor Carrier Safety Administration, DOT. Notice of revised final disposition. Qualification of Drivers; Eligibility Criteria and Applications; Diabetes Exemption. *Fed Reg* 2005;70(Nov. 8):67777–67781.

37. Federal Motor Carrier Safety Administration diabetes exemptionn application. www.fmcsa.dot.gov/documents/safetyprograms/Diabetes/diabetes-exemption-package.pdf. Accessed July 3, 2007.

38. Federal Motor Carrier Safety Administration, DOT. Advance notice of proposed rulemaking request for comments. Qualifications of Drivers; Diabetes Standard. *Fed Reg* 2006;71(March 17):13801–13805.

9

Psychiatric Disorders

KURT T. HEGMANN, MD, MPH

The CDME processes are currently undergoing substantial changes. As of June 2007, the schedule for the FMCSA Medical Review Board is to review psychiatric disorders in 2008. After the MRB reviews a subject, the FMCSA may be advised of suggested changes in the CDME processes by the MRB, after which rule-making may or may not commence. Please be aware of these updating processes.

Psychiatric conditions present a dual challenge of significant accident risk perceptions combined with a lack of major studies involving many diagnoses [1]. The lack of quality data on crash risks combined with nonspecific advisory criteria make the assessment of drivers with psychiatric disorders regarding fitness to drive commercial vehicles a challenging problem for the examining doctor. There appear to be no data on the risks among commercial drivers.

Some data from the general driving population are available. It has been shown that a history of mental illness conferred about a twofold increased risk of accidents (15.3 versus 7.2 accidents per 1 million miles) [2]. Comparable results were found in a 5-year population-based study that demonstrated elevated risks for motor vehicle crashes among those with psychiatric or emotional conditions whether on restrictions (relative risk [RR] = 1.87, 95% confidence interval [CI] = 1.11–3.17) or unrestricted (RR = 1.57, 95% CI = 1.46–1.67) [3]. Those drivers were at still higher risk for at-fault motor vehicle crashes whether on restrictions (RR = 2.98, 95% CI = 1.64–5.07) or unrestricted (RR = 1.85, 95% CI = 1.69–2.01). Also, from that same study, those with learning, memory, or communication problems were at about twice the risk for motor vehicle crashes and more than threefold the risk for at-fault crashes. Another study found that risk of crash was 4.2-fold among those with suicidal ideation but without current antidepressant use [4].

Far more data are available regarding the risks of psychoactive medication use and the general driving population's motor vehicle crash rates than those for disease states. Most of those data concern increased risks associated with use of benzodiazepines, barbiturates, opioids, and antidepressants [5–14].

Psychiatric Disorders and the CDME Certification Process

The regulation which addresses psychiatric issues is:

> *(b)(9) Has no mental, nervous, organic, or functional disease or psychiatric disorder likely to interfere with his/her ability to drive a commercial motor vehicle safely;*

The advisory criteria explain that emotional or adjustment problems contribute directly to an individual's level of memory, reasoning, attention, and judgment. These types of disorders can cause drowsiness, dizziness, confusion, weakness, or paralysis that may lead to uncoordination, inattention, loss of functional control, and susceptibility to crashes while driving. If severe fatigue or headaches, impaired coordination, recurring physical ailments, or chronic pain as well as conditions that are periodically incapacitating it may be grounds for disqualification. Somatic and psychosomatic complaints should be thoroughly examined.

The degree to which an individual is able to appreciate, evaluate, and adequately respond to environmental strain and emotional stress is critical when assessing an individual's mental alertness and flexibility to cope with the stresses of commercial motor vehicle driving.

The examiner should remember that individuals who live under chronic emotional upsets may have deeply ingrained maladaptive or erratic behavior patterns. Excessively antagonistic, instinctive, impulsive, openly aggressive, paranoid, or severely depressed behavior greatly interfere with the driver's ability to drive safely. Those individuals who are highly susceptible to frequent states of emotional instability (schizophrenia, affective psychoses, paranoia, anxiety, or depressive neurosis) may warrant disqualification.

Careful consideration should be given to the side effects and interactions of medications in the overall qualification determination.

There are no specific, mandatory psychiatric criteria. However, there are many disorders, conditions, and medication uses that are recommended for disqualification by the conference report [13].

Recommendations

The procedure proposed by the U.S. Department of Transportation (DOT) conference report on psychiatric disorders [15] for handling psychiatric problems was similar to that recommended by the conference report on neurologic disorders (Table 9-1). The procedure would likely work with virtually any medical problem and organ system.

Although the mechanism proposed in the conference report has not been implemented, it provides a valuable framework for handling psychiatric problems; however, one caveat should be kept in mind: The conference report "strongly" recommended a neurologic, psychiatric, or neuropsychological evaluation for any central nervous system (CNS) problem or medical condition that has the potential to cause CNS damage or in anyone with a family history of a degenerative neurologic disorder. As written, this is an impractical recommendation owing to the number of referrals required and the poor likelihood ratio for that approach. It probably is more appropriate to refer individuals with mildly active psychiatric problems for consideration of their ability to drive. If there is a substantially active problem, then a referral probably is unnecessary because the person is not likely to be qualified to drive. Referral to an appropriate individual to confirm the American Psychiatric Association's *Diagnostic and Statistical Manual,* 4th edition (DSM-IV) diagnosis and a joint determination of whether to disqualify the individual is likely needed in uncertain circumstances. Neuropsychological evaluation and tests may be ordered as well, depending on the situation. The conference report notes that no data or little data exist for many disorders, and thus the report is a summation of "educated guesses" and recommendations from a panel of experts.

Table 9-1. Commercial Driver Medical Examination Guidelines for Psychiatric Disorders

---

1. Commercial driver medical examination reveals a problem.

2. Referral to a psychiatrist, neurologist, or neuropsychologist to confirm *DSM-IV* diagnosis; some are disqualified at this step.

3. Neuropsychological or other psychometric testing may be performed; some are disqualified at this step.

4. A road test may be done to confirm the ability to drive.

Source: Adapted from the U.S. Department of Transportation, Federal Highway Administration. *Conference on Psychiatric Disorders and Commercial Drivers.* Publication No. FHWA-MC-91-006. Washington: U.S. DOT, Federal Highway Administration, Office of Motor Carriers, 1991.

Because the conference report is somewhat dated, other country's approaches may be helpful for comparative purposes. In Canada [16], the following factors are recommended to assess fitness to drive: (1) the psychiatric condition is stable and not in the acute phase, (2) functional cognitive impairment is assessed as minimal, (3) there is consistent compliance with prescribed psychotropic medication, (4) the maintenance dose of medication does not cause noticeable sedation, (5) insight is present to self-limit at times of symptoms of relapse and seek prompt assessment, and (6) the family is supportive of driving.

Great Britain handles psychiatric problems in a somewhat similar manner. Drivers with relapsing, recurrent, or progressive psychiatric disorders are required to be reported and investigated [17]. As well, other disorders are to be reported to the agency "if causing or felt likely to cause symptoms affecting safe driving."

Psychotropic Medications

Many psychiatric patients take multiple medications simultaneously (*polypharmacy*). This may present additional problems in evaluations, but it also may simplify other cases as signifying higher risk and likelihood of disqualification. An observational but uncontrolled study failed to confirm the impression that individuals taking selective serotonin reuptake inhibitors (SSRIs) are more likely to perform better on tests such as reaction times; instead, only 11.4 percent were believed to have passed all tests administered, and there were no differences between SSRIs, monoamine oxidase inhibitors (MAOIs), and tricyclic antidepressants [18]. Although definitive disqualification of such complex prospective drivers is not delineated in the conference report, these data and other information suggest that those requiring multiple medications to control psychiatric problems deserve at least an additional opinion, if not outright disqualification, as an inference on severity of the problems.

Benzodiazepines have been associated with an elevated risk for motor vehicle accidents in a number of studies. Of further concern is one study by Barbone and colleagues [5] that showed a similarly increased risk associated with short-acting medications. The risk associated with minor tranquilizer use has been estimated to be as high as 4.9, although most studies have found much smaller estimates of elevated risk.

One other group of medications to be mentioned is the antihistamines, because these are occasionally prescribed as anxiolytics. They have long been considered to be sedating and thus place a driver at increased risk of motor vehicle accidents. Some reports have drawn this association [8–11]. Newer, selective antihistamines for allergies are thought to be less sedating, yet there also is a study by O'Hanlon and Ramaekers [10] that shows some sedating effects of the newer antihistamine agents on measures of driver performance.

The Australia driving standards note that, regarding prescription and over-the-counter drugs, "In all cases when health professionals are prescribing or dispensing medication (including OTC and 'alternative' medications), they should consider any possible effects on driving skills and inform the patient [1]. Failure to do so may have medicolegal consequences for the practitioner in the event of a crash involving the patient, particularly in the case of commercial vehicle drivers." An individualized approach was recommended for most psychiatric conditions. For acute or chronic psychosis, personality or psychiatric disorders with aggression, violence, and other actions that may be hazardous to driving, psychoactive drug use that may impair driving, judgment, or perceptual cognitive or motor function affected by a mental disorder, or if the examining physician feels significant risk of a prior psychotic condition relapsing. A conditional license is available if: (1) the condition is well controlled, (2) the patient is compliant, and (3) the medication minimizes the risk of cognitive or other side effects that might affect driving.

The Canadian Medical Association (CMA) has written that "Physicians who prescribe drugs known to have an effect on sensory, mental or physical functions have a clear responsibility to warn their patients that these drugs may affect their ability to drive safely" [16].

The DVLA in Great Britain notes that "Doctors have a duty of care to advise their patients of the potential dangers of adverse effects from medication and interactions with other substances, especially alcohol" [17]. As well, they note that "any person who is driving or attempting to drive on the public highway, or other public place whilst unfit due to any drug, is liable to prosecution."

The conference report recommends that use of a number of medications should result in disqualification (Table 9-2). When dealing with an examinee who uses one or more of these medications, the commercial driver medical examiner likely will need to send the driver to a psychiatrist to determine whether he or she can drive safely, because most commercial driver medical examiners are unlikely to routinely prescribe these medications for psychiatric conditions and, as such, are unlikely to be familiar with their effects. The conference report recommends that use of benzodiazepines for anxiolytic purposes, use of tricyclic antidepressants, and use of barbiturates should be disqualifying. The only exception noted is that an individual who is treated effec-

Table 9-2. Psychiatric Medications and Conditions

Recommended Disqualifying	May Be Qualified*
Benzodiazepines	Buspirone
Hypnotics	Short-acting hypnotics and < 2 weeks' use
Barbiturates	
Tricyclic antidepressants	Amitriptyline, 25 mg every night Fluoxetine Bupropion
Antipsychotics	Stable on lithium > 3 months after electroconvulsive therapy Valproic acid Carbamazepine
Psychosis	Psychosis but symptom free > 1 year Anorexia nervosa Bulimia Personality disorders

*Psychiatric evaluation prior to clearance is recommended.
Source: Adapted from the U.S. Department of Transportation, Federal Highway Administration. *Conference on Psychiatric Disorders and Commercial Drivers.* Publication No. FHWA-MC-91-006. Washington: U.S. DOT, Federal Highway Administration, Office of Motor Carriers, 1991.

tively with nonsedating anxiolytics such as buspirone may be qualified. Individuals who require hypnotics were recommended to use, under medical supervision, only short-acting drugs with half-lives of less than 5 hours for no more than 2 weeks. If a patient is stable on lithium, he or she may be qualified. Again, however, many commercial driver medical examiners are not likely to be familiar with lithium or the evaluation of bipolar disorder patients and probably would need the assistance of a psychiatrist to judge the driving abilities of most such patients. Antidepressants are believed to be largely disqualifying medications, although it is recognized that some medications are not as sedating or impairing and that an individual taking such a medication may be qualified. The conference report recommended that there be a minimum of 3 months after electroconvulsive therapy prior to CDME certification. However, this also likely requires the judgment of a psychiatrist and an assessment of stability, including an assessment of any potential impairment from medications prescribed. Antipsychotic medications are thought to be disqualifying. Stimulants of the CNS also are believed to be disqualifying, with the possible exception of stimulants used in certain controlled situations such as narcolepsy. However, this conflicts with the conference report on neurologic disorders (see Chapter 7).

One psychoactive drug that is not well assessed with the current examination form is tobacco. Despite significant impacts on health possibly surpassed only by obesity, this is not assessed in the commercial driver certification process unless the examiner either makes specific inquiries with each driver or the clinic revises the examination form to include such question(s).

Australian criteria disqualify patients taking chronic psychoactive medications that "impair driving performance on a long-term basis" [1]. Exceptions are that there is a supportive psychiatric opinion, or the psychotic condition is "so well controlled as to reduce the risk of an exacerbation to that of any member of the general population."

Anxiety Disorders

Aside from the condition itself, there is also a concern about driver impairment from the medications used to treat anxiety disorders. Some evidence partially validates these concerns. A large-scale case-control study found that anxiety increased risks of a motor vehicle crash by 3.2 fold among elderly drivers [19]. As noted previously, an elevated risk of motor vehicle accidents is reported with benzodiazepine use. A population-based case-control study found that benzodiazepines increased the risk for motor vehicle crash in the elderly by 5.2-fold [14]. A list of the medications used to treat anxiety (Table 9-2) as represented in the conference report is updated in Table 9-3 [20]. Buspirone is believed to have the least sedating potential [13].

Generalized anxiety disorder is believed to be potentially impairing, particularly if severe, untreated, or associated with depression, drug use, or other anxiety disorders. Psychiatric referral is recommended by the conference report, and consideration of a driving test with an occupational therapist also is recommended. Some individuals with post-traumatic stress disorder (PTSD) are believed to have a greater potential for motor vehicle accidents. With this disorder, there may be a loss of regard for personal safety, whether the PTSD occurred secondary to a motor vehicle accident. Psychiatric referral and consideration of a driving test were recommended. Agoraphobia warrants the same treatment. Social phobia is believed not to warrant further evaluation.

Great Britain states that drivers with anxiety states with memory, concentration problems, agitation, behavioral disturbance, or suicidal

Table 9-3. Medications for Anxiety and Depression

Antidepressant Medications	Other
Tricyclics	Bupropion
Amitriptyline	Mirtazapine
Desipramine	Nefazodone
Imipramine	Trazodone
Nortriptyline	Amoxapine
Protriptyline-Deprex	Venlafaxine
Trimipramine	Hydroxyzine
	Thioridazine
Selective serotonin reuptake inhibitors	
Citalopram	**Antianxiety Medications**
Fluoxetine	
Paroxetine	Benzodiazepines
Escitalopram	Alprazolam
Sertraline	Clonazepam
	Diazepam
Monoamine oxidase inhibitors	Lorazepam
Phenelzine	Chlordiazepoxide
Tranylcypromine	Doxepin
	Oxazepam
	Clorazepate
	Other
	Buspirone

Source: Adapted from Drugs for depression and anxiety. *Med Lett Drugs Ther* 2002;44(1140):83.

thoughts may be permitted to drive if the person has demonstrated stability for 6 months [17]. Psychiatric reports may be required.

Australia notes that "Chronic sedative use is undesirable in general but in particular is likely to impair the ability to drive. Risks are increased if doses are not stable." Canadian recommendations are that those on mild sedatives and short-acting hypnotics for sleep aids "can usually drive any type of motor vehicle without difficulty" [16].

Attention Deficit Hyperactivity Disorder

Attention deficit hyperactivity disorder (ADHD) and attention deficit disorder (ADD) are increasingly recognized as problems in the adult population. Part of the reason for this interest is that individuals diagnosed as having ADHD 10 to 20 years ago now are entering the workforce. One study reported that ADHD adults "report more driving anger and aggressive expression through the use of their vehicle and less adaptive and constructive anger expression than their non-ADHD peers" [21]. Those findings confirmed a prior investigation in a different study population by the same research group [22]. Quite a few studies that have followed these individuals over time have found an elevated risk for traffic offenses, licensure suspensions, and motor vehicle crashes [23–26]. Nearly all these studies examined only ADHD patients through approximately age 25 years. Most of the elevated risk seems to be in those who were most severely affected as children. Nevertheless, how to evaluate such a prospective commercial driver is uncertain.

Because some features of this disorder are believed to carry over into adulthood, the conference report recommended that examiners evaluating individuals with this past history do the following:

1. Arrange a practical driving test conducted by an occupational therapist.
2. Make collateral contact with employers and others who have observed the examinee in tasks requiring sustained attention.
3. Evaluate the examinee's complete legal and driving records.
4. Review a detailed work history of the examinee, with particular attention to the length of service and the reason for and mode of termination for each employer.

In Canada, the prescription use of amphetamines "such as those used for attention deficit and sleep disorders, may not impair ability to drive." These patients should be followed regularly by the prescribing physician [16].

Depression, Bipolar, and Other Mood Disorders

Depression is a common disorder with a clinical prevalence in the general population estimated to be 3 to 5 percent [27]. Depression also has been associated with an elevated risk for motor vehicle accidents. A study by MacPherson and colleagues [8] estimated that the risk for antidepressant use increased 4.63-fold ($p < 0.001$). A large case-control study found that feeling depressed increased risks of a motor vehicle crash by 2.43-fold and of antidepressant use by 1.7-fold among elderly drivers [28]. A study by Sims et al. found a 2.5-fold increased risk for motor vehicle crashes among those who test as depressed on a rating instrument [29]. On the other hand, in a study by Ray and colleagues [11] that analyzed the risk of cyclic antidepressant use by dose, no elevated risk was found for those using low doses (i.e., amitriptyline at up to 25 mg/d). Beyond this, the risk was increased approximately 2.2-fold [12]. Those findings were confirmed in a review of nine studies that found the sedating antidepressants to impair to a degree comparable to alcohol (0.8 mg/mL or more), but not when taken nocturnally [30]. A study of moderate to severe depression evaluating psychomotor reaction function and times in a hospitalized setting found that only 11.4 percent passed all tests administered, and there were believed to be no significant differences between those using tricyclic antidepressants, MAOIs, or SSRIs [31].

A list of these medications as updated from Table 9-2 is presented in Table 9-3. Generally, the SSRIs and the MAOIs are thought to have less-sedating properties than the tricyclic antidepressants. However, fatigue is a side effect reported in excess compared with placebo for several of these medications in controlled clinical trials. Increased complaints of sedation or fatigue also were seen for nefazodone, trazodone, and mirtazapine. Also of potential concern for the commercial driver medical examiner are the side effects of agitation, anxiety, and insomnia that may occur with bupropion [20], as well as similar effects with use of some of the other medications.

The conference report recommended that drivers with histories of depression, bipolar disorder, and other mood disorders be evaluated by a psychiatrist. Any actively manic, suicidal, or severely depressed individual should not be qualified. Symptoms from severe depression, mania, or a suicide attempt would need to be absent for at least 1 year prior to recertification. All drivers without active disease but with a history of these disorders were recommended to be evaluated every 2 years by a psychiatrist.

Australian guidelines are the same as those for schizophrenia and other disorders noted previously [1].

The CMA recommends that "Patients taking antidepressants . . . should be carefully observed during the initial phase of dose adjustment and advised not to drive if they show any evidence of drowsiness or hypotension. Patients who are stable on maintenance doses can usually drive any class of motor vehicle if they are symptom free" [16].

In Great Britain, drivers with minor anxiety or depression are believed to be capable of being certified, and no notification of the driver licensing agency is necessary [17]. Drivers with depressive states with memory and/or concentration problems, agitation, behavioral disturbance, or suicidal thoughts may be permitted to drive if the person has demonstrated stability for 6 months. Psychiatric reports may be required.

Dissociative Disorders

Individuals with multiple personality disorder are believed to need psychiatric evaluation and a driving test. However, it is difficult to envision a situation in which such a person could be considered qualified. Individuals with psychogenic fugue, psychogenic amnesia, and depersonalization need psychiatric evaluation and further investigation, particularly with respect to their driving record.

Eating Disorders

Eating disorders and personality disorders are mentioned in the conference report as being possibly disqualifying conditions depending on the situation. It was recommended that a psychiatrist evaluate all individuals with a history of these disorders. Patients with active eating disorders should be disqualified. Those with significant malnutrition or fluid/electrolyte disturbances from these disorders were recommended to be stable for 1 year prior to consideration for recertification. All individuals with a past history of these problems were believed to require evaluation every 2 years by a psychiatrist.

Factitious Disorder

Those with factitious disorder should be evaluated carefully because they may engage in behaviors that are very risky in the commercial driving business, such as injecting insulin to induce hypoglycemia, thus attaining the role of the sick. Any active factitious disorder was believed to require psychiatric evaluation, although a remote and inactive problem is believed not to require further evaluation.

Hypomania and Mania

The conference report considered lithium use to be potentially disqualifying, signifying that stable mania was potentially able to be qualified. In Canada, a manic episode is a contraindication to driving [16]. In Great Britain, drivers with hypomania and mania are to cease driving pending outcome of a medical evaluation [17]. They must generally demonstrate 3 years of stability and good functional recovery as well as insight and adherence to treatment to be considered eligible for reinstatement. Psychiatric reports are generally required.

Personality Disorders

Drivers with personality disorders are thought to have an elevated accident risk [1].

The personality disorders considered in the DOT conference report included paranoid, schizoid, schizotypal, antisocial, borderline histrionic, narcissistic, avoidant, dependent, obsessive-compulsive, and passive-aggressive personality disorders. Individuals with histrionic, narcissistic, and dependent personality disorders were not recommended for special evaluations. Those with obsessive-compulsive and passive-aggressive disorders were thought to be somewhat intermediate, with a potential to have an increased risk for motor vehicle accidents. Those diagnosed as having obsessive-compulsive disorder should be asked questions to assess the degree of excess hostility, aggressive tendencies, vulnerability to stress, and past job dysfunction to evaluate the need for further assessment. Passive-aggressive traits deemed worthy of further investigation include recent suicidal or homicidal thoughts, hospitalization in the past 6 months, or a history of arrest for a violent offense. The general approach recommended for evaluating the other problems includes an assessment to confirm accuracy of the diagnosis, assessment of past ability to drive safely, and reliance on collateral interviews to assess the risks of allowing the individual to drive. It is noteworthy that antisocial personality disorder and alcoholism are the two psychological factors thought to most likely result in motor vehicle accidents.

Disorders of impulse control, such as intermittent explosive disorder, kleptomania, pathologic gambling, and pyromania, also were addressed. Intermittent explosive disorder is recommended to be evaluated by a psychiatrist or psychologist, with special attention being paid to hostility, violence, tolerance to stress, unsafe driving practices, school/military/employment records, and violent thought content. Other disorders of impulse control may occur in the setting of other psychological disorders or may occur in individuals with impulsive and risky behaviors that should be assessed by a psychiatrist prior to certification.

A study of "road rage" deserves mention. Although it is not a disorder, it is considered to be associated with several disorders. This study found that factors associated with road rage were male gender, history of illicit drug use, history of evaluation/treatment for emotional problems, and an inverse relationship with years of driving [32].

The CMA notes that "personality disorders may be associated with behavior such as aggression, egocentricity, impulsiveness, resentment of authority, intolerance of frustration and irresponsibility" [16]. In

Great Britain, a license is to be revoked if the disorder is "associated with serious behavior disturbance likely to make the individual a source of danger at the wheel. If psychiatric reports confirm stability, then consideration would be given to restoration of the license" [17].

Schizophrenia and Psychoses

A study of inpatients recovering from acute schizophrenic episodes and expected to be discharged within 2 weeks found that only 10.7 percent were believed to have passed a battery of psychomotor tests, whereas 32 percent were believed to have impairments requiring further evaluation of the ability to drive and 57 percent were considered severely impaired and unqualified to drive. Those treated with clozapine tended to perform better than those treated with usual neuroleptics, though the results were not always statistically significant [33].

Schizophrenia is considered to be a chronic and permanently disqualifying condition, as recommended in the DOT conference report [15]. Those with active psychoses should be prohibited from commercial vehicle operation. It was recommended that individuals be free of psychotic episodes for 1 year prior to consideration for certification. If a person had only a brief psychosis, the option for evaluating the patient 6 months after the event was noted as a possibility. The conference report also recommended reevaluation every 2 years for those whose mental illness histories have psychotic features, and such drivers were instructed to report any psychotic symptoms within 30 days. Many believe that, at least initially, recertification more frequently than every 2 years would be more appropriate and that any patient with psychotic symptoms should report symptoms on the date of occurrence.

The CMA also believes that acute psychosis is "incompatible with safe driving" [16].

Acute psychoses are incompatible with driving in Great Britain [17]. Those with any episode of psychosis are not believed to be able to safely drive unless there is no recurrence for at least 3 years and there is insight into the condition. Chronic schizophrenia is not believed to be incompatible with driving provided the person is stable for 3 years and has insight into his or her condition, there is adherence to treatment, and there are no significant adverse medication effects. A consultant report is generally required.

Patients with acute psychosis are believed to be unqualified in Australia [1]. If a driver is no longer acutely psychotic but the examiner believes that there is a significant risk of relapse, he or she is not qualified.

The CMA recommends that "Patients taking . . . antipsychotics should be carefully observed during the initial phase of dose adjustment and advised not to drive if they show any evidence of drowsiness or hypotension. Patients who are stable on maintenance doses can usually drive any class of motor vehicle if they are symptom free" [16].

Somatoform Disorders

Individuals with body dysmorphic disorder, hypochondriasis, somatization disorder, and undifferentiated somatization disorder are believed not to have difficulty driving.

Those with either conversion disorder or somatoform pain disorder are believed to have an elevated accident potential, so a psychiatric evaluation and consideration of a practical driving test with an occupational therapist are recommended.

Conclusion

In a practical light, a number of disorders discussed previously would seem unlikely to result in licensure for an applicant. Informed, psychiatric evaluation is likely needed for prospective drivers with a number of these conditions. Regardless of the diagnosis or situation, if the commercial driver medical examiner is uncomfortable with an individual's mental aspects, a psychiatric evaluation is warranted. It is probably best to communicate with the psychiatrist prior to such a consultation, because many are unfamiliar with the CDME requirements. However, should the psychiatrist establish that the person can drive safely and the examiner still has lingering doubts, one may consider: (1) (re)contacting the psychiatrist, (2) informing him or her of the concerns, and (3) requesting a letter in writing from the psychiatrist stating that there is no increased risk of a motor vehicle accident with this applicant (if there is a belief that the CDME would affirm certification of the driver). In individuals for whom there is no such concern or in individuals with a history of a problem that has been silent for years, certification would seem to be justifiable.

References

1. Assessing Fitness to Drive. Interim Review Report. Austroads, National Transportation Commission, Melbourne, Australia, 2005. Update to Assessing Fitness to Drive 2003. www.austroads.com.au/cms/AFTD%20web%20Aug%202006.pdf. Accessed May 27, 2007.

2. Waller JA. Chronic medical conditions and traffic safety. *N Engl J Med* 1965;273(26):1413–1420.

3. Diller E, Cook L, Leonard D, Reading J, Dean JM, Vernon D. Evaluating drivers licensed with medical conditions in Utah, 1992–1996. NHTSA Technical Report DOTHS 809 023. Washington: National Highway Traffic Safety Administration, June 1999.

4. Lam LT, Norton R, Connor J, Ameratunga S. Suicidal Ideation, antidepressive medication and car crash injury. *Accid Anal Prev* 2005;37(2):335–339.

5. Barbone F, McMahon AD, Davey PG, et al. Association of road-traffic accidents with benzodiazepine use. *Lancet* 1998;352:1333–1336.

6. Koepsell TD, Wolf ME, McCloskey L, et al. Medical conditions and motor vehicle collision injuries in older adults. *J Am Geriatr Soc* 1994;42(7):695–700.

7. Laux LF, Brelsford J. Age-related changes in sensory, cognitive, psychomotor, and physical functioning and driving performance in drivers aged 40 to 92. Washington: AAA Foundation for Traffic Safety, 1990:1–58.

8. MacPherson RD, Perl J, Stramer GA, et al. Self-reported drug-usage and crash-incidence in breathalyzed drivers. *Accid Anal Prev* 1984;2:139–148.

9. Morris LN, Allman RM, Owsley C, et al. Vehicle crashes and positive urine drug screens among older drivers. *Clin Epidemiol Health Care Res II* 1992;4:827A.

10. O'Hanlon JF, Ramaekers JG. Antihistamine effects on actual driving performance in a standard test: A summary of Dutch experience, 1989–1994. *Allergy* 1995;50(3):234–242.

11. Ray WA, Thapa PB, Shorr RI. Medications and the older driver. *Clin Geriatr Med* 1993;9(2):413–438.

12. Ray WA, Fought RL, Decker MD. Psychoactive drugs and the risk of injurious motor vehicle crashes in elderly patients. *Am J Epidemiol* 1992;136:873–883.

13. Skegg DCG, Richards SM, Doll R. Minor tranquilisers and road accidents. *Br Med J* 1979;1:917–919.

14. McGwin G Jr., Sims RV, Pulley L, Roseman JM. Relations among chronic medical conditions, medications, and automobile crashes in the elderly: A population-based case-control study. *Am J Epidemiol* 2000;152(5):424–431.

15. U.S. Department of Transportation, Federal Highway Administration. *Conference on Psychiatric Disorders and Commercial Drivers.* Publication No. FHWA-MC-91-006. Washington: U.S. DOT, Federal Highway Administration, Office of Motor Carriers, 1991.

16. Canadian Medical Association. *Determining Medical Fitness to Operate Motor Vehicles CMA Driver's Guide*, 7th ed. www.cma.ca/index.cfm/ci_id/18223/la_id/1.htm. Accessed May 27, 2007.

17. Driver and Vehicle Licensing Agency. *At-a-Glance Guide to the Current Medical Standards of Fitness to Drive.* Swansea, England: Drivers Medical Unit, DVLA. www.dvla.gov.uk/. Accessed May 27, 2007.

18. Grabe HJ, Wolf T, Grätz S, Laux G. The influence of polypharmacological antidepressive treatment on central nervous information processing of de-

pressed patients: Implications for fitness to drive. *Neuropsychobiology* 1998; 37:200–204.

19. Sagberg F. Driver health and crash involvement: A case-control study. *Accid Anal Prev* 2006;38(1):28–34.

20. Drugs for depression and anxiety. *Med Lett Drugs Ther* 2002;44(1140):83.

21. Richards TL, Deffenbacher JL, Rosen LA, Barkley RA, Rodricks T. Driving anger and driving behavior In adults with ADHD. *J Atten Disord* 2006; 10(1):54-64.

22. Richards T, Deffenbacher J, Rosen L. Driving anger and other driving-related behaviors in high and low ADHD symptom college students. *J Attn Disord* 2002;6(1):25–38.

23. Barkley RA, Guevremont DC, Anastopoulos AD, et al. Driving-related risks and outcomes of attention deficit hyperactivity disorder in adolescents and young adults: A 3- to 5-year follow-up survey. *Pediatrics* 1993; 92(2):212–218.

24. Nada-Raja S, Langley JD, McGee R, et al. Inattentive and hyperactive behaviors and driving offenses in adolescence. *J Am Acad Child Adolesc Psychol* 1997;36:515–522.

25. Barkley RA, Murphy KR, Depaul GJ, Bush T. Driving in young adults with attention deficit hyperactivity disorder: Knowledge, performance, adverse outcomes, and the role of executive functioning. *J Int Neuropsychol Soc* 2002;8:655–672.

26. Barkley RA. Driving impairments in teens and adults with attention-deficit/hyperactivity disorder. *Psychiatr Clin North Am* 2004;27(2):233–260.

27. Myers JK, Weissman MM, Tischler GE, et al. Six-month prevalence of psychiatric disorders in three communities. *Arch Gen Psychiatry* 1984;41:959–970.

28. Sagberg F. Driver health and crash involvement: A case-control study. *Accid Anal Prev* 2006;38(1):28–34.

29. Sims RV, McGwin G Jr, Allman RM, Ball K, Owsley C. Exploratory study of incident vehicle crashes among older drivers. *J Gerontol A Biol Sci Med Sci* 2000;55(1):M22–27.

30. Ramaekers JG. Antidepressants and driver impairment: Empirical evidence from a standard on-the-road test. *J Clin Psychiatry* 2003;64(1):20–29.

31. Grabe HJ, Wolf T, Grätz S, Laux G. The influence of polypharmacological antidepressive treatment on central nervous information processing of depressed patients: Implications for fitness to drive. *Neuropsychobiology* 1998;37(4):200–204.

32. Fong G, Frost D, Stansfeld S. Road rage: A psychiatric phenomenon? *Soc Psychiatry Psychiatr Epidemiol* 2001;36:277–286.

33. Grabe HJ, Wolf T, Grätz S, Laux G. The influence of clozapine and typical neuroleptics on information processing of the central nervous system under clinical conditions in schizophrenic disorders: Implications for fitness to drive. *Neuropsychobiology* 1999;40:196–201.

10

Renal Disease

Natalie P. Hartenbaum, MD, MPH

Although there is no regulation that directly addresses drivers with renal disease, a number do so indirectly, including the cardiac, hypertension, respiratory, psychiatric, and neurologic standards. As part of the regulatory review of medical standards and guidelines, the FMCSA has an expert panel on renal disease planned. The FMCSA addressed renal disease in two FAQs where they explain that finding proteinuria might indicate renal disease and the examiner may disqualify, issue a time-limited certification, or certify depending on whether the examiner believed the proteinuria could affect safe driving. They also recommended that the driver should be referred for follow-up regardless of the certification decision. In another FAQ, FMCSA indicated that although there is no guidance on patients on kidney dialysis, the examiner should require a letter from the treating doctor (nephrologist) outlining the condition, medications, and recommendation regarding certification. As with any opinion from a treating provider, the examiner may or may not accept this recommendation. Examiners are reminded that restrictions other than those on the preprinted form are disqualifying.

In evaluating the fitness of a commercial driver with renal disease, it is important not only to consider the renal disease itself but also to assess other coexisting medical conditions. Drivers who also have diabetes, hypertension, or heart disease may be at higher risk of complications or sudden impairment than drivers with renal disease may alone. In addition, the fluid shifts and electrolyte disturbances before or after dialysis may impair the driver.

There is little in the literature on the risk of motor vehicle crashes in individuals with renal disease. Some literature suggests impairments in cognitive functioning in patients on dialysis as well as those with end-stage renal disease not on dialysis [1–4].

The type of dialysis may play a role in the maintenance of cognitive function. In one study, cognitive function was restored transiently after hemodialysis but maintained close to normal during continuous peritoneal dialysis [5,6]. Memory and cognitive function appears to improve after transplant [7].

Renal failure can result in a number of physiologic and clinical abnormalities. Among dialysis patients age 20–64, overall mortality rates are more than eight times greater than those found in the general Medicare population, mostly due to cardiovascular causes [8].

The first step in the evaluation must be to assess the degree of renal impairment. Results from laboratory studies, including electrolyte levels, blood urea nitrogen level, creatinine level, and creatinine clearance, should be reviewed, as should the degree of proteinuria, if present. There is some evidence that older drivers with proteinuria have an increased risk of motor vehicle accidents [9].

More than 50 percent of patients undergoing dialysis continue to have hypertension [10]. The old advisory criteria for hypertension suggest that as part of the evaluation of the severity of hypertension, renal function should be evaluated. The criteria further suggest that individuals with a creatinine level >2.5 mg/dL not be certified to drive commercial vehicles in interstate commerce. This however was not included in the advisory criteria revised in 2003 [11].

Cardiovascular disease is the leading cause of death in patients with end-stage renal disease [8]. This increase continues even after renal transplantation although it is lower than in patients on dialysis. By 18 months after development of chronic kidney disease, approximately 12 percent of patients, including those on dialysis, have an acute myocardial infarction, at 18 months, and 56 percent will have developed congestive heart failure [8]. Cardiac arrest risk is higher in those on dialysis that chronic kidney disease patients who are not; 24 percent at 3 years. The single greatest cause of mortality in dialysis patients is arrhythmias, estimated at 27 percent.

Anemia also is common in patients with end-stage renal disease. The degree of anemia should be evaluated in a commercial driver because it leads to many of the problems seen in these patients. Such problems include fatigue and exercise intolerance as well as cardiac ischemia through a decreased amount of oxygen delivered to the cardiac tissue.

A mixed sensory and motor neuropathy, often more severe in the legs than in the arms, is common in patients with uremia. This often will respond to dialysis [12]. Diabetic neuropathy may be superimposed on the uremic neuropathy and will not improve with dialysis.

Abnormalities that may be seen in individuals with renal failure and affect their ability to concentrate include fatigue, impaired mentation, sleep disorders, restless legs syndrome (resulting in sleep disturbance), and peripheral neuropathies. In more severe cases, seizures or coma may occur if the uremia is not treated properly.

Two types of dialysis are used: hemodialysis or peritoneal dialysis. Hemodialysis is more common and usually requires 9 to 12 hours of treatment per week, often divided into three sessions per week. Frequently, an artificial shunt is used, and thus the incidence of infection or sepsis is high. The significant interruption in normal activities of daily living and altered body image may lead to depression. During dialysis, fluxes in osmolality and electrolytes may lead to a dialysis disequilibrium syndrome or arrhythmias. Hypotension is common. Electrolyte disturbances also may result in muscle cramps. The development of dialysis dementia is another concern.

Heparin is used during the dialysis procedure and may lead to subdural hematoma and retroperitoneal, gastrointestinal, pericardial, or pleural hemorrhage. Long-term dialysis patients have increased mortality due to myocardial infarction and cerebrovascular accidents, both serious concerns in a commercial driver. Dialysis is best performed in a consistent setting, a difficulty for many long-haul truckers. Arranging dialysis in different locations over the course of several weeks may be a logistical impossibility. A reliable schedule also is required and may present difficulty. Commercial drivers whose routes are solely local, short haul, or intermittent may be able to coordinate their work schedule around their dialysis schedule. Medical examiners, however, are unable to restrict drivers to operating only under these conditions. If it is determined that such a driver should be medically qualified, only short-term certification to monitor the disease process and work routine should be considered.

The other main method of dialysis is continuous ambulatory peritoneal dialysis (CAPD). For this method, patients instill dialysate fluid into the peritoneal cavity, seal the catheter, and continue with normal activities. The fluid is removed and replaced every 4 to 6 hours. A cyclic dialysate delivery device allows continuous exchange at night. Advantages over hemodialysis include the more gradual shifts in fluid and electrolyte levels and the avoidance of heparinization. Longer treatment times may be a disadvantage to some patients. Complications include catheter infection, peritonitis, and moderate protein loss. Because CAPD is performed by the patient, the requirement for compliance to avoid infection or other complications is significant.

Patients who undergo renal transplantation often will return to a near-normal lifestyle. One of the greatest risks for these individuals is transplant rejection. Such patients should be able to obtain care in the event of infection or rejection in a reasonable period of time. The risk of rejection is highest in the first year after transplantation. For a commercial driver, one concern should be the potential side effects of the medication in addition to its immunosuppressive effects. Steroids at higher doses can cause confusion, and cyclosporine can lead to tremor. As with all medication use in commercial drivers, it is important for examiners to be in contact with the treating physician to obtain an understanding of the medication and any potential interference with the safe operation of a vehicle.

Even with treatment, only about 10 to 20 percent of chronic renal failure patients are totally rehabilitated by dialysis, and another 30 to 40 percent of nondiabetic patients are returned to a functional level. Mean mortality for all end-stage renal disease patients is approximately 18 percent per year. In those younger than age 45 with no complicating medical problems, mortality with treatment falls below 5 percent per year.

As examiners under the federal program, we are unable to limit geographic range or duration of driving or impose other restrictions. Patients often complain of weakness or fatigue the day after they are dialyzed, and the examiner will be unable to control for this.

Other Standards and Guidelines

In general, guidelines from other transportation modes and countries advise against certifying individuals on dialysis or after renal transplantation for performing safety-sensitive operations unless their condition is fully stabilized and thoroughly evaluated. The Federal Aviation Administration considers renal dialysis as a cause for denial of licensure except under limited circumstances.

Australia's guidelines for commercial drivers indicate an individual is not eligible for an unconditional license if they have end-stage renal disease requiring dialysis or if predialysis the GFR is <20 percent. A conditional license can be granted if a renal specialist indicates the condition is stable and there are limited comorbidities [13].

The Canadian Medical Association indicates that drivers should not drive if their dialysis treatment interferes with safe driving or if they have a complicating medical problem. Individuals who have adequate cognitive and sensorimotor abilities can driver any class of vehicle even if on hemodialysis or peritoneal dialysis. They note that the commercial driver must be under the supervision of a nephrologist or an internist and have an annual medical review and be able to receive appropriate dialysis therapy. They note that hemodialysis is generally not a feasible treatment modality for a long-distance driver [14].

In the United Kingdom, the Driver and Vehicle Licensing Agency's [15] medical group assesses commercial drivers on peritoneal or hemodialysis on an individual basis.

Conclusion

End-stage renal disease has the potential to cause impairment in a commercial driver by a number of mechanisms. It is important to evaluate not only the degree and stability of renal impairment but also the presence and status of any coexisting diseases. Information from all treating physicians should be reviewed, and arrangements should be made with the primary-treating physician that commercial driving status be reviewed with significant changes in medical stability. A 1998 accident with multiple fatalities involved a driver who was medically qualified and 2 months later began renal dialysis. No evaluation of the individual's ability to perform commercial driver functions occurred at that time or after long-term absences to stabilize his disease. Final determination of the actual cause of the accident is still pending, but the contribution of his medical condition has many people discussing the inadequacy of the current medical certification system.

References

1. Dobbs BM. Medical conditions and driving: A review of the scientific literature (1960–2000). Report DOT HS 809 690. National Highway Traffic Safety Administration. September 2005.
2. Murray AM, Tupper DE. Knopman DS, Gilbertson DT, Pederson SL, Li S, Smith GE, Hochhalter AK, Collins AJ, Kane RL. Cognitive impairment in hemodialysis patients is common. *Neurology* 2006;67(2):216–223.
3. Pereira AA, Weiner DE, Scott T, Sarnak MJ. Cognitive function in dialysis patients. *Am J Kidney Dis* 2005;45(3):448–462.
4. Kurella M, Chertow GM, Luan J, Yaffe K. Cognitive impairment in chronic kidney disease. *J Amer Geriatrics Soc* 2004;52(11):1863–1869.
5. Buocristiani LRI, Brown AL, Byrne J, et al. Better preservation of cognitive faculty in continuous ambulatory peritoneal dialysis. *Peritoneal Dialysis Int* 1993;13 (Suppl 2):S202–205.
6. Tilki HE, Akpolat T, Tunali G, Kara A, Onar MK. Effects of haemodialysis and continuous ambulatory peritoneal dialysis on P300 cognitive potentials in uraemic patients. *Upsala J Medl Sci* 2004;109(1):43–48.
7. Griva K, Thompson D, Jayasena D, Davenport A, Harrison M, Newman S, Stanton P. Cognitive functioning pre- to post-kidney transplantation—a prospective study. *Nephrology Dialysis Transplant* 2006;21(11):3275–3282.
8. U.S. Renal Data System, USRDS 2006 Annual Data Report: Atlas of End-Stage Renal Disease in the United States, National Institutes of Health,

National Institute of Diabetes and Digestive and Kidney Diseases, Bethesda, MD, 2006.

9. Stewart RB, Moore MT, Marks RG, et al. *Driving Cessation and Accidents in the Elderly: An Analysis of Symptoms, Diseases, Cognitive Dysfunction and Medicationsx* Washington: AAA Foundation for Traffic Safety, 1993.

10. Pastan S, Bailey J. Medical progress: Dialysis therapy. *N Engl J Med* 1998;338:1428–1437.

11. Federal Motor Carrier Safety Administration, DOT. Motor Carrier Safety Regulations, Miscellaneous Technical Amendments. *Fed Reg* 2003;68(Sept. 30):56196–56208.

12. Onyekachi I. Current concepts: Care of patients undergoing hemodialysis. *N Engl J Med* 1998;339:1054–1062.

13. Austroads. Assessing Fitness to Drive For Commercial and Private Vehicle Drivers. Sydney, Australia, 2003. www.austroads.com.au/aftd/downloads/AFTD_2003_FA_WEBREV1.pdf. Accessed May 21, 2007.

14. Canadian Medical Association. *Determining Medical Fitness to Operate Motor Vehicles,* 7th ed. Ottawa: CMA, 2006. www.cma.ca/index.cfm/ci_id/18223/la_id/1.htm. Accessed May 21, 2007.

15. Driver and Vehicle Licensing Agency. At-a-Glance Guide to the Current Medical Standards of Fitness to Drive. Swansea, England: Drivers Medical Unit, DVLA. Last updated February 2007. www.dvla.gov.uk/media/pdf/medical/aagv1.pdf. Accessed May 21, 2007.

11

Substance Abuse and Medication Use

Natalie P. Hartenbaum, MD, MPH

The CDME processes are currently undergoing substantial changes. The FMCSA Medical Expert Panel on the Licit Use of Schedule II Medications presented their findings in January 2007, the Medical Review Board made their recommendations in April 2007. They are included in this chapter but as of publication date have not been adopted by the FMCSA. Please be aware of these updating processes.

Few areas have undergone as many changes in the commercial driver medical certification area as medication use and abuse and substance abuse. Two of the 13 medical standards have addressed substance abuse since implementation of the standards. For a period of time, drug and alcohol testing were a part of the periodic examination process. The new examination reporting form emphasizes the importance of reviewing the use of both prescription and nonprescription medications and the potential impact on safety that these medications may have. Included on the form is a statement that the medical examiner must review and discuss with the driver the "potential hazards including over-the-counter medications, while driving."

Drug and alcohol testing by the U.S. Department of Transportation (DOT) was begun in 1989 and 1994, respectively, after several high-profile accidents in which these substances were implicated as the probable cause. Although the medical review officer (MRO) is responsible for determining whether there is a legitimate medical explanation for a laboratory nonnegative test result, the examiner is required to determine whether the driver is using any substance that may pose a fitness-for-duty concern. There are several situations in which the MRO's and the examiner's paths may cross, and it is recognized that at times physicians may seem to serve as both MRO and examiner simultaneously. In practice, the two roles should be separate and the physician should "take off one hat and put on the other" when acting as either examiner or MRO.

This chapter does not discuss the MRO process except where it overlaps with a fitness-for-duty determination. Additional information on 49 CFR Part 40 or 49 CFR 382, the DOT or Federal Motor Carrier Safety Administration (FMCSA) regulations, respectively, can be found through the DOT (www.dot.gov) or FMCSA (www.fmcsa.dot.gov) Internet sites. Another excellent resource is the DOT's Office of Drug and Alcohol Policy Compliance (www.dot.gov/ost/dapc/).

The Federal Motor Safety Regulations that address substance abuse and alcohol misuse [49 CFR 391.41(b)] state that a person is physically qualified to drive a commercial motor vehicle (CMV) if that person

> *(12)(i) Does not use a controlled substance identified in 21 CFR 1308.11 Schedule I, an amphetamine, a narcotic, or any other habit-forming drug.*
> *(ii) Exception. A driver may use such a substance or drug, if the substance or drug is prescribed by a licensed medical practitioner who:*
> > *(A) Is familiar with the driver's medical history and assigned duties; and*
> > *(B) Has advised the driver that the prescribed substance or drug will not adversely affect the driver's ability to safely operate a commercial motor vehicle; and*
> *(13) Has no current clinical diagnosis of alcoholism.*

Drivers who test positive under the DOT controlled substance testing regulations [1] must be removed from service until they have completed evaluation, treatment, and return to duty testing.

Advisory Criteria, Interpretations, Frequently Asked Questions, and Conference Reports

The advisory criteria found on the medical examination reporting form or the FMCSA Website [2] for this part further explain the exception permitting drivers who are using a "Schedule I controlled substance, an amphetamine, a narcotic, or any other habit-forming drug." Examiners must determine whether the medication or the medical condition it is treating may impair the driver's safe operation of the CMV. It is advised that a written statement be obtained from the prescribing provider. The controlled substances referenced in 49 CFR 391(b)12(i) are found in 21 CFR 1308.11 [3] (Figure 11-1). Methadone is specifically mentioned in the advisory criteria as well as in the interpretations [4] and FMCSA's Frequently Asked Questions [5] as not being subject to

---

Figure 11-1. Title 21—Food and Drugs. Section 1308.11 Schedule I.

TITLE 21—FOOD AND DRUGS

CHAPTER II—DRUG ENFORCEMENT ADMINISTRATION, DEPARTMENT OF JUSTICE
PART 1308—SCHEDULES OF CONTROLLED SUBSTANCES—
Sec. 1308.11 Schedule I.

(a) Schedule I shall consist of the drugs and other substances, by whatever official name, common or usual name, chemical name, or brand name designated, listed in this section. Each drug or substance has been assigned the DEA Controlled Substances Code Number set forth opposite it.

(b) Opiates. Unless specifically excepted or unless listed in another schedule, any of the following opiates, including their isomers, esters, ethers, salts, and salts of isomers, esters and ethers, whenever the existence of such isomers, esters, ethers and salts is possible within the specific chemical designation (for purposes of paragraph (b)(34) only, the term isomer includes the optical and geometric isomers):

(1) Acetyl-alpha-methylfentanyl (N-[1-(1-methyl-2-phenethyl)-4-piperidinyl]-N-phenylacetamide) 9815
(2) Acetylmethadol 9601
(3) Allylprodine 9602
(4) Alphacetylmethadol (except levo-alphacetylmethadol also known as levo-alpha-acetylmethadol, levomethadyl acetate, or LAAM) ... 9603
(5) Alphameprodine 9604
(6) Alphamethadol 9605
(7) Alpha-methylfentanyl (N-[1-(alpha-methyl-beta-phenyl)ethyl-4-piperidyl] propionanilide; 1-(1-methyl-2-phenylethyl)-4-(N-propanilido) piperidine) 9814
(8) Alpha-methylthiofentanyl (N-[1-methyl-2-(2-thienyl)ethyl-4-piperidinyl]-N-phenylpropanamide) 9832
(9) Benzethidine 9606
(10) Betacetylmethadol 9607
(11) Beta-hydroxyfentanyl (N-[1-(2-hydroxy-2-phenethyl)-4-piperidinyl]-N-phenylpropanamide) 9830
(12) Beta-hydroxy-3-methylfentanyl (other name: N-[1-(2-hydroxy-2-phenethyl)-3-methyl-4-piperidinyl]-N-phenylpropanamide. 9831
(13) Betameprodine 9608
(14) Betamethadol 9609
(15) Betaprodine 9611
(16) Clonitazene 9612
(17) Dextromoramide 9613
(18) Diampromide 9615
(19) Diethylthiambutene 9616
(20) Difenoxin 9168
(21) Dimenoxadol 9617

Figure 11-1. Title 21—Food and Drugs. Section 1308.11 Schedule I. *(continued)*

(22) Dimepheptanol 9618
(23) Dimethylthiambutene 9619
(24) Dioxaphetyl butyrate 9621
(25) Dipipanone 9622
(26) Ethylmethylthiambutene 9623
(27) Etonitazene 9624
(28) Etoxeridine 9625
(29) Furethidine 9626
(30) Hydroxypethidine 9627
(31) Ketobemidone 9628
(32) Levomoramide 9629
(33) Levophenacylmorphan 9631
(34) 3-Methylfentanyl (N-[3-methyl-1-(2-phenylethyl)-4-piperidyl]- N-
      phenylpropanamide) 9813
(35) 3-methylthiofentanyl (N-[(3-methyl-1-(2-thienyl)ethyl-4-
      piperidinyl]-N-phenylpropanamide) 9833
(36) Morpheridine 9632
(37) MPPP (1-methyl-4-phenyl-4-propionoxypiperidine) 9661
(38) Noracymethadol 9633
(39) Norlevorphanol 9634
(40) Normethadone 9635
(41) Norpipanone 9636
(42) Para-fluorofentanyl (N-(4-fluorophenyl)-N-[1-(2-phenethyl)-4-
      piperidinyl] propanamide 9812
(43) PEPAP (1-(-2-phenethyl)-4-phenyl-4-acetoxypiperidine 9663
(44) Phenadoxone 9637
(45) Phenampromide 9638
(46) Phenomorphan 9647
(47) Phenoperidine 9641
(48) Piritramide 9642
(49) Proheptazine 9643
(50) Properidine 9644
(51) Propiram 9649
(52) Racemoramide 9645
(53) Thiofentanyl (N-phenyl-N-[1-(2-thienyl)ethyl-4-piperidinyl]-
      propanamide 9835
(54) Tilidine 9750
(55) Trimeperidine 9646

(c) Opium derivatives. Unless specifically excepted or unless listed in another schedule, any of the following opium derivatives, its salts, isomers, and salts of isomers whenever the existence of such salts, isomers, and salts of isomers is possible within the specific chemical designation:

(1) Acetorphine 9319
(2) Acetyldihydrocodeine 9051

(continues)

Figure 11-1. Title 21—Food and Drugs. Section 1308.11 Schedule I. *(continued)*

(3)	Benzylmorphine	9052
(4)	Codeine methylbromide	9070
(5)	Codeine-N-Oxide	9053
(6)	Cyprenorphine	9054
(7)	Desomorphine	9055
(8)	Dihydromorphine	9145
(9)	Drotebanol	9335
(10)	Etorphine (except hydrochloride salt)	9056
(11)	Heroin	9200
(12)	Hydromorphinol	9301
(13)	Methyldesorphine	9302
(14)	Methyldihydromorphine	9304
(15)	Morphine methylbromide	9305
(16)	Morphine methylsulfonate	9306
(17)	Morphine-N-Oxide	9307
(18)	Myrophine	9308
(19)	Nicocodeine	9309
(20)	Nicomorphine	9312
(21)	Normorphine	9313
(22)	Pholcodine	9314
(23)	Thebacon	9315

(d) Hallucinogenic substances. Unless specifically excepted or unless listed in another schedule, any material, compound, mixture, or preparation, which contains any quantity of the following hallucinogenic substances, or which contains any of its salts, isomers, and salts of isomers whenever the existence of such salts, isomers, and salts of isomers is possible within the specific chemical designation (for purposes of this paragraph only, the term ``isomer'' includes the optical, position and geometric isomers):

(1) Alpha-ethyltryptamine 7249
Some trade or other names: etryptamine; Monase; [alpha]-ethyl-
1H-indole-3-ethanamine; 3-(2-aminobutyl) indole; [alpha]-ET;
and AET
(2) 4-bromo-2,5-dimethoxy-amphetamine 7391
Some trade or other names: 4-bromo-2,5-dimethoxy-[alpha]-
methylphenethylamine; 4-bromo-2,5-DMA
(3) 4-Bromo-2,5-dimethoxyphenethylamine 7392
Some trade or other names: 2-(4-bromo-2,5-dimethoxyphenyl)-1-
aminoethane; alpha-desmethyl DOB; 2C-B, Nexus
(4) 2,5-dimethoxyamphetamine 7396
Some trade or other names: 2,5-dimethoxy-[alpha]-
methylphenethylamine; 2,5-DMA
(5) 2,5-dimethoxy-4-ethylamphetamine 7399
Some trade or other names: DOET

Figure 11-1. Title 21—Food and Drugs. Section 1308.11 Schedule I. *(continued)*

---

(6) 4-methoxyamphetamine 7411
Some trade or other names: 4-methoxy-[alpha]-
methylphenethylamine; paramethoxyamphetamine, PMA
(7) 5-methoxy-3,4-mdthylenedioxy-amphetamine 7401
(8) 4-methyl-2,5-dimethoxy-amphetamine 7395
Some trade and other names: 4-methyl-2,5-dimethoxy-[alpha]-
methylphenethylamine; "DOM"; and "STP"
(9) 3,4-methylenedioxy amphetamine 7400
(10) 3,4-methylenedioxymethamphetamine (MDMA) 7405
(11) 3,4-methylenedioxy-N-ethylamphetamine (also known as
N-ethyl-alpha-methyl-3,4(methylenedioxy)phenethylamine,
N-ethyl MDA, MDE, MDEA 7404
(12) N-hydroxy-3,4-methylenedioxyamphetamine (also known as
N-hydroxy-alpha-methyl-3,4(methylenedioxy)phenethylamine,
and N-hydroxy MDA 7402
(13) 3,4,5-trimethoxy amphetamine 7390
(14) Bufotenine 7433
Some trade and other names: 3-([beta]-Dimethylaminoethyl)-5-
hydroxyindole; 3-(2-dimethylaminoethyl)-5-indolol; N,
N-dimethylserotonin; 5-hydroxy-N,N-dimethyltryptamine;
mappine
(15) Diethyltryptamine 7434
Some trade and other names: N,N-Diethyltryptamine; DET
(16) Dimethyltryptamine 7435
Some trade or other names: DMT
(17) Ibogaine 7260
Some trade and other names: 7-Ethyl-6,6[beta],7,8,9,10,12,13-
octahydro-2-methoxy-6,9-methano-5H-pyrido [lsqb]1',2':1,2[rsqb]
azepino [lsqb]5,4-b[rsqb] indole; Tabernanthe iboga
(18) Lysergic acid diethylamide 7315
(19) Marihuana 7360
(20) Mescaline 7381
(21) Parahexyl—7374; some trade or other names: 3-Hexyl-1-hydroxy-
7,8,9,10-tetrahydro-6,6,9-trimethyl-6H-dibenzo[b,d]pyran;
Synhexyl
(22) Peyote 7415
Meaning all parts of the plant presently classified botanically as
Lophophora williamsii Lemaire, whether growing or not,
the seeds thereof, any extract from any part of such plant, and
every compound, manufacture, salts, derivative, mixture, or
preparation of such plant, its seeds or extracts (Interprets
21 USC 812(c), Schedule I(c)(12))
(23) N-ethyl-3-piperidyl benzilate 7482
(24) N-methyl-3-piperidyl benzilate 7484

(continues)

Figure 11-1. Title 21—Food and Drugs. Section 1308.11 Schedule I. *(continued)*

(25) Psilocybin 7437
(26) Psilocyn 7438
(27) Tetrahydrocannabinols 7370
     Meaning tetrahydrocannabinols naturally contained in a plant
     of the genus Cannabis (cannabis plant), as well as synthetic
     equivalents of the substances contained in the cannabis plant, or
     in the resinous extractives of such plant, and / or synthetic
     substances, derivatives, and their isomers with similar chemical
     structure and pharmacological activity to those substances
     contained in the plant, such as the following:
          1 cis or trans tetrahydrocannabinol, and their optical isomers
          6 cis or trans tetrahydrocannabinol, and their optical isomers
          3, 4 cis or trans tetrahydrocannabinol, and its optical isomers
     (Since nomenclature of these substances is not internationally
     standardized, compounds of these structures, regardless of
     numerical designation of atomic positions covered.)
(28) Ethylamine analog of phencyclidine 7455
     Some trade or other names: N-ethyl-1-phenylcyclohexylamine,
     (1-phenylcyclohexyl)ethylamine, N-(1-phenylcyclohexyl)
     ethylamine, cyclohexamine, PCE
(29) Pyrrolidine analog of phencyclidine 7458
     Some trade or other names: 1-(1-phenylcyclohexyl)-pyrrolidine,
     PCPy, PHP
(30) Thiophene analog of phencyclidine 7470
     Some trade or other names: 1-[1-(2-thienyl)-cyclohexyl]-piperidine,
     2-thienylanalog of phencyclidine, TPCP, TCP
(31) 1-[1-(2-thienyl)cyclohexyl]pyrrolidine 7473
     Some other names: TCPy

     (e) Depressants. Unless specifically excepted or unless listed in another
schedule, any material, compound, mixture, or preparation which contains
any quantity of the following substances having a depressant effect on the
central nervous system, including its salts, isomers, and salts of isomers
whenever the existence of such salts, isomers, and salts of isomers is possible
within the specific chemical designation:

(1) gamma-hydroxybutyric acid (some other names include GHB;
    gamma-hydroxybutyrate; 4-hydroxybutyrate; 4-hydroxybutanoic
    acid; sodium oxybate; sodium oxybutyrate) 2010
(2) Mecloqualone 2572
(3) Methaqualone 2565

     (f) Stimulants. Unless specifically excepted or unless listed in another
schedule, any material, compound, mixture, or preparation which contains
any quantity of the following substances having a stimulant effect on the central nervous system, including its salts, isomers, and salts of isomers:

Figure 11-1. Title 21—Food and Drugs. Section 1308.11 Schedule I. *(continued)*

(1) Aminorex (Some other names: aminoxaphen; 2-amino-5-phenyl-2-oxazoline; or 4,5-dihydro-5-phenyl-2-oxazolamine) 1585
(2) Cathinone 1235
     Some trade or other names: 2-amino-1-phenyl-1-propanone, alpha-aminopropiophenone, 2-aminopropiophenone, and norephedrone
(3) Fenethylline 1503
(4) Methcathinone (Some other names: 2-(methylamino)-propiophenone; alpha-(methylamino)propiophenone; 2-(methylamino)-1-phenylpropan-1-one; alpha-N-methylaminopropiophenone; monomethylpropion; ephedrone; N-methylcathinone; methylcathinone; AL-464; AL-422; AL-463 and UR1432), its salts, optical isomers and salts of optical isomers . 1237
(5) (±)cis-4-methylaminorex ((±)cis-4,5-dihydro-4-methyl-5-phenyl-2-oxazolamine) 1590
(6) N-ethylamphetamine 1475
(7) N,N-dimethylamphetamine (also known as N,N-alpha-trimethyl-benzeneethanamine; N,N-alpha-trimethylphenethylamine) 1480

  (g) Temporary listing of substances subject to emergency scheduling. Any material, compound, mixture or preparation which contains any quantity of the following substances:

(1) N-[1-benzyl-4-piperidyl]-N-phenylpropanamide (benzylfentanyl), its optical isomers, salts and salts of isomers 9818
(2) N-[1-(2-thienyl)methyl-4-piperidyl]-N-phenylpropanamide (thenylfentanyl), its optical isolers, salts and salts of isomers 9834
(3) N-benzylpiperazine (some other names: BZP; 1-benzylpiperazine), its optical isomers, salts and salts of isomers— 7493
(4) 1-(3-trifluoromethylphenyl)piperazine (other name: TFMPP), its optical isomers, salts and salts of isomers— 7494
(5) 2,5-dimethoxy-4-(n)-propylthiophenethylamine (2C-T-7), its optical isomers, salts and salts of isomers— 7348

---

this exception, and commercial drivers on methadone should be found medically unqualified.

   An examiner may determine use through interview, available history, or body fluid testing. If testing is done, it is not performed as DOT-required testing (do not use a federal form), but any positive screening test should be confirmed. The advisory criteria indicate that if the driver is found to be medically unqualified owing to prohibited drug use, he or she can only return once a second examination finds that the driver is no longer using that substance. An evaluation

by a substance abuse professional, completion of a drug rehabilitation program, and a negative drug test result may be required of a
driver who was not qualified because of substance use. If a driver is
found not to be medically qualified because of a regulated test that
is MRO positive, a return to duty would have to include all of the
components required by the DOT and FMCSA drug testing regulations. The examiner also may certify the driver for less than 2 years
if there is a concern that there may be a recurrence of impairing or
illegal substance use. As with all of the advisory criteria, the examiner is referred to the conference reports, for this standard, the neurologic [6] and psychiatric [7] reports.

For drivers found not to be medically qualified because of alcohol
use, it is explained that "current clinical diagnosis" refers to a "current
alcoholic illness or those instances where the individual's physical condition has not fully stabilized." This would seem not to include individuals who are abstinent and have no other alcohol-related medical
conditions but who may be considered recovering alcoholics. Individuals who have physical signs of or provide a history consistent with alcohol problems should be referred to a specialist and, after evaluation
and/or treatment, if indicated, should then be medically certified.

There was a great deal of confusion when DOT-mandated controlled substance testing was first implemented. At the time, the form
included options that would allow the examiner to indicate whether
the testing was performed "in accordance with subpart H" and
whether controlled testing was performed as part of the medical examination. This was important because if the testing was part of the examination, then the examiner should not sign the medical certificate until
the drug test results were reviewed and an MRO-negative report was
obtained. The drug testing and examination now are totally separate
procedures, and the only time they might ordinarily be performed at
the same office visit would be in the preplacement setting [8]. The drug
test, but not the examination, can be performed prior to an offer of employment. The interpretations [4] explain that when a driver presents
for both the drug test and the examination, the examination is completed first; if the driver meets the medical criteria, the medical certificate should be prepared. The collection for controlled substance testing
then is performed. It is the motor carrier's responsibility to ensure that
a verified negative test from the MRO has been obtained prior to having the driver operate CMVs. The examiner should not hold the card
pending the controlled substance test result.

The interpretations also addresses whether a driver who tests positive for alcohol or a controlled substance under part 382 needs a new
medical examination. Provided that the driver was evaluated by a sub-

stance abuse professional (SAP) who did not determine that the driver had a current clinical diagnosis of alcoholism, a new examination is not required. If it is determined that the driver has a diagnosis of alcoholism, then the driver is not qualified. Again, the motor carrier is responsible for ensuring that the driver is medically qualified. This may be done through the SAP, but some carriers may choose to have the driver obtain a new medical certificate.

There are instances in which an examiner is performing an examination on a driver for one company and has previously provided MRO services on the same driver for another company. The interpretations explain that the examiner may decline to qualify the driver if "the medical examiner determines, based on other evidence besides the drug test, including, but not limited to, knowledge of the prior positive test result, that the driver continues to use prohibited drugs (49 CFR 391.43)." Many examiners in this situation will require information from a SAP prior to completing the certificate. The carrier is responsible for querying past employers about previous positive tests, and now must also ask about tests performed as preemployment. Any recommendation from the SAP regarding follow-up testing should also follow that driver to a new employer.

An examiner may have knowledge that could impact a fitness determination obtained while acting as an MRO for a different carrier. This may occur when a driver has a laboratory-positive test but the MRO determines that there is a legitimate medical explanation for the test result yet has concerns about whether that substance may impair the driver. 49 CFR Part 40 (49 CFR Part 40.327) directs the MRO to report information obtained in the verification process to an employer, physician, or other health care provider "responsible for determining the medical qualification of the employee under an applicable DOT agency safety regulation." This can be done without employee consent if it is determined that the information may result in the individual being medically unqualified because of a safety risk. Initially this was believed to prohibit reporting of the safety concern to a medical examiner for an employer other than the one for whom the test was performed. The September 2001 Q & A issued by the Office of Drug and Alcohol Policy Compliance [9] explains that if the MRO knew the identity of the physician responsible for determining whether the driver was physically qualified under FMCSA regulations for another employer, they could provide the information to that examiner. If the MRO serves as the medical examiner for another company, he or she can "take off" the MRO hat and essentially notify him- or herself as examiner for the other company that there may be a safety concern and that the driver would need to be evaluated [10].

The MRO may report a negative test conducted under DOT regulations when the employee is unable to provide a urine specimen in the preplacement, return-to-duty, or follow-up situation (49 CFR Part 40.195). If the MRO determines that a permanent or long-term preexisting condition prevents the individual from providing a sufficient urine specimen, he or she can conduct an examination, or have an examination conducted by a physician acceptable to the MRO, to determine whether there is clinical evidence of illicit drug use. Although conditions may be met to report the test result as negative, the medical condition resulting in this inability to provide a urine specimen may cause the driver *not* to meet the medical criteria.

When state laws were passed legalizing medicinal marijuana, there were questions on how this would affect federal drug testing policies. Federico Peña, then secretary of the U.S. DOT, stated on December 12, 1996, that "any safety-sensitive transportation worker—such as a pilot, railroad engineer, or bus driver—who tests positive under our program may not use Proposition 215 or Proposition 200 as an excuse or defense" [11]. He also explained that the MRO should not find that the presence of these substances, even *with* the report of a recommendation of a physician, is due to a legitimate medical use. Use of these substances is not consistent with federal approved use.

During a medical examination, if the driver admits to frequent alcohol use or responses on a TWEAK, CAGE, or other screening tool suggests that the driver may have an alcohol problem, the examiner should refer the driver for additional evaluation prior to signing the medical certificate [5].

The current regulation permits a driver to use certain medications when prescribed by a license health care professional who states the individual is able to drive safely. Two FAQs address the use of legally prescribed medications. One advises that although a medication may be legally prescribed, the driver could be disqualified if the medication could impair. The second indicates that even with a statement from the treating health care provider, the examiner may decide not to certify the driver.

Only a few medications are mentioned by name in the regulation or advisory criteria. Methadone, as discussed earlier, and insulin are indicated to be disqualifying although drivers may apply for an exemption from the insulin criteria. Also noted to be disqualifying in the advisory criteria is antiseizure medications. This has caused some confusion as many antiseizure medications may be prescribed for conditions other than seizure control. The FAQs clarify this by explaining that antiseizure medication used for the prevention of seizures is disqualifying. There also is a question that noted that a driver taking medical marijuana cannot be certified.

Another medication addressed in the FAQs is modafinil (Provigil). The initial recommendation from the FMCSA was that commercial motor vehicle operators on this medication should not be qualified. It was explained that this medication has several side effects and may interact with other medications. In addition, it could alter concentration or may cause the individual to be unaware that they are tired. Recently the recommendation for modafinil was updated to indicate that drivers should be not be qualified until they have been monitored closely for at least 6 weeks while taking modafinil. Both the treating physician and medical examiner should agree that modafinil is effective in preventing daytime somnolence and that there are no significant side effects. Commercial motor vehicle drivers on modafinil should be recertified annually. This would both evaluate the medication and the underlying medical condition.

On the FMCSA's medical program Website, examiners are advised that while Exenatide (Byetta) is permitted under FMCSA rules, when used in conjunction with a sulfonylurea it has an increased risk of hypoglycemia. Drivers who are on Exenatide should provide a note from their treating provider and should be monitored more closely.

Several of the conference reports discussed medications. The no-longer current Conference on Cardiac Disorders and Commercial Drivers [12] suggested that antihypertensives with a higher incidence of drowsiness be avoided, including clonidine, methyldopa, guanabenz, reserpine, and prazosin. They also suggested that medications that can cause postural hypotension should be used with caution. The more recent Cardiovascular Panel Guidelines [13] recommended that medications used to treat hypertension that predispose to precipitous declines in blood pressure, syncope, fatigue or excessive electrolyte shifts be avoided.

Headache medications that might cause sedation such as barbiturates, antihistamines, and analgesics were concerns in the neurology report [6].

Pulmonary conference [14] participants recommended against the use of antitussives and antihistamines for at least 12 hours prior to driving owing to their sedating side effects. This report noted that alternatives are available and "commercial drivers can and should avoid potentially sedating antihistamines."

The most extensive recommendations are in the Conference on Psychiatric Disorders and Commercial Drivers [7], in which all but the nonsedating anxiolytics were recommended to be disqualifying. It also was advised that only short-acting hypnotics be used, and for less than 2 weeks only. Drivers on antidepressants and antipsychotics were recommended to be referred to a psychiatrist for evaluation of both the condition and the medication side effects. Stimulants were also recommended to be disqualifying unless reviewed because although they can improve performance of simple tasks, they can impair performance of complex tasks.

Additional Considerations

Controlled Substances and Alcohol

The 2005 National Survey on Drug Use and Health [15] found that an estimated 19.7 million Americans were current (used in month preceding interview) illicit drug users. Marijuana was the most commonly used: 74.2% of illicit drug users, many of those also used other illicit drugs. An estimated 10.5 million people reported driving under the influence of controlled substances, and most of those (77 percent) also had driven under the influence of alcohol.

Federally mandated drug and alcohol testing is believed to serve as a deterrent in commercial drivers. The most recent published data showed that the positive in 2003 for controlled substances were 2.0 percent and for alcohol were 0.2 percent for levels greater than 0.04, about the same since 1997 [16].

In one study of voluntary roadside testing, Washington state's Operation Trucker Check found that truck drivers are still using substances that may impair safe operation of the CMV [17]. Voluntary testing, not falling into any of the federal testing categories, for controlled substances was requested of 1,079 drivers; 822 actually submitted urine specimens, 19 percent declined testing. Of the 822 drivers, 21 percent were positive for illicit, prescription, or over-the-counter medications; 9.5 percent were positive for central nervous system stimulants other than nicotine or caffeine; and 4.3 percent tested positive for cannabinoids.

Some of the physical findings an examiner may encounter in an individual with excessive alcohol use are spider angiomas, conjunctival injection, palmar erythema, tremor, hepatomegaly, gynecomastia, and testicular atrophy. Slurred speech, unsteady gait, lack of attention to personal hygiene, tremor, and memory deficits may be observed when controlled substances or alcohol is abused.

Several tools can be used to screen for possible alcohol misuse [18]. One is the CAGE questionnaire. Positive responses to two or more of the following questions may indicate that further evaluation may be warranted:

1. Have you ever felt you should Cut down on your drinking?
2. Have people Annoyed you by criticizing your drinking?
3. Have you ever felt bad or Guilty about your drinking?
4. Have you ever had a drink first thing in the morning to steady your nerves or get rid of a hangover (Eye-opener)?

Others tools include the TWEAK scale and the Alcohol Use Disorders Identification Test (AUDIT) (Figure 11-2).

Figure 11-2. TWEAK Scale

T   **Tolerance:** How many drinks does it take to make you feel high? _____ No. of drinks

   Score 2 points if four or more drinks for women, six or more for men

W   **Worry:** Have close friends or relatives worried or complained about your drinking in the past year? _____Yes _____No

   Score 2 points for a "yes."

E   **Eye-Opener:** Do you sometimes have a drink in the morning when you first get up? _____Yes _____No

   Score 1 point for a "yes."

A   **Amnesia (Blackouts):** Has a friend or family member ever told you about things you said or did while you were drinking that you could not remember? _____Yes _____No

   Score 1 point for a "yes."

K(C)   **Cut Down:** Do you sometimes feel the need to cut down on your drinking? _____Yes _____No

   Score 1 point for a "yes."

A total score of 2 or more points indicates a likely drinking problem.

Alcohol Use Disorders Identification Test (AUDIT)

---

1. How often do you have a drink containing alcohol?
   _____ never (0)
   _____ monthly or less (1)
   _____ 2 to 4 times a month (2)
   _____ 2 to 3 times per week (3)
   _____ 4 or more times per week (4)

(continues)

Figure 11-2. TWEAK Scale *(continued)*

2. How many drinks containing alcohol do you have on a typical day when you are drinking?
   _____ not applicable (0)
   _____ 1 or 2 (0)
   _____ 3 or 4 (1)
   _____ 5 or 6 (2)
   _____ 7 to 9 (3)
   _____ 10 or more (4)

3. How often do you have six or more drinks on one occasion?
   _____ not applicable/never (0)
   _____ less than monthly (1)
   _____ monthly (2)
   _____ weekly (3)
   _____ daily or almost daily (4)

4. How often during the past year have you found that you were not able to stop drinking once you had started?
   _____ not applicable/never (0)
   _____ less than monthly (1)
   _____ monthly (2)
   _____ weekly (3)
   _____ daily or almost daily (4)

5. How often during the past year have you failed to do what was normally expected from you because of drinking?
   _____ not applicable/never (0)
   _____ less than monthly (1)
   _____ monthly (2)
   _____ weekly (3)
   _____ daily or almost daily (4)

6. How often during the past year have you needed a first drink in the morning to get yourself going after a heavy drinking session?
   _____ not applicable/never (0)
   _____ less than monthly (1)
   _____ monthly (2)
   _____ weekly (3)
   _____ daily or almost daily (4)

7. How often during the past year have you had a feeling of guilt or remorse after drinking?
   _____ not applicable/never (0)
   _____ less than monthly (1)
   _____ monthly (2)
   _____ weekly (3)
   _____ daily or almost daily (4)

Figure 11-2. TWEAK Scale *(continued)*

8. How often during the past year have you been unable to remember what happened the night before because you had been drinking?
   ____ not applicable/never (0)
   ____ less than monthly (1)
   ____ monthly (2)
   ____ weekly (3)
   ____ daily or almost daily (4)

9. Have you or someone else been injured as a result of your drinking?
   ____ no (0)
   ____ yes, but not during the past year (2)
   ____ yes, during the past year (4)

10. Has a relative, friend, doctor, or other health worker been concerned about your drinking or suggested you cut down?
    ____ no (0)
    ____ yes, but not during the past year (2)
    ____ yes, during the past year (4)

____ TOTAL SCORE

Score by adding the value in the parentheses next to your selected response.

A sum of or greater than 8 is considered positive for alcohol dependence or abuse.

Findings that might lead an examiner to consider a diagnosis of drug use include needle tracks, a perforated nasal septum, a long curved fifth fingernail, dilated pupils (e.g., amphetamine, barbiturate, cocaine, marijuana, or lysergic acid diethylamide [LSD] use or opiate withdrawal), or constricted pupils (e.g., opiate use).

Prescription and Over-the-Counter Medications

Probably one of the most challenging areas for the medical examiner is determining whether a medication might impair. This includes both those prescribed by a health care professional and those purchased over the counter. The examiner is required to review with the driver any medications he or she may be taking and to discuss potential hazards. This should include advising drivers to read all package inserts, with special attention to precautions on driving or operating heavy machinery. A search of an electronic version of the *Physician's Desk Reference* found more than 700 medications with warnings similar to "Use caution when driving a motor vehicle or operating machinery." Drivers also should be made aware that medications that list fatigue or sedation as side effects may not be safe to use while operating a CMV. In addition, it must be remembered, and the driver must be advised, that many over-the-counter medications contain alcohol and that side effects can be increased when certain medications are used with even small amounts of alcohol or other medications. The driver should not use these medications while driving until he or she and their physician are certain that there are no impairing side effects.

Examiners should discuss the effect a medication may have with the treating provider, but, unfortunately, the provider may not be aware or may be unable to assess the risk that a specific medication may have on safety. Similar to alcohol, an individual often is unable to determine whether he or she is impaired or the degree of impairment with a particular medication. By relying on subjective observations and whether drivers report them to a prescribing provider or the medical examiner is much like permitting individuals who have had several drinks to get behind the wheel because they do not believe they are impaired [19].

The examiner must educate drivers and providers on the well-documented risks of impairment with certain medications. Medications in several classes, including the first-generation antihistamines, benzodiazepines, antidepressants, anxiolytics, narcotics, and some of the nonnarcotic analgesics, have a high incidence of sedation as a side effect. Other side effects examiners must consider include dizziness, confusion, fatigue, seizures, headaches, and hypotension. Potential interactions among medications the driver might be using also should be evaluated. The National Highway Traffic Safety Administration found that narcotics, long-acting benzodiazepines in therapeutic doses, barbiturates, first-generation antihistamines, and some antidepressants had a high potential for significant driving impairment [20]. Drivers and health care providers should be encouraged to avoid use of these potentially impairing medications whenever possible by utilizing alternatives that do not have an undesirable side effect profile.

All medications must be used as approved by the Food and Drug Administration (FDA). Drivers should be instructed to always use medications as prescribed, not to increase the dose except under supervision, and to avoid driving until they know how the medication might affect them. They also should inform their health care provider of any and all medications, including herbal or alternative treatments, because side effects may be additive.

It is important that the examiner not only focus on the medication but on the underlying condition. Although the driver may be on a medication that has the potential to impair performance and the prescribing provider insists that the individual is not impaired, the underlying medical condition itself may interfere with safe operation of a CMV.

Over the years, the DOT repeatedly has reminded those in the transportation industries "of potential threat to public safety caused by the on-duty use of some over-the-counter and prescription medication by persons performing some safety sensitive duties." Employee training was recommended. As a result of studying more than 100 accidents in all modes of transportation that involved prescription or over-the-counter medications that could potentially impair the operator, the National Transportation Safety Board (NTSB) recommended that the DOT develop a list of approved medications/classes of medications and forbid the use of medications not on the list for twice the dosage interval, except where individually assessed [21]. The NTSB recommends against relying on the individual's subjective assessment and reports of this assessment to the treating provider. The NTSB stated in the 2000 safety recommendation that "vehicle operators using such medications might not always be in a position to judge the extent and effect of such impairment; a vehicle operator whose judgment is adversely affected by a medication may decide, inappropriately, that he or she is not impaired."

Although the FDA has made labeling for over-the-counter medications more consistent, there is still concern that this may not be sufficient to adequately warn of potential hazards for those performing services in commercial transportation operations. There is no FDA requirement for labeling directed toward consumers for prescription medications. The package inserts that may be provided to the individual are directed at health care providers and are difficult to read and understand. Although labels may include precautions for driving and operating heavy machinery, this is based on subjective reports of sedation or drowsiness and not on specific tests that measure degree of impairment. Even if it were possible to get drivers and health care providers to read the labels and consider the potential impairment, subjective reports of side effects do not correlate with actual performance decrements [22].

The NTSB and FDA held a joint public meeting in November 2001 [22] to review the effects of medications on commercial operations. The main issues addressed in that meeting were

1. How to increase awareness of the public about the possible impairment caused by prescription and over-the-counter drug products
2. How to identify products that cause impairment
3. How to help the public avoid taking products that will cause impairment while driving
4. Whether relabeling those prescription and over-the-counter products helps the issue

Based on information from that meeting, the FDA planned to review and update labeling for several of the benzodiazepines and benzodiazepine-like hypnotics with intermediate and longer half-lives. They also will consider whether standard testing of the effect on driving performance should be required during drug development for potentially sedating drugs. The FDA did not indicate that it planned to review warnings on over-the-counter medication other than the new over-the-counter labeling. A public education campaign to give further attention to the need for consumers to comply with all labeling warnings, including those about drowsiness and driving, was mentioned as a consideration [23].

In one study [24], driving simulator performance after a prototypic sedating antihistamine was worse than an illegal level of alcohol for driving. Importantly, in this study, subjective feelings of drowsiness did not correlate with impairment. The National Highway Traffic Safety Administration conducted a review of the scientific literature in 2004 [25] and found that there is overwhelming evidence that first-generation antihistamines produce objective signs of skills performance impairment as well as subjective symptoms of sedation. There remained some evidence that even the second-generation antihistamines may cause sedation and impair performance, at least in some individuals. The evidence was slight and ambiguous that there was a connection between the earlier antihistamines and traffic accidents. More than 60 percent of allergy sufferers had taken over-the-counter medications for their allergies, and in one survey, most indicated they were unaware of the difference between the sedating and nonsedating options [21]. With several of the newer antihistamines available over the counter, it is very important to stress that driver select these over the older ones.

Benzodiazepine, especially at higher dosages and those that have longer-acting duration of actions, appear to be associated with an increased risk of motor vehicle crashes [26–29]. One study found a 5.1 relative risk of injurious road accidents with flurazepam, comparable to a

.10 percent blood alcohol concentration and a 3.1 relative risk, comparable to a .08 blood alcohol level with diazepam [29].

Sleep aids clearly should not be used if the individual may need to drive during the time the medication is intended to assist the individual in sleeping. A letter from the Food and Drug Administration warned health care providers that 13 sleep medications could result in complex behaviors such as sleep driving, driving while not fully awake, and with no memory of driving [30]. Menzin et al. [31] estimated that the use of a driving-impairing sleep medication would result in about 503 excess accidents per 100,000 drivers during a 14-day period.

Some of the medications used to treat Parkinson's disease such a pergolide (which has since been removed from the market), pramexole, and ropinirole (also used in restless leg syndrome) have been associated with sleep attacks. These are unpredictable and have occurred up to 1 year after beginning the medication [32].

One of the most challenging areas for the medical examiner is the narcotics. The FMCSA convened a medical expert panel to review the literature for Schedule II medications [33]. For many of the key questions, the panel had a difficult time reaching an evidence-based conclusion, due to the paucity of evidence that met the inclusion criteria. There was evidence that first-time doses of Schedule II opioids had deleterious effects on driving performance as well as cognitive and psychomotor function. The panel recommended that until the National Registry of Certified Medical Examiners (NRCME) was fully implemented, the exception for drivers on Schedule II opioids be eliminated. Once the NRCME had been formed, examiners should be provided standardized forms and specific guidance to aid in determining whether an individual would be able to safely operate a commercial motor vehicle on specific medications. Additional recommendations included expanding the drug testing panel to include synthetic opioids and to conduct additional reviews on the benzodiazepines.

The Medical Review Board [34] considered the panel's recommendations but made different suggestions to the FMCSA (see Figure 11-3). They suggested modifying the standard to specifically include Schedule II medications and benzodiazepines. They also recommended limiting the exception to those situations where the medication is prescribed by a licensed physician (MD, DO) and the medical examiner also would need to be a physician. The examiner would be required to review a specific form developed by the FMCSA. The examiner would also have to inform the driver that if he or she does not take the substance or drug as prescribed, they are using the substance or drug

Figure 11-3. The MRB Recommended Changes to the Exception for Licit Use of Schedule II Drugs [34]

The following are the existing guidelines, with the MRB's recommended changes marked in bold.

An individual is considered medically fit to drive if he/she:

b(12)(i) Does not use a controlled substance or drug identified in 21 CFR 1308.11 Schedule I, an amphetamine, **a benzodiazepine,** a narcotic, **a Schedule II medication,** or any other habit-forming substance or drug; (b)(12)(ii) Exception. A driver may use such a licit substance or drug if the substance or drug is prescribed for that individual for a legitimate medical reason **by a licensed physician (medical doctor [MD] or doctor of osteopathy [DO]) who:**
is familiar with the driver's medical history and assigned duties; and has warned the driver that the prescribed substance or drug **may** adversely affect the driver's ability to safely operate a CMV; **and:**
the driver is independently evaluated by a Commercial Driver Medical Examiner (CDME) who also:
is a licensed physician (MD or DO);
is familiar with the driver's medical history and assigned duties;
has warned the driver that the prescribed substance or drug may adversely affect the driver's ability to safely operate a CMV; and
has informed the driver that if the driver does not take the substance or drug as prescribed, the driver is using the substance or drug improperly and is not covered by this exception.
reviews a form for this purpose that is signed by the driver.*

Specifically excluded from the exception are drivers who:

- use substances or drugs administered parenterally (e.g., intravenously, transdermally, subcutaneously, intrathecally, or intramuscularly);
- have initiated or increased doses of one of these substances or drugs within the past two weeks after such changes;
- have a history of substance, drug or alcohol abuse, or addiction; or
- require the ingestion of substances or drugs while driving.

Factors to be considered by the CDME in determining whether to certify the driver include:

- -driving history;
- -psychiatric and psychologic history;
- -dose(s) of the prescribed substance or drug;
- -underlying and comorbid conditions; and
- -duration of action and pharmacokinetics of the prescribed substance or drug.

---

*The driver questionnaire would address the medication, purpose, side effects, proper usage, and whether it may have an impairing effect. If the driver does feel impaired, the driver must sign that he/she will stop driving. The questionnaire must have the driver assert that his/her statements are true and spell out the consequences of an untruthful declaration.

improperly, and is not covered by this exception. Specifically excluded from the exception would be drivers who use substances or drugs administered parenterally (e.g., intravenously, transdermally, subcutaneously, intrathecally, or intramuscularly). Driving also would not be permitted when the medication of concern is initiated or dosage increased within the past 2 weeks; the driver has a history of substance, drug, or alcohol abuse or addiction; or if the medication would be ingested while driving.

There are many other resources that have reviewed medications and their effects on driving but in all the challenge is determining whether an individual is at risk while taking a specific medication. In the medication section of another NHTSA report, Medical Conditions and Driving: A Review of the Literature (1960–2000) [35], in addition to similar finding to earlier reports on benzodiazepines and antihistamines, it was reported that among the antidepressants, amitriptyline and doxepin were highly sedating with driving impairment comparable to 0.10 blood alcohol. Trazodone also was found to be highly sedating while Imipramine was moderately sedating.

Another resource the examiner could use in determining whether to certify a driver on potentially impairing medication is from the International Council on Alcohol, Drugs and Traffic Safety (ICADTS) [36]. Medications were placed in Category III if they were likely to produce severe effects or presumed to be potentially dangerous (Figure 11-4). They suggested that individuals be advised not to drive while taking these medications.

After two accidents at Baltimore-Washington International train station, the Federal Transit Administration commissioned the creation

Figure 11-4. Some of the Medications Listed in Category III from the International Council on Alcohol, Drugs and Traffic Safety (ICADTS) [36]

Morphine	Diazepam
Fentanyl	Chlordiazepoxide
Meperidine	Oxazepam
Pentazocine	Lorazepam
Buprenorphine	Aprazolam
Tramadol	Meprobamate
Phenobarbital	Flurazepam
Primidone	Midazolam
Phenytoin	Zopiclon
Chlorpromazine	Trazodone
Thioridazine	Diphenhydramine

of a Prescription and Over-the-Counter Tool Kit [37]. Although intended for the transit industry, the information is relevant to any transportation mode. This kit includes sample policies on the use of medications, training aids, several lists of medications that are permitted or not by various federal and private agencies, and an extensive reference list.

There are a tremendous number of medications, and more added regularly, that may cause sedation or other cognitive impairment. For the majority of these, there have not been studies that specifically look at driving risk and therefore the examiner and treating health care professionals are left to rely on surrogate measures such as cognitive and psychomotor function. Where both driving and surrogate measures have been assessed, there is not always a consistent relationship between psychomotor impairment and driving impairment. Unlike alcohol where there is a direct relationship between blood levels and performance, this has not been clearly demonstrated with medications [38]. With some medication, an individual may develop tolerance and the greater concern with driving is the intermittent use, especially those with longer half-lives. Although some medications might not cause impairment as prescribed, an individual frequently will use a medication differently than directed, skipping doses, increasing the frequency or dosage, or as frequently frustrates medical review officers, using the medication for different reasons than for what the medication was initially intended (for instance, hydrocodone prescribed 6 months earlier for back pain, more recently used for a different musculoskeletal injury without consulting a health care provider). Patients frequently will use multiple potentially impairing medications together such as pain medications and muscle relaxants, increasing the risk of impairment.

The examiner is in the difficult position of trying to determine whether a particular medication or medications will interfere with a particular driver's performance. Many have utilized questionnaires (Figure 11-5) or have a discussion with the prescribing physician. Whenever possible, the driver should be on medications that do not impair. When new long-term medications are started that carry the warning or precaution against driving or operating heavy machinery, the commercial driver should refrain from driving until he or she is aware of how the medication might affect his or her abilities. For acute or intermittent use of medications that might impair, the driver should only use those with shorter half-lives and not while they would be pharmacologically active while she or he would or might be required to drive.

Figure 11-5. Sample Medication Questionnaire

OccuMedix, Inc

MEDICATION QUESTIONNAIRE

Re: _____ *S.S. Number* _____ *Date:* _____

Dear Doctor:

The above patient/driver is being evaluated to determine whether he/she meets the medical standards of the Federal Motor Carrier Safety Administration (FMCSA) to operate a commercial motor vehicle. The Federal Regulation that addresses the use of medications which may impair safe operation of a commercial motor vehicle is;

§ 391.41(b)(12) - **A person is physically qualified to drive a commercial motor vehicle if that person:**
   (i) **Does not use a controlled substance identified in 21 CFR 1308.11 Schedule I, an amphetamine, a narcotic, or any other habit-forming drug.**
   (ii) **Exception. A driver may use such a substance or drug, if the substance or drug is prescribed by a licensed medical practitioner who:**
      (A) **Is familiar with the driver's medical history and assigned duties; and**
      (B) **Has advised the driver that the prescribed substance or drug will not adversely affect the driver's ability to safely operate a commercial motor vehicle; and**
      (C) **Has no current clinical diagnosis of alcoholism.**

The FMCSA explains that a commercial driver "must have the perceptual skills to monitor a sometimes complex driving situation," and "the judgment skills to make quick decisions." There is increasing recognition that both prescription and nonprescription medications can impair the performance of tasks requiring concentration, such as driving. Certain classes of medications, including benzodiazepines, anxiolytics, narcotic, and some nonnarcotic analgesics, sedating antihistamines, and sedatives, can impair performance on tasks such as driving to as great a degree as alcohol. Similar to alcohol, the individual using these medications may not be aware that they are impaired and therefore may not be able to adequately assess their ability to perform safely. It is important to consider potential side effects such as sedation or dizziness especially when the medication carries a precaution such as "not to drive or operate machinery." This precaution is found with both prescription and over-the-counter medications. This is especially relevant in the commercial driver who is held to a higher standard because they may operate larger

(continues)

Figure 11-5. Sample Medication Questionnaire *(continued)*

vehicles, passenger-carrying vehicles, or vehicles carrying hazardous materials. The commercial driver also is on the road more hours each day, exposing the public to a greater risk if the driver becomes impaired. Whenever possible, medications should be utilized that do not have potentially impairing side effects. It is important not only to review the medication and its side effects, but also the status of the underlying disease process.

The Federal Highway Administration has sponsored several conferences to address medical conditions and commercial driving. In the conference on Psychiatric Disorders and the Commercial Driver, participants recommended that:

- Individuals requiring anxiolytic medications should be precluded from commercial driving. This recommendation would not apply to patients treated effectively with nonsedating anxiolytics such as buspirone.
- Individuals requiring hypnotics should only use drugs with half lives of less than 5 hours for less than 2 weeks under medical supervision and only at the lowest effective dose.
- Some antidepressants do produce impairment that can be mitigated over time but not completely removed with chronic use. Individuals on antidepressants that may interfere with performance should not be allowed to drive commercial vehicles. Amitriptyline was specifically mentioned as an antidepressant to be avoided due to its sedating effects.
- Given strong evidence of impaired psychomotor performance associated with the use of all antipsychotic drugs, drivers should only be qualified after the effects of the illness and the neuroleptic have been reviewed by a psychiatrist familiar with the regulations and safety risks associated with medications and commercial driving.
- Lithium, in a stable, chronic dose and plasma level, is permissible for regularly monitored asymptomatic drivers.
- CNS stimulants, in therapeutic doses, impair driving by a variety of mechanisms. A person using these drugs should not be medically qualified to drive commercially. Legitimate medical use (ADHD, for example) with no demonstrable impairment or dosage escalation tendency, may receive an exemption after expert review.

MEDICATION QUESTIONNAIRE

Please provide the following information:

1. How long have you been treating this patient?

_____

2. Please list medications, dosage, and duration of treatment at the current dose. _____

_____

_____

Figure 11-5. Sample Medication Questionnaire *(continued)*

3. Have there been any side effects such as sedation or decreased concentration? Yes ☐ No ☐

If so, please explain _____

_____

_____

4. Will use of this (these) medication(s) likely interfere with safe operation of a commercial motor vehicle? Yes ☐ No ☐

If so, please explain and discuss whether alternate medications have been considered: _____

_____

_____

5. What condition(s) is/are being treated with these medications? _____

_____

Are these conditions likely to interfere with the safe operation of a commercial motor vehicle? Yes ☐ No ☐

6. Considering the complex mental requirements of operating a commercial motor vehicle (CMV), **and after reviewing the included federal regulations and conference report recommendation,** do you believe your patient can safely operate a CMV while taking the medications? Yes ☐ No ☐

Additional Comments:

_____

_____

_____

_____

Physician Name _____ Signature_____

Phone #_____ Date _____

References

1. U.S. Department of Transportation, Office of the Secretary. Procedures for transportation workplace drug and alcohol testing programs: Final rule. *Fed Reg* 2000;65(Dec. 19):79461–79579. www.dot.gov/ost/dapc/NEW_DOCS/part40.html?proc. Accessed May 22, 2007.
2. Federal Motor Carrier Safety Administration, DOT. Motor Carrier Safety Regulations, Miscellaneous Technical Amendments. *Fed Reg* 2003;68(Sept. 30):56196–56208.
3. Code of Federal Regulations. 21 CFR 1308.11. Revised April 1, 2003.
4. Interpretations of Regulations Federal Motor Carrier Safety Administration. www.fmcsa.dot.gov/rulesregs/fmcsr/fmcsrguide.htm. Accessed May 22, 2007.
5. FMCSA Frequently Asked Questions—Medical. www.fmcsa.dot.gov/rules-regulations/topics/medical/faq.asp. Accessed May 22, 2007.
6. U.S. Department of Transportation, Federal Highway Administration. Conference on Neurological Disorders and Commercial Drivers. Publication No. FHWA-MC-88-042. Washington: U.S. DOT, Federal Highway Administration, Office of Motor Carriers, 1988.
7. U.S. Department of Transportation, Federal Highway Administration. Conference on Psychiatric Disorders and Commercial Drivers. Publication No. FHWA-MC-91-006. Washington: U.S. DOT, Federal Highway Administration, Office of Motor Carriers, 1991.
8. Commercial driver's license program and controlled substances and alcohol use and testing—Conforming and technical amendments. *Fed Reg* 1997;62(July 11):37150–37153.
9. Office of Drug and Alcohol Policy Compliance. Questions and Answers, September 2001. www.dot.gov/ost/dapc/questions/part40questions.pdf. Accessed May 24, 2007.
10. Hartenbaum NP. MROs, medical examiner and positive drug tests. *CDME Review*, Fall 2002.
11. Peña F. Statement on the Use of Proposition 200 and 215, December 12, 1996. Washington: U.S. DOT, Office of the Assistant Secretary of Public Affairs, 1996.
12. U.S. Department of Transportation, Federal Highway Administration. Conference on Cardiac Disorders and Commercial Drivers. Publication No. FHWA-MC-88-040. Washington: U.S. DOT, Federal Highway Administration, Office of Motor Carriers, 1987.
13. Blumenthal R, Braunstein J, Connolly H, Epstein A, Gersh BJ, Wittels EH. Cardiovascular Advisory Panel Guidelines for the Medical Examination of Commercial Motor Vehicle Drivers. FMCSA-MCP-02-002. Washington: U.S. Department of Transportation, Federal Motor Carrier Safety Administration, October 2002.
14. U.S. Department of Transportation, Federal Highway Administration. Conference on Respiratory/Pulmonary Disorders and Commercial Drivers. Publication No. FHWA-MC-91-004. Washington: U.S. DOT, Federal Highway Administration, Office of Motor Carriers, 1991.

15. 2005 National Survey on Drug Use and Health. Department of Health and Human Services, SAMHSA, Office of Applied Studies. September 2006. www.oas.samhsa.gov/nsduh/2k5nsduh/2k5Results.pdf. Accessed May 24, 2007.

16. U.S. Department of Transportation, Federal Motor Carrier Safety Administration. Analysis Brief May 2005. Drug and Alcohol Testing Survey 2003 Results. www.fmcsa.dot.gov/facts-research/research-technology/analysis/drug-testing-update-2003.htm. Accessed May 24, 2007.

17. Couper FJ, Pemberton M, Jarvis A, Hughes M, Logan BK. Prevalence of drug use in commercial tractor-trailer drivers. *J Forensic Sci* 2002;47(3):562–567.

18. LoBuono C. Dealing with the alcohol controversy. *Patient Care* 2000;5:211–225.

19. Meltzer EO. Performance effects of antihistamines. *J Allergy Clin Immunol* 1990;86:613–619.

20. Jones RK, Shinar D, Walsh JM. State of Knowledge of Drug Impaired Driving. NHTSA August 2003. DOT HS 809 642. www.nhtsa.dot.gov/people/injury/research/StateofKnwlegeDrugs/StateofKnwlegeDrugs/index.html. Accessed May 27, 2007.

21. National Transportation Safety Board. Safety Recommendation. Public Meeting: Safety Recommendations to be Issued to the DOT and Other Agencies Concerning the Use of Medications by Vehicle Operators, January 5, 2000.

22. Transcripts from FDA/NTSB Public Meeting: Transportation Safety and Potentially Sedating or Impairing Medications 01N-0397. www.fda.gov/ohrms/dockets/dockets/01n0397/01n0397.htm. Accessed May 26, 2007.

23. Correspondence from Steven Galson, MD, MPH, Deputy Director, Center for Drug Evaluation and Research, FDA, to Marion C. Blakey, Chairman, National Transportation Safety Board, June 21, 2002.

24. Weiler JM, Bloomfield JR, Woodworth GG, et al. Effects of fexofenadine, diphenhydramine, and alcohol on driving performance: A randomized, placebo-controlled trial in the Iowa Driving Simulator. *Ann Intern Med* 2000;132:354–363.

25. Moskowitz H, Wilkinson CJ. Antihistamines and driving-related behavior: A review of the evidence for impairment. Department of Transportation, NHSTA. May 2004. Report No. DOT HS 809 714. www.nhtsa.dot.gov/people/injury/research/StateofKnwlegeDrugs/StateofKnwlegeDrugs/index.html. Accessed May 27, 2007.

26. Barbone F, McMahon AD, Davey PG, et al. Association of road-traffic accidents with benzodiazepine use. *Lancet* 1998;352:1331–1336.

27. Hemmelgarn B, Suissa S, Huang A, Boivin JF, Pinard G. Benzodiazepine use and the risk of motor vehicle crash in the elderly. *JAMA* 1997;278:27–31.

28. Verster JC, Volkerts ER, Verbaten MN. Effects of alprazolam on driving ability, memory functioning and psychomotor performance: A randomized, placebo-controlled study. *Neuropsychopharmacology* 2002;27(2):260–269.

29. Neutel IC. Benzodiazepine-related traffic accidents in young and elderly patients. *Human Psychopharmacology* 1998;13:S115–S124.
30. FDA Press Release. FDA Requests Label Change for All Sleep Disorder Drug Products. March 14, 2007. www.fda.gov/bbs/topics/NEWS/2007/NEW01587.html. Accessed May 27, 2007.
31. Menzin J, Lang K, Levy P, Levy E. A general model of the effects of sleep medications on the risk and cost of motor vehicle accidents and its application to France. *Pharmacoeconomics* 2001;19:69–78.
32. Frucht S, Rogers JD, Greene PE, Gordon MF, Fahn S. Falling asleep at the wheel: Motor vehicle mishaps in persons taking pramipexole and ropinirole. *Neurology* 1999;52:1908–1910.
33. Expert Panel Commentary and Recommendations: Licit Schedule II Drug Use and Commercial Motor Vehicle Driver Safety (Comprehensive Review). www.mrb.fmcsa.dot.gov/documents/Schedule_II_Commentary.pdf. Accessed May 27, 2007.
34. Federal Motor Carrier Safety Administration, Medical Review Board. www.mrb.fmcsa.dot.gov/042507_meeting_MRBchanges.htm. Accessed June 1, 2007.
35. Dobbs BM. Medical Conditions and Driving: A Review of the Literature (1960–2000). NHSTA. September 2005. www.nhtsa.dot.gov/people/injury/research/Medical_Condition_Driving/. Accessed May 27, 2007.
36. Alvarez JF, de Gier JJ, Christophersen AS. The ICADTS Working Group on Prescribing and Dispensing Guidelines for Medicinal Drugs Affecting Driving Performance. March 2001. www.icadts.org/reports/ICADTSpresguiderpt.pdf. 2006 Update and Drug www.icadts.org/medicinal.html. Accessed May 27, 2007.
37. Sarles RL. Prescription and Over the Counter Medications Tool Kit. Federal Transit Administration. FTA-MA-5020-03-1. March 2003. http://transit-safety.volpe.dot.gov/Publications/order/singledoc.asp?docid=223. Accessed May 27, 2007.
38. Transportation Research Board. Transportation Research Circular E-C096. Drugs and Traffic; A Symposium, June 20–21, 2005, Woods Hole, Massachusetts. May 2006. http://onlinepubs.trb.org/onlinepubs/circulars/ec096.pdf. Accessed May 27, 2007.

Additional References

Aronoff GM, Erdil M, Hartenbaum NP. Medications, driving, and work. In Talmage JB, Melhorn JM. *A Physician's Guide to Return to Work.* Chicago: AMA Press, 2005.
Baselt RC. *Drug Effects on Psychomotor Performance.* Foster City, CA: Biomedical Publications. 2001
Couper FJ, Logan BK. Drugs and Human Performance Fact Sheets. NHTSA 2004. www.nhtsa.dot.gov/people/injury/research/job185drugs/drugs_web.pdf. Accessed May 27, 2007.

FTA Drug and Alcohol Update. http://transit-safety.volpe.dot.gov/Safety/DATesting/Newsletters/default.asp. Accessed May 27, 2007.
Transportation Research Board. Transportation Research Circular May 2006. Number E-C096. Drugs and Traffic; a symposium. June 20–21, 2005.

III

Commercial Drivers' Health: Risks and Hazards

Natalie P. Hartenbaum, MD, MPH

Similar to many occupations, operating a commercial motor vehicle has a unique set of occupational hazards. In addition to the obvious risk from motor vehicle crashes, their exposures and hazards include ergonomic hazards, exposure to diesel exhaust, noise, long hours, and a challenging lifestyle to maintain good health. Truck drivers have a higher incidence of many chronic diseases such as diabetes and cardiac disease. It is important to remember that the professional driver has many tasks beyond entering the vehicle and steering. The FMCSA provides a very detailed description of the many factors that may affect a driver's health on the medical examination form.

Responsibilities, work schedules, physical and emotional demands, and lifestyles among commercial drivers vary by the type of driving that they do. Some of the main types of drivers include the following: turn around or short relay (drivers return to their home base each evening); long relay (drivers drive 9–11 hours and then have at least a 10-hour off-duty period); straight through haul (cross country drivers); and team drivers (drivers share the driving by alternating their 5-hour driving periods and 5-hour rest periods.)

The following factors may be involved in a driver's performance of duties: abrupt schedule changes and rotating work schedules, which may result in irregular sleep patterns and a driver beginning a trip in a fatigued condition; long hours; extended time away from family and friends, which may result in lack of social support; tight pickup and delivery schedules, with irregularity in work, rest, and eating patterns; adverse road, weather, and traffic conditions, which may cause delays and lead to hurriedly loading or unloading cargo in order to compensate for the lost time; and environmental conditions such as excessive vibration, noise, and extremes in temperature. Transporting passengers or hazardous materials may add to the demands on the commercial driver.

There may be duties in addition to the driving task for which a driver is responsible and needs to be fit. Some of these responsibilities are: coupling and uncoupling trailer(s) from the tractor, loading and unloading trailer(s) (sometimes a driver may lift a heavy load or unload as much as 50,000 lbs. of freight after sitting for a long period of time without any stretching period); inspecting the operating condition of tractor and/or trailer(s) before, during and after delivery of cargo; lifting, installing, and removing heavy tire chains; and lifting heavy tarpaulins to cover open top trailers. The above tasks demand agility, the ability to bend and stoop, the ability to maintain a crouching position to inspect the underside of the vehicle, frequent entering and exiting of the cab, and the ability to climb ladders on the tractor and/or trailer(s).

In addition, a driver must have the perceptual skills to monitor a sometimes complex driving situation, the judgment skills to make quick decisions, when necessary, and the manipulative skills to control an oversize steering wheel, shift gears using a manual transmission, and maneuver a vehicle in crowded areas.

Another description of the standard skills required of a tractor-trailer operator was developed by the Professional Truck Driver Institute which includes the basic skills needed for tractor-trailer drivers [1] (Figure III-1).

Figure III-1. Primary Functions/Duties: Long-Distance Hauler

---

1. Read and Interpret Control Systems.
2. Perform Vehicle Inspections.
3. Exercise Basic Control.
4. Execute Shifting.
5. Back and Dock Tractor-Trailer.
6. Couple Trailer.
7. Uncouple Trailer.
8. Perform Visual Search.
9. Manage and Adjust Vehicle Speed.
10. Manage and Adjust Vehicle Space Relations.
11. Check and Maintain Vehicle Systems/Components.
12. Diagnose and Report Malfunctions.
13. Identify Potential Driving Hazards and Perform Emergency Maneuvers.
14. Identify and Adjust to Difficult and Extreme Driving Conditions.
15. Handle and Document Cargo.
16. Deal with Accident Scenes and Reporting Procedures.
17. Deal with Environmental Issues.
18. Plan Trips/Make Appropriate Decisions.
19. Use Effective Communication and Public Relations Skills.
20. Manage Personal Resources/Deal with Life on the Road.
21. Record and Maintain Hours of Service Requirement.

Source: Professional Truck Driver Institute [1].

It is estimated that there were around 224,000 million miles traveled by truck and buses in 2005. There are several estimates of the number of licensed commercial motor vehicle operators. In 2004, the FMCSA conducted surveys that estimated there were 10,400,000 truck and bus drivers who held medical certificates [2] and about 11,400,000 total commercial driver license holders (CDL) (this would not include drivers who are required to have a medical certificate but not a CDL).

Those working in the transportation and material moving occupational group had the highest number of fatalities in 2004 [3] (Figure III-2). In 2005, transportation and warehousing had the highest days away from work, job transfer, or restriction days [4] (Figure III-3). According to the Federal Motor Carrier Safety Administration, there were 5,510 total fatalities in trucks and buses with a fatality rate of 0.184 fatalities per 100 million vehicle miles traveled (VMT) in 2005. The injury rate was 4.55 per 100 million VMT [5].

Figure III-2. Number and Rate of Fatal Occupational Injuries by Major Occupational Groups, 2004

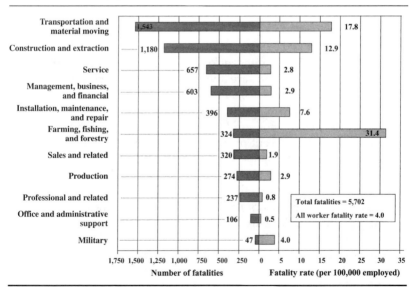

Rate = (Fatal work injuries/Employment) × 100,000. Employment data based on the 2004 Current Population Survey (CPS) and Department of Defense (DOD) figures.

Source: US Department of Labor, Bureau of Labor Statistics, Current Population Survey, Census of Fatal Occupational Injuries, and US Department of Defense, 2004.

Figure III-3. Incidence Rates for Cases with Days Away from Work, Job Transfer, or Restriction by Case Type and Selected Industry Sector, 2005

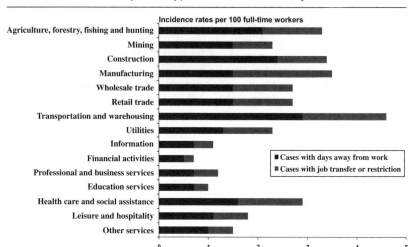

Source: Bureau of Labor Statistics, U.S. Department of Labor, October 2006.

The Occupational Safety and Health Administration (OSHA) indicate that about 475,000 large trucks with a gross vehicle weight rating of more than 10,000 pounds are involved in crashes each year. These results in approximately 5,360 fatalities and 142,000 injuries, about 74 percent were occupants of other vehicles (usually passenger cars), 3 percent were pedestrians, and 23 percent were occupants of large trucks. In about 70 percent of these, the unsafe actions of automobile drivers are a contributing factor [6].

The FMCSA and the National Highway Traffic Safety Administration (NHTSA) conducted the Large Truck Crash Causation Study (LTCCS) evaluating factors that contributed to crashes. Many of the factors had little to do with driver health. Of the nearly 1,000 injuries and fatal crashes evaluated involving large trucks that occurred between April 2001 and December 2003, the top associated driver factor was prescription drug use (Figure III-4) factor [7].

Many of the injuries driver sustained are similar to the general working population with about 50 percent of injuries being sprains and strains with bruises, fractures, cuts and lacerations, soreness and pain, and multiple traumatic injuries other common injuries. Causes include overexertion, contact with object, being struck by an object, falling (on the same level), and transportation accidents [6].

Figure III-4. Estimated Number of Trucks in All Crashes by Associated Factor

Top 20 Factors for Drivers	Number of Trucks	Percent
Prescription Drug Use	37,000	26.3
Traveling Too Fast for Conditions	32,000	22.9
Unfamiliar with Roadway (Less Than 6 Times in 6 Months)	30,000	21.6
Over-the-Counter Drug Use	24,000	17.3
Inadequate Surveillance	19,000	13.2
Fatigue	18,000	13.0
Under Work-Related Pressure	13,000	9.2
Illegal Maneuver	13,000	9.1
Inattention	12,000	8.5
External Distraction Factors	11,000	8.0
Inadequate Evasive Action	9,000	6.6
Aggressive Driving Behavior (Tailgating, Weaving, Other)	9,000	6.6
Unfamiliar with Vehicle (Less Than 6 Times in 6 Months)	9,000	6.5
Following Too Closely	7,000	4.9
False Assumption of Other Road Users' Actions	7,000	4.7

Source: Large Truck Crash Causation Study [7].

Although there has been attention paid to driver's risks of injuries and fatalities, until recently, there has been little focus on driver's health and well-being. Their lifestyle, unique set of stressors, and exposures can lead to an increased incidence of many chronic diseases.

Unlike many studies that focused on general highway issues, a conference on driver health was held at Wayne State University in 2003. It provided an overview of the trucking industry, summarized the current knowledge of truck driver health and safety, and identified areas for future research. It was organized by Wayne State University and sponsored by the National Institute for Occupational Safety and Health (NIOSH), the Owner-Operator Independent Drivers Association, the International Brotherhood of Teamsters, and the Trucking Industry Program and the Trucking Industry Benchmarking Program at Wayne State University [8]. They reported that in 2004, U.S. truck drivers were seven times more likely to die on the job and 2.5 times more likely to suffer an occupational injury or illness than the average worker.

Some of the specific areas addressed at that conference are discussed later. Among the research needs identified at this conference were evaluation of fatigue and its management, evaluation of an association between work characteristics and driver health, relationship between driver compensation and safety, means to increase driver access to health services, and comparison of health risk and work characteristics of U.S. drivers to those of other countries.

Another extensive look at driver health was conducted as a result of revising the hours of service (HOS) regulations. The 2004 revision of the HOS rules were challenged in a lawsuit that alleged that the FMCSA did not adequately account for driver health issues. As part of the response, the FMCSA contracted with a research team to review and summarize the literature on commercial driver health, wellness, and fatigue, primarily as they relate to the number of hours worked and the structure of the work schedule. Several observations on driver health were made [9].

1. Lung cancer is likely caused by exposure to diesel exhaust and the longer that exposure lasts, the more likely it is that a cancer will develop. It is likely that there is also a relationship between diesel exhaust and bladder cancer but this is less robust.
2. There is some evidence that cardiovascular disease is caused in part by truck driving. Risk increases with the duration of driving and disruption of sleep cycle.
3. Noise-induced hearing loss may be the result of a lifetime working as a commercial driver.
4. There is likely a causative relationship between professional driving and vertebral disorders. This may be due to whole body vibration but could not be established based on published literature.
5. It is suggested that there is a causal relationship between commercial driving and other musculoskeletal disorders but also not proven in the literature.
6. An increase in gastrointestinal (GI) symptoms has been documented in drivers, however, there was insufficient evidence to implicate circadian disruption and varying shift assignments.
7. The literature suggests, but does not establish, that disruption of circadian rhythm may have negative impacts on the general health of workers. Drivers may experience an improvement in subjective health complaints if stabilized to a day schedule but this does not occur if stabilized to night or evening schedules.

8. There was no definitive information concerning (a) the relationship between reproductive health and duration of driving, (b) the effects of prolonged work hours, or (c) increasing driving from 10 to 11 hours while decreasing overall work time from 15 to 14 hours on the general health of workers.

Structure of the Trucking System

There are essentially three segments in the U.S. trucking industry, government entities, private carriers, and for-hire motor carriers. The industry was deregulated in 1980 and after that the industry shifted from predominantly unionized to less than 15 percent unionized in 2003. With deregulation, inflation-adjusted wages have fallen [8].

Another significant change in the industry was the revised HOS regulations. This increased the minimum daily off-duty time, yet allowed drivers to spend more total time working and more time behind the wheel. Current regulations increased driving time from 10 to 11 hours but require between 8 and 10 hours off.*

A 2006 report updated an assessment of the trucking industry. Two of the greatest challenges in the trucking industry are fuel costs and a shortage of drivers. Both driver turnover and difficulty attracting new drivers contribute to this shortage. Driver income has been falling below other similar positions and drivers are leaving the industry for more traditional jobs. Some companies are reporting 100 percent turnover in drivers. These challenges are leading to consolidation in the industry as the smaller carriers are less able to compete [10].

Equipment

There are many types of trucks a driver may operate. An extensive description can be found on Wikipedia [11]. In general, they are categorized as light, medium, or heavy. Another general category is straight or articulated. A straight truck is one that has the engine, cab, and cargo space built on a single chassis, or frame, regardless of the number of wheels. An articulated vehicle consists of a power unit, the tractor, and one to three attached trailers. Vehicles can be designed for specific tasks such as to carry liquids or gases, cargo, bottles, livestock, refrigerated cargo, or other specific material. Seventy percent of the nation's trucks are used mainly in local areas.

*The US Court of Appeals recently vacated the 11 drive time and 34 restart provision of the 2005 Hours of Service Rule requiring the FMCSA to provide an explanation of these two provisions. Final outcome is still pending.

Schedules

Typical work schedules vary. Hours are long and often unpredictable. On turnaround or short relay, a driver may drive 4 to 5 hours, leave the truck he or she has driven, and return in another vehicle. On long relays, a driver will drive up to 11 hours; take a 10-hour break, and then return. Straight-through hauling is often cross country, with 11 hours of driving and 10-hour rest stops. Drivers may drive as part of a team and utilize a sleeper berth to obtain part or all of their sleep. Straight-haul and sleeper-haul drivers often are on the road for days to weeks.

Current HOS regulations initially introduced in 2003 [12] and revised in 2005 [13] (Figure III-5) allow drivers to work as much as 84 hours in a 7-day period. Drivers were previously limited to 70 hours of work time within any 7-day interval, but a new "restart" provision allocates a fresh set of work hours to a driver after 34 hours of continuous off-duty time.*

Drivers are not covered under overtime provisions of the Fair Labor Standards Act, requiring time-and-a-half pay for hours worked in excess of 40 hours per week. In general, truckers are paid by the mile and may not be paid for waiting or time loading or unloading.

It is recognized that drivers often will exceed the legal operating time, often encouraged or required to do so by their employers. In January 2007, a proposed rule [14] was announced that would require electronic on-board recorders (EOBRs) for those carriers with serious HOS violations. It was estimated that during the first 2 years the rule would be enforced, approximately 930 carriers with 17,500 drivers would fall under this requirement. The rule also would encourage other carriers to voluntarily install the recorders and incentives are anticipated.

Health Issues

Several international studies have looked at overall driver health. A large Danish study found that truck drivers had a higher mortality rate over a 10-year period from lung cancer and multiple myeloma than unskilled laborers in other occupations [15]. Another Danish study found that compared to the male working-age population, both truck and bus drivers had especially high age standardized hospital admission ratios for lung cancer, ischemic heart disease, cerebrovascular disease, chronic obstructive pulmonary disease, and prolapsed cervical or lumbar discs [16].

---

*The US Court of Appeals recently vacated the 11 drive time and 34 restart provision of the 2005 Hours of Service Rule requiring the FMCSA to provide an explanation of these two provisions. Final outcome is still pending.

Figure III-5. Provisions of the 2005 Hours or Service Regulations and Changes from 2003*

2003 Rule Property-Carrying CMV Drivers Compliance Through 09/30/05	2005 Rule Property-Carrying CMV Drivers Compliance on & After 10/01/05
May drive a maximum of 11 hours after 10 consecutive hours off duty.	NO CHANGE
May not drive beyond the 14th hour after coming on duty, following 10 consecutive hours off duty.	NO CHANGE
May not drive after 60/70 hours on duty in 7/8 consecutive days. • A driver may restart a 7/8 consecutive day period after taking 34 or more consecutive hours off duty.	NO CHANGE
Commercial Motor Vehicle (CMV) drivers using a sleeper berth must take 10 hours off duty, but may split sleeper-berth time into two periods provided neither is less than 2 hours.	CMV drivers using the sleeper berth provision must take at least 8 consecutive hours in the berth, plus 2 consecutive hours either in the sleeper berth, off duty, or any combination of the two.

Passenger-carrying carriers/drivers are not subject to the new hours-of-service rules. These operations must continue to comply with the hours-of-service limitations specified in 49 CFR 395.5.

Short-Haul Provision

Drivers of property-carrying CMVs that do not require a Commercial Driver's License for operation and who operate within a 150 air-mile radius of their normal work reporting location:

- May drive a maximum of 11 hours after coming on duty following 10 or more consecutive hours off duty
- Are not required to keep records-of-duty status (RODS)
- May not drive after the 14th hour after coming on duty 5 days a week or after the 16th hour after coming on duty 2 days a week

Employer must:

- Maintain and retain accurate time records for a period of 6 months showing the time the duty period began, ended, and total hours on duty each day in place of RODS.

Drivers who use these described short-haul provisions are **not** eligible to use 100 air-mile provision 395.1(e) or the current 16-hour exception in 395.1(o).

*The US Court of Appeals recently vacated the 11 drive time and 34 restart provision of the 2005 Hours of Service Rule requiring the FMCSA to provide an explanation of these two provisions. Final outcome is still pending.

Source: FMCSA, 2005. Hours of Service. www.fmcsa.dot.gov/rules-regulations/truck/driver/hos/cards2005.htm. Accessed June 22, 2007.

Fatigue

Fatigue is a significant issue in the life of the trucker. Morrow and Crum [17] reported that they found that almost one-half of the drivers they studied reported starting a new work week tired more often than not. In one study, the Truck Driver Fatigue Management Survey [18], conducted by the FMCSA, 51–65 percent of drivers reported having experienced yawning, feeling drowsy, eyelids heavy, feeling sleepy, and struggling to be alert while driving. Many less-reported serious driving consequences from drowsiness include nodding off or falling asleep (13%), having a near miss (9%), running off the road (6%), or colliding with something (3%).

Drivers will use many different techniques to manage their fatigue both on and off the job. Off the job, they will try to "get a good night's sleep" although for many this is not possible or effective. On the job, some of the activities they would engage in while driving included stretching/changing positions, adjusting ventilation, having a caffeinated drink, listening to music or the radio, talking on the cell phone or CB radio, or eating while driving [18]. Some of the nondriving, on-the-job techniques a driver might use to manage fatigue include stopping to eat, napping, resting without sleep, or walking around.

A majority of drivers indicated that having more control over their schedules (76%), working fewer hours (70%), and sleeping regular hours (62%) would help lessen fatigue. Many drivers also felt that having fatigue monitoring technologies (64%) and receiving training in fatigue management (43%) would be helpful [18].

One of the interesting findings is that there is large interindividual differences in susceptibility to fatigue [11,19]. Fatigue can lead to accidents and those drivers who report poor quantity or quality of sleep were found to be at fault more often than those who reported good sleep [20].

As part of the Literature Review on Health and Fatigue Issues Associated with Commercial Motor Vehicle Driver Hours of Work [9], some of the conclusions reached regarding fatigue were:

- Falling asleep at the wheel is a common experience for truck drivers. In one study almost one-fifth reported falling asleep at least twice in the preceding 3 months [21]. Driving while fatigued increased the risk of close calls.
- Night driving is associated with poor sleep, more falling asleep accidents [22], and poorer driving performance.
- Long-haul drivers get poor sleep with 44 percent of long-haul driver's sleep occurring during the work shifts [23].

- Reduced sleep at night is associated with poorer daytime performance and with inadequate recovery.
- Time of day is far more important than hours of driving in predicting observed fatigue.
- Night sleep is important for recovery and insufficient recovery is related to close calls.

Shift schedules can impact subjective fatigue. In one study [24], while night-shift drivers may feel more tired than day-shift workers they do not perform worse on tests such as the psychomotor vigilance test. The literature is inconclusive whether shift work is associated with depression, cancer, or sickness absence [5].

Obstructive Sleep Apnea

Drivers, including commercial drivers, with obstructive sleep apnea (OSA) are at an increased risk of motor vehicle crashes [25–27]. OSA may be more common in the commercial driver than the general population [28, 29]. Similarly to fatigue, there is significant variability in risk of crashes in those with OSA although those who report feeling tired do appear to be at a higher risk [30]. For the commercial driver medical examiner, subjective inquiries on tiredness may not be sufficient to identify those drivers at increased risk of OSA or crashes due to OSA. Objective measures or a combination of objective measures and subjective reports may improve identification. Such methods suggested by the Joint Task Force of the American College of Chest Physicians, American College of Occupational and Environmental Medicine, and the National Sleep Foundation may improve detection. [28]

The Truck Driver Fatigue Management Survey [18] also looked at driver health–related demographics. They found that almost 50 percent of the drivers surveyed had a body mass index (BMI) in the obese range, nearly double that in the general population. Despite this high rate of obesity, only 5.6 percent of drivers indicated they had been diagnosed as having a sleep disorder; 89 percent of the diagnoses were sleep apnea and only 67 percent of these drivers were currently being treated.

Pulmonary Disorders

Truck drivers may have significant exposures to diesel exhaust. In addition to increased risk of lung cancer, the exposure also may be associated with chronic respiratory diseases such as asthma, respiratory symptoms such as wheezing, reduction in pulmonary function, and allergic inflammation [31].

New Environmental Protection Agency standards may reduce driver exposure. Starting in 2007, all new trucks must be equipped with diesel particulate filters (DPFs). These filters are designed to cut soot emissions by 90 percent. There is concern, however, that these filters may lead to equipment malfunctions and will increase the cost of a new truck [32].

Mental Stress

The long hours, schedule demands, and extended time away from family and friends can lead to stress. Owner-operators are under additional stress from financial pressures to pay the loan or lease payments on their truck. Package drivers are required to make a large number of deliveries on a very tight schedule and like bus driver also must deal with the public. Other sources of stress for drivers include required waiting in their trucks for long and unpredictable periods of time before being brought in to the dock to load or unload; denied opportunities for food, water, and restroom facilities; and being treated disrespectfully by shipping and receiving personnel [8].

Improving Driver Health

In a study surveying 2,945 male drivers and 353 female drivers done at a trade show for truckers, 54 percent of male truck drivers smoked cigarettes (versus 30 percent of U.S. white males), 92 percent did not exercise regularly, 50 percent were overweight (versus 25 percent of U.S. white males), and 66 percent were not aware that they had high blood pressure (versus 46 percent of the U.S. population). Of the surveyed truck drivers, 23 percent tested positive on one measure of alcoholism [33].

Although it has long been noted that the commercial driver is often not in optimal health, few studies have been done to examine this issue or address methods to improve driver health. A driver wellness program was designed and piloted by a consortium of private, government, and industry organizations for drivers [34]. Some interesting data in the pretest survey showed

1. Major health concerns of drivers were lack of family time, lack of exercise, weight, fatigue, poor diet, and stress.
2. Drivers were in the ready or trying to improve behavior in eating, exercise, stress management, self-care, and sleep stages.

3. Drivers most concerned about health were long-haul drivers 40 to 60 years old and those who did not currently exercise or eat well.
4. Drivers who felt they were in control or were responsible for their own health tended to have better lifestyle habits (i.e., lower weight, more exercise, healthier eating, no tobacco).

After the program, physical improvement measures showing statistical significance were BMI (from obese as a group to overweight), pulse, diastolic blood pressure, aerobic fitness level (the most improved), strength fitness level, and flexibility fitness level. The program itself had a 96 percent satisfaction rate, with 100 percent recommending the program to others.

The intention of the government and private sectors to actively address the underlying health of this critical workforce is the most noteworthy outcome of such a small study. This is a small step, but an important one.

Conclusion

Although many advances have been made in recognizing issues in driver health and safety, there are still many questions that remain. At the recent Conference on Future Truck and Bus Safety Research Opportunities [35], it was noted while individual risk factors such as those listed in Figure III-6, have been shown to correlate with a

---

Figure III-6. Individual Risk Factors That Have Been Shown to Correlate with Increase in Crash Risk

---

- Driver physical and medical characteristics
  - obesity
  - sleep disorders
- Driver performance capabilities
  - attentional demands
  - useful field of view
- Driver personalities and off-duty behavior
- Carrier operational and management practices
  - training practice
  - safety practices
- Driving actions and behavior
- Vehicle factors
- Situational and environmental factors

---

varying increase in crash risk, there was not a model to evaluate relative or interactive effects of these individual risks.

Their recommendations included:

- Research should be conducted on the prevalence and nature of factors contributing to driver occupational injuries and illnesses that are unrelated to crashes.
- The relationship between health and wellness and driver performance should be measured, individual and corporate benefits associated with healthy lifestyles quantified, and a regulatory framework, working environment, and incentives that promote healthier lifestyles created.
- Current medical requirements should be examined and updated, including a review of the effects of prescription and over-the-counter medications on driver performance.

References

1. Professional Truck Driver Institute. Skill standards for entry-level tractor-trailer drivers. www.ptdi.org/errata/SKILLSTANDARDS_ENTRYLEVEL .pdf. Accessed June 14, 2007.
2. Commercial Motor Vehicle Fact Sheets—FMCSA—April 2005. www .fmcsa.dot.gov/facts-research/facts-figures/analysis-statistics/ driverfacts.htm. Accessed June 14, 2007.
3. US Department of Labor, Bureau of Labor Statistics, Current Population Survey, Census of Fatal Occupational Injuries, and US Department of Defense, 2004. www.bls.gov/iif/oshcfoiarchive.htm#2004charts. Accessed June 14, 2007.
4. Bureau of Labor Statistics, US Department of Labor, October 2006. www.bls.gov/iif/oshwc/osh/os/osch0032.pdf. Accessed June 14, 2007.
5. Motor Carrier Safety Progress Report, Federal Motor Carrier Safety Administration. www.fmcsa.dot.gov/facts-research/facts-figures/analysis-statistics/MCSPR-03-31-07.htm. Accessed June 13, 2007.
6. OSHA Safety and Health Topics—OSHA Assistance for the Trucking Industry. Industry hazards. www.osha.gov/SLTC/trucking_ industry/hazards.html. Accessed June 14, 2007.
7. Federal Motor Carrier Safety Administration. Report to Congress on the large truck crash causation study. March 2006. www.fmcsa.dot.gov/facts-research/research-technology/report/ltccs-2006.pdf. Accessed June 14, 2007.
8. Saltzman GM, Belzer MH. *Truck Driver Occupational Safety and Health, a Conference Report and Selective Review of the Literature.* DHHS (NIOSH) Publication No. 2007–120. June 2007. www.cdc.gov/niosh/docs/ 2007-120/. Presentations from conference at www.ilir.umich.edu/TIBP/ truckdriverOSH/index.cfm. Accessed June 15, 2007.

9. Orris P, Buchannon S, Dinges D, Bergoffen G. Literature Review on Health and Fatigue Issues Associated with Commercial Motor Vehicle Driver Hours of Work. Synthesis 9. Transportation Research Board. 2005. http://trb.org/publications/ctbssp/ctbssp_syn_9.pdf. Accessed June 15, 2007.

10. Fox B, Zadecky L. Assessing the motor carrier industry and its segments: Current and prospective issues. 2006. http://ai.fmcsa.dot.gov/Carrier ResearchResults/PDFs/IndustryProfiles/MotorCarrierAssessment Report_final.pdf. Accessed June 14, 2007.

11. Wikipeida. List of truck types. http://en.wikipedia.org/wiki/List_of _truck_types. Accessed June 22, 2007.

12. Department of Transportation, Federal Motor Carrier Safety Administration, 49 CFR Parts 385, 390, and 395, Hours of Service of Drivers; Driver Rest and Sleep for Safe Operations, *Fed Reg* 2003;68(81):22456–22517.

13. Department of Transportation. Federal Motor Carrier Safety Administration. 49 CFR Parts 385, 390, and 395. Hours of Service of Drivers; Final Rule. *Fed Reg* 2005;70(164):49978–50073.

14. Department of Transportation. Federal Motor Carrier Safety Administration. Electronic on-board recorders for hours-of-service compliance: Proposed rule. *Fed Reg* 2007;72(11):2339–2394.

15. Hansen ES. A follow-up study on the mortality of truck drivers. *American Journal of Industrial Medicine* 1993;23(5):811–821.

16. Hannerz H, Tuchsen F. Hospital admissions among male drivers in Denmark. *Occupational and Environmental Medicine* 2001;58(4):253–260.

17. Morrow PC, Crum MR. Antecedents of fatigue, close calls, and crashes among commercial motor-vehicle drivers. *Journal of Safety Research* 2004;35(1):59–69.

18. Dinges D, Maislin G. Truck Driver Fatigue Management Survey. FMCSA. FMCSA-RRR-06-0. May 2006. www.fmcsa.dot.gov/facts-research/ research-technology/report/Truck-Driver-Fatigue-Management-Survey-Report.pdf. Accessed June 17, 2007.

19. Van Dongen HPA, Baynard MD, Maislin G, Dinges TF. Systematic interindividual differences in neurobehavioral impairment from sleep loss: Evidence of trait-like differential vulnerability. *Sleep* 2004;27(3):423–433.

20. Hanowski RJ, et al. *Impact of Local/Short Haul Operations on Driver Fatigue: Final Project Report.* 2000. DOT-MC-00-203. Federal Motor Carrier Safety Administration.

21. Hakkanen H, Summala H. Driver sleepiness related problems, health status, and prolonged driving among professional heavy-vehicle drivers. *Transportation Human Factors* 2000;2(2):151–171.

22. Wylie CD, Shultz T, Miller JC, Mitler MM, Mackie RR. *Commercial Motor Vehicle Driver Fatigue and Alertness Study.* Report No. FHWA-MC-97-002. FHWA 1997.

23. Balkin T, Thome D, Sing H, Thomas M, Redmond D, Wesensten N, Williams J, Hall S, Belenky G. *Effects of Sleep Schedules on Commercial Motor Vehicle Driver Performance.* Department of Transportation, Federal Motor Carrier Safety Administration. FMCSA-MCRT-00-015. 2000.

24. Williamson A, Friswell R, Feyer AM. *Fatigue and Performance in Heavy Truck Drivers Working Day Shift, Night Shift or Rotating Shifts.* National Transportation Commission, 2004.

25. Howard ME, Desai AV, Grunstein RR, et al. Sleepiness, sleep-disordered breathing, and accident risk factors in commercial vehicle drivers. *Am J Respir Crit Care Med* 2004;170:1014–1021.

26. Shiomi T, Arita AT, Sasanabe R, et al. Falling asleep while driving and automobile accidents among patients with obstructive sleep apnea—Hypopnea syndrome. *Psychiatry Clin Neurosci* 2002;56:333–334.

27. Teran-Santos J, Jimenez-Gomez A, Cordero-Guevara J. The association between sleep apnea and the risk of traffic accidents. Cooperative Group Burgos- Santander. *N Engl J Med* 1999;340:847–851.

28. Hartenbaum N, Collop N, Rosen IM, Phillips B, George CF, Rowley JA, Freedman N, Weaver TE, Gurubhagavatula I, Strohl K, Leaman HM, Moffitt GL, Rosekind MR. Sleep apnea and commercial motor vehicle operators: Statement from the Joint Task Force of the American College of Chest Physicians, American College of Occupational and Environmental Medicine, and the National Sleep Foundation. *J Occup Environ Med* 2006; Sept;48(9 Suppl):S4–S37.

29. Moreno CR, Carvalho FA, Lorenzi C, et al. High risk for obstructive sleep apnea in truck drivers estimated by the Berlin Questionnaire: Prevalence and associated factors. *Chronobiol Int* 2004;21:871–879.

30. Lindberg E, Carter N, Gislason T, Janson C. Role of snoring and daytime sleepiness in occupational accidents. *Am J Respir Crit Care Med* 2001;164: 2031–2035.

31. Hoek G, Brunekreef B, et al. Association between mortality and indicators of taffic-related air pollution in the Netherlands: A cohort study. *Lancet* 2002;360(9341):1203–1209.

32. Gilroy R. Soot-filter performance is key to success of 2007 engines. *Transport Topics* 2006;Feb.

33. Korelitz JJ, Fernandez AA, Uyeda VJ, Spivey GH, Browdy BL, Schmidt RT. Health habits and risk factors among truck drivers visiting a health booth during a trucker trade show. *Am J Health Promotion* 1993;8(2):117–123.

34. Roberts S, York J. *Design Development and Evaluation of Driver Wellness Programs.* Federal Motor Carrier Safety Administration. Final Report. June 2000. www.fmcsa.dot.gov/facts-research/research-technology/report/driver-wellness.htm. Accessed June 25, 2007.

35. Transportation Research Board Conference Proceedings 38. *Future Truck and Bus Safety Opportunities.* March 2005. http://onlinepubs.trb.org/onlinepubs/conf/CP38.pdf. Accessed June 17, 2007.

INDEX

Abdomen, physical requirements for, 19, 31
Abdominal aortic aneurysm,
123
Accidents
factors causing, 293, 301
injuries and deaths from,
291-292
number and rate of, 291-292
Acromegaly, 231
Addison's disease, 230, 231
Advisory criteria, FMCSA, 44-
69
Age requirements, 75
AIDS, 174
Air conditioning, 92
Alcohol misuse
advisory criteria regarding,
257
incidence of, 268
and medical examination,
264-265
physical signs of, 268
regulations regarding, 257
screening tools for, 266, 268-
271
testing for, 256, 268
Alcoholism, 41, 74, 174, 176,
245
advisory criteria regarding,
54
and medical examination, 70
regulations regarding, 257
Alexia, 174
Allergies, 137
Alpha-glucosidase inhibitors,
209
Alprazolam, 241, 277
Alzheimer's disease, 174, 177
Americans with Disabilities
Act, 4
Amitriptyline, 239, 241, 277
Amnesia, 174
psychogenic, 244
transient global, 188
Amoxapine, 241
Amyotrophic lateral sclerosis,
183
Analgesics, 267
Anaphylaxis, idiopathic, 137
Anemia, in renal disease, 251
Aneurysms
aortic, 123
brain, 189
Angina pectoris, 80, 109
and certification, 111

Angioedema, 137-138
Angioplasty, 89-90
Ankylosing spondylitis, 159
Anorexia nervosa, 239
ANSI standard, 88
Antianxiety agents, 241
Anticoagulant therapy
for atrial fibrillation, 119-120
See also Coumadin
Antidepressants, 242-243, 268
Antihistamines, 237-238, 267,
274, 277
Antihypertensives, 174, 267
Antipsychotics, 239, 268
Antisocial personality disor-
der, 245
Antitussives, 267
Anxiety disorders, 240-241
drugs used to treat, 241
Anxiolytics, 239-240, 267
Aortic regurgitation, 114-115
recommendations regard-
ing, 116
Aortic stenosis, 114
recommendations regard-
ing, 115
Aphasia, 174
Apnea, 79, 85
See also Obstructive sleep
apnea (OSA)
Apnea/hypopnea index (AHI),
139
Arrhythmias, 118-122
in renal disease, 251
ventricular, 120
Arthritis, 39
advisory criteria regarding,
49
psoriatic, 158
reactive, 159
rheumatoid, 158
Asthma, 137, 144, 299
Ataxia, cerebellar, 162, 176
Atrial fibrillation, 119-120
Atrioventricular block, 121
Attention deficit disorder
(ADD), 241
Attention deficit hyperactivity
disorder (ADHD), 241-242
AUDIT (Alcohol Use Disor-
ders Identification Test),
269-271
Avandia, 200

Back disorders, 161, 162
Barbiturates, 238, 239, 267

Benign essential tremor, 179
Benign familial chorea, 178
Benzodiazepines, 237, 238, 239,
240, 274-275, 277
Bipolar disorder, 243
Bladder cancer, 294
Blepharospasm, 178, 194
Blood pressure disorders. See
Hypertension
Body dysmorphic disorder, 247
Body Mass Index (BMI), 15
Brain
aneurysm in, 190
benign tumor of, 162
trauma to, 188-189
Bronchitis, 140, 144
Brugada syndrome, 120
Bulimia, 239
Bundle branch block, 120
Buprenorphine, 277
Bupropion, 239, 241, 243
Bursitis, 161
Buspirone, 239, 241
Byetta, 267

CAGE questionnaire, 266, 268-
271
Canadian National Safety
Code for Motor Carriers,
13, 90-91, 92
Cancer
bladder, 294
of CNS, 162
lung, 145-146, 294, 299
Carbamazepine, 239
Cardiac myopathies, 117-118
Cardiovascular disorders
advisory criteria regarding,
100-101
angina pectoris, 109, 111
arrhythmias, 118-122
cardiac myopathies, 117-118
as cause of accidents, 99
causes of, 294
congenital, 122-123
coronary heart disease, 104,
105
disqualifying conditions,
101
hypertension. See Hypertension
incapacitation risk from,
102-103
ischemic heart disease, 104-
110, 111
medications for, 125-126

305

Cardiovascular disorders,
  continued
  myocardial infarction, 106-
    107, 108-109, 111
  questions for assessing, 103
  regulations concerning, 100
  renal disease and, 251
  valvular disorders, 112-117
  vascular disease, 123-125
Cardiovascular system
  advisory criteria on, 46-47
  physical requirements for,
    18-19, 31, 38-39, 78-79, 80
Cardioverter defibrillator, as
  disqualifier, 101, 122
Carpal tunnel syndrome (CTS),
  160
Cataracts, 194
CB radios, 70
Cerebellar ataxia, 162, 176
Cerebellar degeneration, 176
Cerebrovascular disease, 174,
  176-177
CHADS2 model, 119
Chest X-rays, 71
Chief Medical Officer, 8
Chlordiazepoxide, 241
Chlorpromazine, 277
Chronic disease, 97-98
Chronic obstructive pul-
  monary disease (COPD),
  135-136
Circadian rhythm, disruption
  of, 294
Citalopram, 241
Clonazepam, 241
Clonidine, 267
Clorazepate, 241
Cluster headaches, 174, 179
Cognitive screen, for neuro-
  logic disorders, 171-173
Color blindness, 194
Commercial Driver's License,
  8-9
Commercial motor vehicle
  categories of, 25
  defined, 12, 24
Common cold, 140
Compensation, direct, 25
Conflict resolution, 55-57, 73
  reconsideration, 79
Congenital heart disease, 122-
  123
Congenital myopathy, 175
Congestive heart failure, 118
  renal disease and, 251
Construction apraxia, 174
Continuous ambulatory peri-
  toneal dialysis, 252
Controlled substances
  list of, 258-263
  See also Substance abuse
Conversion disorder, 247
Cor pulmonale, 146
Coronary artery bypass graft
  (CABG), 79-79, 80, 101

Coronary heart disease (CHD),
  104, 105
Coumadin, 70-71, 124-125, 145
CPR (cardiopulmonary resus-
  citation), 88
Cranial nerves, testing of, 172
Cranial neuralgia, 174
Creatinine, 251
Creutzfeldt-Jakob disease, 174
Crohn's disease, 159
Cushing's syndrome, 230, 231

Deep venous thrombosis
  (DVT), 123-124, 133, 145
Defibrillator, 101, 122
Dementia, 162, 174, 177-178
  from dialysis, 252
Depersonalization, 244
Depressants, as controlled substances, 262
Depression, 174, 177
  as accident risk factor, 242-
    243
  drugs used to treat, 241
  incidence of, 242
Dermatomyositis, 175, 183
Desipramine, 241
Diabetes, 17, 38
  as accident risk, 199-200,
    203-204
  advisory criteria on, 45-46
  assessment of patient, 210-
    213
  changes in criteria regard-
    ing, 5-6
  damage caused by, 210
  diagnostic criteria for, 207
  drug therapy for, 209
  incidence of, 199
  insulin use, 4, 5, 6, 17, 20, 32,
    201, 212, 266
  licensure differences across
    jurisdictions, 204-206
  management of, 208-210
  medical evaluation checklist
    for, 222-228
  neuropathy in, 251
  recommendations regard-
    ing, 201-202
  regulations regarding, 32-33,
    86
  screening for, 202, 207-208
  types of, 202
  urine testing for, 71, 202, 211
  waiver programs for, 4, 5, 6,
    89, 213-221, 229
  waiver study programs for,
    67-69, 91
Diabetes insipidus, 230, 231
Dialysis, 91, 250
  hemodialysis, 251-252
  peritoneal, 252
Diazepam, 241, 275, 277
Dipeptidyl-peptidase-4 inhibitors, 209
Diphenhydramine, 277

Diplopia, 174, 194
Direct compensation, 25
Discogenic disease, 161, 162
Dissociative disorders, 244
Doxepin, 241, 277
Driver investigation history
  file, 65-66
Driver qualification file
  driver investigation history
    in, 65-66
  exemptions to requirements
    for, 66-69
  general requirements of, 64-
    66
  for LCV driver-instructors,
    66
  medical certification card in,
    75, 87
Drivers
  age requirement for, 75
  cardiac risks of, 99
  certification requirement of,
    54-55
  demands on, 289
  duties and functions of, 33,
    43
  exemptions affecting, 66-69
  fatigue and, 298-299
  hazards and risks of, 289
  health hazards of, 298-300
  health studies of, 293-294,
    296
  improving health of, 300-301
  injury rates of, 291-292
  injury types of, 292-293
  intrastate, 87
  licensure of, 8, 9
  maximum hours for, 297
  mental stress of, 300
  multiple-employer, 67
  need for medical certificate,
    75
  physical qualifications for,
    24-28, 37, 69-70, 85-86
  qualification file for, 64-69
  regulations regarding, 72-73
  responsibilities of, 289-290
  returning to work, 73
  schedules of, 296
  school bus, 6
  state requirements for, 84
Driving record, 88
Drug testing, 4
Drug toxicities, 178
Drug use. *See* Medication use;
  Substance abuse
Dyskinesia, 162
Dyspnea, 132
Dystonia musculorum deformans, 178
Earphones, 70
Ears, physical requirements
  for, 18, 30
Eating disorders, 244
Ejection fraction, 108
Electroconvulsive therapy, 239

Employer
  access to medical evaluation by, 77
  qualification file of, 64-69, 75
Encephalitis, 174, 175
End-stage renal disease, 251
Endocrine disorders
  advisory criteria for, 201
  diagnostic criteria for, 200
  hypothalamic-pituitary-adrenocortical axis disorders, 231
  regulation regarding, 200-201
  thyroid disorders, 229-231
  See also Diabetes
Enthesopathies, 158
Entrapment neuropathies, 160-161
Epilepsy, 17, 40, 83
  as accident risk, 185
  advisory criteria regarding, 50, 168-169
  as disqualifier, 185, 186
  incidence of, 184
  recommendations regarding, 187
Escitalopram, 241
Excessive daytime sleepiness, 85
Exempt intracity zone
  defined, 26
  driver qualification file exemptions in, 66-67
Exemption, 90
  authority to grant, 81
  defined, 77
  request for, 87, 89, 91
  terms of, 82
Exenatide, 267
Exercise tolerance test (ETT), 86, 108
Extrapyramidal disorders, 178-179
Extremities, physical requirements for, 20, 32

Factitious disorder, 244
Fatigue, 298-299
Febrile seizures, 185
Federal Highway Administration (FHWA), 4
Federal Motor Carrier Safety Administration (FMCSA), 4
  advisory criteria of, 44-69
  described, 80-81
  frequently asked questions of, 74-92
  Website of, 23-24
Federal Motor Carrier Safety Regulations (FMCSRs), availability of, 86
Fentanyl, 277
Fibrillation, 119-120

Fluoxetine, 239, 241
Flurazepam, 274, 277
Focal dystonias, 179
Foreign medical examinations, 71, 90-91
Frontal-lobe disorders, 174
Functional capacity, cardiac, 113

General appearance, physical requirements for, 18, 30
Generalized anxiety disorder, 240
Genital-urinary system, physical requirements for, 19, 31
Giant cell arteritis, 160
Gout, 159-160
Government employees, exemption for, 90
Granulomatous meningitis, 174
Guanabenz, 267

Hallucinogens, 260-262
Head and eyes, physical requirements for, 18, 30
Headaches, 179
  evaluation of, 180
  medications for, 267
Hearing
  advisory criteria regarding, 52-53
  causes of loss of, 294
  criteria for, 3, 17, 18, 40, 76
  tests of, 92, 168, 169, 180-181
Hearing aids, 4
Heart
  advisory criteria on, 46-47
  functional capacity assessment, 113
  physical requirements for, 18-19, 31, 38-39, 78-79, 80
  transplantation of, 125
  See also Cardiovascular disorders; Cardiovascular system
Heavy-metal toxicity, 174
Hematuria, 82
Hemianopia, 174
Hemineglect, 174
Hemodialysis, 251-252
  side effects of, 252
Hemoptysis, 144
Heparin, 124, 252
HIPAA (Health Insurance Portability and Accountability Act)
  coverage of DOT medical examinations, 81, 86, 92
  privacy guarantee of, 77
  release form under, 21
Huntington's disease, 162, 174, 178, 179

Hydrocephalus, 174
Hydroxyzine, 241
Hyperglycemia, 212
Hypersensitivity pneumonitis, 137
Hypertension, 82
  as accident risk factor, 110
  advisory criteria regarding, 47-49, 101-102
  current criteria for, 15, 19, 39, 87
  diagnosis and treatment of, 77-78
  exemption regarding, 78
  former criteria for, 3
  recommendations regarding, 112
  regulations regarding, 31
  in renal disease, 251
  revised criteria for, 7
  stages of, 48, 84, 101-102
Hyperthyroidism, 230
Hypertrophic cardiomyopathy (HCM), 117-118
Hypnotics, 239, 267, 274
Hypocalcemia, 230
Hypochondriasis, 247
Hypoglycemia, 204, 211, 212
  risk factors for, 213
Hypomania, 244
Hypothalamic-pituitary-adrenocortical axis disorders, 231
Hypothyroidism, 174, 176, 229, 230

Idiopathic dilated cardiomyopathy, 118
Imipramine, 241, 277
Inclusion-body myositis, 183
Infectious diseases, effects of, 140, 144
Inflammatory bowel disease, 159
Influenza, 140, 144
Insulin use, 4, 5, 6, 17, 20, 32, 201, 212, 266
Interstate commerce, defined, 26
Intrastate
  commerce, 26
  drivers, 87
Isaac's syndrome, 183
Ischemic heart disease (IHD)
  angina pectoris, 109, 111
  evaluation for, 104-105
  incidence of, 104
  myocardial infarction, 106-107, 108-109, 111
  risk factors for, 105-106

Januvia, 209

Kidney disease. *See* Renal disease

Labyrinthine fistula, 174, 191
Labyrinthitis, 191, 192
LCV driver-instructor qualification files, 66
Legal incompetence, 174
Licencia Federal de Conductor, 13, 72, 90
Limb impairment
  advisory criteria regarding, 155-156
  regulations regarding, 152
  waivers for, 6, 44
Limbs
  advisory criteria for, 44-45
  loss of, 152-155
  physical requirements for, 31, 38, 151-152, 156
Lithium, 239, 244
Long form, 14, 21
Long QT syndrome, 120
Lorazepam, 241, 277
Loss of limb
  advisory criteria regarding, 153-155
  regulations regarding, 151-152
Low back pain (LBP), 161
Lungs
  advisory criteria on, 47
  cancer of, 145-146, 294, 299
  physical requirements for, 31, 39, 84
  transplantation of, 146
  See also Respiratory system
Lupus. *See* Systemic lupus erythematosus (SLE)

Major psychiatric disorder, 174
Mania, 244
Marijuana
  incidence of use of, 268
  medical, 91, 266, 267
Medical certificate (card), 14, 16, 28-29, 42
  advisory criteria regarding, 57-62
  in driver qualification file, 75, 87
  expiration of, 82
  medical criteria for, 83
  receipt of, 85
  regulations regarding, 71
  replacement of, 76
  requirement to carry, 21, 86-87
  requirement to hold, 76, 77, 87
  scope of, 75
  signature of, 77
Medical examination, 3, 83
  acceptance of foreign, 71, 90-91
  advisory criteria for, 15-16
  changes to process, 4
  certificate for, 14

conflict resolution for, 55-57, 73, 79
  fee for, 83
  payment for, 92
  personnel qualified to perform, 4, 13-14
  privacy issues, 81, 92
  regulations regarding, 28-29, 72
  reporting of results of, 14-15
Medical examination form, truthfulness on, 93
Medical examination report, 34-36
  employee access to, 81
  employer access to, 77, 92
  privacy issues regarding, 77, 81, 86, 92
Medical examiners
  duties and knowledge of, 82
  foreign, 71
  and HIPAA, 86
  instructions to, 38-41, 43-44
  interpretations of standards by, 44-69
  personnel qualified to serve as, 4, 13-14, 78
  qualifications of, 4, 13-14, 80
  regulations regarding, 71
  responsibilities of, 69
  restrictions on responsibilities of, 70
  standards followed by, 85
Medical Review Officers (MROs), 82-83
Medical Review Board (MRB), 7-8
  service on, 93
Medication use, 88
  antihistamines, 237-238, 267, 274
  antihypertensives, 174, 267
  anxiolytics, 274-275, 277
  antiparkinsonism, 275
  employee training regarding, 272-273
  exenatide, 267
  headache medications, 267
  insulin, 4, 5, 6, 17, 20, 32, 201, 212, 266
  and medical examination, 271-273
  methadone, 53, 70, 78, 257, 265, 266
  modafinil, 74-75, 133-134, 267
  opioids, 275
  proposed changes to regulations on, 273-277
  psychiatric, 237-243, 267-268, 274-275
  questionnaire regarding, 279-281
  sedation as effect of, 278
  sulfonylureas, 208, 201, 267
Meigs' syndrome, 178

Meniere's disease, 84, 89, 169, 174, 191, 192
Meningitis, 175-176
  granulomatous, 174
Mental disorders. *See* Psychiatric disorders
Meperidine, 277
Meprobamate, 277
Metabolic encephalopathy, 174
Metabolic muscle disease, 175
Methadone, 53, 70, 78, 257, 265, 266
Methyldopa, 267
Mexico, driver's license of, 13, 72
Midazolam, 277
Migraines, 174
Mirtazapine, 241, 243
Mitral regurgitation, 114
Mitral stenosis, 112-114
Modafinil, 74-75, 133-134, 267
Monoamine oxidase inhibitors (MAOIs), 237, 241, 243
Monocular vision, 194-195
Mood disorders, 242-243
Morphine, 277
Motor Carrier Safety Act of 1935, 3
Motor nerves, testing of, 172
Motor neuron disease, 162, 175, 183
Multiple dystrophy, 175
Multiple sclerosis, 162, 174, 176, 181-182
Multiple-employer drivers, 67
Musculoskeletal disorders, 39
  acute and subacute, 163
  advisory criteria regarding, 49, 153-163
  and crash risk, 150-151
  examination in, 164-165
  history taking in, 174
  long-distance driving as risk factor for, 294
  regulations regarding, 151-153
  self-treatment for, 151
  vertebral disorders, 294
Musculoskeletal system, physical requirements for, 20, 32
Myasthenia gravis, 183
Myocardial disease, 117-118
Myocardial infarction (MI)
  and certification, 111
  defined, 108-109
  evaluation after, 108
  renal disease and, 251
  risk for, 106-107
Myoclonus, 179
Myopathies, 159, 162
  congenital, 183
  inflammatory, 183
Myotonia, 175, 183
Narcolepsy, 74-75, 78, 85, 133, 181-182

Neck disorders, 162
Nefazodone, 241, 243
Nervous system tumors, 174
    proposed procedure for, 175,
        190-191
Neurologic disorders, 162-163,
    167
    advisory criteria regarding,
        168-170
    appeal procedure for, 178
    cognitive screen for, 171-173
    disqualifying conditions,
        173-195
    recommendations regard-
        ing, 170-171
    regulations regarding, 167-
        168
Neurological systems, physical
    requirements for, 19-20,
        31-32
Neuromuscular disorders, 39,
    162, 175, 183
    advisory criteria regarding,
        49
Neuromuscular junction disor-
    der, 162
Neuropathies
    diabetic, 251
    entrapment, 160-161
    peripheral, 162, 175, 183
    sensory and motor, 251
Night blindness, 194
Nitroglycerin, 80
Nonfunctioning labyrinth, 174,
    191
Nortriptyline, 241

Obsessive-compulsive disor-
    der, 245
Obstructive sleep apnea
    (OSA), 132, 133, 187
    as accident risk, 299
    diagnosis of, 139
    effects of, 138-139, 140
    and fitness for duty, 142-143
    screening recommendations
        for, 141-142
    treatment of, 140, 145
Opiates and opium derivatives
    as controlled substances,
        258-260
    legality of, 275, 277
Organic-solvent toxicity, 174
Orthopedic disease, 39
    advisory criteria regarding,
        49
Oscillopsia, 174
Osteoarthritis, 158
Osteoporosis, 160
Oxazepam, 241
Oxygen therapy, 81

Pacemakers, 101, 121
Paget's disease, 159
Panhypopituitarism, 230
Paraplegia, 189

Parathyroid disorders, 230
Parkinson's disease, 174, 177-
    178
    medication for, 275
    proposed procedure for, 175,
        184
    somnolence in, 184
Paroxetine, 241
Passive-aggressive disorders,
    245
Pentazocine, 277
Percutaneous coronary inter-
    ventions (PCIs), 109-110
    and certification, 111
Pergolide, 275
Peripheral neuropathy, 162,
    175, 183
Peripheral vascular disease,
    123
Peritoneal dialysis, 252
Personality disorders, 239, 245-
    246
Phenelzine, 241
Phenobarbital, 277
Pheochromocytoma, 230
Physical examination
    personnel qualified to per-
        form, 13-14
    instructions for, 17-20
    regulations regarding per-
        forming, 29-33, 72
    reporting of results of, 14-
        15, 20-21
Pick's disease, 174
Pilot program
    defined, 88
    initiating, 87
Pilots, air, 80, 83
Pituitary disorders, 230
Pneumonectomy, 144-145
Pneumonia, 144
Pneumothorax, 136-137
Polymyalgia rheumatica, 160
Polymyositis, 183
Polypharmacy, 237
Post-traumatic stress disorder
    (PTSD), 240
Pramexole, 275
Prazosin, 267
Primidone, 277
Privacy, of medical results, 77,
    81, 86, 92
Progressive supranuclear
    palsy, 174
Prosthetic valve repair, 115, 117
Proteinuria, 78, 250
Provigil, 74-75, 134, 267
Psoriatic arthritis, 158
Psoriatic spondylitis, 159
Psychiatric disorders, 40
    as accident risk, 234
    anxiety disorders, 240-241
    advisory criteria regarding,
        51
    attention disorders, 241-242
    disqualifying, 239

dissociative disorders, 244
drug therapies for, 237-240,
    241
eating disorders, 244
factitious disorder, 244
hypomania and mania,
    244
mood disorders, 242-243
personality disorders, 245-
    246
psychosis, 239, 246-247
recommendations regard-
    ing, 236-237
regulation regarding, 235
schizophrenia and psy-
    choses, 246-247
somatoform disorders, 247
Psychogenic amnesia, 244
Psychogenic fugue, 244
Psychosis, 239, 246-247
Pulmonary disorders, 132, 299-
    300
    allergies and asthma, 137-
        138
    COPD, 135-136
    dyspnea, 132
    evaluation for, 134-135
    guidelines regarding, 133-
        134
    infectious diseases, 140, 144
    medications for, 146-147
    obstructive sleep apnea
        (OSA), 132, 133, 138-143,
        145, 299
    pneumothorax, 137
    secondary conditions, 144-
        146
Pulmonary emboli, 124, 133,
    145
Pulmonary function tests
    (PFTs), 135

Radiculopathy, 162
*Rauenhorst v. Dept. of Trans-
    portation,* 5
Reactive arthritis, 159
Reciprocity, NAFTA, 13
Reconsideration, after disquali-
    fication, 79
Rectal examination, 31
Reiter's syndrome, 159
Religious beliefs, 69
Renal disease, 250
    anemia in, 251
    assessment of, 251
    dialysis in, 250-251
    cardiovascular effects of, 251
    effects of, 251-252
    international standards re-
        garding, 253-254
    neuropathies in, 251
    transplant to treat, 252-253
Repaglinide, 209
Report
    form, medical (long form),
        14-15, 21

Report , *continued*
 of medical examination, 34-36
 of physical examination, 14-15, 20-21
Reserpine, 267
Respiratory system
 advisory criteria on, 47
 diseases of. *See* Pulmonary disorders
 physical requirements for, 19, 39, 81, 84
 See also Lungs
Return-to-work rules, 73
Rheumatic disease, 39
 advisory criteria regarding, 49
Rheumatic fever, 178
Rheumatoid arthritis (RA), 158
Risk, exposure to, 97
Road rage, 245
Ropinirole, 275
Rosiglitazone, 200

Safe, Efficient, Flexible and Efficient Transportation Equity Act: A Legacy for Users (SAFETEA-LU), 5, 7-8
Schizophrenia, 246-247
School bus drivers, 6
Sciatica, 161
Scleroderma, 160
Sedative use, 174, 277-278
Seizure disorders. *See* Epilepsy
Selective serotonin reuptake inhibitors (SSRIs), 237, 241, 243
Sensory nerves, testing of, 172
Sertraline, 241
Shift work sleep disorder, 133
Sinus node dysfunction, 121
Sitagliptin, 209
Sjogren's syndrome, 158
Skill Performance Evaluation (SPE) certificate, 6, 73
 advisory criteria regarding, 57-62, 153-155
 form of, 62-63
Sleep apnea. *See* Obstructive sleep apnea (OSA)
Sleep disorders, 74-75, 78, 85, 133, 181-182
 circadian rhythm disruption and, 294
 fatigue and, 298-299
Somatization disorder, 247
Somatoform disorders, 247
Spasmic torticollis, 178
Spinal cord injuries, 189-190
Spinal muscular atrophy, 183
Spine, physical requirements for, 20, 32
Spondylitis, 158
 ankylosing, 159
 psoriatic, 159

States, adoption of FMCSA criteria by, 24
Stents, 89-90
Stiff-man syndrome, 183
Stimulants, as controlled substances, 262-263
Streptomycin, 144
Stress, 300
Stroke, 174, 176-177
 fibrillation and, 119
Subarachnoid hemorrhage, 190
Subdural hematoma, 174
Substance abuse
 advisory criteria regarding, 53-54, 257
 as disqualifier, 41, 91
 list of controlled substances, 258-263
 and medical examination, 70, 263-265
 physical signs of, 271
 regulations regarding, 257
 testing for, 256, 268
Sulfonylureas, 208, 201, 267
Syncope, 187-188
 causes of, 121-122
Syphilis, 174
Systemic lupus erythematosus (SLE), 158, 160

Tachycardia, 80
 multifocal atrial, 120
Tarsal tunnel syndrome, 161
Temporal arteritis, 160
Tendinitis, 161
Thiazolidinediones, 209
Thioridazine, 241, 277
Thoracic aortic aneurysm, 123
Throat, physical requirements for, 18, 30
Thyroid disorders, 229-231
Thyrotoxicosis, 230
Tics, 179
Tobacco use, 240
Torsion dystonias, 178
Torticollis, 178
Tracheostomy, 145
Tramadol, 277
Tranquilizers, 174
Transient global amnesia, 188
Transient ischemic attacks (TIAs), 176-177
Transplant
 heart, 125
 lung, 146
 kidney, 252-253
Tranylcypromine, 241
Trazodone, 241, 243, 277
Tremors, 179
Tricyclics, 237, 238, 239, 241, 242-243
Trimipramine, 241
Trucking
 equipment for, 295
 health issues related to, 293-294, 296-297
 interstate, 26

intrastate, 26, 87
 maximum hours for, 297
 scheduling of, 296
 structure of system, 295
Truthfulness, importance of, 93
Tuberculosis, 144
TWEAK scale, 269

Ulcerative colitis, 159
Uremia, 251
Urinalysis
 regulations regarding, 71
 requirements for, 19, 31
Uveitis, 159

Valproic acid, 239
Valvular heart disease, 112
 aortic regurgitation, 114-115
 aortic stenosis, 114, 115
 mitral regurgitation, 114
 mitral stenosis, 112-114
 prosthetic valve repair, 115, 117
Vascular disease, 39, 123-125
 advisory criteria regarding, 49
Venlafaxine, 241
Ventricular tachycardia (V-tach), 80, 120
Vertigo, 84, 179, 191-192
Vestibulopathies, 191-192
Viscera, physical requirements for, 19, 31
Vision, 4-5, 40, 168
 and accident risk, 192
 advisory criteria regarding, 52
 corrective lenses and, 168, 169
 criteria for, 16, 18, 20
 monocular, 194
 testing of, 1920193
 waiver of requirements, 6, 73, 89, 193-194
 waiver study programs for, 67-69, 91
Vitamin B12 deficiency, 174

Waiver
 authority to grant, 81
 defined, 76-77
 limb, 6, 44
 programs, 4, 5, 6
 request for, 77, 87, 89, 91
 response to request for, 83
Warfarin, 70-71, 124-125, 145
Whistleblowing, 87
Wilson's disease, 162, 178
Wolff-Parkinson-White syndrome, 120
Work load
 fatigue and, 298-299
 maximum, 296-297

X-rays, chest, 71

Zopiclone, 277